THE THEORY OF CAPITALIST DEVELOPMENT

THE THEORY OF CAPITALIST DEVELOPMENT

Principles of Marxist Political Economy

Paul M. Sweezy

AAKAR

The Theory of Capitalist Development
Paul M. Sweezy

First Aakar Edition 2016
Reprinted 2018
Reprinted 2023

ISBN 978-93-5002-420-1

Published in agreement with Monthly Review Press, New York for South Asia.

Published by
AAKAR BOOKS
28 E Pocket IV, Mayur Vihar Phase I
Delhi 110 091, India
www.aakarbooks.com

Printed at
D.K. Fine Art Press, Delhi

PREFACE

THERE exists in English no reasonably comprehensive analytical study of Marxian Political Economy. This book is intended to fill the gap. It is, however, neither complete nor exhaustive; many important topics have been altogether omitted, and others have been passed over with no more than a brief reference. Nevertheless, I hope it will contribute to a better understanding of an important body of social thought which in the past has too often suffered from ignorant and superficial treatment. I have not tried to gloss over difficulties, but neither have I gone out of my way to dwell upon complex theoretical problems unless they seemed to be directly related to the task in hand.

Throughout the book I have quoted frequently and extensively from the works of Marx and his followers. This unquestionably makes for an awkward style of presentation, but it has seemed unavoidable. It is not possible to take for granted an acquaintance with the literature of Marxism; much of the most important work, even of Marx himself, has never been translated into English, while many relevant books and periodicals are available only in the larger libraries. Moreover, interpretations of Marxian theories have differed widely, and I am anxious that my own interpretations, however much some readers may disagree with them, shall at any rate not give the impression of being made up out of whole cloth. Quotations from *Capital* are taken from the three-volume edition published by Charles Kerr & Co. of Chicago. I have felt free to simplify the punctuation in the passages quoted, and in several cases, all of which are recorded in the footnotes, I have altered the translation itself to convey more accurately the meaning of the German original.

Besides presenting and analyzing the views of other writers I have also attempted to solve certain theoretical problems which have long been the subject of controversy, and to bring within the framework of Marxian theory a variety of issues which it seems to me have hitherto received inadequate analysis. In the latter connection the reader's attention is particularly directed to Chapter x (Realization Crises), Chapter xii (Chronic Depression?), Chapter xiv (The Development of Monopoly Capital), Chapter xv (Monopoly and the Laws of Motion of Capitalism), and Chapter xviii (Fascism). The arrangement of the subject matter follows a definite pattern, starting from the most abstract problem of Political Economy—the theory of value—and proceeding by successive stages to the pressing problems of present-day world society.

Many friends and colleagues have been kind enough to read all or parts of the manuscript in various stages of completion and to offer valuable criticisms and suggestions. Among them I should like particularly to mention Drs. Erich Roll, Lewis Feuer, Franz Neumann, Alan R. Sweezy, Robert K. Merton, Svend Laursen, Stanley Moore, and Mr. Paul Baran. The criticisms of my wife, Maxine Yaple Sweezy, have been especially helpful, though she can legitimately complain that they have not always been accepted. My greatest debt is to Dr. Shigeto Tsuru, with whom I have had the good fortune to have many discussions over a period of years not only on the topics covered in this book but also on a wide range of related subjects. Dr. Tsuru has read the entire manuscript and has helped me in innumerable ways to improve both form and content. It is a great pleasure for me to be able to include an Appendix by him explaining and comparing the reproduction schemes of Quesnay, Marx, and Keynes. This Appendix should, I think, be of great interest to economists.

Needless to say, none of the above-named persons is in any way responsible for the views which I have expressed or for analytical errors which may remain.

I have included as a second Appendix a translation of several pages from Rudolf Hilferding's book *Das Finanzkapital* (first published in 1910) under the title 'The Ideology of Imperialism.' The idea is widespread in English-speaking countries that Marxism failed to understand and foresee the ideological trends which have reached their climax in the present-day fascist states. Even a brief excerpt from this well-known work of the period before the First World War should do much to dispel this groundless impression.

With regard to footnotes, the following practice has been adopted: those containing references and nothing more are relegated to the back of the book; all others appear at the bottom of the page.

Acknowledgments are gratefully made to the following publishers for permission to quote as follows:

Charles Kerr & Co., Chicago, from Karl Marx, *Capital*, 3 Vols.; from Karl Marx, *A Contribution to the Critique of Political Economy;* and from Louis B. Boudin, *The Theoretical System of Karl Marx.*

Macmillan and Company, New York, from Lionel Robbins, *The Nature and Significance of Economic Science;* and from Joan Robinson, *The Economics of Imperfect Competition.*

McGraw-Hill Book Co., New York, from J. A. Schumpeter, *Business Cycles*, Vol. I.

Methuen & Co., Ltd., London, from Adam Smith, *An Inquiry into the Nature and Causes of the Wealth of Nations*, Vol. I.

International Publishers, New York, from Karl Marx, *The Class Struggles in France;* from Karl Marx and Friedrich Engels, *Correspondence*, 1846-95, *a Selection with Commentary and Notes;* from V. I. Lenin, *Imperialism;* from V. I. Lenin, *Left-Wing Communism: an Infantile Disorder;* from Joseph Stalin, *Leninism;* and from Maurice Dobb, *Political Economy and Capitalism.*

PAUL M. SWEEZY

Dunster House,
Cambridge, Mass.
1 *August* 1942.

PREFACE TO 1956 PRINTING

When this book went out of print several years ago, neither the original publisher nor the author thought that the demand would again be sufficient to warrant a new edition. Conditions have changed, however. Abroad, the increasingly brisk competition between the systems has stimulated renewed interest in Marxian ideas; while at home relaxation of the tensions of cold war and witch hunt has allowed this interest to be expressed more freely than was possible in the late 1940s and early 1950s. As a result, a need for usable and reliable introductory material on Marxism has made itself felt, and the demand for *The Theory of Capitalist Development* has correspondingly grown. The point has now been reached where a new printing seems called for.

My first inclination was to prepare a revised and expanded second edition, but on more mature consideration I decided against it. Not that the book lacks faults and deficiencies—far from it. But it seemed to me that a serious attempt to remedy the bigger ones would go beyond the scope of an introduction and might badly impair the value of the book for the purpose for which it was first intended. Since, to my knowledge, no comparable text has been published in English in the intervening period, I concluded that *The Theory of Capitalist Development* in its original form still has a useful function to perform.

For the rest, I confess to a certain prejudice against too much alteration of a book once published. The late Professor Schumpeter, to whom this book indirectly owes a great deal, including its title, aptly wrote in the preface to the English translation of his *Theory of Economic Development:* "Books, like children, become independent beings when once they leave the parents' home. They lead their own lives, while the authors lead their own also. It will not do to interfere with those who become strangers to the house." I am content to follow his advice (and example) and to leave this work as it came into the world.

Paul M. Sweezy

Cambridge, Mass.
22 October 1956

CONTENTS

INTRODUCTION

INTRODUCTION

SOCIETY is more than a number of individuals. It is a number of individuals among whom certain definite and more or less stable relations exist. The form of society is determined by the character and form of these relations. The social sciences comprise all those branches of knowledge which have as their aim the study and understanding of these relations and their changes in the course of time.

All this, it will be said, is obvious to the point of banality. And so it is. But it is as well to remember that the most obvious things are frequently the most important. Those who neglect the obvious do so at their own peril. Let us take the modern science of economics as a case in point.

Economics, by common consent, is a social science; one has only to consult a university catalogue to convince oneself. Its subject matter is drawn from the field of the production and distribution of the goods and services which people need and want. From these two premises it would seem to be a legitimate conclusion that economics studies the social (inter-personal) relations of production and distribution. What these relations are, how they change, and their place in the totality of social relations would seem to be the indicated subjects of inquiry.

But do economists see matters in this way? Let us glance briefly at the work of Professor Lionel Robbins, *The Nature and Significance of Economic Science* (1st ed., 1932), for enlightenment. Professor Robbins's book is not chosen as an extreme example, but merely as a convenient summary of views which are widely held among modern economists. Does Professor Robbins regard economics as a social science in the sense that it deals primarily with relations between people?

'The definition of Economics which would probably command most adherents . . . is that which relates it to the study of the causes of material welfare,' he tells us (p. 4). This, surely, is not a very promising definition, since it suggests all kinds of natural and applied sciences which the economist could scarcely be expected to master. We may, therefore, be thankful that Professor Robbins decides to reject this approach. In order to get at the essence of the matter, he next proceeds to consider 'the case of isolated man dividing his time between the production of real income and the enjoyment of leisure.' (p. 12) Here is our good friend Robinson Crusoe, and Professor Robbins finds his behavior very instructive. Without returning to the mainland, Professor Robbins works out a definition of economics: 'Economics is the science which studies human behaviour as a relationship between ends and scarce means which have alternative uses.' (p. 15)

This does not look very much like the definition of a science of social relations. It purports to be rather a definition of a science of human behavior in general. We are not, therefore, surprised to find that this science produces results which are generally relevant to all forms of society, that is to say, under the most different conditions as regards the kind of relations existing between the members of society. 'The generalisations of the Theory of Value,' according to Professor Robbins, 'are as applicable to the behaviour of isolated man or the executive authority of a communist society, as to the behaviour of man in an exchange economy.' (p. 19) The same thing, no doubt, could be said of the generalizations of physiology. Professor Robbins hardly goes so far as to affirm that economics is not a social science, but he has an evident distaste for the view that it is. If one took the point of view of the classical economists, he says, 'It was possible to regard the subject-matter of Economics as something social and collective.' With the more recent appreciation of the importance of individual choice, however, 'this approach becomes less and less convenient.' (p. 69) Furthermore, he tells us that instead of studying the aggregate output of society and its division—that is to say, the result of the social relationships of production—'we regard [the economic system] as a series of interdependent but conceptually discrete relationships *between men and economic goods*.'* (p. 69) In other words, the economic system is not considered primarily in terms

* Italics added.

of relations between men and men (social relations) but in terms of relations between men and things.

It would be a mistake to conclude that the modern economist does not concern himself at all with the social relations of production. On the contrary, he is continually engaged in researches which have an obviously social character. He will perhaps point to these researches as proof that charges brought against him on this score are unfounded. But this misses the essential point which we are trying to make. It is, of course, perfectly true that in applying or using the conceptual apparatus of economic theory, social relations are inevitably encountered and must be brought into the discussion. The point we are concerned to emphasize is that this conceptual apparatus is intended to be so constructed as to transcend any particular set of social relations. Consequently the latter enter the picture only incidentally, as it were, and at the level of application. We say incidentally because they need not enter at all. The fact that economic theory is supposed to be equally applicable to Robinson Crusoe and to various types of social economy proves this. To put the matter otherwise, economic theorizing is primarily a process of constructing and interrelating concepts from which all specifically social content has been drained off. In actual application the social element may be (and usually is, since Robinson Crusoe is mostly serviceable and interesting in the preliminary stages of theorizing) introduced by way of *ad hoc* assumptions specifying the field of application.

Let us attempt to make our meaning clear by examining the particular concept 'wages,' which plays a role in all modern economic theories. The term is taken from everyday language in which it signifies the sums of money paid at short intervals by an employer to hired workmen. Economic theory, however, has emptied out this social content and has redefined the word to mean the product, whether expressed in value or in physical terms, which is imputable to human activity engaged in a productive process in general. Thus Robinson Crusoe, the self-employed artisan, and the small peasant proprietor as well as the factory laborer all earn wages in this sense, though in common parlance, of course, only the last-named is properly to be regarded as the recipient of wages. In other words, 'wages' becomes a universal category of economic life (the struggle to overcome scarcity) instead of a category relevant to a particular historical form of society.

In investigating the present economic system, economists introduce either explicitly or by implication such institutional and social assumptions as are necessary in order that wages take the form of money payments by employers to hired workmen. What lies behind this form, however, is derived from the productivity theorems, which in themselves are entirely empty of social content. From this point it is an easy and natural step to treat wages as 'really' or 'in essence' the marginal productivity of labor and to regard the relation between employer and worker as expressed in the actual wage payment as incidental and in itself of no particular significance. Thus Professor Robbins states that 'the exchange relationship [in this case between employer and worker] is a *technical* incident . . . subsidiary to the main fact of scarcity.' (p. 19)

Nor is this the end of the matter. Once the point of view just set forth has been adopted, it is extraordinarily difficult, even for the most cautious, to avoid slipping into the habit of regarding the productivity 'wage' as in some sense the right wage, that is to say the income which the worker would receive under a fair and just economic order. We do not refer to the justifications of the present economic system which the older economists were in the habit of putting forward in terms of the productivity theory. They were too blatant and obvious and have long since gone out of fashion. We are referring to a much more subtle use of the productivity theory as a standard of desirability by critics of the *status quo*. Both Professor Pigou and Mrs. Robinson, for example, hold that the worker is exploited if he receives as wages less than the value of the marginal physical product of his labor.[1] Thus the present economic system is by implication criticized to the extent that it falls short of conformity with a model constructed from concepts which are altogether lacking in social content. Something which bears a striking resemblance to the eighteenth-century natural-law manner of judging society is thus smuggled through the back door by those who would carefully avoid bringing it openly into the front hall.

It would be possible to make a like analysis and to come to

broadly similar results if we were to examine such other central concepts of economic theory as rent, interest, profits, capital, et cetera. But the point is probably sufficiently clear by now. In each case the concepts are borrowed from everyday language, the social content is drained off, and the resulting universal categories are applied indifferently to all kinds of economic systems. These systems are then judged to differ from one another largely in unessential matters of form, as far as the economist is concerned. And it may even be, as we have seen, that they are evaluated not in social terms, but by reference to abstract models which are felt to be of prior logical importance.

It seems obvious that in this way the economist avoids a systematic exploration of those social relations which are so universally regarded as having a relevance to economic problems that they are deeply imbedded in the everyday speech of the business world. And it is even more obvious that the basic point of view which modern economics has adopted unfits it for the larger task of throwing light on the role of the economic element in the complex totality of relations between man and man which make up what we call society.

It seems reasonable to suppose that the state of affairs which has been briefly sketched in the foregoing paragraphs has more than a little to do with what may fairly be described as a widespread feeling of dissatisfaction with economists and their works. This being the case, it might appear that the most fruitful procedure would be to launch upon a detailed investigation of the central tenets and beliefs of modern economics from the point of view of its shortcomings as a truly social science of human relations. Critical analysis of this kind, however, is at best a thankless task, and it is commonly open to the justifiable charge of failure to offer anything constructive in place of what it rejects. We have, therefore, decided to abandon the terrain of received doctrine, having convinced ourselves that there is reason to be restless there, and to explore another approach to the study of economic problems, namely, that which is associated with the name of Karl Marx.

In what follows, consequently, we shall be concerned very largely with Marxian economics. This should not be taken to imply that there is any intention of revealing 'what Marx really meant.' On this score we make the simplifying, though perhaps not obvious, assumption that he meant what he said, and we set ourselves the more modest task of discovering what, if anything, can be learned from Marx.

PART ONE

VALUE AND SURPLUS VALUE

I

MARX'S METHOD

Discussions of methodology in economics, as in other fields, are likely to be tiresome and unrewarding. Nevertheless, to avoid the problem altogether is to risk serious misunderstanding. In this chapter, therefore, we shall attempt as briefly as possible to set forth the chief elements in Marx's approach to economics. This is the more important in Marx's case since many of his original and significant contributions are precisely of a methodological character. Lukacs, one of the most penetrating of contemporary Marxists, has even gone so far as to assert that 'orthodoxy in questions of Marxism relates exclusively to method.' [1]

1. The Use of Abstraction

From a formal point of view Marx's economic methodology may appear strikingly similar to that of his classical predecessors and his neo-classical successors. He was a strong adherent of the abstract-deductive method which was such a marked characteristic of the Ricardian school. 'In the analysis of economic forms,' he wrote in the Preface to *Capital*, 'neither microscopes nor chemical reagents are of use. The force of abstraction must replace both.' Moreover, Marx believed in and practiced what modern theorists have called the method of 'successive approximations,' which consists in moving from the more abstract to the more concrete in a step-by-step fashion, removing simplifying assumptions at successive stages of the investigation so that theory may take account of and explain an ever wider range of actual phenomena.

When we inquire further, however, we find striking differences between Marx and the representatives of the classical and neo-classical tradition. The principle of abstraction is itself powerless to yield knowledge; the difficult questions concern the manner of its application. In other words, one must somehow decide what to abstract from and what not to abstract from. Here at least two issues arise. First, what problem is being investigated? And, second, what are the essential elements of the problem? If we have the answer to these questions, we shall surely know what we cannot abstract from, and, within these limits, we shall be able to frame our assumptions according to criteria of convenience and simplicity. Now, we need go no further than the first question to convince ourselves that economists have not always been in agreement on their objectives. The problems which several well-known economists have set themselves for investigation may be cited: 'the nature and causes of the wealth of nations' (Adam Smith); 'the laws which regulate the distribution of the produce of the earth' (Ricardo); 'man's actions in the ordinary business of life' (Marshall); 'price and its causes and its corollaries' (Davenport); 'human behaviour as a relationship between ends and scarce means which have alternative uses' (Robbins). No doubt there is overlapping here, but it is doubtful if any two could be regarded as identical. From this it follows that no two investigators will handle their materials—including the manner in which they apply the weapon of abstraction—in exactly the same way. One may abstract from a difference which another is trying to explain, yet each may be justified from the point of view of the problem which he is studying. This must be particularly kept in mind by the student of Marx, since his objective—'to lay bare the economic law of motion of modern society' [2]—is radically different from that of non-Marxian schools of thought.

Even after the investigator's task has been determined, however, there is still no sovereign formula to guide his footsteps. As Hegel very correctly remarked in the Introduction to his *Philosophy of History:* in the 'process of scientific understanding, it is of importance that the essential should be distinguished and brought into relief in contrast with the so-called non-essential. But in order to render this possible we must know what *is essential* . . .' [3] To bring the essential into relief and to make possible its analysis: that is the specific task of abstraction. But where to start? How to distinguish the essential from the non-essential? Methodology can pose these questions, but unfortunately it cannot provide ready-made answers. If it could, the 'process of scientific understanding' would be a far more routine matter than it actually is. In practice, it is necessary to formulate hypotheses about what is essential, to work these hypotheses through, and to check the conclusions against the data of experience. If we are to understand the achievement of a particular scientist we must, therefore, try to identify his key hypotheses and to see, if possible, where he gets them from and how he develops their implications. It need hardly be pointed out that this is not always an easy matter, but in the case of Marx we know enough about his intellectual development to make the attempt.

As a student at the university, Marx concentrated in jurisprudence and philosophy and planned to enter upon an academic career. His 'radical' leanings—though at the time he was not even a socialist—prevented his getting a teaching position, and in 1842 he accepted the editorship of the newly founded *Rheinische Zeitung*. In this capacity he came into contact for the first time with actual social problems and also with new social ideas, particularly the socialist and communist ideas which were emanating from France in such quantities in the 1830s and 1840s. In a controversy with the *Augsburger Zeitung*, Marx was somewhat discomfited to discover that he did not know what to think of socialism; he therefore resolved at the first opportunity to give the subject the serious study which he was convinced it merited. The opportunity was not long in coming; in a few months the *Rheinische Zeitung* was shut down by the authorities, and Marx found himself a free agent. He immediately plunged into an intensive study of socialism and communism, of French history, and of English political economy. It was during the next few years, spent mostly in Paris and Brussels, that he broke with his philosophic past and achieved the mature point of view from which he was to write his later economic works. In short, his approach to economics was shaped and determined long before he decided to make the study of economics his primary concern.

We have in the justly famous Preface to *The Critique of Political Economy* a statement by Marx concerning his intellectual development during these crucial years. Though many readers will be familiar with this preface, it may perhaps not be amiss to reproduce a portion of it here. (The italics are added.)

I was led by my studies [he wrote] to the conclusion that legal relations as well as forms of state could neither be understood by themselves, nor explained by the so-called general progress of the human mind, but that they are rooted in the material conditions of life which are summed up by Hegel after the fashion of the English and French of the eighteenth century under the name 'civil society'; *the anatomy of that civil society is to be sought in political economy*. The study of the latter which I had taken up in Paris, I continued at Brussels . . . The general conclusion at which I arrived and which, *once reached, continued to serve as the leading thread in my studies*, may be briefly summed up as follows: In the social production which men carry on they enter into definite relations that are independent of their will; these relations of production correspond to a definite stage of development of their material powers of production. The sum total of these relations of production constitutes the economic structure of society—the real foundation on which rise legal and political superstructures and to which correspond definite forms of social consciousness. The mode of production in material life determines the general character of the social, political, and spiritual processes of life. It is not the consciousness of men that determines their existence, but, on the contrary, their social existence determines their consciousness. At a certain stage of their development, the material forces of production in society come in conflict with the existing relations of production, or—what is but a legal expression for the same thing—with the property relations within which they had been at work before. From forms of development of the forces of production these relations turn into their fetters. Then comes the period of social revolution. With the change of the economic foundation the entire immense superstructure is more or less rapidly transformed.

It is apparent from this that Marx's primary interest was society as a whole, and, more especially, the process of social change. Political Economy—the 'anatomy' of society—is significant not primarily for its own sake but because it is in this sphere that the impetus to social change is to be found. It must be emphasized, because the contrary has so often been asserted, that Marx was not trying to reduce everything to economic terms. He was rather attempting to uncover the true interrelation between the economic and the non-economic factors in the totality of social existence.

Once having reached the conclusion that the key to social change is to be found in movements of the mode of production, Marx was in effect committed to an exhaustive study of political economy from the standpoint of the laws governing changes in the mode of production. 'To lay bare the economic law of motion of modern society' now became the scientific goal to which he devoted most of the remainder of his life.

How, given this objective, could one recognize the essential aspects of the problem? Marx retained, because they seemed to stand up under searching studies into the actuality of historical development, those elements of Hegel's thought which emphasized process and development through the conflict of opposed or contradictory forces. Unlike Hegel, however, he traced decisive historical conflicts to roots in the mode of production; that is, he discovered them to be what he called class conflicts. Thus the *Communist Manifesto* (1847), after an introductory note, begins: 'The history of all hitherto existing society is the history of class struggles.' The economic forces at work manifest themselves in class conflicts under capitalism as under earlier forms of society. It follows that the essential economic relations are those which underlie and express themselves in the form of class conflict. These are the essential elements which must be isolated and analysed through the method of abstraction.

Even this hypothesis, however, could lead to divergent procedures. The classical economists were also very much interested in the economic roots of class conflicts—in a sense this is exactly what 'the distribution of the produce of the earth' meant to Ricardo—but the social antagonism which occupied most of their attention, both intellectual and emotional, was the conflict between industrial capitalists and landlords. Consequently they placed great, sometimes predominant, emphasis on land and the income derived from the ownership of land. Indeed, without a knowledge of 'the true doctrine of rent,' Ricardo asserted, 'it is impossible to understand the effect of the progress of wealth on profits and wages, or to trace satisfactorily the influence of taxation on different classes of the community . . .'[4] Marx recognized the tendency to lay primary emphasis on land and rent, but he regarded it as misguided. 'Nothing seems more natural,' he wrote, 'than to start with rent, with landed property, since it is bound up with land, the source of all production and all existence, and with the first form of production in all more or less settled communities, viz., agriculture.'[5] Nevertheless, he added at once, 'nothing could be more erroneous.' His reason for adopting this attitude is the key to his subsequent procedure. In capitalist society,

> agriculture comes to be more and more merely a branch of industry and is completely dominated by capital . . . *Capital is the all-dominating power of bourgeois society*. It must form the starting point as well as the end and be developed before land ownership is . . .
>
> It would thus be impractical and wrong to arrange the economic categories in the order in which they were the determining factors in the course of history. Their order of sequence is rather determined by the relation which they bear to each other in modern bourgeois society, and which is the exact opposite of what seems to be their natural order or the order of their historical development. What we are interested in is not the place which economic relations occupy in the historical succession of different forms of society . . . We are interested in their organic connection within modern bourgeois society.[6]

The italicized sentence is particularly important. That 'capital is the all-dominating economic power of bourgeois society' meant to Marx, as it would have meant to one of the classical economists, that the primary economic relation is that between capitalists and workers. As he expressed the point in another place, 'The relation betwen wage labor and capital determines the entire character of the mode of production.'[7] Even before he began his researches for the *Critique* and for *Capital*, he had expressed the same judgment in the *Manifesto:* 'Society as a whole is more and more splitting up into two great hostile camps, into two great classes facing each other—bourgeoisie and proletariat.' This relation must form the center of investigation; the power of abstraction must be employed to isolate it, to reduce it to its purest form, to enable it to be subjected to the most painstaking analysis, free of all unrelated disturbances.

The adoption of this position requires a procedure involving at least two fairly distinct steps.

First, all social relations except that between capital and labor must be provisionally assumed away, to be reintroduced, one at a time, only at a later stage of the analysis.

Second, the capital-labor relation itself must be reduced to its most significant form or forms. This is not a quantitative question; it does not mean that the most frequent, or modal, forms of the relation must be selected for analysis. Significance, in this context, is a question of the structural characteristics and tendencies of the whole society. Marx, as is well known, selected the forms of capital-labor relation which arise in the sphere of industrial production as the most significant for modern capitalist society. Capitalists and workers are alike reduced to certain standard types, from which all characteristics irrelevant to the relation under examination are removed. 'Individuals are dealt with,' he wrote in the Preface to *Capital*, 'only in so far as they are the personifications of economic categories, embodiments of particular class relations and class interests.'

What is the nature of this capital-labor relation? In form it is an exchange relation. The capitalist buys labor power from the worker; the worker receives money from the capitalist with which he acquires the necessaries of life. As an exchange relation, it is clearly a special case of a large class of such relations which have a common form and structure. It is evident, therefore, that the study of the capital-labor relation must begin with an analysis of the general phenomenon of exchange.

In this way we arrive at the actual starting point of Marx's Political Economy. Part I of the first volume of *Capital*, which summarizes the earlier *Critique of Political Economy*, is entitled 'Commodities.' Whatever is customarily intended for exchange rather than for direct use is a commodity; the analysis of commodities, therefore, involves the analysis of the exchange relation and its quantitative aspect (exchange value); it includes, moreover, an analysis of money. As we shall see later on, some of Marx's most interesting results arise out of the treatment of commodities.

Having laid the necessary foundation with the analysis of commodities, Marx proceeds to his main task. *Almost the entire remainder of the first volume of* Capital *is devoted to the capital-labor relation in its 'isolated' and 'purified' forms.* In other words, Volume I begins and remains on a high level of abstraction.

It is difficult for those unacquainted with Marx's method to believe that this statement can be meant seriously. They point to the wealth of factual and historical material which is such an outstanding feature of Volume I. Does this not mean that Marx was, in fact, just the reverse of abstract? This reasoning misses the point. The legitimate purpose of abstraction in social science is never to get away from the real world but rather to isolate certain aspects of the real world for intensive investigation. When, therefore, we say that we are operating on a high level of abstraction we mean that we are dealing with a relatively small number of aspects of reality; we emphatically do not mean that those aspects with which we are dealing are not capable of historical investigation and factual illustration. A cursory check-up is sufficient to indicate that the great bulk of the factual material introduced by Marx in Volume I relates directly to the capital-labor relation and is of an illustrative or historical character. It constitutes, therefore, a confirmation rather than a contradiction of the statement that Volume I begins and remains on a high level of abstraction.

The establishment of this fact allows us to draw an important corollary, namely, that the results achieved in Volume I have a provisional character. In many cases, though not necessarily in all, they undergo a more or less extensive modification on a lower level of abstraction, that is to say, when more aspects of reality are taken into account.* It follows that the tendencies or laws enunciated in Volume I are not to be interpreted as direct predictions about the future. Their validity is relative to the level of abstraction on which they are derived and to the extent of the modifications which they must undergo when the analysis is brought to a more concrete level. Recognition of this fact would have saved a great deal of sterile controversy. As an ex-

* This aspect of Marx's method is well treated by Henryk Grossmann in the Introduction to his book *Das Akkumulations- und Zusammenbruchsgesetz des kapitalistischen Systems*, 1929.

ample we may cite the famous 'law of the increasing misery of the proletariat,' which Marx called 'the absolute general law of capitalist accumulation.' [8] Anti-Marxists have always maintained the falsity of this law and have deduced from this the incorrectness of Marx's analysis of capitalism.* Some Marxists, on the other hand, have been equally concerned to demonstrate the truth of the law,† and so a controversy producing much heat and little light has raged for more than a half century. Both sides are guilty of the same misunderstanding of Marx's method. The law in question is derived on a high level of abstraction; the term 'absolute' used in describing it is used in the Hegelian sense of 'abstract'; it constitutes in no sense a concrete prediction about the future. Moreover, in this particular case, Marx says as much in perfectly clear language, so that misinterpretation seems peculiarly difficult to condone. Having stated the law, he immediately adds, 'Like all other laws it is modified in its working by many circumstances, the analysis of which does not concern us here.' It would be impossible to have a plainer warning not to interpret the law as a concrete prediction. A proper regard to problems of method would have rendered this misunderstanding, along with many others, unnecessary.

We need not discuss the whole plan of *Capital*. For present purposes, it is only necessary to point out that the intent of Volumes II and III was to take into account factors which were consciously left out of Volume I, that is to say, to bring the analysis to progressively lower levels of abstraction. At the same time, and in a sense paradoxically, Volumes II and III contain relatively less factual material than Volume I. This is accounted for by their unfinished state. In compiling Volumes II and III from Marx's manuscripts, Engels found a great deal of illustrative material, but it was 'barely arranged, much less worked out.' [9] Volume I, on the other hand, Marx prepared for the press himself, so that he was able to integrate his factual and theoretical materials in a way which Engels could not possibly have accom-

* Grossmann cites a large number of examples. *Das Akkumulations- und Zusammenbruchsgesetz des kapitalistischen Systems*, pp. 23 ff.

† Perhaps the most recent example is the pamphlet by Alex Bittelmann and V. J. Jerome, *Leninism—the only Marxism Today* (1934). This pamphlet is a criticism of Lewis Corey's *Decline of American Capitalism* (1934).

plished for the later volumes without going far beyond the functions of an editor, a course which he wisely declined to pursue.

We have discussed Marx's use of abstraction in general terms and do not propose at this stage to enter into particular cases. It is well to note, however, that a great many criticisms of Marx's economics are, consciously or unconsciously, based upon a rejection of the assumptions with which he works. Our discussion should help to establish criteria by which to judge the validity of these criticisms. In each case, the following three questions should be asked about the simplifying assumptions (or abstractions) which give rise to criticism: (1) are they framed with a proper regard for the problem under investigation? (2) do they eliminate the non-essential elements of the problem? (3) do they stop short of eliminating the essential elements? If all three of these questions can be answered in the affirmative, we may say that the principle of appropriate abstraction has been observed. This principle is of great assistance in testing the relevance and validity of a considerable range of Marx criticism.

2. The Historical Character of Marx's Thought

Marx's method, says Lukacs, 'is in its innermost essence historical.' [10] This is certainly correct, and no discussion of the problem which fails to emphasize it can be regarded as satisfactory.*

For Marx, social reality is not so much a specified set of relations, still less a conglomeration of things. It is rather the process of change inherent in a specified set of relations. In other words, social reality is the historical process, a process which, in principle, knows no finality and no stopping places.† Social systems, like individuals, go through a life cycle and pass from the scene when 'from forms of development of the forces of production' they 'turn into their fetters.' The process of social change, however, is not purely mechanical; it is rather the product of human

* One of the best discussions in English of this aspect of Marx's thought, and, indeed, of all the problems treated in this chapter, will be found in Karl Korsch, *Karl Marx* (1938).

† 'There is a continual movement of growth in productive forces, of destruction in social relations, of formation in ideas; the only immutable thing is the abstraction of movement—*mors immortalis*.' Marx, *The Poverty of Philosophy*, International Publishers ed., p. 93.

action, but action which is definitely limited by the kind of society in which it has its roots. 'Men make their own history,' Marx wrote, 'but they do not make it just as they please; they do not make it under circumstances chosen by themselves, but under circumstances directly found, given and transmitted from the past.' [11] Society both is changing and, within limits, can be changed.

Consistent adherence to this position leads to a consistently historical approach to social science. Moreover—and this is but another aspect of the same thing—it leads to a critical approach to every form of society, including the present. The importance of this point is difficult to overstress. It is a characteristic feature of non-Marxian thought that it can comprehend the transitory character of all earlier social orders, while this same critical faculty fails when it is a question of the capitalist system itself. This is, no doubt, true to a certain extent of all historical epochs, but, as we shall see later on, there are special reasons why it applies with peculiar force to our own.* For the typical modern thinker, as Marx expressed it, 'there has been history, but there is no longer any.' [12] Lukacs' remark in this connection is striking:

> This un- and anti-historical core of bourgeois thought appears in its most glaring form when we consider the *problem of the present as a historical problem* . . . The complete incapacity of all bourgeois thinkers and historians to comprehend world-historical events of the present as world history must remain an unpleasant memory to all level-headed people since the world war and the world revolution.[13]

Nothing that has happened since 1922 could lead one to alter this judgment; rather the contrary. Marxists, on the other hand, consistently interpret contemporary events in a world-historical context. The difference is obviously not a question of intelligence; it is a question of method and approach.

Most people take capitalism for granted, just as they take the solar system for granted. The eventual passing of capitalism, which is often conceded nowadays, is thought of in much the same way as the eventual cooling of the sun, that is to say, its relevance to contemporary events is denied. From this point

* See below, pp. 34-40.

of view one can understand and criticize what happens within the framework of the system; one can neither understand nor evaluate what happens to the system itself. The latter fact not infrequently takes the form of a simple denial that one can meaningfully talk about social systems. Great historical events, however, generally concern whole social systems. The result is that to the typical modern mind they assume a catastrophic character, with all that this implies in the way of emotional shock and intellectual confusion.

To the Marxist, on the other hand, the specific historical (i.e. transitory) character of capitalism is a major premise. It is by virtue of this fact that the Marxist is able, so to speak, to stand outside the system and criticize it as a whole. Moreover, since human action is itself responsible for the changes which the system is undergoing and will undergo, a critical attitude is not only intellectually possible, it is also morally significant—as, for example, a critical attitude toward the solar system, whatever its shortcomings, would not be—and, last but not least, practically important.

II

THE QUALITATIVE-VALUE PROBLEM

1. Introduction

The first chapter of *Capital* is entitled 'Commodities.' It has already been pointed out that a commodity is anything that is produced for exchange rather than for the use of the producer; the study of commodities is therefore the study of the economic relation of exchange. Marx begins by analysing 'simple commodity production,' that is to say a society in which each producer owns his own means of production and satisfies his manifold needs by exchange with other similarly situated producers. Here we have the problem of exchange in its clearest and most elementary form.

In starting from simple commodity production, Marx was following a well-established tradition of economic theory, but this should not be allowed to obscure the sharp break which divides his analysis from that of the classical school. In the case of Adam Smith, for example, exchange is tied in the closest possible way to the main technological fact of economic life, namely, the division of labor. According to Smith, division of labor is the foundation of all increases in productivity; it is even the basis of the human economy, what distinguishes the latter from the life of the beasts. But Smith is unable to conceive of division of labor independently of exchange; exchange, in fact, is prior to and responsible for division of labor. The following passage sums up Smith's theory of the relation between division of labor and exchange:

> This division of labor, from which so many advantages are derived, is not originally the effect of any human wisdom, which foresees and intends that general opulence to which it gives occasion. It is the necessary, though very slow and gradual consequence of a certain propensity in human nature which has in

view no such extensive utility; the propensity to truck, barter, and exchange one thing for another.[1]

This 'propensity to truck, barter, and exchange,' moreover, is peculiar to human beings: 'Nobody ever saw a dog make a fair and deliberate exchange of one bone for another with another dog.' [2] Exchange and division of labor are in this manner indissolubly bound together and shown to be the joint pillars supporting civilized society. The implications of this position are clear: commodity production, rooted in human nature, is the universal and inevitable form of economic life; economic science is the science of commodity production. From this point of view the problems of economics have an exclusively quantitative character; they begin with exchange value, the basic quantitative relation between commodities established through the process of exchange.

Turning now to Marx, we see at the very outset the difference in approach which marks off his political economy from that of Adam Smith. Marx does not deny the existence of a relation between commodity production and the division of labor, but it is by no means the hard and fast relation depicted by Smith. The difference in points of view is clearly brought out in the following passage:

This division of labor is a necessary condition for the production of commodities, but it does not follow conversely, that the production of commodities is a necessary condition for the division of labor. In the primitive Indian community there is social division of labor without production of commodities. Or, to take an example nearer home, in every factory the labor is divided according to a system, but this division is not brought about by the operatives' mutually exchanging their individual products. *Only such products can become commodities with regard to each other as result from different kinds of labor, each kind being carried on independently and for the account of private individuals.*[3]

Division of labor is deprived of none of the importance which was attributed to it by Smith, but it is emphatically denied that division of labor is necessarily tied to exchange. Commodity production, in other words, is not the universal and inevitable form of economic life. It is rather one possible form of economic life, a form, to be sure, which has been familiar for many centuries and which dominates the modern period, but none the less a historically conditioned form which can in no sense claim to be a direct manifestation of human nature. The implications of this view are striking. Commodity production itself is withdrawn from the realm of natural phenomena and becomes the valid subject of socio-historical investigation. No longer can the economist afford to confine his attention to the quantitative relations arising from commodity production; he must also direct his attention to the character of the social relations which underlie the commodity form. We may express this by saying that the tasks of economics are not only quantitative, they are also qualitative. More concretely, in the case of exchange value there is, as Adam Smith saw, the quantitative relation between products; hidden behind this, as Marx was the first to see, there is a specific, historically conditioned, relation between producers. Following Petry, we may call the analysis of the former *the quantitative-value problem*, the analysis of the latter *the qualitative-value problem.**

The great originality of Marx's value theory lies in its recognition of these two elements of the problem and in its attempt to deal with them simultaneously within a single conceptual framework. The same considerations, however, account in no small degree for the great difficulty in understanding the theory which is almost invariably experienced by those brought up in the main tradition of economic thought. For this reason it has seemed advisable to separate Marxian value theory into its two component parts and attempt to deal with them one at a time. Consequently in this chapter we shall discuss the qualitative-value problem, leaving the more familiar quantitative problem for consideration in the next chapter.

* Franz Petry, *Der Soziale Gehalt der Marxschen Werttheorie* (1916). This little book, the only one ever published by its author, who was killed in the First World War at the age of 26, deserves much more attention than it has received. A similar distinction is made in the excellent note on value theory by Alfred Lowe, 'Mr. Dobb and Marx's Theory of Value,' in the English *Modern Quarterly*, July 1938.

2. Use Value

'Every commodity,' Marx wrote, 'has a twofold aspect, that of use value and exchange value.'[4]

In possessing use value a commodity is in no way peculiar. Objects of human consumption in every age and in every form of society likewise possess use value. Use value is an expression of a certain relation between the consumer and the object consumed. Political economy, on the other hand, is a social science of the relations between people. It follows that 'use value as such lies outside the sphere of investigation of political economy.'[5]

Marx excluded use value (or, as it now would be called, 'utility') from the field of investigation of political economy on the ground that it does not directly embody a social relation. He enforces a strict requirement that the categories of economics must be social categories, i.e. categories which represent relations between people. It is important to realize that this is in sharp contrast to the attitude of modern economic theory. As previously noted, Lionel Robbins says—and in this he is merely formulating the practice of all non-Marxian schools—'We regard [the economic system] as a series of interdependent but conceptually discrete relationships *between men and economic goods.*'[6] From this starting point, it follows, of course, that use value or utility takes a central position among the categories of economics. But it should not be overlooked in any comparison of Marxian and orthodox economics that their respective starting points are in this respect diametrically opposed. Nor should it be made a matter of reproach against Marx that he failed to develop a subjective value theory, since he consciously and deliberately dissociated himself from any attempt to do so.*

This does not mean that use value should play no role in economics. On the contrary, just as land, though not an economic category itself, is essential to production, so use value is a pre-

* The best criticism of subjective value theory from the Marxist standpoint, and at the same time a very valuable contribution to the understanding of Marx's value theory, is Rudolf Hilferding, 'Böhm-Bawerk's Marx-Kritik,' *Marx Studien*, Bd. 1, 1904.

requisite to consumption and, as Petry correctly remarks, is in no sense excluded by Marx from the causal chain of economic phenomena.[7]

3. Exchange Value

In possessing exchange value relative to one another, commodities show their unique characteristic. It is only as commodities, in a society where exchange is a regular method of realizing the purpose of social production, that products have exchange value. At first sight it might seem that even less than in the case of use value have we here to do with a social relation. Exchange value appears to be a quantitative relation between things, between the commodities themselves. In what sense, then, is it to be conceived as a social relation and hence as a proper subject for the investigation of the economist? Marx's answer to this question is the key to his value theory. The quantitative relation between things, which we call exchange value, is in reality only an outward form of the *social* relation between the commodity owners, or, what comes to the same thing in simple commodity production, between the producers themselves. The exchange relation as such, apart from any consideration of the quantities involved, is an expression of the fact that individual producers, each working in isolation, are in fact working for each other. Their labor, whatever they may think about the matter, has a social character which is impressed upon it by the act of exchange. In other words, the exchange of commodities is an exchange of the products of the labor of individual producers. What finds expression in the form of exchange value is therefore the fact that the commodities involved are the products of human labor in a society based on division of labor in which producers work privately and independently.

Strictly speaking, the concept exchange value applies 'only when commodities are present in the plural,'[8] since it expresses a relation *between* commodities. An individual commodity, however, possesses the social quality which manifests itself quantitatively in exchange value. A commodity in so far as we center our attention on this social quality is called by Marx a plain 'value.' Late in Chapter 1 of *Capital,* he says: 'When, at the beginning of this chapter, we said, in common parlance, that a commodity is both a use value and an exchange value, we were, accurately speaking, wrong. A commodity is a use value or object of utility, and a value.'[9]

As a use value, a commodity is a universal feature of human existence, present in every and all forms of society. As a value, a commodity is a feature of a specific historical form of society which has two main distinguishing characteristics: (1) developed division of labor, and (2) private production. In such an order—and in none other—the labor of producers eventuates in commodities or, neglecting the universal aspect of commodities (utility), in values.

It is essential to realize that it was this analysis of the social characteristics of commodity production, and not an arbitrary preconception or an ethical principle, which led Marx to identify labor as the substance of value.* We must now examine this more closely.

4. Labor and Value

The requirement that all economic categories must represent social relations led Marx directly to labor as the 'value that lies hidden behind'[10] exchange value. 'Only one property of a commodity,' as Petry expressed it, 'enables us to assume it as the bearer and expression of social relations, namely its property as *the product of labor*, since as such we consider it no longer from the standpoint of consumption but from the standpoint of production, as materialized human activity . . .'[11] In what sense, then, are we using the concept 'labor'?

Labor also has two aspects, the one corresponding to the use value and the other to the value of the commodity which it produces. To the commodity as a use value corresponds labor as useful labor.

* In the notes on Wagner quoted above, Marx described his procedure in part as follows: 'What I . . . start from is the simplest social form in which the labor product is found in present society, and that is "commodity." I analyse it, and first of all in *the form in which it appears.* Here I find that on the one hand in its natural form it is a *useful thing* alias *use value,* on the other hand the *bearer of exchange value . . .* Further analysis of the latter shows me that exchange value is only a "phenomenal *form,*" an independent method of displaying the value contained in the commodity, and then I proceed to the analysis of the latter . . .' *Das Kapital* (Marx-Engels-Lenin ed.) I, p. 847.

> The coat is a use value that satisfies a particular want. Its existence is the result of a special sort of productive activity, the nature of which is determined by its aim, mode of operation, subject, means and result. The labor, whose utility is thus represented by the value in use of its product, or which manifests itself by making its product a use value, we call useful labor.[12]

Thus tailoring creates a coat, spinning creates yarn, weaving creates cloth, carpentering creates a table, et cetera. These are all different varieties of useful labor. But it would be incorrect to assume that useful labor is the only source of use value; nature co-operates both actively and passively in the process of producing use value. 'As William Petty put it, labor is its father and the earth its mother.' [13]

If, now, we abstract from the use value of a commodity it exists simply as a value. Proceeding in a similar fashion to abstract from the useful character of labor, what have we left?

> Productive activity, if we leave out of sight its special form, viz., the useful character of the labor, is nothing but the expenditure of human labor power. Tailoring and weaving, though qualitatively different productive activities, are each a productive expenditure of human brains, nerves, and muscles, and in this sense are human labor. Of course, this labor power which remains the same under all its modifications must have attained a certain pitch of development before it can be expended in a multiplicity of modes. But the value of a commodity represents human labor in the abstract, the expenditure of human labor in general.[14]

Thus, what use value is to value in the case of commodity, useful labor is to abstract labor in the case of productive activity. When Marx says that labor is the substance of value, he always means, therefore, labor considered as abstract labor. We may sum up the qualitative relation of value to labor with the following statement:

> On the one hand all labor is, speaking physiologically, an expenditure of human labor power, and in its character of identical abstract human labor, it creates and forms the values of commodities. On the other hand, all labor is the expenditure of

human labor power in a special form and with a definite aim, and in this, its character of concrete useful labor, it produces use values.[15]

5. Abstract Labor

Abstract labor which is represented in the value of commodities is a concept which has an important place in Marx's thinking. It must be admitted, however, that it is not an easy concept to comprehend; and for this reason it seems wise to consider the matter in further detail.

It may be well to remove at once any misunderstandings of a purely verbal character. To many the expression 'abstract labor' suggests something slightly mysterious, perhaps not a little metaphysical and unreal. As should be clear from the last section, however, nothing of the sort was intended by Marx. Abstract labor is abstract only in the quite straightforward sense that all special characteristics which differentiate one kind of labor from another are ignored. Abstract labor, in short, is, as Marx's own usage clearly attests, equivalent to 'labor in general'; it is what is common to all productive human activity.

Marx did not think he was the first to introduce the idea of labor in general into political economy. For example, in speaking of Benjamin Franklin, whom he regarded as 'one of the first economists, after Wm. Petty, who saw through the nature of value,' he had the following to say:

> Franklin is unconscious that by estimating the value of everything in labor, he makes abstraction from any difference in the sorts of labor exchanged, and thus reduces them all to equal human labor. But although ignorant of this, yet he says it. He speaks first of 'the one labor,' then of 'the other labor,' and finally of 'labor,' without further qualification, as the substance of the value of everything.[16]

And in another connection, he remarks that 'it was a tremendous advance on the part of Adam Smith to throw aside all limitations which mark wealth-producing activity and to define it as labor in general, neither industrial, nor commercial, nor agricultural, or one as much as the other.'[17] Ricardo, as Marx was well aware, adopted the same point of view and followed it out with greater consistency than Smith. In this, as in many other cases, Marx started from a basic idea of the classical school, gave it precise and explicit expression, developed it, and utilized it in the analysis of social relations in his own original and penetrating fashion.

It is important to realize that the reduction of all labor to a common denominator, so that units of labor can be compared with and substituted for one another, added and subtracted, and finally totalled up to form a social aggregate, is not an arbitrary abstraction, dictated in some way by the whim of the investigator. It is rather, as Lukacs correctly observes, an abstraction 'which belongs to the essence of capitalism.'[18] Let us examine this more closely.

Capitalist society is characterized by a degree of labor mobility much greater than prevailed in any previous form of society. Not only do workers change their jobs relatively frequently, but also the stream of new workers entering the labor market is quickly diverted from declining to rising occupations. As Marx expressed it, 'We see at a glance that, in our capitalist society, a given portion of human labor is, in accordance with the varying demand, at one time supplied in the form of tailoring, at another in the form of weaving. This change may possibly not take place without friction, but take place it must.'[19] Under these circumstances, the various specific kinds of labor in existence at any given time and the relative quantities of each become matters of secondary importance in any general view of the economic system. Much more significant is the total size of the social labor force and its general level of development. On these depend the productive potentialities of society, whether the latter be manifested in the production of consumer's goods or in the production of implements of war. This is a conclusion which commands universal assent in the modern world; it flows from such common facts of experience that no one would think of denying it. It is important to observe, however, that in arriving at this conclusion we were obliged to abstract from the differences between specific forms of labor, an abstraction which is inevitably implied in the very notion of a total labor force available to society. We are likely to forget or overlook this only because the differences are *practically* of secondary importance.

In the course of a methodological discussion, Marx emphasizes this point in the following terms:

> . . . This abstraction of labor is but the result of a concrete aggregate of different kinds of labor. The indifference to the particular kind of labor corresponds to a form of society in which individuals pass with ease from one kind of work to another, which makes it immaterial to them what particular kind of work may fall to their share. Labor has become here, not only categorically but really, a means of creating wealth in general and is no longer grown together with the individual into one particular destination. This state of affairs has found its highest development in the most modern of bourgeois societies, the United States. It is only here that the abstraction of the category 'labor,' 'labor in general,' labor *sans phrase*, the starting point of modern political economy, becomes realized in practice.[20]

To sum up, we may say that the reduction of all labor to abstract labor enables us to see clearly, behind the special forms which labor may assume at any given time, an aggregate social labor force which is capable of transference from one use to another in accordance with social need, and on the magnitude and development of which society's wealth-producing capacity in the last resort depends. The adoption of this point of view, moreover, is conditioned by the very nature of capitalist production which promotes a degree of labor mobility never before approached in earlier forms of society.

6. The Relation of the Quantitative to the Qualitative in Value Theory

We are now in a position to see precisely what is implied in the thesis that abstract labor is the substance of value. A commodity appears at first glance to be merely a useful article which has been produced by a special kind of workman, working privately and in isolation from the rest of society. This is correct so far as it goes. But investigation reveals that the commodity in question has this in common with all other commodities (i.e.

they are all values), namely, that it absorbs a part of society's total available labor force (i.e. they are all materialized abstract labor). It is this characteristic of commodities (which presupposes use value and manifests itself in exchange value) that makes of 'commodity' the starting point and central category of the political economy of the modern period.

We have reached these conclusions through a purely qualitative analysis, and it may appear that they have little bearing on the quantitative problem. This, however, is not so. The truth is that the basic significance as well as the main tasks of quantitative-value theory are determined by the qualitative analysis. Here we shall merely indicate the reasons for this, leaving more detailed treatment for the next chapter.

From a formal point of view it appears that quantitative-value theory is concerned solely with discovering the laws which regulate the relative proportions in which commodities exchange for one another. This is, indeed, the way in which orthodox theory regards the matter; it is simply a question of exchange value.* But for Marx, as we already know, exchange value is merely the 'phenomenal form' behind which hides value itself. The question therefore arises: what, beyond the mere determination of exchange ratios, is the quantitative-value problem? The analysis presented above provides us with an answer.

The fact that a commodity is a value means that it is materialized abstract labor, or, in other words, that it has absorbed a part of the total wealth-producing activity of society. If now we reflect that abstract labor is susceptible of measurement in terms of time units, the meaning of value as a quantitative category distinct from exchange value becomes apparent. As Marx stated it, 'Magnitude of value expresses . . . the connection that exists between a certain article and the portion of the total labor time of society required to produce it.'[21]

The main task of quantitative-value theory emerges from this

* Cf., for example, the following statement made by Joan Robinson in the Introduction to her book, *The Economics of Imperfect Competition:* 'The main theme of this book is the analysis of value. It is not easy to explain what the analysis of value is . . . The point may be put like this: You see two men, one of whom is giving a banana to the other, and is taking a penny from him. You ask, How is it that a banana costs a penny rather than any other sum?' (p. 6)

definition of value as a magnitude. It is nothing more nor less than the investigation of the laws which govern the allocation of the labor force to different spheres of production in a society of commodity producers. How Marx carried through this task will be treated in the next chapter.

Before returning to the further implications of Marx's qualitative analysis, it is well to remark that the two concepts, 'socially necessary labor' and 'simple labor,' which have stood in the forefront of nearly every attack on Marx's economics, both pertain to the quantitative aspect of value theory and hence will come up for subsequent consideration. That critics of Marx have concentrated their attention on this aspect of the theory, and at that one-sidedly, is no accident; their attitude towards the value problem has disposed them to a preoccupation with exchange ratios to the neglect of the character of the social relations which lie hidden beneath the surface. Hence lengthy critiques of socially necessary labor, but hardly a word about abstract labor.

7. The Fetish Character of Commodities

Our analysis of commodities has led us to see in exchange value a relation between producers in a definite system of division of labor, and in the particular labor of individuals a component part of the aggregate labor force of society. In other words, we have looked beneath the forms of social organization to discover the substance of social relations. That we are able to do this, however, is no indication that the forms are unimportant. On the contrary, they are of the greatest importance. Reality is perceived in terms of form. Where, as here, there is a gap between form and substance which can be bridged only by critical analysis, the understanding plays queer tricks. Error and fantasy are readily accepted as obvious common sense and even provide the basis for supposedly scientific explanation. An incapacity to comprehend, a false consciousness, permeates, to a greater or lesser extent, the structure of thought. This principle applies with peculiar force to commodities and commodity production. The thinking to which this form of social organization gives rise frequently bears only a remote and perverted relation to the real social relations which underlie it. In his doctrine of Commodity Fetishism, Marx was the first to perceive this fact and to realize its decisive importance for the ideology of the modern period.

In commodity production, the basic relation between men 'assumes, in their eyes, the fantastic form of a relation between things.' * This reification of social relations is the heart and core of Marx's doctrine of Fetishism.

In the mist-enveloped regions of the religious world . . . the productions of the human brain appear as independent beings endowed with life, and entering into relation both with one another and with the human race. So it is in the world of commodities with the products of men's hands. This I call the Fetishism which attaches itself to the products of labor, so soon as they are produced as commodities, and which is therefore inseparable from the production of commodities.

This fetish character of the commodity world has its origin . . . in the peculiar social character of the labor which produces commodities.

As a general rule, articles of utility become commodities only because they are products of private individuals or groups of individuals who carry on their work independently of each other. The sum total of the labor of all these private individuals forms the aggregate labor of society. Since the producers do not come into contact with each other, the specific social character of each producer's labor does not show itself except in the act of exchange. In other words, the labor of the individual asserts itself as a part of the labor of society only through the relations which the act of exchange establishes directly between the products and indirectly, through them, between the producers. To the latter, therefore, the social relations between the labor of private individuals appear for what they are, i.e. not as the direct social relations of persons in their work, but rather as material relations of persons and social relations of things.[22]

In earlier periods of history, when the relations of production had a direct personal character, such a reification of social relations was obviously impossible. Even in the early stages of commodity production itself 'this mystification is as yet very simple' [23] and is therefore easily seen through. It is, in fact, only

* *Capital* I, p. 83. 'Fantastic' is, of course, meant in its literal sense.

when commodity production becomes so highly developed and so widespread as to dominate the life of society that the phenomenon of reification of social relations acquires decisive importance. This occurs under conditions of relatively advanced capitalism such as emerged in Western Europe during the seventeenth and eighteenth centuries.* Here the impersonalization of productive relations is brought to its highest pitch of development. The individual producer deals with his fellow men only through 'the market,' where prices and amounts sold are the substantial realities and human beings merely their instruments. 'These quantities vary continually, independently of the will, foresight, and action of the producers. To them their own social movement takes the form of the movement of things which rule the producers instead of being ruled by them.' † This is, indeed, 'a state of society in which the process of production has the mastery over man instead of being controlled by him,'[24] and in which, therefore, the real character of the relations among the producers themselves is both distorted and obscured from view.

Once the world of commodities has, so to speak, achieved its independence and subjected the producers to its sway, the latter come to look upon it in much the same way as they regard that other external world to which they must learn to adjust themselves, the world of nature itself. The existing social order becomes in the apt expression of Lukacs, a 'second nature' which stands outside of and opposed to its members.[25]

The consequences for the structure of thought are both extensive and profound. Here we shall have to be content with a few suggestions which may serve to illustrate the possibilities for critical interpretation which are opened up by the doctrine of Fetishism.

The application of the ideas and methods of natural science

* Cf. the discussion of this point by Lukacs, op. cit. pp. 96-7. Lukacs has developed and applied the doctrine of Fetishism probably as skilfully and successfully as any Marxist writer.

† *Capital* I, p. 86. A correction has been made in the translation. This feature of developed commodity production finds precise formulation in the modern theory of pure competition in which it is assumed that each producer treats all prices as data. His function as an economic subject is to adjust himself to price changes as best he can.

to society is one of the most striking features of the capitalist period. While the development of the natural sciences themselves was certainly in part responsible, nevertheless, the deeper roots of the phenomenon must be sought in the changed attitude towards society which was the reflex of the flowering of commodity production. In the field of political economy the results of the transition are most clearly observable in the eighteenth-century doctrines of the Physiocrats in France and the classical school in England. The *loi naturelle* of the Physiocrats, the 'invisible hand' of Adam Smith, their common faith in the wisdom of *laissez-faire* as an economic policy, all attest to a profound belief in the impersonal and automatic character of the economic order. This bias against conscious social action in economic affairs which grew up in the eighteenth century remained a very prominent feature of capitalist ideology until quite recently.* Its specific roots in the characteristics of commodity production, as well as its connection with cognate doctrines of natural law and social automatism, are brilliantly illuminated by Marx's theory of Fetishism.

Reification of social relations has exercised a profound influence on traditional economic thinking in at least two further important respects. In the first place, the categories of the capitalist economy—value, rent, wages, profit, interest, et cetera—have been treated as though they were the inevitable categories of economic life in general. Earlier economic systems have been looked upon as imperfect or embryonic versions of modern capitalism and judged accordingly. It requires but little reflection to see that this procedure slurs over significant differences between social forms, encourages an unhistorical and sterile taxonomy, and leads to misleading and at times even ludicrous judgments. Thus, it has been common for economists to denounce medieval prohibitions of usury as irrational and misguided because (in modern capitalism) interest plays an important part in

* The decline of *laissez-faire* in recent times is fundamentally attributable to the growth of monopoly and imperialism, a subject which we are obviously not prepared to discuss at this stage of the analysis. The cause and implications of monopoly and imperialism will be explored in Part IV below. The specifically ideological aspect of the process is briefly but profoundly analysed by Rudolf Hilferding in the passage which is included in the present work as Appendix B.

regulating the productive mechanism. Or, to take another example, we find Keynes evaluating pyramid building in ancient Egypt and cathedral building in medieval Europe in terms appropriate to a public-works program in twentieth-century England.[26] It cannot, of course, be denied that certain features are common to all forms of social economy, but to comprehend them all in a single set of categories and hence to ignore their specific differences is in a very real sense a negation of history. That modern economics has consistently pursued this course is the best evidence of its subordination to the fetishism inherent in commodity production.

In the second place, the attribution of independent power to things is nowhere more clear than in the traditional division of 'factors of production' into land, labor, and capital, each of which is thought of as 'producing' an income for its owners. Here, as Marx expressed it,

> we have the complete mystification of the capitalist mode of production, the transformation of social conditions into things, the indiscriminate amalgamation of the material conditions of production with their historical and social forms. It is an enchanted, perverted, topsy-turvy world in which Monsieur le Capital and Madame la Terre carry on their goblin tricks as social characters and at the same time as mere things.*

It is true that in the Ricardian theory of value and distribution, the highwater mark of classical political economy, the foundation for a rational view of capitalist productive relations had been laid. But Ricardo himself was never able to raise himself above a narrowly limited outlook; † and his followers, alarmed by the vistas which were opened up to them, quickly retreated into the world of illusion from which he had all but given them the means of escape. Thenceforth, it was only critics of the existing social order, like Marx, who cared to take up where Ricardo had left off by laying bare the real social relations underlying the forms of commodity production. What contact

* *Capital* III, p. 966. The entire section on 'The Trinitarian Formula,' in which this passage occurs, should be read in this connection.

† Marx justly remarked of Ricardo that 'The "parallelograms of Mr. Owen" seem to be the only form of society outside of the bourgeois form with which he was acquainted.' *Critique*, pp. 69-70.

with social relations the post-Ricardians allowed themselves was effectually dissolved by the rise of subjective value theory in the final third of the nineteenth century.*

Turning from political economy in a narrow sense, it is apparent that the commodity-producing form constitutes the most effective possible veil over the true class character of capitalist society. Everyone appears first of all as a mere commodity owner with something to sell—this is true of landowners, capitalists, and laborers alike. As commodity owners they all stand on a perfectly equal footing; their relations with each other are not the master-servant relations of a regime of personal status, but the contractual relations of free and equal human beings. It does not appear to the worker that his own lack of access to the means of production is forcing him to work on terms dictated by those who monopolize the means of production, that he is therefore being exploited for the benefit of others just as surely as the serf who was forced to work a certain number of days on the lord's land in return for the privilege of working a strip of land for himself. On the contrary, the world of commodities appears as a world of equals. The labor power of the worker is alienated from the worker and stands opposed to him as any commodity to its owner. He sells it, and so long as true value is paid all the conditions of fair and equal exchange are satisfied.

This is the appearance. Those who regard capitalist forms as natural and eternal—and, generally speaking, this includes most of those who live under capitalist forms—accept the appearance as a true representation of social relations. On this foundation there has been erected the whole vast superstructure of ethical and legal principles which serve at once to justify the existing order and to regulate men's conduct towards it. It is only by means of a critical analysis of commodity production, an analysis that goes beneath the superficial forms to the underlying relations of man to man, that we can see clearly the historically relative character of capitalist justice and capitalist legality, just as it is only by such an analysis that we can see the historical character of capitalism itself. This illustration, while it cannot

* Cf. the excellent essay by Maurice Dobb, 'The Trend of Modern Economics,' in his *Political Economy and Capitalism* (1937).

be pursued further here, shows that the doctrine of Fetishism has implications which far transcend the conventional limits of economics and economic thinking.

If commodity production has fostered the illusion of its own permanence and hidden the true character of the social relations which it embodies, it has at the same time created the economic rationality of modern times without which a full development of society's productive forces would be unthinkable. Rationality, in the sense of a deliberate adaptation of means to ends in the economic sphere, presupposes an economic system which is subject to certain objective laws which are not altogether unstable and capricious. Given this condition, the individual can proceed to plan his affairs in such a way as to achieve what is, from his own standpoint and from the standpoint of prevailing standards, an optimum result.

That this condition is fulfilled by commodity production does not mean that the system is to be regarded as a planned or rational whole. On the contrary, the development of commodity production under capitalist conditions displays on the one hand an intense rationalization of its part-processes and an ever increasing irrationality in the behavior of the system as a whole. It is clear that we have to do here with one of the most comprehensive contradictions of the capitalist order. A social system which has sway over man educates him to the point where he has the capacity to control his own destiny. At the same time it blinds him to the means of exercising the power which is within his grasp and diverts his energies increasingly into purely destructive channels. The study of this process will claim our attention in later chapters of this book; here it suffices to point out that qualitative-value theory with its corollary in the doctrine of Commodity Fetishism is the essential first step in the Marxian analysis of capitalism. He who has not understood this has understood little of Marx's critical method.

III

THE QUANTITATIVE-VALUE PROBLEM

1. The First Step

In every society, from the most primitive to the most advanced, it is essential that labor be applied to production and that goods be distributed among the members of society. What changes in the course of history is the way in which these productive and distributive activities are organized and carried out. As Marx expressed it,

> Every child knows that if a country ceased to work, I will not say for a year, but for a few weeks, it would die. Every child knows too that the mass of products corresponding to the different needs require different and quantitatively determined masses of the total labor of society. That this necessity of distributing social labor in definite proportions cannot be done away with by the *particular form* of social production, but can only change the *form it assumes*, is self-evident. No natural laws can be done away with. What can change in changing historical circumstances, is the *form* in which these laws operate. And the form in which this proportional division of labor operates, in a state of society where the interconnection of social labor is manifested in the *private exchange* of the individual products of labor, is precisely the *exchange value* of these products.[1]

Exchange value is thus an aspect of the laws governing the allocation of productive activity in a commodity-producing society. To discover the implications of this form of production, in terms of social relations and social consciousness, was the task of qualitative-value theory discussed in the preceding chapter. To discover the nature of these laws in quantitative terms is the task of quantitative-value theory, and it is in this sense that value theory has constituted the traditional starting point of modern political economy. If we bear this in mind we shall realize that the investigation of exchange value itself is only the beginning of economic science and not, as some writers have maintained, its ultimate objective.

Commodities exchange against each other on the market in certain definite proportions; they also absorb a certain definite quantity (measured in time units) of society's total available labor force. What is the relation between these two facts? As a first approximation Marx assumes that there is an exact correspondence between exchange ratios and labor-time ratios, or, in other words, that commodities which require an equal time to produce will exchange on a one-to-one basis. This is the simplest formula and hence a good starting point. Deviations which occur in practice can be dealt with in subsequent approximations to reality.

Two obvious qualifications need to be introduced at once. In the first place, it is not true that 'if the value of a commodity is determined by the quantity of labor spent on it, the more idle and unskilful the laborer, the more valuable would his commodity be because more time would be required in its production.'[2] No more labor than that which is 'socially necessary,' that is to say necessary under the existing social conditions, is to be counted in the determination of value. 'The labor time socially necessary is that required to produce an article under the normal conditions of production, and with the average degree of skill and intensity prevalent at the time.'[3] It should be noted that the concept of 'socially necessary labor' is concerned solely with the quantity of labor performed, and has nothing to do with use value or utility.

Secondly, labor more skilled than average (or 'simple') labor must have a correspondingly greater power of producing value. 'Skilled labor counts only as simple labor intensified, or rather as multiplied simple labor, a given quantity of skilled labor being considered equal to a greater quantity of simple labor.'[4] The quantitative relation between an hour of simple labor and an hour of any given type of skilled labor is observable in the relative values of the commodities which they produce in one hour. This does not mean, of course, that the relation between two types of labor is *determined by* the relative values of their products. To argue in this way would be circular reasoning. The relation between the two types of labor is theoretically susceptible to measurement independently of the market values of their products. There are two possible cases here: either the skilled laborer is more proficient because of superior natural ability, or the skilled laborer is more proficient because of superior training. Let us examine these in turn.

If the difference between two workers is a question of natural ability, as a rule the superiority of the more skilled will manifest itself regardless of the line of production in which he may be engaged. In order, therefore, to establish a quantitative relation of equivalence between the two workers, it is only necessary to put them in the same line of production, where their relative effectiveness can be easily measured in purely physical terms. Once the required ratio has been established in this way, it can be used to reduce these two kinds of labor to a common denominator in value-creating terms, no matter how freely the workers in question may move from industry to industry. There is nothing artificial in this solution of the problem in a society in which a high degree of labor fluidity is an established fact.

If, on the other hand, the difference between two workers is a question of training, then it is clear that the superior worker expends in production not only his own labor (which we can assume would have the quality of simple labor in the absence of training) but also indirectly that part of the labor of his teachers which is responsible for his superior productivity. If the productive life of a worker is, say, 100,000 hours, and if into his training went the equivalent of 50,000 hours of simple labor (including his own efforts during the training period), then each hour of his labor will count as one and one-half hours of simple labor. This case, therefore, presents no more difficulties than the first.

In practice, differences in skill are likely to be the result of a combination of differences in ability and differences in training. These more complex cases present no new questions of principle and can be handled in accordance with the methods outlined for the two basic cases.

The influence exerted by ability and training makes itself felt only slowly and imperfectly, and frequently in ways which are not obvious. It is for this reason that Marx remarked that 'the different proportions in which different sorts of labor are reduced to unskilled labor as their standard, are established by a process that goes on behind the backs of the producers, and, consequently, appear to be fixed by custom.' [5]

Critics of Marx's (and Ricardo's) theory of value have always maintained that the reduction of skilled to simple labor involves circular reasoning. The argument seems to be that the greater value-creating power of the more skilled worker is *deduced from* the greater value of his product. If this were so the criticism would, of course, be valid, but our analysis has shown that there is no need to rely on such fallacious reasoning. A more substantial attack on the theory would center attention on the assumption that differences in natural ability remain more or less constant even though workers are shifted about from one line of production to another. It is clearly not difficult to think of cases which violate this assumption; there are individuals who have great ability in some *special* line of activity but whose *general* productive capacity is in no way remarkable—for example, opera singers, star baseball players, mathematicians, and so forth. But these are exceptional cases which should not be allowed to distort our view of the labor force as a whole. So far as the vast majority of productive workers is concerned, specialized talents are not of great importance; the qualities which make a good worker—strength, dexterity, and intelligence—do not differ greatly from one occupation to another. No more than this need be granted to establish the essential commensurability of simple and skilled labor.

Having demonstrated the theoretical feasibility of reducing skilled to simple labor, we may follow Marx in abstracting from the conditions in the real world which make such a reduction necessary. 'For simplicity's sake we shall henceforth account every kind of labor to be unskilled, simple labor; by this we do no more than save ourselves the trouble of making the reduction.' [6] From the point of view of the problems which he set himself to investigate, differences between skilled and unskilled labor were not essential. To ignore them, hence, is an *appropriate abstraction* within the meaning of that term explained in Chapter I above. This is not to imply that such an abstraction would always be appropriate. If Marx had been interested in explaining differences in wages, for example, it clearly would have been illegitimate.*

It would be a serious error, though one which is frequently committed, to suppose that the whole of Marx's quantitative-value theory is contained in Chapter I of *Capital.* That chapter, it will be recalled, is entitled 'Commodities,' and its emphasis is overwhelmingly on what we have called the qualitative-value problem. So far as the quantitative-value problem is concerned, it makes no attempt to go beyond the first approximation contained in the proposition that commodities exchange for one another in proportion to the quantity of socially necessary labor embodied in each. Moreover, even in respect to this first approximation the circumstances under which it would be unconditionally valid are not investigated. It is evident that we have in Chapter I no more than a first step into the field of quantitative-value theory. Subsequent steps are left, in accordance with the plan of *Capital,* until a later stage of the work. Here we shall attempt to round out Marx's basic ideas on the subject of value not because it is essential to do so for the immediately succeeding chapters, which are based on Volume I, but because this seems to be the best way of avoiding misunderstandings which might otherwise arise.

2. The Role of Competition

Let us first inquire under what conditions exchange ratios would correspond exactly to labor-time ratios. Adam Smith's famous deer-beaver example, which was also used by Ricardo, provides a convenient starting point.

> In that early and rude state of society which precedes both the accumulation of stock and the appropriation of land, the proportion between the quantities of labor necessary for acquiring different objects seems to be the only circumstance which can afford any rule for exchanging them for one another. If among a nation of hunters, for example, it usually costs twice the labor

* In this connection Marx's practice does not differ essentially from that of modern economists. As Hicks expresses it, 'if changes in relative wages are to be neglected, it is quite legitimate to assume all labor homogeneous.' J. R. Hicks, *Value and Capital* (1939), pp. 33-4.

to kill a beaver which it does to kill a deer, one beaver should naturally exchange for or be worth two deer. It is natural that what is usually the produce of two days' or two hours' labor, should be worth double of what is usually the produce of one day's or one hour's labor.[7]

Adam Smith's hunters are what Marx would have called simple commodity producers, each hunting with his own relatively simple weapons, in forests which are open to all, and satisfying his needs by exchanging his surplus catch against the products of other hunters. Why, under these circumstances, would deer and beaver exchange in proportion to the quantity of time required to kill each? It is easy to supply a proof of what Adam Smith took for granted.

A hunter by spending two hours of his time can have either one beaver or two deer. Let us imagine now that one beaver exchanges for one deer 'on the market.' Under the circumstances any one would be foolish to hunt beaver. For in one hour it is possible to catch a deer and thence, by exchange, to get a beaver, whereas to get a beaver directly would require two hours. Consequently this situation is unstable and cannot last. The supply of deer will expand, that of beaver contract until nothing but deer is coming on the market and no takers can be found. Following this line of reasoning it is possible to show by exclusion that only one exchange ratio, namely one beaver for two deer, does constitute a stable situation. When this ratio rules in the market, beaver hunters will have no incentive to shift to deer hunting, and deer hunters will have no incentive to shift to beaver hunting. This, therefore, is the equilibrium ratio of exchange. The value of one beaver is two deer and *vice versa*. Adam Smith's proposition is thus demonstrated to be correct.

To get this result two implicit assumptions are necessary, namely, that hunters are prepared to move freely from deer to beaver if by so doing they can improve their position; and that there are no obstacles to such movement. In other words the hunters must be both willing and able to compete freely for any advantages which may arise in the course of exchange by shifting their labor from one line to another. Given this kind of competition in a society of simple commodity production, supply and demand will be in equilibrium only when the price of every commodity is proportional to the labor time required to produce it. Conversely prices proportional to labor times will be established only if the forces of competitive supply and demand are allowed to work themselves out freely. The competitive supply-and-demand theory of price determination is hence not only not inconsistent with the labor theory; rather it forms an integral, if sometimes unrecognized, part of the labor theory.

Marx does not touch on this point in the first chapter of *Capital;* like the classics, he always tended to take it for granted. But in various other parts of his economic writings he deals with 'supply and demand'—an expression which was used merely to summarize the competitive forces at work on the market—and always in the sense of a mechanism for eliminating deviations between market prices and values: what Oskar Lange aptly terms an 'equilibrating mechanism.' [8] Thus in Volume III, where several pages are devoted to the subject, we read that 'The relation of demand and supply explains, therefore, on the one hand only the deviations of market prices from market values, and on the other hand the tendency to balance these deviations, in other words, to suspend the effect of the relation of demand and supply.' [9] And the point is made even more clearly in *Value, Price, and Profit* as follows: 'At the moment when supply and demand equilibrate each other, and therefore cease to act, the *market price* of a commodity coincides with its real value.' [10]

3. The Role of Demand

Marx is often accused of having ignored the role of demand, in the sense of consumers' needs and desires, in determining quantitative-value relations. The issue is unimportant so long as discussion is confined to exchange ratios in a simple commodity-producing society like Adam Smith's hunters, for under these conditions the pattern of consumers' wants plays no part in the determination of equilibrium values. If beaver and deer are both useful—'nothing can have value without being an object of utility' [11]—they must exchange in proportion to their respective labor times regardless of the relative intensity of the desire for each.

We have already expressed the opinion, however, that the

quantitative-value problem is broader than the mere question of exchange ratios, that it includes an investigation of the quantitative allocation of society's labor force to different spheres of production in a society of commodity producers. When the problem is thus broadly conceived, consumers' demands can no longer be neglected. If, for example, beaver are used only for making fur hats while deer provide the community's basic food, a great deal more labor will go into hunting deer than into hunting beaver. Thus, if it is desired to know *both* the exchange ratio *and* the distribution of labor, it is necessary to have two kinds of information: first, information on the relative labor cost of beaver and deer; and, second, information on the relative intensity of demand for beaver and deer. Given these two kinds of information, it is possible to determine what may be called the general economic equilibrium of the society in question. It is an 'equilibrium' because it defines the state of affairs which, in the absence of any change in the basic conditions, will persist; and it is 'general' because not only the relative value of beaver and deer is established, but also the quantities of beaver and deer produced and the distribution of the society's labor force are established.

When the tasks of quantitative-value theory are thought of in this broad sense, the pattern of consumer wants cannot be neglected. It is just here, however, that the charge of ignoring demand cannot be successfully maintained against Marx. The contrary impression seems to be so widespread that a lengthy quotation from Volume III may not be out of place.

> If this division of labor among the different branches of production is proportional, then the products of the various groups are sold at their values . . . or at prices which are modifications of their values . . . due to general laws. It is indeed the law of value enforcing itself, not with reference to individual commodities or articles, but to the total products of the particular social spheres of production made independent by division of labor. Every commodity must contain the necessary quantity of labor, and at the same time only the proportional quantity of the total social labor time must have been spent on the various groups. For the use value of things remains a prerequisite. The use value of the individual commodities depends on the particular need

which each satisfies. But the use value of the social mass of products depends on the extent to which it satisfies in quantity a definite social need for every particular kind of product in an adequate manner, so that the labor is proportionately distributed among the different spheres in keeping with these social needs, which are definite in quantity . . . The social need, that is the use value on a social scale, appears here as a determining factor for the amount of social labor which is to be supplied by the various particular spheres . . . For instance, take it that proportionally too much cotton goods have been produced, although only the labor time necessary for this total product under the prevailing conditions is realized in it. But too much social labor has been expended in this line, in other words a portion of this product is useless. The whole of it is therefore sold only as though it had been produced in the necessary proportion. This quantitative limit of the quota of social labor available for the various particular spheres is but a wider expression of the law of value, although the necessary labor time assumes a different meaning here. Only so much of it is required for the satisfaction of the social needs. The limitation is here due to the use value. Society can use only so much of its total labor for this particular kind of product under the prevailing conditions of production.[12]

If Marx recognized so clearly the part played by demand in determining the allocation of social labor, it may well be asked why, in terms of his entire systematic theory, he treated this factor so briefly and, one might even say, casually; why did he not work along the lines of his contemporaries, Jevons, Walras, and Menger, in developing a theory of consumers' choice? There are two fundamental reasons for Marx's apparent neglect of this problem.

In the first place, under capitalism effective demand is only partly a question of consumers' wants. Even more important is the basic question of income distribution which in turn is a reflection of the relations of production or, in other words, of what Marxists call the class structure of society. Marx was very emphatic on this point:

We remark by the way that the 'social demand,' in other words that which regulates the principle of demand, is essentially conditioned on the mutual relations of the different economic classes and their relative economic positions; that is to say, first, on the ratio of total surplus value to wages, and, second, on the division of surplus value into its various parts (profit, interest, ground rent, taxes, etc.). And this shows once more that absolutely nothing can be explained by the relation of supply and demand unless the basis has first been ascertained on which this relation rests.[13]

And again:

> It would seem . . . that there is on the side of demand a definite magnitude of social wants [of the working class] which require for their satisfaction a definite quantity of certain articles on the market. But the quantity demanded by these wants is very elastic and changing. Its fixedness is but apparent. If the means of subsistence were cheaper, or money wages higher, the laborers would buy more of them, and a greater 'social demand' would be manifested for this kind of commodities . . . The limits within which the *need for commodities on the market*, the demand, differs quantitatively from the *actual social need*, varies naturally for different commodities; in other words, the difference between the demanded quantity of commodities and that quantity which would be demanded, if the money prices of the commodities, or other conditions concerning the money or living of the buyers, were different.[14]

In so far as one accepts the position that market demand is dominated by income distribution—and it is difficult to see how this can be denied at least for the case of modern capitalism—it would seem that we cannot very well escape the conclusion that the problems of value should be approached via the relations of production rather than via the subjective valuations of consumers. As we have already seen in the last chapter, the labor theory is constructed to take full account of the productive relations specific to simple commodity production. In the next chapter we shall see how the theory of surplus value carries on this approach for the case of capitalism, which is a more advanced form of commodity production.

This consideration alone, however, would hardly be sufficient to explain the degree to which Marx neglects consumers' wants. For even though their importance is limited, nevertheless there is no doubt that they do play a part in determining the allocation of society's productive efforts. A second factor must be taken into account. In Chapter 1 it was emphasized that Marx was primarily interested in the process of social change: more specifically, in *Capital* he was investigating 'the economic law of motion of modern society.' From this point of view anything which is in itself relatively stable and merely reacts to changes elsewhere not only can but must be given a subordinate place in the analytical scheme. It is clear that Marx thought of consumers' wants as falling in the category of reactive elements in social life. Wants, in so far as they do not spring from elementary biological and physical needs, are a reflection of the technical and organizational development of society, not *vice versa.* 'The mode of production in material life determines the general character of the social political and spiritual processes of life. It is not the consciousness of men that determines their existence, but on the contrary, their social existence determines their consciousness.' * If one is interested in economic change and if one accepts the position that subjective factors play an essentially passive role in the process of change, one can scarcely deny that Marx was justified in neglecting consumers' wants as he did.

Orthodox economists, though most of them approach the problem of value via a theory of consumers' choice, have generally been obliged in practice to recognize the primacy of production and income distribution whenever they tackle questions of economic evolution. Schumpeter may be taken as an example. In his recent treatise on *Business Cycles*, he states:

> We will, throughout, act on the assumption that consumers' initiative in changing their tastes—i.e., in changing that set of data which general theory comprises in the concepts of 'utility functions' or 'indifference varieties'—is negligible and that all change in consumers' tastes is incident to, and brought about by, producers' action.[15]

And a little further on, Schumpeter remarks that even spontaneous changes in consumers' tastes are unlikely to be of im-

* *Critique*, pp. 11-12. Cf. also the following: 'Production thus produces consumption: first, by furnishing the latter with material; second, by determining the manner of consumption; third, by creating in consumers a want for its products as objects of consumption. It thus provides the object, the manner and the moving spring of consumption.' *Critique*, p. 280.

portance unless they cause shifts in real income. Schumpeter in effect admits that for the problems in which he is interested—business cycles and the developmental tendencies of the capitalist system—the theory of consumers' choice is of little or no relevance.

Nearly all modern business-cycle analysts follow the same course, though few as consciously as Schumpeter. The 'Keynesians' * for example, pay little attention to subjective-value problems except when they speak *ex professo* of 'pure theory,' which, since it is furthest removed from real problems, is naturally the last stronghold of obsolete ideas. Demand plays a very important role in their analysis, but what they have to say about it is dominated by the distribution of income, that is to say by the existing relations of production. It is perhaps no exaggeration to say that the importance of the Keynesian contribution stems largely from the fact that here for the first time since Ricardo orthodox economics accords to the real relations of capitalist production reasonable weight in the analysis of the capitalist process. It would be a further step forward if the Keynesians could be brought to realize that this is what they are doing.†

We see that Marx's relative neglect of the problems of consumers' choice finds ample support in recent trends in economic thinking.

4. 'Law of Value' vs. 'Planning Principle'

We are now in a position to see that what Marx called 'the law of value' summarizes those forces at work in a commodity-

* Those who are in agreement with the fundamental doctrines of J. M. Keynes. The latter's *General Theory of Employment, Interest and Money* is undoubtedly the most important work by an English economist since Ricardo's *Principles*. The writings of Keynes and his followers mark the emergence of Anglo-American economics from roughly a century of relative sterility. That this phenomenon is the direct outcome of the latest phase of capitalist development goes without saying.

† It has been shown that even Marshall was aware of the primary significance of production in shaping wants. Cf. Talcott Parsons, 'Wants and Activities in Marshall,' *Quarterly Journal of Economics*, November 1931. The structure of Marshall's theory, however, seems to be unaffected by this awareness.

producing society which regulate (a) the exchange ratios among commodities, (b) the quantity of each produced, and (c) the allocation of the labor force to the various branches of production. The basic condition for the existence of a law of value is a society of private producers who satisfy their needs by mutual exchange. The forces at work include, on the one hand, the productivity of labor in the various branches of production and the pattern of social needs as modified by the distribution of income; and, on the other hand, the equilibrating market forces of competitive supply and demand. To use a modern expression, the law of value is essentially a theory of general equilibrium developed in the first instance with reference to simple commodity production and later on adapted to capitalism.

This implies that one of the primary functions of the law of value is to make clear that in a commodity-producing society, in spite of the absence of centralized and co-ordinated decision-making, there is order and not simply chaos. No one decides how productive effort is to be allocated or how much of the various kinds of commodities are to be produced, yet the problem does get solved and not in a purely arbitrary and unintelligible fashion. It is the function of the law of value to explain how this happens and what the outcome is. Marx makes this point in an important passage near the end of *Capital:*

> Since individual capitalists meet one another only as owners of commodities, and every one seeks to sell his commodity as dearly as possible (being apparently guided in the regulation of his production by his own arbitrary will), the internal law enforces itself merely by means of their competition, by their mutual pressure upon each other, by means of which the various deviations are balanced. Only as an internal law, and from the point of view of the individual agents as a blind law, does the law of value exert its influence here and maintain the social equilibrium of production in the turmoil of its accidental fluctuations.[16]

It follows that in so far as the allocation of productive activity is brought under conscious control, the law of value loses its relevance and importance; its place is taken by the principle of planning.* In the economics of a socialist society the theory of planning should hold the same basic position as the theory of value in the economics of a capitalist society. Value and planning are as much opposed, and for the same reasons, as capitalism and socialism.

5. Value and Price of Production

Price, as Marx uses the term in Volume I of *Capital*, is merely the money expression of value. As such its analysis belongs to the theory of money, which we shall not attempt to present in this work. In Volume III, however, there is the quite different concept of 'price of production.' Prices of production are *modifications* of values. Since, however, the differences between prices of production and values are attributable to certain features of capitalism that have not yet been taken into account, we shall postpone the discussion of the subject until a later stage of the argument (see Chapter VII below).

Only one point in this connection needs to be made here. As we shall see, prices of production are derived *from* values according to certain general rules; the deviations are neither arbitrary nor unexplained. The view that has dominated Anglo-American Marx criticism since Böhm-Bawerk,[17] namely, that the theory of production price contradicts the theory of value, is hence the very opposite of the truth. Not only does the theory of production price not contradict the theory of value; it is based directly on the theory of value and would have no meaning except as a development of the theory of value.

6. Monopoly Price

The introduction of monopoly elements into the economy of course interferes with the operation of the law of value as the

* This contrast is correctly drawn by the former Soviet economist Preobrashensky: 'In our country where the centralized planned economy of the proletariat has been established and the law of value limited or replaced by the planning principle, foresight and knowledge play an exceptional role as compared with the capitalist economy.' E. Preobrashensky, *The New Economics* (1926, in Russian), p. 11. I am indebted to Mr. Paul Baran for calling my attention to this passage.

regulator of the quantitative relations of production and exchange. 'When we speak of monopoly price,' Marx remarked, 'we mean in a general way a price which is determined only by the eagerness of purchasers to buy and by their solvency, independently of the price which is determined by the general price of production and by the value of the product.'[18] In other words, the monopolist's control over supply enables him to take advantage of demand conditions. In this case, therefore, demand acquires a special significance, and both price and quantity produced (hence also the allocation of labor) are different from what they would be in a regime of competition. Moreover, and this is the most serious aspect of monopoly from an analytical point of view, the discrepancies between monopoly price and value are not subject to any general rules, as is the case with the discrepancies between production price and value. Later, when we investigate monopolistic tendencies in capitalist society we shall find, however, that this arbitrary element in price determination under monopolistic conditions is less troublesome than might at first be thought. So far as the functioning of the system as a whole is concerned, we shall discover that the kind, if not the extent, of changes caused by monopoly can be reasonably well analysed and interpreted.*

Before we leave the subject of monopoly price, one point in particular needs to be stressed. Quantitative-value relations are disturbed by monopoly; qualitative-value relations are not. In other words, the existence of monopoly does not in itself alter the basic social relations of commodity production: the organization of production through the private exchange of the individual products of labor. Nor does it change the essential commensurability of commodities: that is to say, the fact that each represents a certain portion of the time of the total social labor force, or, to use Marx's terminology, that each is a congelation of a certain amount of abstract labor. This is an important point, for it means that even under monopoly conditions we can continue to measure and compare commodities and aggregates of commodities in terms of labor-time units in spite of the fact that the precise quantitative relations implied in the law of value no longer hold.

* See Chapter xv below.

IV

SURPLUS VALUE AND CAPITALISM

It is important not to confuse commodity production in general with capitalism. It is true that only under capitalism 'all or even a majority of the products take the form of commodities,'[1] so that capitalism can certainly be said to imply commodity production. But the converse is not true; commodity production does not necessarily imply capitalism. In fact a high degree of development of commodity production is a necessary precondition to the emergence of capitalism. In order, therefore, to apply our theory of value to the analysis of capitalism it is first necessary to inquire carefully into the special features which set this form of production off from the general concept of commodity production.

1. Capitalism

Under simple commodity production, to which we have so far largely confined our attention, each producer owns and works with his own means of production; under capitalism ownership of the means of production is vested in one set of individuals while the work is performed by another. Both means of production and labor power, moreover, are commodities; that is to say, both are objects of exchange and hence bearers of exchange value. It follows that not only the relations among owners but also the relations between owners and non-owners have the character of exchange relations. The former is characteristic of commodity production in general, the latter of capitalism only. We may therefore say that the buying and selling of labor power is the *differentia specifica* of capitalism. As Marx expressed it:

> The historical conditions of its existence are by no means given with the mere circulation of money and commodities. It can spring into life only when the owner of the means of produc-

tion and subsistence meets in the market with the free laborer selling his labor power. And this one historical condition comprises a world's history. Capital, therefore, announces from its first appearance a new epoch in the process of social production.* [2]

In simple commodity production the producer sells his product in order to purchase other products which satisfy his specific wants. He starts with Commodities, turns them into Money, and thence once again into Commodities. Commodities constitute the beginning and end of the transaction which finds its rationale in the fact that the commodities acquired are qualitatively different from those given up. Marx designates this circuit symbolically as *C-M-C*. Under capitalism, on the other hand, the capitalist, acting in his capacity as a capitalist, goes to market with Money, purchases Commodities (labor power and means of production), and then, after a process of production has been completed, returns to market with a product which he again converts into Money. This process is designated as *M-C-M*. Money is the beginning and end; the rationale of *C-M-C* is lacking, since money is qualitatively homogeneous and satisfies no wants. Indeed it is evident that if the *M* at the beginning has the same magnitude as the *M* at the end, the whole process is pointless. It follows that the only meaningful process from the standpoint of the capitalist is *M-C-M'*, where *M'* is larger than *M*. The qualitative transformation of use value is here replaced by the

* This is often expressed by saying that capitalism, unlike earlier economic systems, is based upon free labor. The question may occur to the reader whether by this criterion the modern fascist economy is capitalist. The answer is certainly in the affirmative. The most thorough study of National Socialist Germany yet to be made answers this question in the following manner: 'Freedom of the labor contract means . . . primarily a clear distinction between labor and leisure time, which introduces the element of calculability and predictability into labor relations. It means that the worker sells his labor power for a time only, which is either agreed upon or fixed by legislative acts . . . Such freedom of the labor contract still exists in Germany . . . The distinction between labor and leisure is as sharp in Germany as it is in any democracy, even though the regime attempts to control the worker's leisure time . . . Every attempt of the National Socialist lawyers to supersede the labor contract by another legal instrument (such as community relations) has failed, and . . . all relations between employer and employee are still contractual ones.' Franz Neumann, *Behemoth* (1942), pp. 338-9.

quantitative expansion of exchange value as the objective of production. In other words, the capitalist has reason for laying out money for labor power and means of production only if he can thereby acquire a larger amount of money. The increment of money, the difference between *M'* and *M*, is what Marx calls surplus value; * it constitutes the income of the capitalist as capitalist and furnishes 'the direct aim and determining incentive of production.' [3]

It is of the utmost importance not to overlook the implications of this analysis. For Marx the decisive importance of surplus value is due to the specific historical form of capitalist production. The following passage brings this point into sharp relief:

> The simple circulation of commodities—selling in order to buy—is a means of carrying out a purpose unconnected with circulation, namely, the appropriation of use values, the satisfaction of wants. The circulation of money as capital is, on the contrary, an end in itself, for the expansion of value takes place only within this constantly renewed movement. The circulation of capital has therefore no limits. Thus the conscious representative of this movement, the possessor of money, becomes a capitalist. His person, or rather his pocket, is the point from which the money starts and to which it returns. *The expansion of value, which is the objective basis or main-spring of the circulation M-C-M, becomes his subjective aim,* and it is only in so far as the appropriation of ever more and more wealth in the abstract becomes the sole motive of his operations that he functions as a capitalist, that is, as capital personified and endowed with consciousness and a will. *Use values must therefore never be looked upon as the real aim of the capitalist; neither must the profit on any single transaction. The restless never-ending process of profit-making alone is what he aims at.*[4]

One need only contrast this statement with the all but universal view of orthodox economists that the acquisition of surplus value as an incentive of production derives from an innate characteristic of human nature (the so-called 'profit motive') to see how deep is the gulf separating Marxian from orthodox political economy. We shall have frequent occasion, in later chapters, to

* The German word is *Mehrwert*, literally 'more value.'

revert to this point; until it has been thoroughly grasped there can be no question of a genuine understanding of Marx.

2. The Origin of Surplus Value

In order to discover the origin of surplus value it is first necessary to analyse the value of the commodity labor power. When we say that labor power is a commodity, we do not imply that labor is itself a commodity. The distinction is an important one and must be carefully borne in mind; it may be clarified as follows. The capitalist hires the worker to come to his factory on a certain day and be prepared to perform whatever tasks are set before him. In so doing he is buying the worker's capacity to work, his labor power; but so far there is no question of the expenditure of brain and muscle which constitutes actual labor. The latter enters the picture only when the worker is set into motion on a specific task. Labor, in other words, is the use of labor power, just as, to use Marx's analogy, digestion is the use of the power to digest.

In the strictest sense labor power is the laborer himself. In a slave society this is obvious, since what the purchaser buys is the slave and not his labor. Under capitalism, however, the fact that the labor contract is legally limited or terminable, or both, obscures the fact that what the worker is doing is selling himself for a certain stipulated period of time. Nevertheless this is the reality of the matter, and the concept of a day's labor power is probably best understood to mean simply a laborer for a day.

Now since labor power is a commodity it must have a value like any other commodity. But how is the value of 'this peculiar commodity' determined? Marx answers this question in the following manner:

> The value of labor power is determined, as in the case of every other commodity, by the labor time necessary for the production and consequently also the reproduction of this special article . . . Given the individual, the production of labor power consists in his reproduction of himself or his maintenance. Therefore the labor time requisite for the production of labor power reduces itself to that necessary for the production of those means of subsistence; in other words, the value of labor power is the

value of the means of subsistence necessary for the maintenance of the laborer . . . His means of subsistence must . . . be sufficient to maintain him in his normal state as a laboring individual. His natural wants, such as food, clothing, fuel, and housing vary according to the climatic and other physical conditions of his country. On the other hand the number and extent of his so-called necessary wants . . . are themselves the product of historical development and depend, therefore, to a great extent on the degree of civilization of a country . . .[5]

We shall return to this problem below; * for the present the following point is to be particularly noted: that the value of labor power reduces to the value of a more or less definite quantity of ordinary commodities.

We are now ready to proceed with the analysis of surplus value. The capitalist comes into the market with money and buys machinery, materials, and labor power. He then combines these in a process of production which results in a certain mass of commodities which are again thrown upon the market. Marx assumes that he buys what he buys at their equilibrium values and sells what he sells at its equilibrium value. And yet at the end he has more money than he started with. Somewhere along the line more value—or surplus value—has been created. How is this possible?

It is clear that surplus value cannot arise from the mere process of circulation of commodities. If every one were to attempt to reap a profit by raising his price, let us say by 10 per cent, what each gained as a seller he would lose as a buyer, and the only result would be higher prices all around from which no one would benefit. It seems to be equally obvious that the materials entering into the productive process cannot be the source of surplus value. The value which the materials have at the outset is transferred to the product at the conclusion, but there is no reason to assume that they possess an occult power to expand their value. The same is true, though perhaps less obviously, of the buildings and machines which are utilized in the productive process. What differentiates buildings and machinery from materials is the fact that the former transfer their value to the final product more slowly, that is to say, over a succession of produc-

* See pp. 87 ff.

tion periods instead of all at once as in the case of materials. It is, of course, true that materials and machinery can be said to be *physically* productive in the sense that labor working with them can turn out a larger product than labor working without them, but physical productivity in this sense must under no circumstances be confused with value productivity. From the standpoint of value there is no reason to assume that either materials or machinery can ultimately transfer to the product more than they themselves contain. This leaves only one possibility, namely that labor power must be the source of surplus value. Let us examine this more closely.

As we have already seen, the capitalist buys labor power at its value, that is to say, he pays to the worker as wages a sum corresponding to the value of the worker's means of subsistence. Let us suppose that this value is the product of six hours' labor. This means that after production has proceeded for six hours the worker has added to the value of the materials and machinery used up—a value which we know reappears in the product—an additional value sufficient to cover his own means of subsistence. If the process were to break off at this point the capitalist would be able to sell the product for just enough to reimburse himself for his outlays. But the worker has sold himself to the capitalist for a day, and there is nothing in the nature of things to dictate that a working day shall be limited to six hours. Let us assume that the working day is twelve hours. Then in the last six hours the worker continues to add value, but now it is value over and above that which is necessary to cover his means of subsistence; it is, in short, surplus value which the capitalist can pocket for himself.

> Every condition of the problem is satisfied, while the laws that regulate the exchange of commodities have been in no way violated. For the capitalist as buyer paid for each commodity, for the cotton, the spindle, and the labor power, its full value. He sells his yarn . . . at its exact value. Yet for all that he withdraws . . . more from circulation than he originally threw into it.[6]

The bare logic of this reasoning can be expressed in a simpler manner. In a day's work the laborer produces more than a day's means of subsistence. Consequently the working day can be divided into two parts, necessary labor and surplus labor. Under conditions of capitalist production the product of necessary labor accrues to the laborer in the form of wages, while the product of surplus labor is appropriated by the capitalist in the form of surplus value. It is to be noted that necessary labor and surplus labor as such are phenomena which are present in all societies in which the productiveness of human labor has been raised above a certain very low minimum, that is to say, in all but the most primitive societies. Furthermore, in many non-capitalist societies (e.g. slavery and feudalism) the product of surplus labor is appropriated by a special class which in one way or another maintains its control over the means of production. What is specific to capitalism is thus not the *fact* of exploitation of one part of the population by another, but the *form* which this exploitation assumes, namely the production of surplus value.

3. The Components of Value

From the foregoing analysis it is apparent that the value of any commodity produced under capitalist conditions can be broken down into three component parts. The first part, which merely represents the value of the materials and machinery used up, 'does not, in the process of production, undergo any quantitative alteration of value.'[7] and is therefore called 'constant capital.' It is represented symbolically by the letter c. The second part, that which replaces the value of labor power, does in a sense undergo an alteration of value in that 'it both reproduces the equivalent of its own value, and also produces an excess, a surplus value, which may itself vary, may be more or less according to circumstances.'[8] This second part is therefore called 'variable capital' and is represented by the letter v. The third part is the surplus value itself, which is designated by s. The value of a commodity may, in keeping with this notation, be written in the following formula:

$$c + v + s = \text{total value}$$

This formula, moreover, is not limited in its applicability to the analysis of the value of a single commodity but can be directly extended to cover the output during a certain period of time, say a year, of an enterprise or of any group of enterprises up to and including the whole economy.

Two comments may be made in this connection. First, it should be noted that the formula just presented is in effect a simplified version of the modern corporate income statement. Total value is equivalent to gross receipts from sales, constant capital to outlay on materials plus depreciation, variable capital to outlay on wages and salaries, and surplus value to income available for distribution as interest and dividends or for reinvestment in the business. Marx's value theory thus has the great merit, unlike some other value theories, of close correspondence to the actual accounting categories of capitalistic business enterprise.

Second, if the formula be extended to take in the entire economy it provides us with a conceptual framework for handling what is usually called the national income. Nevertheless, it is necessary not to overlook the differences between the Marxian income concepts and those which are employed by most modern investigators. If we use capital letters to designate aggregate quantities, we can say that modern theorists, when they speak of gross national income, commonly include $V + S$ plus that part of C which represents depreciation of fixed capital, but exclude the rest of C. By net national income, they mean simply $V + S$, which includes all payments to individuals plus business savings. Comparing Marxian with classical terminology we find a different type of discrepancy. By 'gross revenue' Ricardo, for example, understood what modern theorists call net income, that is to say, $V + S$, while 'net revenue' to Ricardo signified surplus value alone, that is to say the sum of profits and rent.*

4. The Rate of Surplus Value

The formula $c + v + s$ constitutes the analytic backbone, so to speak, of Marx's economic theory. In the remainder of this chapter we shall define and discuss certain ratios which are derived from it.

The first of these ratios is called the rate of surplus value, is

* For further discussion of the relation between the value formula and income concepts, see Appendix A below.

defined as the ratio of surplus value to variable capital, and is denoted by s':

$$\frac{s}{v} = s' = \text{rate of surplus value}$$

The rate of surplus value is the capitalist form of what Marx calls the rate of exploitation, that is to say, the ratio of surplus labor to necessary labor. Thus suppose that the working day is 12 hours, and that 6 hours are necessary labor and 6 hours surplus labor. Then in any society in which the product of surplus labor is appropriated by an exploiting class, we shall have a rate of exploitation given by the following ratio:

$$\frac{6 \text{ hrs.}}{6 \text{ hrs.}} = 100 \text{ per cent}$$

Under capitalism the product of labor assumes the value form. If we assume that in one hour the worker produces a value of \$1, the rate of surplus value will be given by

$$\frac{\$6}{\$6} = 100 \text{ per cent}$$

which is, of course, numerically identical with the rate of exploitation. The two concepts, rate of exploitation and rate of surplus value, can often be used interchangeably, but it is important to remember that the former is the more general concept applicable to all exploitative societies while the latter applies only to capitalism.

The magnitude of the rate of surplus value is directly determined by three factors: the length of the working day, the quantity of commodities entering into the real wage, and the productiveness of labor. The first establishes the total time to be divided between necessary and surplus labor, and the second and third together determine how much of this time is to be counted as necessary labor. Each of these three factors is in turn the focal point of a complex of forces which have to be analysed in the further development of the theory. The rate of surplus value may be raised either by an extension of the working day, or by a lowering of the real wage, or by an increase in the productiveness of labor, or, finally, by some combination of the three movements. In case of an increase in the length of the working day, Marx speaks of the production of absolute surplus value, while either a lowering of the real wage or an increase in productivity, leading to a reduction of necessary labor, results in the production of relative surplus value.

Marx almost always works with the simplifying assumption that the rate of surplus value is the same in all branches of industry and in all firms within each industry. This assumption implies certain conditions which are never more than partially realized in practice. First there must be a homogeneous, transferable, and mobile labor force. This condition has already been discussed at considerable length in connection with the concept of abstract labor; * if it is satisfied we can speak of 'a competition among the laborers and an equilibration by means of their continual emigration from one sphere of production to another.' [9] Second, each industry and all the firms within each industry must use just the amount of labor which is socially necessary under the existing circumstances. In other words it is supposed that no producers operate with an exceptionally high or exceptionally low level of technique. To the extent that this condition is not satisfied, some producers will have a higher (or lower) rate of surplus value than the social average, and these divergences will not be eliminated by the transferability and mobility of labor as between occupations and firms.

It is important to understand that the assumption of equal rates of surplus value is based, in the final analysis, upon certain very real tendencies of capitalist production. Workers do move out of low-wage areas into higher-wage areas, and producers do try to avail themselves of the most advanced technical methods. Consequently the assumption can be said to be no more than an idealization of actual conditions. As Marx expressed it:

Such a general rate of surplus value—as a tendency, like all other economic laws—has been assumed by us for the sake of theoretical simplification. But in reality it is an actual premise of the capitalist mode of production, although it is more or less obstructed by practical frictions causing more or less considerable

* See above, pp. 30 ff.

differences locally, such as the settlement laws for English farm laborers. But in theory it is the custom to assume that the laws of capitalist production evolve in their pure form. In reality, however, there is but an approximation. Still this approximation is so much greater to the extent that the capitalist mode of production is normally developed, and to the extent that its adulteration with remains of former economic conditions is outgrown.[10]

5. The Organic Composition of Capital

The second ratio to be derived from the formula $c + v + s$ is a measure of the relation of constant to variable capital in the total capital used in production. Marx calls this relation the organic composition of capital. Several ratios would serve to indicate this relation, but the one which seems most convenient is the ratio of constant capital to total capital. Let us designate this by the letter q. Then we have:

$$\frac{c}{c + v} = q = \text{organic composition of capital}$$

In non-technical language the organic composition of capital is a measure of the extent to which labor is furnished with materials, instruments, and machinery in the productive process.

As in the case of the rate of surplus value, the factors which determine the organic composition of capital at any time are themselves subject to a variety of causal influences. Certain important aspects of the problem will be discussed as we proceed. For the present we need only note that the rate of real wages, the productivity of labor, the prevailing level of technique (closely related to the productivity of labor), and the extent of capital accumulation in the past all enter into the determination of the organic composition of capital.

The assumptions which Marx makes concerning the organic composition of capital will be considered in the next section in connection with the rate of profit.

6. The Rate of Profit

To the capitalist the crucial ratio is the rate of profit, in other words, the ratio of surplus value to total capital outlay. If we designate this by p, we have:

$$\frac{s}{c + v} = p = \text{rate of profit}$$

Several things need to be pointed out in connection with this ratio. In the first place, in directly identifying surplus value with profit we are assuming that no part of surplus value has to be paid over to the landlord in the form of rent. This is an assumption which Marx makes until Part VI of Volume III of *Capital*, where he first introduces the problem of rent. This procedure Marx explained in a letter to Engels setting forth a preliminary outline of *Capital*. 'In the whole of this section [at the time called 'Capital in General'] . . . landed property is taken as = 0; that is, nothing as yet concerns landed property as a particular economic relation. This is the only possible way to avoid having to deal with everything under each particular relation.' [11] Since it is beyond the rather limited scope of the present work to attempt a discussion of the theory of rent, we shall adhere to the assumption in question throughout.

In the second place, the formula $s/(c + v)$, strictly speaking, shows the rate of profit on the capital actually used up in producing a given commodity. In practice the capitalist usually calculates the rate of profit on his total investment for a given period of time, say a year. But total investment is generally not the same as capital used up during a year since the turnover time of different elements of total investment varies widely. Thus, for example, a factory building may last for fifty years, a machine for ten years while the outlay on wages returns to the capitalist every three months. In order to simplify the theoretical exposition, and to bring the rate of profit formula into conformity with the usual concept of an annual rate of profit, Marx makes the assumption that all capital has an identical turnover period of one year (or whatever unit period is chosen for the purposes of analysis). This implies that the productive process requires a year, that the materials, machinery, and labor power bought at the beginning of the year are exhausted by the end, and that the product is then sold and all outlays recovered with the addition of surplus value. This is not to say that Marx ignores questions connected with varying turnover periods any more than he ignores the problem of rent; on the contrary, a large part of Volume II is devoted to complications arising from the differences in turnover times of different elements of capital. But here again, in order to restrict the scope of our discussion and to focus attention on the essential elements of the theory, we shall retain the assumption given above throughout the present work.

As for the factors determining the rate of profit, it is easy to demonstrate that they are identical with the factors determining the rate of surplus value and the organic composition of capital. In mathematical language, the rate of profit is a function of the rate of surplus value and the organic composition of capital. Remembering the definitions $s' = s/v$, $q = c/(c + v)$, and $p = s/(c + v)$, it follows by simple manipulation that

$$p = s'(1 - q).^{*}$$

Thus, in spite of the fact that the rate of profit is the crucial variable from the point of view of the behavior of the capitalist, for purposes of theoretical analysis it must be looked upon as dependent upon the two more primary variables, the rate of surplus value and the organic composition of capital. This is the procedure which Marx in effect adopted and which will be followed in our subsequent investigations.†

Just as in the case of the rate of surplus value, so also in the case of the rate of profit the assumption of general equality as between industries and firms is made. The necessary conditions are strictly parallel in the two cases. To the mobility of labor

* As follows:

$$p = \frac{s}{c+v} = \frac{sv}{v(c+v)} = \frac{sc + sv - sc}{v(c+v)} = \frac{s(c+v) - sc}{v(c+v)}$$

$$= \frac{s(c+v)}{v(c+v)} - \frac{sc}{v(c+v)} = \frac{s}{v} - \frac{s}{v}\cdot\frac{c}{c+v} = s'(1-q).$$

† See particularly Chapter VI below.

away from low-wage areas to higher-wage areas corresponds the mobility of capital from low-profit areas to higher-profit areas, while in both instances a general equality in the level of technique is required. Any capitalist who is able to maintain an advantage in point of technical methods is able to enjoy a higher rate of surplus value and therefore also a higher rate of profit than his fellows. The justification for the two assumptions is therefore virtually the same, though it is perhaps true that in practice, and in the absence of monopoly, capital is both more homogeneous and more mobile than labor.

At this point we encounter for the first time an interesting theoretical problem. If both rates of surplus value and rates of profit are everywhere equal, then it follows that, if the exchange of commodities is to take place in accordance with the law of value, organic compositions of capital must also be everywhere the same. This can be readily demonstrated by assuming two commodities with equal values and equal rates of surplus value but with different organic compositions of capital. For example, the value of commodity A is made up of $10c + 20v + 20s = 50$, and that of B is made up of $30c + 10v + 10s = 50$. The rate of surplus value is in each case 100 per cent and their respective values are identical; presumably they should exchange for each other on a one-to-one basis. Yet if this happens it is obvious that the capitalist producing A will have a profit rate of 66⅔ per cent, while the capitalist producing B will have a profit rate of only 25 per cent. This could not be a position of equilibrium.

It will be recalled that the equality in rates of surplus value and in rates of profit was predicated upon actual tendencies at work in capitalist production, tendencies which arise from the force of competition. Can we perhaps assert that there is also an actual tendency to equality in organic compositions of capital so that the difficulty can be overcome by making a similar assumption here? The answer is no. Within a given industry there is undoubtedly a tendency for organic compositions of capital to be equal as between firms. But as between industries producing entirely different commodities by widely varying methods no such tendency exists. For example there is obviously nothing to bring the ratios of constant to variable capital in the steel and clothing industries into conformity.

The conclusion is therefore inescapable that in the real world of capitalist production the law of value is not directly controlling. It is entirely unjustifiable, however, to draw the inference from this fact, as critics of Marx invariably do, that the theory of value must be scrapped and a new basis sought for analysing the workings of the capitalist system.* It is perfectly legitimate to postulate a capitalist system in which organic compositions of capital are everywhere equal and hence the law of value does hold, and to examine the functioning of such a system. Whether or not this procedure is valid cannot be decided *a priori;* it must be tested by dropping the assumption of equal organic compositions and investigating the extent to which the results which have been attained require to be modified. If the modifications should prove to be of negligible importance, the analysis based on the law of value would be vindicated; if, on the other hand, they should turn out to be so great as to alter the essential character of the results, then indeed we should have to abandon the law of value and look for a fresh starting point.

Marx's method conforms to the procedure just outlined. Throughout the first two volumes of *Capital,* he ignores differences in organic compositions, which is another way of saying that he assumes that they do not exist. Then in Volume III he abandons this assumption and attempts to show that, from the point of view of the problems which he was attempting to solve, the modifications which result are of a relatively minor character. There is no doubt that the proof which Marx gives for this latter proposition is in some respects unsatisfactory, but by substituting an adequate proof we shall demonstrate that both his method and his conclusions are sound.†

Alone among critics of Marx's theoretical structure, Bortkiewicz grasped the full significance of the law of value and its

* By far the best statement of this point of view is that of Böhm-Bawerk, *Karl Marx and the Close of his System.* It is hardly an exaggeration to say that subsequent critiques of Marxian economics have been mere repetitions of Böhm's arguments. The one great exception is the critique of Ladislaus von Bortkiewicz, which will be considered at various points as we proceed.

† See Chapter VII below.

use. Moreover, as we shall see, it was Bortkiewicz who laid the basis for a logically unobjectionable proof of the correctness of Marx's method, a fact which entitles him to be considered not only as a critic but also as an important contributor to Marxian theory. Bortkiewicz's statement on the question at issue is worth quoting at this stage of the analysis:

> The fact that the law of value is not valid in the capitalistic economic order depends, according to Marx, on a factor, or series of factors, which does not constitute but rather covers up the essence of capitalism. Assuming that the organic composition of capital were the same in all spheres of production, the law of value would be directly controlling for the exchange of commodities without stopping the exploitation of workers by capitalists and without substituting any other motive for the capitalists' search for profits in determining the size, direction, and technique of production.[12]

Here we have in a nutshell the reason for assuming equal organic compositions of capital. This assumption is not to be confused with the assumptions of equal rates of surplus value and equal rates of profit, however. The latter have their justification in actual tendencies at work in a competitive capitalist economy; the former involves a deliberate abstraction from conditions which undoubtedly exist in the real world. Its full justification can be demonstrated, therefore, only at a later stage, when the consequences of letting it drop are examined.

PART TWO

THE ACCUMULATION PROCESS

V

ACCUMULATION AND THE RESERVE ARMY

1. Simple Reproduction

It is useful, and even necessary, for theoretical purposes to imagine a capitalist system which runs on year in and year out in the same channels and without change. This enables us to comprehend the structure of relations obtaining in the system as a whole in their clearest and simplest form. To follow this procedure is not to imply, however, that there ever was or could be a real capitalist system which remained the same year after year. Indeed when we examine the case from which change is supposed to be absent, it will appear that some of the most essential elements of capitalism as it really exists have been deliberately ignored.

François Quesnay, the leader of the Physiocrats, was the first economist to attempt a systematic presentation of the structure of relations existing in capitalist production. His famous *Tableau Economique* (1758) for this reason alone was a milestone in the development of economic thought—Marx called it 'incontestably the most brilliant idea of which political economy had hitherto been guilty.'[1] Marx was greatly influenced by Quesnay and regarded his own scheme for analysing the structure of capitalism, which in its most elementary form he called 'Simple Reproduction,' as an improved version of the *Tableau*.*

* A letter from Marx to Engels, dated 6 July, 1863, opens as follows: 'If you find it possible in this heat, look at the enclosed *Tableau economique* which I substitute for Quesnay's Table, and tell me of any objections you may have to it. It embraces the whole process of reproduction.' *Selected Correspondence*, p. 153. In *Capital* Marx abandoned the diagrammatic form of the scheme accompanying this letter, but the ideas are there with the exposition greatly expanded. See particularly Volume I, Chapter XXIII and Volume II, Chapter XX. For a discussion of the relation between Quesnay's *tableau* and Marx's reproduction schemes, see Appendix A below.

Simple Reproduction refers to a capitalist system which preserves indefinitely the same size and the same proportions among its various parts. For these conditions to be satisfied capitalists must every year replace all capital worn out or used up and spend all of their surplus value on consumption; and workers must spend all of their wages on consumption. If these requirements were not fulfilled there would take place either an accumulation or a depletion of the stock of means of production, and this is excluded by hypothesis. We can see the reasons for these statements more easily if we represent Simple Reproduction in the notational language introduced in the last chapter.

Suppose that all industry is divided into two great branches: in I means of production are produced, and in II consumption goods are produced. For some purposes it is convenient to subdivide the consumption goods branch into one producing workers' consumption goods, or wage goods, and one producing capitalists' consumption goods, or what may be called luxury goods.* While we shall want to work with a three-branch reproduction scheme in Chapter VII below, a two-branch scheme is simpler and fully adequate to our present purposes.

Let c_1 and c_2 be the constant capital engaged respectively in I and II; similarly let v_1 and v_2 be the variable capital, s_1 and s_2 the surplus value, and w_1 and w_2 the product measured in value of the two branches respectively.

Then we shall have the following table representing the total production:

$$\text{I} \qquad c_1 + v_1 + s_1 = w_1$$

$$\text{II} \qquad c_2 + v_2 + s_2 = w_2$$

For the conditions of Simple Reproduction to be satisfied, the constant capital used up must be equal to the output of the producers' goods branch, and the combined consumption of capitalists and workers must be equal to the output of the consumers' goods branch. This means that

$$c_1 + c_2 = c_1 + v_1 + s_1$$

$$v_1 + s_1 + v_2 + s_2 = c_2 + v_2 + s_2$$

* The distinction as drawn by Marx is between 'necessities of life' and 'articles of luxury.' *Capital* II, Chap. XX, Sec. 4.

By eliminating c_1 from both sides of the first equation and $v_2 + s_2$ from both sides of the second equation, it will be seen that the two reduce to the following single equation:

$$c_2 = v_1 + s_1$$

This, then, may be called the basic condition of Simple Reproduction. It says simply that the value of the constant capital used up in the consumption goods branch must be equal to the value of the commodities consumed by the workers and capitalists engaged in producing means of production. If this condition is satisfied, the scale of production remains unchanged from one year to the next.

Before proceeding, let us examine the reproduction scheme in somewhat more detail. Perhaps its greatest importance lies in the fact that it provides a unified framework for analysing the interconnections of output and income, a problem which was never systematically or adequately dealt with by the classical economists. Production is divided into two broad categories: output of means of production and output of means of consumption. Taken together these constitute the aggregate social supply of commodities. Income, on the other hand, may be said to be divided into three categories; the income of the capitalist which must be spent on means of production if he is to maintain his position as a capitalist, the income of the capitalist which he is free to spend for consumption (surplus value), and the income of the worker (wages). Since, however, there are capitalists and workers in both of the great branches of production, it is perhaps better to say that income is divided into six categories, three for each branch. Taken together these constitute the aggregate demand for commodities. Now it is obvious that in equilibrium aggregate supply and aggregate demand must balance, but what is not so obvious is the interrelation between the various elements of the two aggregates which will just suffice to create such a balance. It is one of the most important functions of the reproduction scheme to throw light on this problem. In fulfilling this function, it may be noted in passing, the reproduction scheme lays the groundwork for an analysis of *discrepancies* between aggregate supply and aggregate demand which, of course, manifest themselves in general disturbances of the productive process.*

Each of the items in the reproduction scheme has a twofold character in that it represents an element of demand and at the same time an element of supply. Consider c_1; it constitutes a part of the value of the output of means of production and it also constitutes a part of the receipts of the capitalists of department I derived from the sale of means of production and normally destined to be spent for fresh means of production. Thus c_1 represents both supply of and demand for means of production. The requisite exchanges always take place among the capitalists of Department I; value to the amount of c_1 pursues, so to speak, a circular course emerging from one end of the means of production branch and circling back to enter the same branch at the beginning of the next production period. The next item is v_1 which represents that part of the value of output of means of production which replaces wages; it is thus supply of means of production. On the other hand v_1 is also the wages of the workers engaged in producing means of production and as such it obviously constitutes demand for means of consumption. Here there is no matching of the supply and demand elements. Exactly the same holds, under the assumption of Simple Reproduction, for s_1 as for v_1 except that here we have to do with the surplus value of the capitalists in Department I. We complete the analysis of Department I with a supply of means of production equal to $v_1 + s_1$ undisposed of, and with a demand for means of consumption of the same magnitude unsatisfied. Now let us turn to Department II, the production of means of consumption. A part of the output of consumption goods equal to c_2, representing the value of means of production used up in turning out consumption goods, corresponds to demand for fresh means of production by the capitalists of Department II. Here again there is no direct matching between supply and demand. It is otherwise with v_2 and s_2; these represent both supply of and demand for consumption goods. As in the case of c_1 the necessary exchanges can take place altogether within one department, this time Department II. Department II is thus left with an 'un-

* See Chapter x below.

sold' supply of consumption goods equal to c_2 and an unsatisfied demand for means of production of the same magnitude.

Coming now to the relations between the two departments we note that I has a supply of means of production and a demand for means of consumption equal to $v_1 + s_1$, and II has a demand for means of production and a supply of means of consumption equal to c_2. It is apparent that the two departments can, so to speak, do business with each other, and provided that $v_1 + s_1$ is exactly equal to c_2 their mutual exchanges will clear the market for both means of production and means of consumption and bring aggregate supply and aggregate demand into balance.

This reasoning brings us again to the equilibrium condition of Simple Reproduction by a method which should have the advantage of laying bare the inherent logic of the reproduction scheme. The reproduction scheme is in essence a device for displaying the structure of supplies and demands in the capitalist economy in terms of the kinds of commodities produced and the functions of the recipients of incomes. It should be added, however, that no causal inferences can be drawn from the scheme as such; the scheme provides a framework, not a substitute, for further investigation.

2. The Roots of Accumulation

The reader may have reflected that the capitalist who lives in the imaginary world of Simple Reproduction does not manifest the characteristics which were attributed to capitalists in the last chapter. There it was pointed out that 'use values must never be looked upon as the real aim of the capitalist,' yet we have now constructed a system in which capitalists receive the same income year in and year out and always consume it down to the last dollar. Clearly under such circumstances use values would have to be regarded as the aim of the capitalist.

The conclusion is inescapable that Simple Reproduction involves abstraction from what is most essential in the capitalist, namely, his concern to expand his capital. He gives effect to this by converting a portion—frequently the major portion—of his surplus value into additional capital. His augmented capital then enables him to appropriate still more surplus value, which he in turn converts into additional capital, and so on. This is the process known as accumulation of capital; it constitutes the driving force of capitalist development.

The capitalist, as Marx observed, 'shares with the miser the passion for wealth as wealth. But that which in the miser is a mere idiosyncrasy, is, in the capitalist, the effect of the social mechanism of which he is but one of the wheels.' [2] It is of the utmost importance to grasp this point. The circulation form *M-C-M'*, in which the capitalist occupies the key position, is *objectively* a value-expansion process. This fact is reflected in the *subjective* aim of the capitalist. It is not at all a question of innate human propensities or instincts; the desire of the capitalist to expand the value under his control (to accumulate capital) springs from his special position in a particular form of organization of social production. A moment's reflection will show that it could not be otherwise. The capitalist is a capitalist and is an important figure in society only in so far as he is the owner and representative of capital. Deprived of his capital, he would be nothing. But capital has only one quality, that of possessing magnitude, and from this it follows that one capitalist is distinguishable from another only by the magnitude of the capital which he represents. The owner of a large amount of capital stands higher in the social scale than the owner of a small amount of capital; position, prestige, power are reduced to the quantitative measuring rod of dollars and cents. Success in capitalist society therefore consists in adding to one's capital. 'To accumulate,' as Marx expressed it, 'is to conquer the world of social wealth, to increase the mass of human beings exploited by him, and thus to extend both the direct and the indirect sway of the capitalist.' [3]

Given the urge to accumulate, an additional, reinforcing factor of hardly less importance enters into the motivation of the capitalist. The greatest amount of surplus value and hence also the greatest power to accumulate goes to the capitalist who employs the most advanced and efficient technical methods; consequently the striving for improvements is universal. But new and better methods of production require increased capital outlays and render obsolete and hence valueless existing means of production. In Marx's words, the development of capitalist production makes it constantly necessary to keep increasing the amount of capital laid out in a given industrial undertaking, and competition makes the immanent laws of capitalist production to be felt by each individual capitalist as external coercive laws. It compels him to keep constantly extending his capital, in order to preserve it, but extend it he cannot except by means of progressive accumulation.[4]

We see that the Marxian analysis relates capital accumulation to the specific historical form of capitalist production. The way to success and social preferment lies through accumulation, and he who refuses to enter the race stands in danger of losing out altogether.

Corresponding to this analysis of accumulation, Marx sketched in the outlines of a theory of capitalists' consumption:

At the historical dawn of capitalist production—and every capitalist upstart has personally to go through this historical stage—avarice and the desire to get rich are the ruling passions. But the progress of capitalist production not only creates a world of delights; it lays open in speculation and the credit system, a thousand sources of sudden enrichment. When a certain stage of development has been reached, a conventional degree of prodigality, which is also an exhibition of wealth and consequently a source of credit, becomes a business necessity to the 'unfortunate' capitalist. Luxury enters into capital's expenses of representation . . . Although, therefore, the prodigality of the capitalist never possesses the bona fide character of the open-handed feudal lord's prodigality, but, on the contrary, has always lurking behind it the most sordid avarice and the most anxious calculation, yet his expenditure grows with his accumulation, without the one necessarily restricting the other. But along with this growth there is at the same time developed in his breast a Faustian conflict between the passion for accumulation and the desire for enjoyment.*

Thus, while the drive to accumulate remains primary, it does not exclude a parallel, and even in part derivative, desire to expand consumption.

* *Capital* I, pp. 650-51. The idea that 'luxury enters into capital's expenses of representation' contains an interesting foreshadowing of Thorstein Veblen's doctrine of 'conspicuous consumption' as expounded in *The Theory of the Leisure Class.*

It is interesting to compare Marx's ideas about the motives behind capitalists' accumulation and consumption with the contemporary orthodox theories which laid stress on 'abstinence' and 'waiting.' According to the abstinence theory, it is painful for the capitalist to 'abstain' from consumption in order to accumulate, and hence interest on capital is to be looked upon as the necessary reward for such abstinence. Against this Marx takes the position that to accumulate capital, that is to say, to increase one's wealth, is a positive end and has 'pleasures' attached to it quite as much as consumption does. It would be just as logical, he suggests, to regard consumption as abstinence from accumulation as *vice versa:*

> It has never occurred to the vulgar economist to make the simple reflection that every human action may be viewed as 'abstinence' from its opposite. Eating is abstinence from fasting, walking abstinence from standing still, working abstinence from idling, idling abstinence from working, etc. These gentlemen would do well to ponder . . . over Spinoza's: 'Determinatio est negatio.'[5]

In short, capitalists want both to accumulate and to consume; when they do either it can be looked upon as abstinence from the other; but looking at the matter in this way explains nothing.

When we come to the 'waiting' theory—Alfred Marshall was the leading exponent of this doctrine—matters are, if anything, worse. The idea here is that ultimately capitalists want to consume everything they own. They do not do so now because if they wait they can consume it with interest in the future. This is the *reductio ad absurdam* of a consistent adherence to the assumption that all economic behavior is directed to the satisfaction of consumption wants. While the abstinence theory merely slurs over the capitalist's drive to accumulate wealth, the waiting theory denies it altogether.

It is not to be overlooked that the abstinence theory was first propounded by Nassau W. Senior in the 1830s and that the earlier economists had generally taken an independent motive to accumulate for granted. Thus Ricardo once wrote to Malthus: 'I consider the wants and tastes of mankind as unlimited. We all wish to add to our enjoyments or to our power. *Consumption adds to our enjoyments, accumulation to our power*, and they *equally promote demand.*'[6] As usual, Ricardo universalizes a feature of capitalist production and applies it to 'mankind' in general, but there is no trace of the abstinence point of view. How can we explain this rather sudden change of front on the part of the political economists? The answer seems to lie in the fact that the abstinence theory, as well as the waiting and time-preference theories after it, operated as a defense of surplus value and hence of the *status quo*. Before about 1830—Marx suggests that the July revolution in France marks the turning point—capitalism, generally speaking, had been an aggressive force attacking many, though certainly not all, aspects of the *status quo*. When the victory had been won, however, it was necessary to turn from attack to defense. Many of the differences between the doctrines of the classical economists and their successors can be understood only when this fact is remembered; not the least of these differences was signalized by the emergence of the abstinence theory of accumulation.

3. Accumulation and the Value of Labor Power—The Problem Stated

It would be possible at this point to present a reproduction scheme, which Marx calls Expanded Reproduction in contrast to Simple Reproduction, showing the interrelation of supplies and demands when accumulation is taken into account, that is to say, when surplus value is no longer entirely consumed by capitalists but is divided into three parts, one being consumed by capitalists, another added to constant capital, and a third added to variable capital. But it seems wiser to postpone the presentation of Expanded Reproduction until Chapter x below, when we shall be ready to inquire more closely into its implications for the problem of crises. For the time being we are interested in investigating the effects of the increased quantity of variable capital, or, what comes to the same thing, the increased demand for labor power, which is implicit in the accumulation process. For this purpose we may simply assume the quantitative relations of supply and demand which are necessary to maintain the equilibrium of Expanded Reproduction without going into the formal structure of the scheme.

We start, then, from the undoubted fact that accumulation involves an increase in the demand for labor power. Now when the demand for any commodity increases, its price also increases; and this entails a deviation of price from value. We know that in the case of an ordinary commodity, say cotton cloth, this will set certain forces in motion to bring price back into conformity with value: cotton-cloth manufacturers will make abnormally high profits, capitalists from outside will be induced to enter the industry, the supply of cotton cloth will be expanded, price will fall until it is once again equal to value and profits are normal. Having stated the general principle in this way, we are at once impressed by a striking fact: labor power is no ordinary commodity! There are no capitalists who can turn to producing labor power in case its price goes up; in fact there is no 'labor-power industry' at all in the sense that there is a cotton-cloth industry. Only in a slave society, like the pre-Civil War South where slave breeding was carried on for profit, can one properly speak of a labor-power industry. In capitalism generally, the equilibrating mechanism of supply and demand is lacking in the case of labor power.

As long as we were dealing with Simple Reproduction it was possible to assume that labor power was selling at its value. There was no contradiction involved in such an assumption since there are no forces operating to produce a deviation between the price of labor power and its value. As soon as accumulation is taken into account, however, this ceases to be the case. Accumulation raises the demand for labor power, and it is no longer legitimate simply to postulate an equality between wages and the value of labor power. Moreover, as we have now seen, the mechanism which can be relied upon to re-establish this identity in the case of all commodities produced for profit is inoperative in the case of labor power. It appears that there are certain difficulties in the way of applying the law of value to the commodity labor power.*

* Marxists have generally overlooked the logical difficulty involved in applying the law of value to the commodity labor power. And, curiously, critics of Marx have with almost equal unanimity neglected this important point. Bortkiewicz, in this as in other respects, presents a special case. He saw the difficulty clearly enough, as the following passage shows: 'Bringing wages under the general law of value, as Marx does, is not

There is more involved in this than a mere terminological quibble. Indeed it is no exaggeration to say that the validity of Marx's whole theoretical structure is called into question. To see why this is so, it is only necessary to recall that surplus value, which is essential to the existence of capitalism, depends upon the existence of a difference between the value of labor power and the value of the commodity which the laborer produces. If there are no forces at work to keep wages equal to the value of labor power, what reason is there for assuming the existence of this vital gap between wages and the value of the product? Might we not just as well assume that wages rise under the stimulus of accumulation until the whole gap is eliminated? Before we consider Marx's answer to these questions it will be necessary to analyse briefly the Ricardian solution to the problem of the relation between wages and the value of labor power, for in this, as in other questions of economic theory, Marx can best be understood by way of a comparison with Ricardo.

Ricardo's quantitative theory of value and profit is very similar, except in matters of terminology, to that of Marx. The same parallelism appears to extend to the theory of wages. 'Labor,' says Ricardo, 'like all other things which are purchased and sold, and which may be increased or diminished in quantity, has its natural and its market price. The natural price of labor is that price which is necessary to enable the laborers, one with another, to subsist and to perpetuate their race, without either increase or diminution.' * Ricardo was very explicit about the forces which operate to keep the market price in line with the natural price:

permissible since this law, so far as it can be assumed to have validity, rests on competition among producers which, in the case of the commodity labor power, is entirely excluded.' 'Wertrechnung und Preisrechnung im Marxschen System,' *Archiv für Sozialwissenschaft und Sozialpolitik*, September 1907, p. 483. Bortkiewicz, however, thought the difficulty could be avoided by dropping the idea that labor power is a commodity like other commodities and simply assuming that the real wage is fixed. It apparently never occurred to him that such an assumption loses all justification the moment accumulation is introduced.

Oskar Lange has recently emphasized the difficulty involved in applying the law of value to the commodity labor power and has pointed out, for the first time so far as I am aware, the implications of the problem for Marx's theoretical structure. 'Marxian Economics and Modern Economic Theory,' *Review of Economic Studies*, June 1935

* *Principles of Political Economy*, p. 71. What Ricardo calls the 'natural

However much the market price of labor may deviate from its natural price, it has, like commodities, a tendency to conform to it.

It is when the market price of labor exceeds its natural price that the condition of the laborer is flourishing and happy, that he has it in his power to command a greater proportion of the necessaries and enjoyments of life . . . *When, however, by the encouragement which high wages give to the increase of population, the number of laborers is increased, wages again fall to their natural price*, and indeed from a reaction sometimes fall below it.[7]

For Ricardo, in short, the mechanism necessary to insure that wages remain at about the conventional subsistence level is furnished by a theory of population. Moreover, the population theory which he had in mind is evidently a special case of the famous Malthusian theory, which was so much in vogue in England during the first half of the nineteenth century. Thus in the classical scheme the supply of all ordinary commodities is regulated by competition among capitalists in such a way as to equate price to value; in the case of the supply of labor precisely the same function is performed by the theory of population. It is in this sense that the theory of population forms an integral part of the theoretical structure of classical political economy.

Marx never wrote much about the factors which determine the size of the population, but this much is certain, that he had no use whatever for the Malthusian theory or any of its variants. He called the theory of population 'the dogma of the economists,'[8] and he scarcely ever mentioned it except to belittle it. Malthus's *Essay on Population* he termed a 'libel on the human race,'[9] and the doctrine it contained 'the Malthusian population fantasy.'[10] The great sensation caused by the *Essay* was due not at all to any originality or scientific interest (both of which it altogether lacked), but 'solely to party interest.'[11] It would probably be impossible to find in all Marx's writings a favorable reference to the classical doctrine of population. Clearly he had no disposition

price of labor' is equivalent to the Marxian concept of the 'value of labor power.' The classics, and Marx in one of his earliest economic works, *Wage Labor and Capital* (1847), did not differentiate between labor and labor power; rather they used the word labor in both senses. Confusion not infrequently resulted from this double use of the word labor.

to adopt *this* method of squaring the theory of value with the unique character of the commodity labor power.

4. Marx's Solution—The Reserve Army of Labor

Marx was, of course, fully aware of the tendency of wages to rise under the impact of capital accumulation.

The requirements of accumulating capital may exceed the increase of labor power or of the number of laborers; the demand for laborers may exceed the supply, and therefore wages may rise. This must, indeed ultimately be the case if the conditions supposed above continue. For since in each year more laborers are employed than in its predecessor, sooner or later a point must be reached at which the requirements of accumulation begin to surpass the customary supply of labor, and therefore a rise of wages takes place.[12]

He was quite certain, however, that such a rise in wages 'can never reach the point at which it would threaten the system itself.' He had therefore to ask: what keeps wages in check so that surplus value and accumulation may continue as the characteristic and essential features of capitalist production? This question is the obverse of that posed above—what keeps wages equal to the value of labor power?—and therefore to answer one is at the same time to answer the other.

Marx's solution to the problem turns around his famous concept of the 'reserve army of labor,' or, as he also termed it, 'relative surplus population.' The reserve army consists of unemployed workers who, through their active competition on the labor market, exercise a continuous downward pressure on the wage level.

The industrial reserve army, during the periods of stagnation and average prosperity, weighs down the active labor army; during the periods of overproduction and paroxysm, it holds its pretensions in check. *Relative surplus population is therefore the pivot upon which the law of demand and supply of labor works.* It confines the field of action of this law within the limits absolutely convenient to the activity of exploitation and to the domination of capital.[13]

The reserve army is recruited primarily from those who have been displaced by machinery, 'whether this takes the more striking form of the repulsion of laborers already employed, or the less evident but not less real form of the more difficult absorption of the additional laboring population through the usual channels.'[14] That Marx thought of the introduction of labor-saving machinery as a more or less direct response on the part of capitalists to the rising tendency of wages is clearly indicated in the following passage:

> Between 1849 and 1859, a rise of wages took place in the English agricultural districts . . . This was the result of an unusual exodus of the agricultural surplus population caused by the demands of war, the vast extension of railroads, factories, mines, etc. . . . Everywhere the farmers were howling and the *London Economist*, with reference to these starvation wages, prattled quite seriously of 'a general and substantial advance.' What did the farmers do now? Did they wait until, in consequence of this brilliant remuneration, the agricultural laborers had so increased and multiplied that their wages must fall again, as prescribed by the dogmatic economic brain? They introduced more machinery and in a moment the laborers were redundant again in a proportion satisfactory even to the farmers. There was now 'more capital' laid out in agriculture than before, and in a more productive form. With this the demand for labor fell not only relatively but absolutely.[15]

So far as the individual capitalists are concerned, each takes the wage level for granted and attempts to do the best he can for himself. In introducing machinery he is therefore merely attempting to economize on his own wage bill. The net effect of all the capitalists' behaving in this way, however, is to create unemployment which in turn acts upon the wage level itself. It follows that the stronger the tendency of wages to rise, the stronger also will be the counteracting pressure of the reserve army, and *vice versa*.

In terms of the movement of the total social capital, mechanization means a rise in the organic composition of capital, i.e. a growth in the expenditures of capitalists on machinery and materials at the expense of labor. It may mean an absolute decline in the demand for labor, or it may mean simply that the demand for labor lags behind the growth of total capital. In the latter case, if population is growing—it does not matter for what reason—the steady expansion of a reserve army, say as a more or less constant proportion of the total working force, is a perfectly logical possibility. Marx seems usually to have had something of this sort in mind; the assumptions underlying this case were, indeed, those which would naturally have suggested themselves to some one writing in the mid-nineteenth century. But the principle of the reserve army is independent of any particular population assumption; it works equally well with a stationary or even a declining population. In this fact we have one of the decisive differences between Marx and his predecessors in the classical school, a subject to which we shall presently return.

In this connection, it is well to note that Marx was not the first to discover the possibility of labor displacement by machinery, or even the first to expose the falsity of the compensation theory which was then, as it is now, so popular among orthdox economists and publicists. Extremely important theoretical work had already been performed by Ricardo (among others) in the famous chapter 'On Machinery' which first appeared in the third edition of the *Principles*. There Ricardo established by a somewhat clumsy but logically watertight argument that labor-saving machinery 'sets free' workers without setting free variable capital for their employment elsewhere, and hence that their re-employment depends primarily on additional accumulation. Though Ricardo did not say so, it is consistent with his reasoning to assume that the rate of displacement exceeds the rate of re-absorption as a result of new accumulation. Marx's great accomplishment was the integration of this principle into the general theory of capital accumulation in such a way as to free the latter from an otherwise fatal dependence on the Malthusian population dogma.

It would, of course, be wrong to assume that either the rate of accumulation or the introduction of labor-saving machinery proceeds at such an even pace as to preserve a nice equilibrium of wages and surplus value. On the contrary, 'with accumulation and the development of the productiveness of labor that accompanies it, the power of sudden expansion of capital also grows.' [16]

A rapid burst of capital accumulation may result from the opening up of a new market or a new industry. In such cases, the reserve army is depleted, and the check on a rise in wages is removed; surplus value, may, indeed, be seriously diminished. 'But as soon as this diminution touches the point at which the surplus labor that nourishes capital is no longer supplied in normal quantity, a reaction sets in: a smaller part of revenue is capitalized, accumulation lags, and the movement of rise in wages receives a check.'[17] Marx is here describing one of the fundamental causes of crises. Alongside of displacement of labor by machinery, crises and depressions take their place as the specific capitalist mechanism for replenishing the reserve army whenever it has been reduced to dangerously small proportions. The elaboration of this theme is left until later.* Here we need only note that through its relation to the reserve army, the problem of crises assumes a central position in Marx's theoretical system. Whereas for the classical theorists, the problem was not so much to explain crises as to explain them away, for Marx capitalism without crises would be, in the final analysis, inconceivable.†

The theory of the reserve army can be illuminated by a simple diagram. Figure 1 is a representation of the industrial process. At the top is the large mass of workers in Industrial Employment. This is fed on the one hand by the stream of new workers finding jobs in capitalist industry for the first time (A), and on the other hand by the unemployed from the Reserve Army who are absorbed into industry (D). Leaving Industrial Employment are, first, the retiring workers who have finished their productive careers (F), and, second, those who are displaced from industry (C) and hence enter the Reserve Army. For the sake of completeness, two further streams are inserted, namely, the new workers who, failing to find employment, immediately join the ranks of the Reserve Army (B); and those who, after a period of unemployment, give up looking for jobs and join the stream of retiring workers (E).

In the prosperity phase of the business cycle Industrial Employment gains at the expense of the Reserve Army; on the other

* Below, Chapter IX.

† In the case of fascism, this principle undergoes a considerable modification. See below, pp. 342-7.

hand crisis and depression witness a contraction of Industrial Employment and a filling up of the Reserve Army.

A similar diagrammatic representation of the classical view of the industrial process would need to show only Industrial Employment with the incoming stream of new workers and the outflow of retiring workers. The level of wages, in this view, depends primarily on the magnitude of the stream of new work-

THE INDUSTRIAL PROCESS

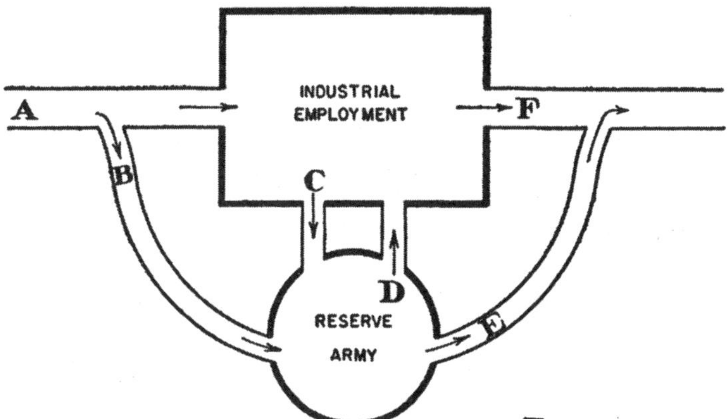

A New Workers
B Unable to find jobs
C Displaced
D Rehired.
E Retiring
F Retiring

FIGURE 1

ers which in turn is a function of population growth. Thus, if we regard the system of production as coextensive with the field of Industrial Employment, it was the classical view that wages were ultimately regulated by factors outside the system (population).

In Marx's theory, however, the system of production includes both Industrial Employment and the Reserve Army. Whatever assumption we care to make about factors outside the system (population), the fact remains that it contains within itself a mechanism for regulating the wage level and hence for maintaining profits.*

* This is not to deny the practical and theoretical significance of the rate of population growth. The problem acquires great importance on a somewhat lower level of abstraction. See below, pp. 222 ff.

Furthermore, since all the streams in Figure 1 are conceived as continuing flows there is no ground for criticism based on the argument that technological unemployment is merely a transitory phenomenon and hence cannot form an integral part of a theory of the productive system.

5. The Nature of the Capitalist Process

Classical political economy, which leaned so heavily on the Malthusian population theory, was always inclined to predict the imminent end of economic progress. The reasoning was majestic and convincing in its simplicity. Accumulation indirectly stimulates the growth of population; increase in numbers forces recourse to inferior lands; the necessaries of life can therefore be produced only at constantly increasing cost in terms of man-hours. This implies a rise in the value of labor and hence of wages as a proportion of the total product; * hence, also, a fall in profit as a proportion of the total product. Eventually it seemed certain that even the absolute amount of profit would commence to fall. Finally, accumulation by capitalists—the motor force of the whole process—'will cease altogether when their profits are so low as not to afford them an adequate compensation for their trouble, and the risk which they must necessarily encounter in employing their capital productively.' [18] This inexorable course of evolution could be temporarily checked by technical and scientific discoveries which would render the production of necessaries less costly. But eventually it must work itself out to its logical conclusion, the stationary state. Economic progress must finally be arrested by two overriding and immutable natural laws: the law of population and the law of diminishing returns. John Stuart Mill, in this connection, speaks gravely of the 'impossibility of ultimately avoiding the stationary state—this irresistible necessity that the stream of human industry should finally spread itself out into an apparently stagnant sea.' [19]

This is a theory of economic evolution deduced with logical precision from a few clearly enunciated initial premises. As the

* It does not, of course, imply any rise in the real wage rate.

final word of classical political economy on the essential tendency of the capitalist system, it possesses an intellectual boldness which is certainly not to be denied. But towards the end of the nineteenth century, facts, like termites eating away the foundation of a stately mansion, brought the whole construction crashing to the ground. The Malthusian theory of population was unable to survive the marked decline in the trend of birth rates which set in during the 1870s in the most advanced western countries. Economists were forced, gradually and reluctantly, to abandon the theory of population and with it the entire classical theory of economic evolution.

Under the circumstances, this was inevitable. But economists gave up much more than was necessary. Instead of searching for a satisfactory theory of economic evolution to replace the discredited classical theory, they proceeded to exclude questions of evolutionary processes from the field of systematic theorizing. From the point of view of the 'statics and dynamics' to which theorists now devoted their attention, even the business cycle looked like a meteorological affair, or at best like a by-product of the congenital inability of the legislative mind to grasp the true principles of money and banking.

Such were the sad consequences of the collapse of classical theory.

The development of Marx's economic theory, however, could lead to no such results. By rejecting from the outset all truck with Malthusianism, Marx protected himself against the evil effects of its collapse. Moreover, by inserting into his theoretical structure the principle of the reserve army in place of the law of population, he not only broke sharply with the classical tradition; he also laid the foundation for a new and amazingly powerful attack on the problems of economic evolution.

Whereas in the classical theory, changes in productive methods are treated as dependent upon essentially fortuitous inventions and discoveries, in Marx's theory they become necessary conditions for the continued existence of capitalist production. For it is chiefly by means of labor-saving technological innovations that the reserve army is recruited, and it is only because of the continued existence of the reserve army that surplus value and the class which it supports can survive. Nor is this the end of the matter. It is not even necessary to accept Marx's theory of historical materialism to agree to the thesis that changes in techniques of production exercise a profound influence on the institutional and ideological structure of society. In the *Communist Manifesto*, Marx said: 'The bourgeoisie cannot exist without constantly revolutionizing the instruments of production, and thereby the relations of production, and with them the whole relations of society.' In *Capital* he rooted this insight in the soil of economic theory. In this way he discovered one of the most important of the 'laws of motion' of capitalism which it was the announced intention of *Capital* to explore.

We have not yet, of course, expounded Marx's theory of economic evolution in all its ramifications; what we have done, however, is to provide the basis for such a theory, the fundamental view of the capitalist process as one which, in principle, involves ceaseless accumulation accompanied by changes in methods of production. It is at once apparent that this view of the capitalist process differs radically from that which underlies the classical theory of economic evolution. The latter is, in principle, unconcerned with changes in methods of production; economic development is viewed exclusively in terms of (gradual) quantitative changes in population, capital, wages, profits, and rent. Social relations remain unaffected; the end product is simply a state of affairs in which all these rates of change equal zero. Since the Marxian view lays primary stress on changes in methods of production, it implies qualitative change in social organization and social relations as well as quantitative change in economic variables as such. The way is thus paved for regarding the 'end product' as a revolutionary reconstitution of society rather than as a mere state of rest.*

* It is necessary to note one important exception to the otherwise valid generalization that modern orthodox economists make no attempt to include evolutionary processes in their systematic theorizing. That exception is J. A. Schumpeter, whose *Theory of Economic Development* (1st German ed. 1912, English translation 1936) represents, in this respect, a sharp deviation from normal.

Schumpeter's theory bears certain striking resemblances to that of Marx. He begins with a demonstration that profit and interest would be absent from the 'Circular Flow,' a concept which corresponds to Marx's Simple Reproduction. It seems probable that Schumpeter would go so far as to maintain that, even in the absence of accumulation, there are forces at work to eliminate the surplus of income over cost from which both entrepreneurial profit and interest are derived. In other words, in the absence of change, income will be imputed entirely to the original factors of production; machines will just replace their own cost, leaving no surplus for their owners.

Entrepreneurs, however, seek to avoid the pauper's fate which awaits them in a stationary state of society by cutting costs, discovering new markets, inventing or popularizing new products—in general, by introducing 'innovations.' Those who are successful enjoy a sort of temporary monopoly position which is the source of entrepreneurial profit. Since money capital provides the wherewithal to wrest resources from their accustomed channels of use and divert them into new channels—and this is the essence of innovation—entrepreneurs are prepared to pay interest to get control of it. Once interest has arisen in one part of the system, being exclusively a monetary phenomenon, it spreads itself over the whole system. Any particular source of profit is bound to be temporary—assuming the absence of permanent barriers to competition—but since fresh innovations are always occurring, profit and interest as such never wholly disappear. To be sure the introduction of innovations does not take place smoothly and continuously, but rather in clusters or groups. This discontinuity in the process of innovation underlies the phenomenon known as the business cycle.

This brief sketch of Schumpeter's theory is sufficient to indicate that for him, as for Marx, changes in methods of production are a basic feature of capitalism and no mere epiphenomena which impinge in a more or less haphazard fashion on the economic process.

In spite of certain obvious similarities between this view and the Marxian view—which Schumpeter himself clearly recognizes—there remain fundamental theoretical differences. For example, there is nothing in Schumpeter analogous to the Reserve Army, and his treatment of the capital-labor relation is altogether different from that of Marx. Moreover, Schumpeter specifically disclaims any intention to proceed from changes in methods of production to 'changes in the economic organization, economic custom, and so on' (p. 61 n). Hence he admits that 'my structure covers only a small part of [Marx's] ground' (p. 60 n).

It is noteworthy that in orthodox circles, Schumpeter's theory of economic development has never commanded anything like the attention which it deserves and that it has been widely misunderstood and misrepresented. In so far as it has achieved recognition it has done so as business-cycle theory rather than as the foundation of a theory of capitalist evolution. In the final analysis, therefore, the example of Schumpeter serves only to emphasize the modern orthodox economist's lack of interest in what Marx called capitalism's 'laws of motion.'

VI

THE FALLING TENDENCY OF THE RATE OF PROFIT

1. Marx's Formulation of the Law

We have seen in the last chapter that the accumulation of capital is accompanied by a progressive mechanization of the process of production. The same amount of labor, working with more elaborate and more efficient equipment, is able to process more materials and turn out an ever increasing volume of finished goods. Looked at from one point of view, this means that the productivity of labor continually grows; from another point of view it means that the organic composition of capital (the ratio of capitalists' outlay on materials and machines to total outlay) also displays a steadily rising trend. From these indisputable trends Marx deduced his famous 'law of the falling tendency of the rate of profit.'

It was shown above * that the rate of profit can be expressed in terms of the rate of surplus value and the organic composition of capital in the following formula:

$$p = s'(1 - q)$$

From this it follows that if we assume the rate of surplus value (s') to be constant, the rate of profit (p) varies inversely with the organic composition of capital (q). In other words, as q rises p must fall. But we have already established the fact that q displays a rising trend in the course of capitalist development; hence there must be at least a tendency for p to fall. As we shall see presently, it may be no more than a tendency, since changes in s' may compensate, or even overcompensate, for the effects of a change in q.

This, very briefly, is the substance of what Marx calls the Theory of the Law (Volume III, Chapter XIII). To him it pos-

* P. 68.

sessed great significance. It demonstrated that capitalist production had certain internal barriers to its own indefinite expansion. On the one hand, a rising organic composition of capital is the expression of growing labor productivity; on the other hand, the falling rate of profit which accompanies it must ultimately choke up the channels of capitalist initiative. Marx very clearly expressed this idea in the following passage, discussing Ricardo's position on the tendency of the rate of profit:

> The rate of profit is the compelling power of capitalist production, and only such things are produced as yield a profit. Hence the fright of the English economists over the decline of the rate of profit. That the bare possibility of such a thing should worry Ricardo shows his profound understanding of the conditions of capitalist production. The reproach moved against him, that he has an eye only to the development of the productive forces . . . regardless of the sacrifices in human beings and capital values incurred, strikes precisely his strong point. The development of the productive forces of social labor is the historical task and privilege of capital. It is precisely in this way that it unconsciously creates the material requirements of a higher mode of production. What worries Ricardo is the fact that the rate of profit, the stimulating principle of capitalist production, the fundamental premise and driving force of accumulation, should be endangered by the development of production itself. And the quantitative proportion means everything here. There is indeed something deeper than this hidden at this point, which he vaguely feels. It is here demonstrated in a purely economic way, that is from a bourgeois point of view, within the confines of capitalist understanding, from the standpoint of capitalist production itself, that it has a barrier, that it is relative, that it is not an absolute but only a historical mode of production corresponding to a definite and limited epoch in the development of the material conditions of production.[1]

2. The Counteracting Causes

Marx enumerates six 'counteracting causes' which 'thwart and annul' the general law of the falling rate of profit, 'leaving to it merely the character of a tendency.'[2] One of these, the sixth, is really concerned with the way in which the rate of profit is calculated and will not be considered here. The other five may be classified according to whether their effect is to keep down the organic composition of capital or to raise the rate of surplus value.* Under the first heading comes Cheapening of the Elements of Constant Capital, while under the second we find Raising the Intensity of Exploitation, Depression of Wages Below Their Value, and Relative Overpopulation. One cause, Foreign Trade, comes under both headings. Let us consider briefly how these various factors operate.

Cheapening of the Elements of Constant Capital. The increased use of machinery, through raising the productivity of labor, lowers the value per unit of constant capital. 'In this way the value of the constant capital although continually increasing, is prevented from increasing at the same rate as its material volume, that is, the material volume of the means of production set in motion by the same amount of labor power. In exceptional cases the mass of the elements of constant capital may even increase while its value remains the same or even falls.' [3] In other words, a given increase in the organic composition of capital, through lowering the value of constant capital, to a certain extent acts as its own corrective. As Marx indicates, the offset may be very substantial, even going to the point of cancelling out the initial increase altogether.

Raising the Intensity of Exploitation. Here Marx stresses lengthening the working day and what would nowadays be called 'speed-up' and 'stretch-out.' Lengthening the working day directly raises the rate of surplus value by increasing the amount of surplus labor without affecting the amount of necessary labor. Speed-up and stretch-out, on the other hand, raise the rate of surplus value through compressing necessary labor into a shorter time and hence leaving a larger proportion of an unchanged working day for surplus labor. The effect in either case is to raise the rate of profit compared to what it otherwise would have been. These methods of raising the rate of surplus value are not necessarily connected with a rising organic composition of capi-

* Remembering the formula $p = s'(1 - q)$ we can see that all forces acting on the rate of profit can be brought into one or the other or both of these classifications.

tal but are rather devices adopted by the capitalists to offset a falling rate of profit if and when they are feasible.

Depression of Wages Below Their Value. The practice of wage cutting, which capitalists are prepared to engage in when possible, Marx merely mentions in passing, since he proceeds on the general assumption that all prices and wages are market-determined, and this assumption rules out the possibility of an aggressive wage policy on the part of the capitalists. This factor, he observes, 'has nothing to do with the general analysis of capital, but belongs in a presentation of competition which is not given in this work.'[4]

Relative Overpopulation. We have already seen in the last chapter how the increasing use of machinery, which in itself means a higher organic composition of capital, sets free workers and thus creates 'relative overpopulation' or the reserve army. Marx stresses the point that the existence of unemployed laborers is conducive to the setting up of new industries with a relatively low organic composition of capital and hence a relatively high rate of profit. When these relatively high rates of profit are averaged in with the rates of profit obtaining in the old industries, they raise the overall rate of profit.* It would seem, however, that a more important effect of the reserve army is that which was discussed in the last chapter, namely, through competition on the labor market with the active labor force, to depress the rate of wages and in this way to elevate the rate of surplus value. For this reason we have classified relative overpopulation as one of the factors which tends to raise the rate of surplus value.

Foreign Trade. It is frequently possible by foreign trade to acquire raw materials and necessities of life more cheaply than they could be produced at home. 'To the extent that foreign trade cheapens partly the elements of constant capital, partly the necessities of life for which the variable capital is exchanged, it tends to raise the rate of profit by raising the rate of surplus value and lowering the value of the constant capital.'[5] This factor, therefore, belongs in both classifications of counteracting causes. Here, again, however, it must be observed that there is

* The formation of a general rate of profit will be discussed in the next chapter.

no necessary connection between the possibilities of foreign trade and changes in the organic composition of capital, so that the inclusion of foreign trade at this point should be regarded in the light of a footnote rather than as an integral part of the analysis.

It will be readily apparent from this brief summary of the main counteracting causes that Marx's analysis is neither systematic nor exhaustive. Like so much else in Volume III it was left in an unfinished state, and it is safe to conclude that if he had lived to prepare the manuscript for the press himself, he would have introduced extensive expansions and revisions at various points. It may not be out of place, therefore, to devote further consideration to the problem of the tendency of the rate of profit in the light of Marx's whole theoretical system. This is the more necessary since the law of the falling tendency of the rate of profit has been the object of numerous criticisms from both followers and opponents of Marx.

3. A Critique of the Law

We have seen that the forces operating on the rate of profit can be summarized in a formula containing two rather complicated variables, the rate of surplus value and the organic composition of capital. We have also seen that the tendency of the rate of profit to fall is deduced by Marx on the assumption that the organic composition of capital rises while the rate of surplus value remains constant. There seems to be no doubt about the propriety of assuming a rising organic composition of capital. Is it justifiable, however, to assume *at the same time* a constant rate of surplus value?

It is necessary to be clear about the implications of the latter assumption. A rising organic composition of capital goes hand in hand with increasing labor productivity. If the rate of surplus value remains constant, this means that a rise in real wages takes place which is exactly proportional to the increase in labor productivity. Suppose that labor productivity is doubled, that is to say, that in the same time labor produces twice as much as previously. Then, since an unchanged rate of surplus value means that the laborer works the same amount of time for himself and the same amount for the capitalist as previously, it follows that both the physical output represented by the wage and the physical output represented by the surplus value have also doubled. In other words, the laborer benefits equally with the capitalist in the increased productivity of his labor. While there can be no logical objection to an assumption which leads to this result, there are nevertheless grounds for doubting its appropriateness.

In the first place, our whole analysis up to this point leads us to expect a rising rate of surplus value. One of the normal concomitants of increasing labor productivity under capitalist conditions is the creation of an industrial reserve army which exercises a depressing effect on wages and in this way tends to elevate the rate of surplus value. This is precisely one of the distinguishing characteristics of capitalism, that past labor in the form of constant capital stands in a competitive relation to living labor and keeps the latter's pretensions in check. The assumption of a constant rate of surplus value with rising labor productivity appears to neglect this effect. It may be said that Marx took account of this problem by including relative overpopulation among the counteracting causes to the falling rate of profit, and from a formal point of view this may be granted. But it seems hardly wise to treat an integral part of the process of rising productivity separately and as an offsetting factor; a better procedure is to recognize from the outset that rising productivity tends to bring with it a higher rate of surplus value. Furthermore, this is what Marx usually does. Two quotations from different parts of Volume I will serve to illustrate his normal approach to the question:

> Like every other increase in the productiveness of labor, machinery is intended to cheapen commodities, and, by shortening that portion of the working day in which the laborer works for himself, to lengthen the other portion that he gives, without an equivalent, to the capitalist. In short, it is a means for producing surplus value.[6]

And another, even more emphatic, statement of the same point:

> But hand-in-hand with the increasing productivity of labor goes, as we have seen, the cheapening of the laborer, therefore a

higher rate of surplus value even when the real wages are rising. *The latter never rise proportionally to the productive power of labor.*[7]

Many other passages expressing the same general view could easily be added; indeed it is perhaps no exaggeration to say that Part IV of Volume I ('The Production of Relative Surplus Value'), which covers more than 200 pages, is very largely devoted to elaborating upon the close relation which exists between labor productivity and the rate of surplus value.

It would appear, therefore, that Marx was hardly justified, even in terms of his own theoretical system, in assuming a constant rate of surplus value simultaneously with a rising organic composition of capital. A rise in the organic composition of capital must mean an increase in labor productivity, and we have Marx's own word for it that higher productivity is invariably accompanied by a higher rate of surplus value. In the general case, therefore, we ought to assume that the increasing organic composition of capital proceeds *pari passu* with a rising rate of surplus value.

If both the organic composition of capital and the rate of surplus value are assumed variable, as we think they should be, then the direction in which the rate of profit will change becomes indeterminate. All we can say is that the rate of profit will fall if the percentage increase in the rate of surplus value is less than the percentage decrease in the proportion of variable to total capital.* (The proportion of variable to total capital is equal to one minus the organic composition of capital. When the organic composition of capital increases, the proportion of variable to total capital decreases.)

Can we say that this condition is generally likely to be satisfied? In other words, is it legitimate to assume that changes in the organic composition of capital will usually be relatively so much larger than changes in the rate of surplus value that the

* We have $p = s'(1 - q)$. Let $1 - q$, the ratio of variable to total capital, be represented by q'. Then the equation can be written $p = s'q'$. Now $dp = s'dq' + q'ds'$. Hence dp is negative, i.e. the rate of profit is falling, if $s'dq'$ (which is essentially negative) is numerically larger than $q'ds'$ (which is essentially positive). This condition can also be written $|ds'/s'| < |dq'/q'|$, which is the form in which it is given in the text.

former will dominate movements in the rate of profit? If so, Marx's assumption of a constant rate of surplus value might be considered a useful device for focusing attention on the most important element in the situation, and the treatment of changes in the rate of surplus value as a 'counteracting cause' could be justified.

Marx himself probably thought in these terms, and this is probably the reason why he formulated the rate of profit problem as he did. Most subsequent Marxist writers have apparently been of the same mind, for the general impression one gets from the literature is that, over any considerable period of time, changes in the organic composition of capital are sure to be enormous, so great in fact as far to outweigh any possible compensating effect of changes in the rate of surplus value.*

This view seems to the present writer to be untenable. In *physical* terms it is certainly true that the amount of machinery and materials per worker has tended to grow at a very rapid rate for at least the last century and a half. But the organic composition of capital is a *value* expression; and, because of steadily rising labor productivity, the growth in the volume of machinery and materials per worker must not be regarded as an index of the change in the organic composition of capital. Actually the general impression of the rapidity of growth of the organic composition of capital seems to be considerably exaggerated.

It should be noted that we are here considering changes in the organic composition of capital after making full allowance for the cheapening of the elements of constant capital which Marx again treats as a 'counteracting cause.' It might seem that it would be preferable to look first at what might be called the 'original' increase in the organic composition, to observe the

* This attitude can be seen very clearly, for example, in the scheme of expanded reproduction developed by Otto Bauer ('Die Akkumulation des Kapitals,' *Neue Zeit*, Jhrg. 31, Bd. 1) in which it is assumed that constant capital grows twice as fast as variable capital while the rate of surplus value remains unchanged. This scheme was taken over by Henryk Grossmann (*Das Akkumulations- und Zusammenbruchsgesetz des kapitalistischen Systems*, 1929) and made the basis of his theory of capitalist breakdown. It is clear that both Bauer and Grossmann accepted the implications of the scheme in so far as it pictures an extremely rapid growth in the organic composition of capital.

effects of this on the rate of profit, and only then to take account of the cheapening of the elements of constant capital which is itself due to the rise in productivity associated with the 'original' increase. It might be held that if this were done, the rate of increase of the organic composition would appear much larger and that this fact is prevented from showing in the statistics only by one of the 'counteracting causes.' It is doubtful, however, whether any useful purpose can be served by such an attempt to preserve Marx's implied distinction between the primary rise in the organic composition and the counteracting (but smaller) fall due to the cheapening of the elements of constant capital. All that can ever be observed is the net change in the organic composition which is the resultant of both forces. It seems better, therefore, to use the expression 'change in the organic composition of capital' only in the net sense which takes account of cheapening of the elements of constant capital. If this is done there will perhaps be less temptation to think of the organic composition in physical instead of value terms.

If these arguments are sound, it follows that there is no general presumption that changes in the organic composition of capital will be relatively so much greater than changes in the rate of surplus value that the former will dominate movements in the rate of profit. On the contrary, it would seem that we must regard the two variables as of roughly co-ordinate importance. For this reason Marx's formulation of the law of the falling tendency of the rate of profit is not very convincing. At the same time we may remark that attempts which have been made to demonstrate that a rising organic composition of capital must be accompanied by a rising rate of profit are equally unconvincing.*

* The most interesting of these was that of Bortkiewicz ('Wertrechnung und Preisrechnung im Marxschen System,' *Archiv für Sozialwissenschaft und Sozialpolitik*, September 1907), who held that 'the mistake in the proof which Marx gives for his law of the falling rate of profit consists primarily in his leaving out of account the mathematical relation between the productivity of labor and the rate of surplus value' (p. 466) and tried to prove that if this factor is taken into account the result must be a rising rate of profit. The proof consists essentially in assuming that capitalists would not introduce methods of production requiring a higher organic composition of capital unless the effect would be to raise the rate of profit. This is true of the individual capitalist, but for the capitalist

This does not mean that there is no tendency for the rate of profit to fall. Not only Marx but classical theorists and modern theorists as well have all regarded a falling tendency of the rate of profit as a basic feature of capitalism. All I have tried to show is that it is not possible to demonstrate a falling tendency of the rate of profit by beginning the analysis with the rising organic composition of capital. Once it is realized, however, that the rising organic composition of capital is itself but a link in a longer causal chain of influences operating on the rate of profit, the apparent dilemma disappears. Behind the rising organic composition of capital lies the process of capital accumulation, and it is here that we should look for forces which tend to depress the rate of profit.

It was explained in the last chapter how the accumulation of capital, taken by itself, operates to increase the demand for labor power and hence to raise wages. Other things remaining equal, such a rise in wages leads to a reduction in the rate of surplus value, and this, in turn, expresses itself in a fall in the rate of profit. Since, as Marx again and again insists, 'the capitalist process of production is essentially a process of accumulation,' [8] it follows that from this fact alone there arises a persistent tendency for the rate of profit to fall. It was also observed in the last chapter, however, that capitalists do not tamely submit to the encroachment on the rate of profit which their own accumulation brings about. They strive through the introduction of machinery and other labor-saving devices to maintain the rate of profit at its former level or even to raise it above its former level. This is where the rising organic composition of capital comes into the picture. Whether their actions will succeed in restoring the rate of profit, or whether they will only act to hasten its fall,

class as a whole the change in the rate of profit is a result of their actions which may be quite different from what each one intended. In the same way when capitalists bid up the price of labor power, each one intends to improve his own situation, yet the net result will be to worsen the lot of all.

The reader interested in following up this question should consult the following: Kei Shibata, 'On the Law of Decline in the Rate of Profit,' *Kyoto University Economic Review*, July 1934, and 'On the General Profit Rate,' ibid. January 1939; also Hans Neisser, 'Das Gesetz der Fallenden Profitrate als Krisen- und Zusammenbruchsgesetz,' *Die Gesellschaft*, January 1931.

is an issue which cannot be settled on general theoretical grounds, if the analysis presented in this section is correct. One thing seems fairly certain, however, and that is that the increase in the organic composition of capital will tend to restore the rate of surplus value and thus to expand the mass of surplus value over what it would have been in the absence of the rise in the organic composition of capital. Hence, even if the effect is to depress the rate of profit still further, the acts of the capitalists in raising the organic composition of capital do not lack a certain objective justification from the point of view of the capitalist class as a whole.

It cannot be too strongly emphasized that the arguments of this section have been concerned with the theoretical foundations of the falling tendency of the rate of profit. There has been no thought of denying the existence or fundamental importance of such a tendency. Nor has there been any intention of denying the validity of Marx's 'counteracting causes.' In practice, one of these, namely the raising of the intensity of exploitation ('speed-up,' 'stretch-out,' Taylorization, et cetera) is particularly important. This is a method of compressing more labor into a given amount of time. For example, what used to require five hours is now accomplished in four as a result of an increase in the speed of machinery. With the working day remaining at, say, ten hours, where necessary labor used to be five hours and surplus labor five hours, the ratio will now be four hours necessary labor and six hours surplus labor. The rate of surplus value has increased from 100 per cent to 150 per cent. The figures are purely illustrative, but the magnitudes involved are not unrealistic, and they show what relatively large changes in the rate of surplus value can result from apparently small changes in the speed of work. Capitalists are always under a temptation to attempt to raise the rate of surplus value in this fashion, and there seems little doubt that the resulting offset to the falling tendency of the rate of profit is continuous and may at times be substantial. No one who neglects this factor can comprehend fully present-day trends in capitalist production.

Finally, before we leave the subject of movements in the rate of profit, it should be pointed out that there are forces other than those which have so far been mentioned which are important in this connection. These forces may be classified as those tending to depress the rate of profit, and those tending to elevate the rate of profit. Among the forces tending to depress the rate of profit we may mention (1) trade unions and (2) state action designed to benefit labor; among the forces tending to elevate the rate of profit we may mention (3) employers' organizations, (4) export of capital, (5) formation of monopolies, and (6) state action designed to benefit capital. (The enumeration is, of course, far from exhaustive.) Let us consider each of these very briefly.

1. *Trade unions.* In combatting the falling tendency of the rate of profit capitalists are equally engaged in attempting to batter down wages. As we have already seen, their chief ally in this war on wages is the industrial reserve army. If the competition of the industrial reserve army on the labor market were allowed to operate without let or hindrance, workers' real incomes might be held down to a low level of subsistence while capitalists reaped all the benefits of advancing productivity, getting both a larger share of the value of output as well as the entire increase in real income. Thus the reserve army is the most important obstacle standing in the way of the workers' realizing a share in the gains of industrial development. In order to overcome this obstacle workers band together in trade unions and in this way secure, so far as possible, control over the supply of labor power. Trade unions are thus the most important instrument by which workers strive to better their condition under capitalist production. At the same time and for the same reasons, however, unions exercise a depressing influence on the rate of profit.

2. *State action designed to benefit labor.* This is a factor of great importance, the roots of which will be discussed more fully below (Chapter XIII). It takes many forms; for example, legal limitation of the working day, unemployment insurance, and, recently in the United States, legislation aimed to safeguard the right of collective bargaining. The first of these generally (though not necessarily) reduces the rate of surplus value, while the second and third are of great assistance to workers in their efforts to maintain wage standards. Many other types of state

action could be mentioned in this connection. Most of them clearly tend to depress the rate of profit.

3. *Employers' organizations.* In so far as such organizations operate to improve the bargaining position of capital vis-à-vis labor, they evidently exercise an upward influence on the rate of profit.

4. *Export of capital.* This is a factor to which Marx devoted little attention, not because it is unimportant but because he did not live to complete his theoretical system. In its direct effect on the home economy, capital export acts to relieve the pressure on the domestic labor market and in this way prevents accumulation from having its full depressing effect on the rate of profit. A more extended discussion of capital export belongs to the theory of world economy to which we return in Chapter XVI.

5. *Formation of monopolies.* Obviously individual capitalists create monopolies in the hope of improving their own rate of profit. Moreover the effect may be an elevation in the general rate of profit. The influence of monopoly on the rate of profit, however, is a complicated subject which must be taken up in detail later on (Chapter XV).

6. *State action designed to benefit capital.* An obvious example of this is provided by protective tariffs. As in the case of monopolies, protective tariffs may have the effect of raising the general rate of profit, but here again the full effect is complex and must be reserved for later treatment (Chapter XVI).

This enumeration of factors operating on the rate of profit, though by no means exhaustive, can serve to show that a wide variety of disparate and apparently unrelated forces have a common focus in their effects on the rate of profit. If the Marxian view that movements in the rate of profit ultimately dominate the functioning of the capitalist system is correct, then this provides us with a unifying principle of first importance. In the analysis of capitalism everything must be carefully scrutinized and tested for its influence on the rate of profit. When this is done, political economy becomes both a more coherent and a more powerful weapon of understanding.

VII

THE TRANSFORMATION OF VALUES INTO PRICES

1. The Problem Stated

It is now time to examine in detail a problem which has occupied a central position in most discussions of Marxian economics since Engels published Volume III of *Capital* in 1894.

Throughout Volume I, Marx develops his analysis as though the law of value were directly controlling for the prices of all commodities. This is legitimate so long as it is assumed that in every branch of production the organic composition of capital is the same. Once this assumption is dropped, however, a serious, some have maintained a fatal, difficulty arises.*

Let us divide industry into three major branches, corresponding to the twofold division employed above in Section 1 of Chapter V. Department I produces means of production, Department II workers' consumption goods (wage goods), and Department III capitalists' consumption goods (luxury goods). For the sake of simplicity we shall assume throughout the whole discussion that all industries within a single department have the same organic composition of capital. To illustrate conditions under which the law of value is valid we assume that as between departments the organic composition of capital is also equal. Taking the rate of surplus value as 100 per cent, we then have a situation such as that depicted in Table I.

Everything is evidently in order. All commodities sell at their values. The conditions of simple reproduction are fulfilled: the amount of constant capital laid out (400) just equals the amount of constant capital produced (400); total wages (200) are just sufficient to buy the quantity of wage goods produced (200); and the surplus value of all departments (200) covers the output of the luxury-goods department (200). Finally all capitalists

* See above, pp. 69-71.

TABLE I

Value Calculation

DEP'T	CONSTANT CAPITAL c	VARIABLE CAPITAL v	SURPLUS VALUE s	VALUE $c+v+s$	RATE OF SURPLUS VALUE s/v	ORGANIC COMPOSITION OF CAPITAL $c/c+v$	RATE OF PROFIT $s/c+v$
I	200	100	100	400	100%	66⅔%	33⅓%
II	100	50	50	200	100%	66⅔%	33⅓%
III	100	50	50	200	100%	66⅔%	33⅓%
Total	400	200	200	800	100%	66⅔%	33⅓%

are enjoying the same rate of profit (33⅓ per cent) and hence none has an incentive to shift from one line of production to another.

In the real world, however, the organic composition of capital is not the same in all industries. For example, it is relatively high in the electric-power industry and relatively low in the clothing industry. In order to bring this fact to light we must alter our assumptions. In Table II, Department III has been left unchanged, but the organic composition of capital in Department I is assumed to be higher and in Department II to be lower.

As before, total production is 800, and the conditions of Simple Reproduction are still satisfied as far as the output of the three departments is concerned. But the effect of changing the organic compositions of capital is clearly seen in the new rates of profit. Whereas before the rates of profit were all equal at 33⅓ per cent, they now stand at 23 per cent, 60 per cent and 33⅓ per cent in the three departments respectively.

Obviously this could not be a position of equilibrium. The capitalists would all want to go into the production of wage goods in order to share in the higher rate of profit obtainable there. And such a migration of capital out of some industries and into others would clearly upset the whole scheme. A position of equilibrium must be characterized by equality in the rates of profit yielded by all the industries in the system. Marx put it strongly when he wrote that 'there is no doubt that, aside from unessential, accidental, and mutually compensating distinctions, a difference in the average rate of profit of the various lines of

TABLE II

Value Calculation

DEP'T	CONSTANT CAPITAL c	VARIABLE CAPITAL v	SURPLUS VALUE s	VALUE $c+v+s$	RATE OF SURPLUS VALUE s/v	ORGANIC COMPOSITION OF CAPITAL $c/c+v$	RATE OF PROFIT $s/c+v$
I	250	75	75	400	100%	77%	23%
II	50	75	75	200	100%	40%	60%
III	100	50	50	200	100%	66⅔%	33⅓%
Total	400	200	200	800	100%	66⅔%	33⅓%

industry does not exist in reality and could not exist without abolishing the entire system of capitalist production.' *

Apparently the attempt to apply the law of value to a situation in which the organic composition of capital differs from industry to industry breaks down. 'It would seem,' Marx said, 'as though the theory of value were irreconcilable with the real phenomena of production, so that we should have to give up the attempt to understand these phenomena.' [1] In the hands of his critics this statement has, figuratively speaking, been reduced to a simpler form: 'The theory of value is irreconcilable with the real phenomena of production.'

Marx himself, however, did not take such a gloomy view of matters. He clearly recognized the dilemma into which the theory of value led; let us examine his efforts to find a way out.†

* *Capital* III, p. 181. As we shall see later, this no longer holds if the economy is assumed to contain elements of monopoly.

† It has been widely supposed that Marx was not aware of the problem under examination until after Volume I had been published, and this has led to the view that the discussion in Volume III of prices of production is no more than a clumsy effort to cover up previously unrecognized errors. For example, H. B. Parkes in his *Marxism: an Autopsy* (1939), a book which contains in convenient form many of the most widespread misinterpretations of Marxism, expresses this view as follows: 'The reason for the assertion that Marx was not trying to explain prices is that when Marx came to write the third volume of *Das Kapital*, he found that some of the theories which he had advanced in the first volume were inapplicable . . .' Actually the first draft of Volume III was completed before Volume I was published. See Engels' Preface to Volume III, p. 11.

2. Marx's Solution

In order to understand Marx's method it is convenient to assume that a process of adjustment is begun from a starting point such as that pictured in Table II. Capitalists will move about in search of the highest possible rate of profit until no one can improve his position by a further move, a state of affairs which will be reached only when the rate of profit is the same for every industry.

Now according to Marx, the total amount of value produced, namely 800, will be the same as before, since there has been no change in the total number of hours of labor expended. Further, both the total amount of capital and the total amount of surplus value will be unaffected. The prices of commodities and the division of surplus value among the capitalists, however, will be different. Capitalists, in other words, will share in the pool of surplus value according to the size of their total capitals instead of, as before, according to the size of their variable capitals. The prices of commodities (what Marx calls 'prices of production') will now be made up of the capital expended in production plus a profit calculated as a certain percentage of the capital outlay. This percentage is nothing but the average rate of profit and is found by dividing total surplus value by total social capital.

In value terms the system looks as follows:

I	$c_1 + v_1 + s_1 = w_1$
II	$c_2 + v_2 + s_2 = w_2$
III	$c_3 + v_3 + s_3 = w_3$
Totals	$C + V + S = W$

The average rate of profit, p, is total surplus value over total capital. That is,

$$p = \frac{S}{C + V}$$

Changing now to price terms, the above scheme becomes

$$
\begin{array}{lc}
\text{I} & c_1 + v_1 + p(c_1 + v_1) = P_1 \\
\text{II} & c_2 + v_2 + p(c_2 + v_2) = P_2 \\
\text{III} & c_3 + v_3 + p(c_3 + v_3) = P_3 \\
\hline
\text{Totals} & C + V + p(C + V) = P
\end{array}
$$

But, of course, $p(C + V) = S$, which means that total surplus value is identical with total profit, and further that total price equals total value. In general, however, individual prices and values differ.

Let us now apply this method of transformation to the data of Table II. The first four columns of Table III reproduce data from Table II; in the remaining columns the transformation is carried out. In this example, p is 200/600 or 33⅓ per cent.

TABLE III

Marx's Price Calculation

DEP'T	CONSTANT CAPITAL	VARIABLE CAPITAL	SURPLUS VALUE	VALUE	PROFIT	PRICE	DEVIATION OF PRICE FROM VALUE
	c	v	s	$c+v+s$	$p(c+v)$	$c+v+p(c+v)$	
I	250	75	75	400	108⅓	433⅓	+33⅓
II	50	75	75	200	41⅔	166⅔	−33⅓
III	100	50	50	200	50	200	0

Comparing Table III with Table II, we see that the price of commodities produced in Department I has risen by 33⅓, the price of commodities produced in Department II has fallen by a like amount, and the price of commodities produced in Department III is unaffected. There has, of course, taken place a corresponding rise in the profits of Department I and fall in the profits of Department II. But the totals of the profits and prices of all departments are respectively equal to the former totals of surplus value and value.

This is Marx's own method of transforming values into prices. Before any general comments can be made it is necessary to test the internal consistency of the results. Tables I and II were both constructed on the hypothesis of Simple Reproduction: the product of Department I was assumed equal to the amount of constant capital used up; the product of Department II was assumed equal to total wages; and the product of Department III was assumed equal to total surplus value. If the procedure used in transforming values into prices is to be considered satisfactory, it must not result in a disruption of the conditions of Simple Reproduction. Going from value calculation to price calculation has no connection with the question whether the economic system as a whole is stationary or expanding. It should be possible to make the transition without prejudicing this question one way or the other.

Let us examine Table III in this light. Table III*a* selects from Table III the relevant items, and it also includes the totals which were omitted from Table III.

TABLE III*a*

Marx's Price Calculation

DEPARTMENT	CONSTANT CAPITAL	VARIABLE CAPITAL	PROFIT	PRICE
I	250	75	108⅓	433⅓
II	50	75	41⅔	166⅔
III	100	50	50	200
Totals	400	200	200	800

A moment's inspection of Table III*a* reveals that the Marxian method of transformation results in a violation of the equilibrium of Simple Reproduction. The total quantity of constant capital used up in production still equals 400, but the constant capital produced in Department I is now priced at 433⅓. There is a discrepancy between the two figures of 33⅓. Similarly, the total wage bill of all three departments amounts to 200, but the output of wage goods in Department II is priced at only 166⅔. Again there is a discrepancy of 33⅓. The fact that total surplus value still covers the output of luxury goods is a mere accident of the way the table has been constructed. In general no such coincidence could be expected.

The discrepancies revealed in Table III*a* could be justified only if we were to make the assumption that workers accumulate capital to the extent of 33⅓ out of their incomes. But, of course, there is no reason why we should make such an assumption, and to have it forced upon us by the mechanics of transforming values into prices is unreasonable. Only one conclusion is possible, namely, that the Marxian method of transformation is logically unsatisfactory.

3. AN ALTERNATIVE SOLUTION *

The source of Marx's error is not difficult to discover. In his price scheme the capitalists' outlays on constant and variable capital are left exactly as they were in the value scheme; in other words, the constant capital and the variable capital used in production are still expressed in value terms. Outputs, on the other hand, are expressed in price terms. Now it is obvious that in a system in which price calculation is universal both the capital used in production and the product itself must be expressed in price terms. The trouble is that Marx went only half way in transforming values into prices. It need occasion no surprise that this procedure leads to contradictory results.

Marx himself was by no means unaware of this possible source of error. In discussing the transformation problem in Volume III he wrote:

> Since the price of production may vary from the value of a commodity, it follows that the cost price [constant capital plus variable capital] of a commodity containing this price of production may also stand above or below that portion of its total value which is formed by the value of the means of production consumed by it. It is necessary to remember this modified significance of the cost price and to bear in mind that there is always the possibility of an error if we assume the cost price of the commodities of any particular sphere is equal to the value of the means of production consumed by it.[2]

At this point, however, he dropped the matter with the remark that 'our present analysis does not necessitate a closer examina-

* The basic work on this subject is Bortkiewicz's paper 'Zur Berichtigung der grundlegenden theoretischen Konstruktion von Marx im dritten Band des "Kapital,"' *Jahrbücher für Nationalökonomie und Statistik*, July 1907. Since this section is essentially nothing but an abbreviated version of Bortkiewicz's argument, specific references have been omitted.

tion of this point.' Nevertheless the problem apparently bothered him, because he returned to it in *Theories of Surplus Value*, where he devoted two full pages to showing how 'the transformation of values into prices of production works doubly,' namely through altering the amount of profit received in a given industry, and through altering the price of input factors, what he called the cost price.[3] In spite of this, Marx reiterated his belief that prices of production could be derived from values: 'This significant deviation of production prices from values—which capitalist production brings about—does not in the least alter the fact that production prices, as before, are determined by values.'[4] It must be said, however, that he never succeeded in proving this contention in a logically convincing manner, although if he had lived to rewrite Volume III it is quite possible that he would have left this subject in a more satisfactory state. In the remainder of this section we shall outline a method of transforming values into prices which is free of the objection to which Marx's method is open.

As a first step, let us assume that the price of a unit of constant capital is x times its value, the price of a unit of wage goods is y times its value, and the price of a unit of luxury goods is z times its value. Further let us call the general rate of profit r—it is important to understand that r is not defined as Marx defined the rate of profit and hence it seems wise not to use the same symbol for both concepts.

Now in value calculation the following three equations describe the conditions of Simple Reproduction:

$$\text{I} \qquad c_1 + v_1 + s_1 = c_1 + c_2 + c_3$$

$$\text{II} \qquad c_2 + v_2 + s_2 = v_1 + v_2 + v_3$$

$$\text{III} \qquad c_3 + v_3 + s_3 = s_1 + s_2 + s_3$$

These equations, when transformed into price terms, become:

$$\text{I} \qquad c_1x + v_1y + r(c_1x + v_1y) = (c_1 + c_2 + c_3)x$$

$$\text{II} \qquad c_2x + v_2y + r(c_2x + v_2y) = (v_1 + v_2 + v_3)y$$

$$\text{III} \qquad c_3x + v_3y + r(c_3x + v_3y) = (s_1 + s_2 + s_3)z$$

And these can be rewritten as:

$$\text{I} \quad (1+r)\ (c_1x + v_1y) = (c_1 + c_2 + c_3)x$$

$$\text{II} \quad (1+r)\ (c_2x + v_2y) = (v_1 + v_2 + v_3)y$$

$$\text{III} \quad (1+r)\ (c_3x + v_3y) = (s_1 + s_2 + s_3)z$$

In these three equations there are four unknown quantities, namely, x, y, z, and r. For a unique solution it is necessary to have the same number of equations and unknowns. Hence we ought to have either one more equation or one less unknown. We might proceed as Marx did by setting total value equal to total price. This would give us the following fourth equation:

$$(c_1 + c_2 + c_3)x + (v_1 + v_2 + v_3)y + (s_1 + s_2 + s_3)z = (c_1 + c_2 + c_3) + (v_1 + v_2 + v_3) + (s_1 + s_2 + s_3)$$

The economic meaning of this equation can be easily seen. So far in our value schemes we have reckoned everything in terms of hours of labor; in other words, one hour of labor has been the unit of account. By assuming that total output in value terms is equal to total output in price terms, we should simply be retaining the same unit of account in the price scheme. There is no logical objection to this way of proceeding, but from a mathematical point of view there is an alternative method which is simpler and hence more attractive.

Instead of calculating the value scheme in terms of units of labor time we might have put it in money terms. Thus the value of each commodity would not be expressed in units of labor but in terms of the number of units of the money commodity for which it would exchange. The number of units of labor necessary to produce one unit of the money commodity would provide a direct link between the two systems of accounting. Let us assume that the value scheme has been cast in money terms and that gold, which we will classify as a luxury good, has been selected as the money commodity. Then one unit of gold (say one thirty-fifth of an ounce) is the unit of value. For the sake of simplicity we will also suppose that the units of other luxury goods have been so chosen that they all exchange against the unit of gold on a one-to-one basis: in other words the unit value of all luxury goods, including gold, is equal to one. Now in going from a value to a price scheme we wish to retain one thirty-fifth of an ounce of gold as the unit of account. The unit of gold will therefore be equal to one in both schemes, and under the assumed conditions the same must be true of all luxury goods. Since we have already assumed that the price of a unit of luxury goods is z times its value, this amounts to setting

$$z = 1$$

and this, in turn, reduces the number of unknowns to three. Since we have three equations the system is now completely determined.

If we now set $1 + r = m$, our three equations finally look as follows:

$$\text{I} \quad m(c_1x + v_1y) = (c_1 + c_2 + c_3)x$$

$$\text{II} \quad m(c_2x + v_2y) = (v_1 + v_2 + v_3)y$$

$$\text{III} \quad m(c_3x + v_3y) = s_1 + s_2 + s_3$$

The actual solution of the equations is, of course, a matter of algebra; what concerns us is the outcome. To express the result most conveniently, the following six expressions are formed:

$$f_1 = \frac{v_1}{c_1} \qquad g_1 = \frac{v_1 + c_1 + s_1}{c_1}$$

$$f_2 = \frac{v_2}{c_2} \qquad g_2 = \frac{v_2 + c_2 + s_2}{c_2}$$

$$f_3 = \frac{v_3}{c_3} \qquad g_3 = \frac{v_3 + c_3 + s_3}{c_3}$$

Remembering that

$$c_1 + c_2 + c_3 = c_1 + v_1 + s_1$$

$$v_1 + v_2 + v_3 = c_2 + v_2 + s_2$$

$$s_1 + s_2 + s_3 = c_3 + v_3 + s_3$$

our equations can be rewritten

$$\text{I} \quad m(x + f_1y) = g_1x$$

$$\text{II} \quad m(x + f_2y) = g_2y$$

$$\text{III} \quad m(x + f_3y) = g_3$$

The solutions * which emerge are then as follows:

$$m = \frac{f_2g_1 + g_2 - \sqrt{(g_2 - f_2g_1)^2 + 4f_1g_1g_2}}{2(f_2 - f_1)}$$

$$y = \frac{g_3}{g_2 + (f_3 - f_2)m}$$

$$x = \frac{f_1ym}{g_1 - m}$$

It will be recalled that we defined m as equal to $r + 1$, and hence r (the rate of profit) is given by

$$r = m - 1$$

These formulas look rather formidable, but actually they are not difficult to apply. As an example of how prices can be derived from values, let us perform the necessary operations on the basic data presented in Table II. The value scheme is as follows:

$$\begin{array}{ll} \text{I} & 250(c_1) + 75(v_1) + 75(s_1) = 400 \\ \text{II} & 50(c_2) + 75(v_2) + 75(s_2) = 200 \\ \text{III} & 100(c_3) + 50(v_3) + 50(s_3) = 200 \end{array}$$

Using the formulas for x, y and m we get

$$x = \tfrac{9}{8}$$

$$y = \tfrac{3}{4}$$

$$m = \tfrac{4}{3}$$

This implies a rate of profit $(m - 1)$ of $33\tfrac{1}{3}$ per cent.

All that remains to be done now is to substitute the actual

* The equations are of the second degree and of rather an unusual sort. The most convenient way of proceeding seems to be to rewrite the first two as linear equations in x and y. Then if there is a solution the condition

$$\begin{vmatrix} (m - g_1) & mf_1 \\ m & (mf_2 - g_2) \end{vmatrix} = 0$$

must be satisfied. The solution for m emerges at once, and from this point everything is plain sailing.

figures in the final set of price equations. The result is shown in Table IIIb.

TABLE IIIb

Correct Price Calculation

DEPARTMENT	CONSTANT CAPITAL	VARIABLE CAPITAL	PROFIT	PRICE
I	281¼	56¼	112½	450
II	56¼	56¼	37½	150
III	112½	37½	50	200
Totals	450	150	200	800

It is clear that price calculation according to what may appropriately be called the Bortkiewicz method, as illustrated in Table IIIb, produces no disturbànce of the equilibrium of Simple Reproduction. The output of Department I equals the constant capital used up; the production of Department II equals wages paid out; and the output of Department III is sufficient to absorb the total surplus value accruing to the capitalists. Furthermore, all capitalists are realizing 33⅓ per cent on their investments. Everything is in order again just as it was in Table I which showed a value scheme on the assumption of equality in the organic composition of capital for all industries.

So far the numerical examples have been worked out on the basis of figures, first presented in Table II, which were specially selected for their simplicity and manageability. There is, however, a certain accidental characteristic of this particular set of figures which might lead to misunderstanding. It will be noted that in Table IIIb total price amounts to 800, exactly the same sum as total value in the earlier tables. One would be tempted to conclude from this that in general the Bortkiewicz method of transforming values into prices leaves the totals unchanged. This, however, is not so, and in order to demonstrate the point it seems desirable to reproduce the tables which Bortkiewicz himself uses to illustrate his method of transformation. Table IV gives a value scheme and Table IVa the corresponding price scheme.

Table IVa is derived from Table IV in the same way that Table IIIb was derived from Table II. We see once again that all the conditions of Simple Reproduction are fully satisfied by this

TABLE IV

Value Calculation [a]

DEPARTMENT	CONSTANT CAPITAL	VARIABLE CAPITAL	SURPLUS VALUE	VALUE
I	225	90	60	375
II	100	120	80	300
III	50	90	60	200
Totals	375	300	200	875

[a] The rate of surplus value is here assumed to be 66⅔ per cent.

TABLE IV*a*

Price Calculation

DEPARTMENT	CONSTANT CAPITAL	VARIABLE CAPITAL	PROFIT	PRICE
I	288	96	96	480
II	128	128	64	320
III	64	96	40	200
Totals	480	320	200	1000

method of transformation. But there is one difference between this case and the earlier one. In Table IV*a* total price (1000) diverges from total value in Table IV (875); whereas in the previous example the two totals were the same. A brief explanation of this difference will show that the earlier example is a special case while the later example must be regarded as possessing general validity.

The problem turns on the organic composition of capital in the gold industry relative to the organic composition of the total social capital before the transformation to price terms has been carried through. This can be readily demonstrated. It is clear, first, that if in the gold industry a relatively high organic composition of capital obtains, the price of gold will be greater than its value. This follows from the fact that in price calculation profit is proportional to total capital whereas in value calculation it is proportional to variable capital alone. Consequently if all other commodities are expressed in terms of gold, their total price must be less than their total value. This can be put otherwise as follows: since *ex hypothesi* the price and the value of a unit of gold are both numerically equal to one, the fact that its price is 'higher' than its value can be expressed only by the fact that the average price of all other commodities is lower than their average value. Put still otherwise, if the organic composition of capital is relatively high in the gold industry, the transformation from value to price will raise the purchasing power of gold. The same reasoning applies, *mutatis mutandis*, to the case where the organic composition of capital in the gold industry is relatively low. In this case total price will be greater than total value. Only in the special case where the organic composition of capital in the gold industry is exactly equal to the social average organic composition of capital is it true that total price and total value will be identical.

These principles can be tested by reference to the numerical examples already presented. In Table II the organic composition of capital in the luxury-goods department (and hence in the gold industry) was 100/150 or 66⅔ per cent, while the organic composition of the total capital was 400/600, also 66⅔ per cent. Hence the transformation to price (Table III*b*) resulted in a total price equal to total value. In the example taken from Bortkiewicz, however, the organic composition of capital in the luxury-goods department was originally 50/140 or 35 5/7 per cent compared to an organic composition of the social capital of 375/675 or 55 5/9 per cent. Since in this case the organic composition of capital in the gold industry was relatively low, the transformation from value to price resulted in a total price greater than total value.

Since there is no reason to assume that the organic composition of capital in the gold industry is equal to the average organic composition of the social capital, it follows that in general the Bortkiewicz method leads to a price total differing from the value total.

It is important to realize that no significant theoretical issues are involved in this divergence of total value from total price. It is simply a question of the unit of account. If we had used the unit of labor time as the unit of account in both the value and the price schemes, the totals would have been the same.*

* The use of the unit of labor time as the unit of account in both schemes underlies the ingenious method of transformation devised by Natalie Moszkowska, *Das Marxsche System* (1929), esp. pp. 3-19.

Since we elected to use the unit of gold (money) as the unit of account, the totals diverge. But in either case the proportions of the price scheme (ratio of total profit to total price, of output of constant capital to output of wage goods, et cetera) will come out the same, and it is the relations existing among the various elements of the system rather than the absolute figures in which they are expressed which are important.

With the help of the Bortkiewicz method we have shown that a system of price calculation can be derived from a system of value calculation. This is the problem in which Marx was really interested. He believed he could solve it by using an average rate of profit calculated directly from the value magnitudes. This was an error, but it was an error which pales into insignificance when compared with his profoundly original achievement in posing the problem correctly. For, by this accomplishment, Marx set the stage for a final vindication of the labor theory of value, the solid foundation of his whole theoretical structure.*

4. A Corollary of the Bortkiewicz Method

A close inspection of the formula for the rate of profit, derived above, reveals a striking fact. The formula in question, it will be recalled, is as follows:

$$r = \frac{f_2 g_1 + g_2 - \sqrt{(g_2 - f_2 g_1)^2 + 4 f_1 g_1 g_2}}{2(f_2 - f_1)} - 1$$

where the following relations hold:

$$f_1 = \frac{v_1}{c_1} \qquad g_1 = \frac{v_1 + c_1 + s_1}{c_1}$$

$$f_2 = \frac{v_2}{c_2} \qquad g_2 = \frac{v_2 + c_2 + s_2}{c_2}$$

$$f_3 = \frac{v_3}{c_3} \qquad g_3 = \frac{v_3 + c_3 + s_3}{c_3}$$

* The significance of the transformation problem is discussed at length in the last two sections of this chapter.

It will be observed that neither f_3 nor g_3 appears in the formula. In other words, the organic composition of capital in Department III (luxury goods) plays no direct role in determining the rate of profit.

This is a result of considerable theoretical interest. It means essentially that the rate of profit depends only upon the conditions of production existing in those industries which contribute directly or indirectly to the make-up of real wages. Conditions existing in industries catering solely to capitalists' consumption are relevant only in so far as they influence conditions in the wage-goods industries. Marx would have agreed that this proposition holds with respect to the rate of surplus value, but his method of transforming values into prices led him to believe that it did not apply to the rate of profit. As Bortkiewicz pointed out, however, the result is in accord with Ricardo's theory of profits, and Marx's criticism of Ricardo on this score was unjustified.*

Bortkiewicz developed this theorem about the rate of profit in two directions. In the first place, he regarded it as conclusive support for the Marxian view that profits constitute a subtraction from the product of labor. In this connection Bortkiewicz substituted the neutral expression 'deduction theory' (*Abzugstheorie*) for Marx's term 'exploitation theory' (*Ausbeutungstheorie*). In the light of this theorem,

> it should be quite clear that the cause of profit as such is to be sought in the wage relation and not in the productive power of capital. If it were a question of this power it would be inexplicable why certain branches of production are excluded from any influence on the height of profits.[5]

Secondly, Bortkiewicz showed how this theorem, relative to the rate of profit, could lead to a refutation of the general validity of Marx's version of the law of the falling tendency of the rate of profit. To demonstrate that there is no necessary connection between variations in the average organic composition of the total social capital and variations in the average rate of profit, one need only assume that the organic composition of capital in Department III rises while everything else remains un-

* Bortkiewicz was at great pains to defend Ricardo against Marx.

changed. The average organic composition of capital must rise, but the rate of profit remains unaffected.

The practical significance of this criticism is not great. In general there is no reason to assume a tendency for the organic composition of capital in the luxury-goods industries to rise more rapidly than the average for all industries. Furthermore, in the real world the industries which cater only to capitalists' consumption are doubtless few and relatively unimportant. The great majority of consumption-goods industries are common to Departments II and III alike.

Some writers have apparently assumed that the main burden of Bortkiewicz's criticism of the law of the falling tendency of the rate of profit rests on grounds which have just been explained.* This is true so far as his article 'On the Rectification of Marx's Fundamental Theoretical Construction in the Third Volume of Capital' [6] is concerned. But in his other papers on Marxian economics, 'Value Calculation and Price Calculation in the Marxian System,' [7] Bortkiewicz puts the chief emphasis on Marx's neglect of 'the mathematical relation between the productivity of labor and the rate of surplus value.' † This latter objection to Marx's formulation of the law of the falling tendency of the rate of profit is certainly the more important of the two. Moreover this objection has nothing to do with the procedure used in transforming values into prices.

5. The Significance of Price Calculation

So far we have discussed the technical aspects of the problem of transforming values into prices. Having observed that Marx's method was faulty, we located the source of his error and proceeded to demonstrate that the problem can be solved in a logically satisfactory manner. What, now, is the significance of the whole issue?

Marx himself, it seems clear, regarded the problem of price calculation as one of distinctly secondary importance. So far as he was concerned, its relevance was limited to two aspects of the economy: (1) the prices of individual commodities, and

* See the articles by Shibata cited in note to p. 105 above.
† See above, p. 104 n.

(2) the relative profits of individual capitalists. To use a modern turn of phrase, these are economic issues of a microscopic nature. They relate to the separate elements of the system, not to the system as a whole. Marx, however, was interested in economic macroscopics: total income, its division among the major social classes, and the manner in which these aggregate quantities behave in the course of the development of the capitalist system. In relation to these larger issues, the question of value calculation *versus* price calculation possessed only an incidental significance, which he could safely afford to neglect.

If Marx's method of solving the transformation problem could be considered valid, there seems to be no doubt that this position would be entirely justified. According to his method, total output, total surplus value, total wages, rate of surplus value, and rate of profit are all undisturbed by the transition from value terms to price terms. Moreover, the forces set in motion by the capitalists' tireless pursuit of increased income and wealth operate quite as strongly and with precisely the same broad effects whether the system be one of value calculation or price calculation.

Our investigation has shown, however, that Marx's method is unsatisfactory, that not only individual prices and profits but also aggregates and their relation to one another may be affected by the transition from value to price. To what extent, if at all, does this fact discredit the conclusions which have been reached in earlier chapters on the assumption of system-wide equality in the organic composition of capitals?

In order to answer the question, let us postulate a value scheme on the assumption of general equality in the organic composition of capitals. Call this value scheme *V*. In this case the corresponding price scheme is identical. Now vary the organic composition of the individual capitals but in such a way as to leave the average unchanged. Call the corresponding price scheme *P*. We know that *V* and *P* will differ in certain particulars. For example, both the total amount of surplus value and the rate of profit may be, say, smaller in *P* than in *V*. But aside from the particular figures involved, it is readily seen that the relationships implied in the two schemes are identical. Capitalists get profits and workers get wages in both; the conditions of Simple Reproduction are the same. In passing from *V* to *P* the system has, so to speak, undergone a transformation which affects only its dimensions. In comparing two equilibrium states, this in itself is a matter of no great import.

Now let the two systems develop under the impact of accumulation. Will their tendential characteristics differ significantly? This is the crux of the problem.

Clearly distinguishable differences, it would appear, might arise from two sources. First, in *P* the organic composition of capital in the gold industry might follow a singular course, let us say rising more steeply than the average for all industries, while *ex hypothesi* in *V* all industries behave similarly in this respect. In such a case the purchasing power of money would act differently in the two systems, or, looking at the matter from the other side, total price would progressively diverge from total value. This, however, as we have already noted, is simply a question of the unit of account which has no deeper theoretical significance. It appears that the first difference can be dismissed without fear of serious consequences.

A second difference between the tendencies of *V* and *P* might arise because of certain relative shifts in the organic composition of capital as between the various industries in *P*, shifts which by assumption are absent from *V*. The average will simultaneously increase in both to the same extent, but in *P* the rate of increase in some industries may be assumed to be rapid while in others it is slow or perhaps even nonexistent. But to make a difference in the broad trends, this internal shifting of the organic composition of capital in *P* will have to be of a certain definite kind. It will have to affect wage-goods industries on balance differently from luxury-goods industries. For, if the particularly sharp increases as well as the failures to increase are distributed in more or less random fashion over the entire field of industry, there will be no reason to assume a particular effect on any of the relevant aggregate quantities.

Shifts which have a special effect on the wage-goods industries are certainly not impossible. Moreover, in principle they need only be shifts which exercise a significant influence on industries which are directly or indirectly relatively more important in the production of wage goods as compared to those which are relatively more important in the luxury-goods field. Consequently it must be admitted that there may be forces present in *P* which are absent from *V*.

But here it is pertinent to pose a question. We already know that *V* exhibits certain fairly definite tendencies. These tendencies are not done away with by the transformation to *P;* at most they are modified. But in which direction are they modified? Are they reinforced? or inhibited? The truth is that there are no grounds on which to base an answer to this question. Under such circumstances there is only one general assumption which has anything to recommend it, namely, that different rates of change in the organic composition of capitals are distributed more or less at random among the various branches of industry. This amounts to assuming that rates of change of the organic composition of capital as between industries are neutral with respect to the trend of the aggregate quantities in which we are primarily interested. And this, finally, amounts to abstracting altogether from such divergent rates of change. This is an appropriate abstraction in the sense already explained in an earlier chapter.*

Once this abstraction has been made, it follows that the patterns of development traced out by *V* and *P* will differ only in minor details. In other words, the laws of motion of capitalist production can, in principle, be discovered and analysed by the use of either value calculation or price calculation. The legitimacy of treating the case where value calculation and price calculation are identical is an obvious corollary.

It appears, therefore, that a correct conception of the transformation problem does not affect the laws of capitalist development reached in earlier chapters.

6. Why Not Start with Price Calculation?

It may be urged that the whole set of problems concerned with value calculation and the transformation of values into prices is excess baggage. The real world is one of price calculation; why not deal in price terms from the outset?

* See above, p. 20.

A Marxist can safely concede something to this point of view. In so far as the problems which are posed for solution are concerned with the behavior of the disparate elements of the economic system (prices of individual commodities, profits of particular capitalists, the combination of productive factors in the individual firm, et cetera) there seems to be no doubt that value calculation is of little assistance. Orthodox economists have been working intensively on problems of this sort for the last half century and more. They have developed a kind of price theory which is more useful in this sphere than anything to be found in Marx or his followers.

One might be tempted to go farther and concede that from the formal point of view it is possible to dispense with value calculation even in the analysis of the behavior of the system as a whole. There is, however, a weighty reason for believing that this would be a mistaken view. The entire social output is the product of human labor. Under capitalist conditions, a part of this social output is appropriated by that group in the community which owns the means of production. This is not an ethical judgment, but a method of describing the really basic economic relation between social groups. It finds its most clear-cut theoretical formulation in the theory of surplus value. As long as we retain value calculation, there can be no obscuring of the origin and nature of profits as a deduction from the product of total social labor. The translation of pecuniary categories into social categories is greatly facilitated. In short, value calculation makes it possible to look beneath the surface phenomena of money and commodities to the underlying relations between people and classes.

Price calculation, on the other hand, mystifies the underlying social relations of capitalist production. Since profit is calculated as a return on total capital, the idea inevitably arises that capital as such is in some way 'productive.' Things appear to be endowed with an independent power of their own. From the point of view of value calculation it is easy to recognize this as a flagrant form of commodity fetishism. From the point of view of price calculation it appears to be natural and inevitable.* It is not only a question of obscuring the basic social relations of

* Cf. above, pp. 37 f.

capitalist production, however. Every one of the theories of profit which have been developed starting from price calculation is open to serious objection. Böhm-Bawerk, the great opponent of Marx's value theory, effectively blasted the theories which rely on the alleged productivity of capital as an explanatory principle. His own theory of time-preference is certainly no more solidly grounded.* It is perhaps significant that modern theorists have largely given up the attempt to explain the origin of profit and now confine themselves to analysing changes in the level of profit and the division of profit among entrepreneurs and interest-receivers.

But despite this attitude of indifference on the part of modern theorists towards the problem of the origin and nature of profit, the issues involved are of profound significance. They affect not only our attitude towards the economic system in which we live but also our choice of the theoretical tools with which we seek to understand it. It is from this circumstance that the dispute over price calculation *versus* value calculation derives its real importance. If we believe, with Marx and the great classical economists, that profit can be understood only as a deduction from the combined product of social labor, there is no way of dispensing with value calculation and the labor theory of value on which it is based.

* Böhm-Bawerk imagined that this theory combined productivity and time preference and in this way avoided his own objections to what he called 'naive' productivity theories. Bortkiewicz, however, showed that the only independent ground for interest adduced by Böhm was time-preference.

Bortkiewicz, apparently alone among Marx critics, regarded the 'deduction' theory of profit and the juxtaposition of value calculation and price calculation as overwhelmingly Marx's most important contributions to economic theory. He took this position because he shared the view expressed in the text, namely, that other theories of profit are unsatisfactory. He developed this theme in an important series of papers which have received much less attention than they deserve. Beside those already cited, the following may be noted: 'Der Kardinalfehler der Böhm-Bawerkschen Zinstheorie,' *Schmoller's Jahrbuch*, 1906; 'Zur Zinstheorie,' ibid. 1907; and 'Böhm-Bawerk's Hauptwerk in seinem Verhältnis zur Sozialistischen Theorie des Kapitalzinses,' *Archiv für die Geschichte des Sozialismus und der Arbeiterbewegung*, 1923.

PART THREE

CRISES AND DEPRESSIONS

VIII

THE NATURE OF CAPITALIST CRISES

MARX never lost sight of the problem of crises. In the *Manifesto*, one of his early works, he spoke of 'the commercial crises that by their periodical return put the existence of the entire bourgeois society on trial, each time more threateningly.' And one of the last things published during his own lifetime, the 'Postscript to the Second Edition' of Volume I of *Capital* (1873), closed on a similar note:

> The contradictory movement of capitalist society impresses itself upon the practical bourgeois most strikingly in the changes of the periodic cycle through which modern industry runs and whose crowning point is the general crisis. The crisis is once again approaching, although as yet but in its preliminary stage; and by the universality of its theatre and the intensity of its action it will drum dialectics even into the heads of the mushroom upstarts of the new, holy Prusso-German empire.[1]

Moreover, throughout the three volumes of *Capital* and the three volumes of *Theories of Surplus Value*, the problem of crises continually recurs. Nevertheless, there is nowhere to be found anything approaching a complete or systematic treatment of the subject in Marx's writings.

There are very good reasons for this lack. Crises are extraordinarily complicated phenomena. They are shaped to a greater or less extent by a wide variety of economic forces. As Marx expressed it, 'the real crisis can be explained only from the real movement of capitalistic production, competition, and credit.'[2] By 'competition' and 'credit' he meant the entire organizational structure of markets and financial machinery which makes the actual economy so much more complicated than the model systems which were analysed in *Capital*. To put the point otherwise, the crisis as a complex concrete phenomenon could not be fully analysed on the levels of abstraction to which *Capital* is confined. What we do find are all the aspects of the crisis problem which emerge on the higher levels of abstraction. These appear from time to time throughout the analysis, though not necessarily in logical order from the point of view of an overall treatment of crises. It is probably safe to say that if Marx had lived to complete his analysis of competition and credit he would have given us a thorough and systematic treatment of crises. As it turned out, however, crises necessarily remained on the list of unfinished business.

Under these circumstances, and in view of the practical importance of the problem, it was natural that Marx's followers should devote a great deal of attention to the theory of crises. On the one hand, they extended Marx's analysis in various respects; on the other hand, they quarreled among themselves about the meaning and relative importance of his scattered contributions to the subject. There can, therefore, be no question of treating crises within the general framework of Marxian economics without taking account of the writings of later Marxists on the subject. In what follows no attempt at complete coverage will be made; rather we shall confine ourselves to drawing upon the most important authors in so far as this will help in rounding out and clarifying the presentation.

1. Simple Commodity Production and Crises

A well-recognized and more or less stable currency, or means of circulation, is a necessary feature of a society which has advanced beyond the stage of occasional barter to the point of regularly satisfying its requirements through the private exchange of individual producers. Whereas the form of the barter transaction is *C-C*, commodity against commodity, under conditions of developed commodity production the form of exchange becomes *C-M-C*, commodity against money and money against commodity. It is thus the function and purpose of money to split the act of exchange into two parts which in the very nature of the case may be separated in time and in space. In the history of civilization the introduction of money represented a great forward step. The producer no longer has to search out some one who has what he wants and at the same time wants what he has. By the use of money he is enabled to sell his product when it is ready and to purchase his requirements at his convenience. In this way much time is saved and genuine specialization, the foundation of increased productivity, becomes possible.

All this is commonplace. But what is perhaps less widely recognized is the fact that the organization of production through private exchange in the manner indicated carries with it the possibility of a crisis of a kind which would be unthinkable in a simpler economy in which labor is organized and products are shared under the direction of a single authority (for example, in the patriarchal family economy, or the economy of the feudal manor). For if producer A sells and then, for whatever reason, fails to buy from B, B, having failed to sell to A, cannot buy from C; and C, having failed to sell to B, cannot buy from D; and so on. Thus a rupture in the process of circulation, which is conditioned upon the separation of purchase and sale, can spread from its point of origin until it affects the entire economy. The familiar result of a crisis, coexistence of stocks of unsaleable commodities and unsatisfied wants, emerges. Every producer has produced more than he can sell. While in earlier forms of society economic disaster was synonymous with unwonted scarcity, here for the first time we meet that peculiarly civilized form of economic crisis, the crisis of overproduction. Of course, in this case it would be absurd to say that the cause of the crisis is overproduction; on the contrary, it is obvious that overproduction is the result of the crisis. In the example given, the 'cause' is to be sought in the circumstances which induced producer A to interrupt the process of exchanging his own products for the products of others. If we can discover why A sold and failed to buy, we shall have laid bare the cause, at least in a proximate sense, of the crisis.

Now actually it is not easy to think of reasons why producers should behave in this disruptive way in a society of simple commodity production. To be sure, it is possible for natural disaster, or war, or some such catastrophic occurrence, to interrupt the circulation of simple commodity production, but the resulting economic crisis is likely to be one of acute shortage rather than one of unsaleable surpluses, and in this respect simple commodity production is not very different from more primitive societies. Hoarding, based on the miser's greed for gold, is a conceivable explanation of a crisis of the sort depicted, and it is well known that hoarding as an end in itself is much more common under conditions approximating simple commodity production than it is in more advanced societies. Hoarding, however, usually takes place gradually and over a long period of time. If it is offset by an adequate increase in the total supply of the money commodity, it will have no noticeable effect on the economy; if it is not, it may exercise a persistently depressive effect on circulation and hence on production. But it is difficult to see how hoarding could produce a crisis of the sudden and violent character with which we are familiar in the modern world. The conclusion seems warranted that, barring external factors like wars and crop failures, crises are possible but rather unlikely, or at most accidental, under simple commodity production.

Essentially this conclusion flows from the basic conditions of simple commodity production. The circulation form *C-M-C* certainly contains the possibility of a crisis, but at the same time it signifies production for consumption; and since consumption is fundamentally a continuous process, there is little reason to expect the possibility to turn into reality.

2. Say's Law

The classical economists showed their lack of historical perspective by a consistent failure to distinguish between simple commodity production and capitalist production. Theorems worked out on the implicit assumptions of simple commodity production were frequently generalized and uncritically applied to capitalist production. One of the clearest examples of this is afforded by the principle which has become famous in economic literature as 'Say's Law of Markets,' so called after the French follower of Adam Smith and contemporary of Ricardo, Jean Baptiste Say.*

* The dubious honor of originality—dubious in this case, at any rate—can hardly be ascribed to Say in spite of the fact that the principle in question is usually associated with his name. So far as the classics are concerned, priority seems to belong to James Mill, father of John Stuart Mill.

Say's Law holds that a sale is invariably followed by a purchase of equal amount; in other words that there can be no interruption of the circulation *C-M-C*, hence no crisis and no overproduction. We have already noted that under simple commodity production such an interruption seems unlikely; Say's Law transforms this into the dogma of impossibility. The correct thesis that crises and overproduction are unlikely under simple commodity production becomes the false thesis that crises and overproduction are impossible under all circumstances. By accepting Say's Law, sometimes explicitly and sometimes tacitly, the classical economists barred the way to a theory of crises; as a result their contributions to the subject were fragmentary, unrelated, and of small permanent value.

No one recognized this more clearly than Marx, and it is hence not surprising that he devoted much attention to a detailed criticism of Say's Law (in its Ricardian version). He wanted to remove all doubt about the nature of the formal possibility of crises and overproduction in commodity-producing societies, and thus to clear the way for a later analysis of the causes of crises. This task is accomplished in the section on Crises in *Theories of Surplus Value*.[3]

Ricardo denied the possibility of general overproduction in the following terms:

> No man produces but with a view to consume or sell, and he never sells but with an intention to purchase some other commodity which may be useful to him, or which may contribute to future production. By producing then, he necessarily becomes either the consumer of his own goods, or the purchaser and consumer of the goods of some other person . . . Productions are always bought by productions, or by services; money is only the medium by which the exchange is effected.[4]

Marx poured ridicule on this reasoning: 'This is the childish babbling of a Say, but unworthy of Ricardo.'[5] Actually one does not have to buy just because one has sold. Sale and purchase are separated both in time and in space. Money is more than the 'medium by which the exchange is effected'; it is the medium by which the exchange is split into the two separate and distinct transactions, sale and purchase. If one sells and fails to buy, the result is crisis and overproduction. 'When we say that the simple form of metamorphosis [i.e. *C-M-C*] contains the possibility of the crisis, we are only saying that in this form itself lies the possibility of the tearing apart and separation of essentially complementary operations.'[6] Ricardo even misrepresents the conditions of simple commodity production, though he obviously means his analysis to apply not only to simple commodity production but to capitalism as well. When we turn to a consideration of the latter, we shall see the full implications of Ricardo's error.

3. Capitalism and Crises

The circulation form *C-M-C*, which is characteristic of simple commodity production, turns into *M-C-M'* under capitalism. From the point of view of circulation this is the fundamental difference between the two.* Let us examine this more closely.

The rationale of *C-M-C* is clear. So far as exchange value is concerned, the *C* at the beginning and the *C* at the end are identical. From the point of view of use value, however, the first *C* possesses for its producer none, or at most a small use value, while the second *C* is desired because of its greater use value. Thus the purpose of the exchange is the acquisition of use value and not the enhancement of exchange value. This is what is meant by saying that simple commodity production is production for consumption, and it is this that explains the unlikelihood of crises and overproduction under conditions of simple commodity production.

M-C-M', the dominant form of circulation under capitalism, is entirely different. The capitalist, acting as a capitalist,† starts his career with money (*M*) in sufficient quantity to function effectively as capital; he throws this into circulation in exchange for labor power and means of production (*C*); and finally, after a process of production has been performed, he reappears on the market with commodities which he transforms back into money

* See above, pp. 57 f.

† It is important not to confuse the capitalist as capitalist and the capitalist as consumer. Ordinarily when we speak of the capitalist without qualification we mean the former.

(M'). Both the M at the beginning and the M' at the end represent exchange value; neither possesses use value. The whole procedure would be pointless, therefore, unless there is a quantitative difference between M and M', in other words unless $M' - M = \Delta M$ is positive. So far as the capitalist is concerned, 'The expansion of value, which is the objective basis or mainspring of the circulation *M-C-M*, becomes his subjective aim, and it is only in so far as the appropriation of ever more and more wealth in the abstract becomes the sole motive of his operations that he functions as a Capitalist.'[7] Here we have a new element which was entirely missing from simple commodity production. For though the miser might share the capitalist's passion for wealth in the abstract, he satisfies it by withdrawing money from circulation; while the capitalist continually throws his money back into circulation and thereby changes the character of the circulation process itself. This is what is meant by saying that capitalism is production for profit, and it is this that explains, as we shall presently see, why capitalism is peculiarly susceptible to crises and overproduction.

Before we consider the relation between *M-C-M'* and crises, it should be noted that the circulation form *C-M-C* does not simply disappear or become irrelevant with the coming of capitalist production. Indeed, for the great majority of people, the laborers, circulation continues to take the form *C-M-C* with all that this implies. The worker begins with a commodity, labor power, which at best has a very limited use value for him; he converts his labor power into money; and finally he uses the money to acquire necessaries and conveniences of life. This is *C-M-C* and the objective is an increase in use value. *M-C-M'* is as foreign to the worker as it is to simple commodity producers. It is therefore entirely mistaken to picture the worker as dominated by the profit motive or to imagine that he shares the capitalist's urge to appropriate 'ever more and more wealth in the abstract.' The worker is motivated by a desire for use values, and what appears to be 'accumulation' on the part of workers (through savings banks, insurance companies, et cetera) has little in common with the accumulation of the capitalist. It springs, rather, from the necessity under which the worker is placed to attempt to insure a flow of use values to himself and his family at a time when his labor power will no longer be saleable.*

The difference of behavior and motivation as between capitalist and worker has, of course, nothing to do with 'human nature.' It springs from the difference between *M-C-M'* and *C-M-C*, that is to say, from the different objective circumstances in which each is placed. Through failure to make this distinction, orthodox economics has frequently been led into one or the other of two opposite errors: the error of supposing that under capitalism *every one* is driven on by a desire to make profits, or the error of supposing that *every one* is interested only in use values and hence that all saving is to be regarded in the light of a redistribution of income through time. A good example of the inconsistencies into which orthodox economics is likely to fall on this account is cited by Marx. He quotes approvingly a statement by MacCulloch: 'The inextinguishable passion for gain, the *auri sacra fames*, will always lead capitalists.' But, Marx quickly adds, 'This view, of course, does not prevent the same MacCulloch and others of his kidney, when in theoretical difficulties, such, for example, as the question of overproduction, from transforming the same capitalist into a moral citizen, whose sole concern is for use values, and who even develops an insatiable hunger for boots, hats, eggs, calico, and other extremely familiar sorts of use values.' [8] Careful consideration of the simple but fundamental characteristics of capitalist society would serve to warn against such pitfalls.

Let us now analyse the relation between *M-C-M'* and the crisis problem. We have already seen that the attention of the capitalist is focused on ΔM; he is interested in seeing that ΔM is as large as possible. Naturally he does not judge success or

* Given an expanding population with a concentration of numbers in the younger age groups, it is possible that 'accumulation' by workers on this account may result in considerable net savings. Against this, however, must be set the dissavings of those whose incomes are below the subsistence level (unemployed, aged, et cetera) and who are therefore obliged to live on charity or relief of one sort or another. It is doubtful if the net savings of the working class as a whole have ever been substantially positive for any considerable period of time. There is hence every reason to believe that the assumption on which Marx always works, namely that workers consume their entire incomes, is fully justified on theoretical as well as empirical grounds.

failure by the absolute size of ΔM, but rather by the size of ΔM relative to the magnitude of his original capital, or, in other words, by the size of the fraction $\Delta M/M$. Since this fraction is obviously nothing but the rate of profit, we may say that the capitalist is interested in maximizing his rate of profit, that this is the immediate objective which he has in view when he embarks his capital in production.

Now so far as the formal possibility of a crisis is concerned, there is no difference between simple commodity production and capitalism. What was said earlier in analysing simple commodity production is equally applicable here. Any interruption in the circulation process, any withholding of buying power from the market, can initiate a contraction in the circulation process which will give rise to the phenomenon of overproduction and which will soon be reflected in a curtailment of production itself. But there is this big difference, that whereas before it was hard to see what would start such a contraction, now at any rate it is clear that if anything happens to ΔM the capitalist will immediately reconsider the desirability of throwing his M into circulation. ΔM constitutes the Achilles' heel of capitalism which was missing from simple commodity production.

For the present two cases will be considered. In the first place, if ΔM disappears or becomes negative the incentive of capitalist production is removed. Capitalists will withdraw their capital, circulation will contract, and a crisis followed by overproduction will set in. This case is pretty clear; it is also, however, an extreme case which is unlikely to have a counterpart in practice. It is true that at times profits do disappear and even give way to losses over the greater part of the whole economy. But this is well recognized as the *result* of a particularly severe crisis; it is, in other words, a depression phenomenon and can scarcely be used to explain the onset of the crisis.

Our second case, therefore, is that of a fall in ΔM or, to use more familiar terminology, in the rate of profit. Supposing that the rate of profit always remains positive so that the motivating factor of capitalist production is never entirely removed, are there still grounds for expecting that at a certain stage capitalists might curtail their operations sufficiently to bring on a crisis? The answer is emphatically yes. As Marx expressed it, under capitalism 'it is not only a question of replacing the same mass of objects of which the capital is composed on the same scale or (in the case of accumulation) on an expanded scale, but of replacing the value of the advanced capital with the *usual* [*gewöhnlichen*] rate of profit.'[9] The usual rate of profit need not be thought of as one definite figure, no more and no less; it is sufficient that it be a fairly well-defined range of figures, say 10 to 15 per cent or 4 to 6 per cent according to circumstances. Once the rate of profit goes below the usual range, a curtailment of operations on the part of capitalists will set in. The reasons for this are not difficult to see.

By the very nature of the circulation process every individual capitalist is continuously called upon to choose between two alternative courses of action: either he must throw his capital back into circulation or he must hold it in its money form. In the long run, it is true, these alternatives do not exist; if he wants to continue as a capitalist, sooner or later he must reinvest his capital. But this does not mean that he must immediately reinvest his capital any more than it means he must always continue to reinvest his capital in the same line of production. It is a generally accepted principle that if the rate of profit goes below the usual level in any particular industry, capitalists will shift their capital out of that industry and into some other. If, however, the rate of profit goes below the usual level in all or nearly all industries at the same time, nothing can be gained by shifting from one to another. When this happens, capitalists are under no compulsion to continue reinvesting under what they must regard as unfavorable conditions; they can postpone reinvesting until conditions are once again favorable, that is to say, until either the rate of profit is back in the usual range or they have reconciled themselves to a new and lower norm for the rate of profit. In the meantime the postponement of reinvestment will have interrupted the circulation process and brought on a crisis and overproduction. The crisis and subsequent depression are, in fact, part of the mechanism by which the rate of profit is restored either completely or partially to its previous level.

It is not true, therefore, that the rate of profit must disappear or become negative in order to produce a crisis. All that is required is a reduction in the rate of profit below its usual level sufficient to induce capitalists to begin holding their capital in money form pending the return of more favorable conditions. In this way the continuity of the circulation process is breached and the crisis precipitated.

It might be thought that, instead of holding on to their money capital, the capitalists would increase their personal consumption when faced with an abnormally low rate of profit. If this happened, the character of the demand for commodities would be changed, but the total would be unaffected, and no interruption of the circulation process would be entailed. To argue in this way, however, is to make the mistake which Marx was so careful to warn against; it is to assume that all at once the capitalist loses his interest in accumulation and becomes 'a moral citizen whose sole concern is for use values'; it is to assume that the capitalist, faced with 'hard times,' seeks compensation in riotous living rather than in the more prosaic but also more realistic way of pulling in his belt; in short, it is to assume away what is most essential to capitalism, the never-ceasing urge to accumulate capital. Marx criticized this line of reasoning very clearly in the following passage:

> It is never to be forgotten that in the case of capitalist production it is not directly a question of use value, but of exchange value, and more particularly of the expansion of surplus value. This is the driving motive of capitalist production, and it is a fine conception which, in order to reason away the contradictions of capitalist production, abstracts from its very basis and makes it into a system of production which is concerned with the immediate consumption of the producers.[10]

The argument of this section may be summed up as follows: the specific form of capitalist crisis is an interruption of the circulation process induced by a decline in the rate of profit below its usual level. It is interesting and also instructive to note that modern business-cycle theory has arrived at a conclusion which, though apparently unrelated, is nevertheless in substance very similar to the Marxian position. Modern theorists start on a lower level of abstraction than Marx: for them the capitalist class is divided into two sections, entrepreneurs who organize and direct the processes of production, and money capitalists who supply the funds, in the form of interest-bearing loans, which the entrepreneurs require for their operations. Entrepreneurs may also own capital, but in so far as they do they are regarded as loaning it at interest to themselves. Under these assumptions the entrepreneur will find it worthwhile to invest capital so long as the rate of profit * which he receives is greater than the rate of interest which he is obliged to pay. Just as soon as the rate of profit falls below the rate of interest, however, the entrepreneur has no more motive to invest; circulation is interrupted, and a crisis ensues.

When the matter is put in this way, it appears that the trouble is that the rate of interest is too high. In a sense this is true, but what it really means is that rather than loan their capital to entrepreneurs at lower rates, capitalists prefer to hold it in money form. There may be various reasons for this preference, but business-cycle theorists seem to be generally agreed that the most important is the capitalists' belief that lower rates of interest would be unlikely to last, in other words, that lower rates would be unusual and abnormal, and hence that from a purely pecuniary point of view it is wiser to postpone lending activities until demand has picked up at the present or perhaps even higher rates.† Of course, if interest rates do not recover as expected after a reasonable lapse of time, capitalists may become reconciled to a new and lower range of rates and may therefore begin lending once again on terms which entrepreneurs can accept.

If now we attempt to formulate this position while abstracting from the separation of capitalists from entrepreneurs we see at once that the refusal of money-capitalists to lend to entrepreneurs at interest rates below what is regarded as normal or usual is essentially the same phenomenon as the refusal of capitalist-entrepreneurs (what Marx calls capitalists without qualification) to invest when the rate of profit falls below the usual range. In general terms these are alternative ways of saying that the capi-

* What we here call the rate of profit is usually termed the marginal efficiency or productivity of capital. The differences between these concepts are not important from the present point of view.

† Holding money in expectation of a higher rate of interest in the future (or, put otherwise, in expectation of lower prices for securities in the future) is what Keynes calls liquidity preference from the speculative motive.

talist class as a whole contracts its investment activities when the rate of return on capital sinks below a certain level which is more or less definite at any particular time and place. The Marxian formulation has the great advantage of emphasizing that this type of behavior springs from the most fundamental characteristics of capitalist production and not from the particular form in which the supply and use of capital funds is organized. This is not to argue that a complete analysis of crises is possible without taking full account of the phenomena of the money market, rate of interest, credit, et cetera. We have only tried to demonstrate what modern business-cycle theory frequently slurs over, namely, that even in the absence of the institutional arrangements which give rise to a money market and a rate of interest, capitalist production would still be subject to crises brought on by fluctuations in the rate of profit. The most important implication of this proof is that no amount of tampering with the monetary system can be expected to do away with capitalist crises.

4. The Two Types of Crises

If the foregoing analysis is correct, it follows that a discussion of the causation of crises must run in terms of the forces operating on the rate of profit. In this connection the law of the falling tendency of the rate of profit has obvious relevance. It was shown in Chapter VI that the process of capital accumulation carries with it a tendency for the rate of profit to decline. If this tendency does not work itself out both continuously and gradually, it seems clear that crises may be the result. This possibility will be considered in the next chapter under the general heading 'Crises Associated with the Falling Tendency of the Rate of Profit.' It is important to realize that the falling tendency of the rate of profit was deduced on the assumption that the conditions of the law of value were fully complied with; * in other words, all commodities were assumed to sell at their equilibrium values throughout the analysis. The falling rate of profit

* The use of price calculation would require no significant modifications of the conclusions reached on the basis of value calculation. See above, pp. 125 ff.

was, therefore, not a symptom of disequilibrium in the value system, though, if it should lead to a crisis, it would then become the cause of such a disequilibrium.

Now if we drop the assumption that all commodities sell at their equilibrium values, another possible source of a fall in profitability emerges. Capitalists may suffer from an inability to sell commodities at their values. This possibility has scarcely been mentioned heretofore, although it is implicit in the theory of value. The point is obvious when applied to a single commodity; if too much is produced, market price falls below value, and profit is reduced or wiped out. If this happens to enough industries at the same time, the outcome is a general fall in the rate of profit followed by a crisis. In this case, however, the decline in profitability is already a symptom of disequilibrium, which is now intensified by the ensuing crisis. The essential difficulty is that of realizing the value which is already, in a physical sense, embodied in finished commodities. Hence this possibility will be considered in detail in Chapter x under the general heading 'Realization Crises.'

It is important to grasp the difference between crises associated with the falling tendency of the rate of profit and realization crises. The practical capitalist is unlikely to see any difference; for him the trouble is always insufficient profitability from whatever source it may arise. But from the point of view of causal analysis, the two types of crises present divergent problems. In the one case we have to do with movements in the rate of surplus value and the composition of capital, with the value system remaining intact; in the other case we have to do with as yet unspecified forces tending to create a general shortage in effective demand for commodities, not indeed in the sense that the demand is insufficient to buy all the commodities offered, but that it is insufficient to buy them all at a satisfactory rate of profit. The starting point of the crisis is in both cases a decline in the rate of profit; but what lies behind the decline in the rate of profit in the one case requires a very different analysis from what lies behind the decline in the rate of profit in the other.

IX

CRISES ASSOCIATED WITH THE FALLING TENDENCY OF THE RATE OF PROFIT

According to Marx, the rate of profit tends to fall in the course of capitalist development because as a general rule the organic composition of capital rises relatively more rapidly than the rate of surplus value.* This may be the case, though reasons were advanced in Chapter vi for doubting the generality of the law. At any rate, to the extent that the rate of profit does manifest a downward tendency for the reason given, it seems clear that we have the basis of a theory of crises. We need not repeat the analysis of the mechanism whereby a fall in the rate of profit beyond a certain point becomes the cause of a crisis.

In a chapter entitled 'Unraveling the Internal Contradictions of the Law,' [1] Marx noted the connection between crises and the tendency of the rate of profit to fall. 'It [a fall in the rate of profit] promotes overproduction, speculation, crises, surplus capital along with surplus population.' [2] And again, 'The barrier of the capitalist mode of production becomes apparent . . . in the fact that the development of the productive power of labor creates in the falling rate of profit a law which turns into an antagonism of this mode of production at a certain point and requires for its defeat periodical crises.' [3] It seems likely that in both these passages Marx had in mind a fall in the rate of profit which is attributable to a rising organic composition of capital; in other words, he had in mind his general law of the falling tendency of the rate of profit.

Some writers have concluded that Marx meant the law of the falling tendency of the rate of profit to be the primary explana-

* Strictly we should speak of the proportion of variable to total capital instead of the organic composition, in this connection. However, if the division of capital into constant and variable is not too far from half and half, the relative fall in the former is little different from the relative rise in the latter.

tory principle so far as crises are concerned.* This is a problem of interpretation which is much complicated by the fact that in the very same chapter in which the above-quoted passages occur, Marx also takes account of declining profitability due to two other separate and distinct causes: (1) a fall in the rate of surplus value consequent upon an increase in wages in value terms,† and (2) the impossibility under certain circumstances of selling commodities at their full values, what we have called the realization problem.‡ Moreover, both of these factors are brought into relation to crises, and at times it is impossible to be sure which kind of a decline in profitability Marx has in mind. Under the circumstances, there is really no way of knowing how much weight he intended to place upon the law of the falling tendency of the rate of profit as an element in the explanation of crises. At times there are indications that he thought of this law as applying only in the long run. For example, in one place, he says: 'In view of the many different causes which bring about a rise or fall in the rate of profit, one would think that the average rate of profit would change every day. But a certain movement in one sphere will counterbalance that of another. We shall examine later on [i.e. in the Part devoted to the law] toward which side these fluctuations gravitate ultimately. But they are slow.'[4] Slow changes in the rate of profit are hardly relevant to the problem of crises, since in the long run capitalists' ideas about what is normal also change. It should be remembered in this connection that the chapter on 'Unraveling the Internal Contradictions of the Law' has, perhaps to a greater degree than most of Volume III, the character of preliminary notes jotted down by Marx for his own guidance in later elaboration of the subjects touched upon, so that definitive judgments are probably out of the question.

So far attention has been confined to the relation between crises and Marx's version of the law of the falling tendency of the rate of profit. In Chapter VI, however, the conclusion was

* See, for example, Maurice Dobb, *Political Economy and Capitalism*, Chapter IV; and Erich Preiser, 'Das Wesen der Marxschen Krisentheorie,' in *Wirtschaft und Gesellschaft* (Festschrift für Franz Oppenheimer, 1924).

† On pp. 294-7. Crises arising from this source are discussed presently.

‡ See the next chapter.

reached that we should be on sounder ground to search for causes of the falling tendency of the rate of profit in the process of capital accumulation with its inherent tendency to raise the demand for labor power and hence the level of wages. If now we turn to Part VII of Volume I ('The Accumulation of Capital') we shall find that Marx had a well-articulated theory of crises running in precisely these terms. It is a curious fact, for which there is no obvious explanation, that the contribution to crisis theory contained in Volume I has been largely neglected by writers on Marxian economics.

We are already familiar with the important place which the reserve army of labor holds in Marx's theoretical analysis of capitalism. That crises play an important role in recruiting the reserve army was briefly indicated in the earlier discussion of this subject. Let us now undertake a closer analysis of this relation.

It is conceivable that if capital accumulation proceeded smoothly and new labor-saving inventions were always available at the right time and in the right quantity, there might exist a more or less stable reserve army which would serve to prevent accumulation from exercising any undue upward pressure on wages. But such a picture is unrealistic. As capitalism develops, sharp fluctuations in the rate of accumulation, partly caused by and partly leading to technical revolutions, become more and more the rule. As Marx expressed it:

With accumulation and the development of the productiveness of labor that accompanies it, the power of sudden expansion of capital also grows; it grows not merely because the elasticity of the capital already functioning increases, not merely because the absolute wealth of society expands, of which capital only forms an elastic part, not merely because credit, under every special stimulus, at once places an unusual part of this wealth at the disposal of production in the form of additional capital; it grows also because the technical conditions of the process of production themselves—machinery, means of transport, etc.—now admit of the rapidest transformation of masses of surplus product into additional means of production. The mass of social wealth, overflowing with the advance of accumulation, and transformable into additional capital, thrusts itself frantically into old branches of production whose market steadily expands, or into newly formed branches, such as railways, etc., the need for which grows out of the development of the old ones. In all such cases, there must be the possibility of throwing great masses of men suddenly on the decisive points without injury to the scale of production in other spheres. Overpopulation supplies these masses.[5]

But if surplus population is a necessary precondition for such rapid bursts of accumulation, it is also true that the latter tend to exhaust the reserve army and lead to a condition in which available labor power is more or less fully utilized. Capitalists are forced to bid against one another for additional workers, wages rise, and surplus value is cut into. Whenever accumulation 'requires an extraordinary addition of paid labor, then wages rise, and, all other circumstances remaining equal, the unpaid labor [surplus value] diminishes in proportion. But as soon as this diminution touches the point at which the surplus labor that nourishes capital is no longer supplied in normal quantity,* a reaction sets in: a smaller part of revenue is capitalized, accumulation lags, and the movement of rise in wages receives a check.'[6] This 'reaction,' characterized as it is by a contraction in investment activity, is nothing more nor less than the crisis.

It seems quite clear that it was this process of declining reserve army, rising wages, and reduced profitability as a cause of crises which Marx had in mind when he formulated his well-known criticism of underconsumption theories in Volume II. The following is the passage in question:

It is purely a tautology to say that crises are caused by the scarcity of solvent consumers, or of a paying consumption. The capitalist system does not know any other modes of consumption but a paying one, except that of the pauper or of the 'thief.' If any commodities are unsaleable, it means that no solvent purchasers have been found for them, in other words, consumers (whether commodities are bought in the last instance for pro-

* Marx here again stresses the necessity for profit to be forthcoming at a normal rate if capitalism is to function smoothly and without interruption. As was pointed out in the last chapter, this is an essential feature of his crisis theory.

ductive or individual consumption). [The reference to 'productive or individual consumption' shows that Marx here meant by 'solvent consumption' what present-day writers call 'effective demand.'] But if one were to attempt to clothe this tautology with a profounder justification by saying that the working class receive too small a portion of their own product, and the evil would be remedied by giving them a larger share of it, or raising their wages, we should reply that crises are precisely always preceded by a period in which wages rise generally and the working class actually get a larger share of the annual product intended for consumption. From the point of view of the advocates of 'simple' (!) common sense, such a period should rather remove a crisis. It seems, then, that capitalist production comprises certain conditions which are independent of good or bad will and permit the working class to enjoy that relative prosperity only momentarily, and at that always as a harbinger of a coming crisis.*

This statement flows naturally from the discussion of crises in Volume I, and it is directed against the kind of crude underconsumption theory which has always enjoyed considerable popularity, particularly among trade unionists. There could be nothing more absurd, however, than to cite this passage as 'proof' that Marx regarded the magnitude of consumption as of no consequence in the causation of crises. We shall go into this aspect of his thought more in detail in our discussion of realization crises.

Crises which are brought on by a reduction in profitability consequent upon a rise in wages are also considered in the chapter on 'Unraveling the Internal Contradictions of the Law' in Volume III. Here 'extreme conditions' are assumed according to which not only the rate of profit but also the absolute amount of profit suffers a reduction. In this case, 'there would be a strong and sudden fall in the average rate of profit, but it would be due to a change in the composition of capital which would not be caused by the development of the productive forces, *but by a rise in the money value of the variable capital (on account of the increased wages) and the corresponding reduction in the*

* *Capital* II, pp. 475-6. Marx adds the following footnote: 'Advocates of the theory of crises of Rodbertus are requested to make a note of this.'

proportion of surplus labor to necessary labor.'* In connection with this case, which clearly continues the Volume I line of thought on crises, Marx made his most detailed analysis of the depression. This discussion is so compact that, with the deletion of a few unessential passages, it can best be presented in his own words.

Once the crisis has broken out,

under all circumstances the equilibrium is restored by making more or less capital unproductive or destroying it. This would affect to some extent the material substance of capital, that is, a part of the means of production, fixed and circulating capital, would not perform any service as capital; a portion of the running establishments would then close down. Of course, time would corrode and depreciate all means of production (except land), but this particular stagnation would cause a far more serious destruction of means of production . . .

The principal work of destruction would show its most dire effects in a slaughtering of the *values* of capitals. That portion of the value of capital which exists only in the form of claims on future shares of surplus value or profit, which consists in fact of creditor's notes on production in its various forms, would be immediately depreciated by the reduction of the receipts on which it is calculated. One portion of the gold and silver money is rendered unproductive, cannot serve as capital. One portion of the commodities on the market can complete its process of circulation and reproduction only by means of an immense contraction of its prices, which means a depreciation of the capital represented by it. In the same way the elements of fixed capital are more or less depreciated. Then there is the added complication that the process of reproduction is based on definite assumptions as to prices, so that a general fall in prices checks and disturbs the process of reproduction. This interference and stagnation paralyses the function of money as a medium of payment, which is conditioned on the development of capital and the resulting price relations. The chain of payments due at certain times is broken in a hundred places, and the disaster is intensified by the collapse of the credit system . . .

* *Capital* III, p. 295. Italics added. It is interesting to note that Preiser (op. cit.) draws heavily on this example in support of his contention that the law of the falling tendency of the rate of profit is central to Marx's crisis theory. He fails to note that Marx is here talking about a kind of fall in the rate of profit different from that implied in the 'law.'

At the same time still other agencies would have been at work. The stagnation of production would have laid off a part of the laboring class and thereby placed the employed part in a condition in which they would have to submit to a reduction of wages even below the average. This operation has the same effect on capital as though the relative or absolute surplus value had been increased at average wages . . . On the other hand, the fall in prices and the competitive struggle would have given to every capitalist an impulse to raise the individual value of his total product above its average value by means of new machines, new and improved working methods, new combinations, which means to increase the productive power of a certain quantity of labor . . . The depreciation of the elements of constant capital itself would be another factor tending to raise the rate of profit. The mass of the employed constant capital, compared to the variable, would have increased, but the value of this mass might have fallen. The present stagnation of production would have prepared an expansion of production later on, within capitalistic limits.

And in this way the cycle would be run once more. One portion of the capital which had been depreciated by the stagnation of its function would recover its old value. For the rest, the same vicious circle would be described once more under expanded conditions of production, in an expanded market, and with increased productive forces.[7]

It is clear from this description of the after-effects of a crisis that Marx regarded depression as more than just hard times; the depression is rather the specific method of remedying the evils (from a capitalist point of view) of prosperity. An accelerated rate of accumulation brings on a reaction in the form of a crisis; the crisis turns into depression; the depression, through filling up the reserve army and depreciating capital values, restores the profitability of production and thereby sets the stage for a resumption of accumulation. A repetition of the whole process is now merely a matter of time. This is, then, really more than a theory of crises; it is essentially a theory of what modern economists call the business cycle as a whole. Marx was fully aware of this:

The course characteristic of modern industry, viz., a decennial cycle (interrupted by smaller oscillations), of periods of average activity, production at high pressure, crisis and stagnation, depends on the constant formation, the greater or less absorption, and the re-formation of the industrial reserve army of surplus population. In their turn the varying phases of the industrial cycle recruit the surplus population and become one of the most energetic agents of its reproduction . . . The whole form of the movement of modern industry depends, therefore, upon the constant transformation of a part of the laboring population into unemployed or half-employed hands. The superficiality of Political Economy shows itself in the fact that it looks upon the expansion and contraction of credit, which is a mere symptom of the periodic changes of the industrial cycle, as their cause. As the heavenly bodies, once thrown into a certain definite motion, always repeat this, so it is with social production as soon as it is once thrown into this movement of alternate expansion and contraction. Effects, in their turn, become causes, and the varying accidents of the whole process, which always reproduces its own conditions, take on the form of periodicity.[8]

It thus appears that Marx regarded the business cycle as the specific form of capitalist development and the crisis as one phase of the cycle. The basic factor which is reflected in this peculiar course of development is a fluctuating rate of accumulation which, in turn, is rooted in the fundamental technical and organizational characteristics of the capitalist system. The chain of causation runs from the rate of accumulation to the volume of employment, from the volume of employment to the level of wages, and from the level of wages to the rate of profit. A fall in the rate of profit below the normal range chokes off accumulation and precipitates a crisis, the crisis turns into depression, and, finally, the depression recreates the conditions favorable to an acceleration in the rate of accumulation.

It should be noted that the conception of the business cycle which emerges from Marx's analysis of capital accumulation is one which is, in principle at least, acceptable to non-Marxian political economy. Indeed it is probably safe to say that there is not a single important element in this theory which does not find its place in some one or more of the many theories of the business cycle elaborated by economists in the last three or four decades.* Fluctuations in the rate of investment, shortages of labor, 'maladjustments' between wages and selling prices, these are all familiar to students of the cycle problem, through naturally the emphasis varies from theory to theory. Even the idea that the business cycle is the inevitable form of capitalist development is widely accepted; such well-known theorists as Spiethoff, Schumpeter, Robertson, and Hansen have been at great pains to emphasize this point. Here, however, orthodox theory has called a halt. It has never seen in the business cycle a threat to the permanence of the capitalist system itself; crisis and depression, instead of being what Kautsky once incisively described as capitalism's *memento mori*, are rather looked upon as restorative forces, unpleasant in the short run but necessary in the long run. Are we to conclude that Marx himself would have agreed?

If he had had no views on crises other than those set forth in this chapter, the answer might be in the affirmative. Such, however, was not the case. The theory of crises propounded in Volume I, and occasionally reverted to in Volumes II and III, is intended to deal with only one side of the whole problem. For it assumes throughout that, until the crisis actually breaks out, all commodities can be sold at their full values. In the language of current theory, it assumes that the crisis is not the result but rather the cause of a shortage of effective demand. The trouble, therefore, is not in any sense a scarcity of markets but an unsatisfactory (from a capitalist standpoint) distribution of income between recipients of wages and recipients of surplus value. To drop this assumption is to open up a new range of possibilities. Until these have been explored, a task which is undertaken in the next chapter, the theory remains incomplete and one-sided; the conclusions which apparently flow from it must not be regarded as definitive.

* This does not imply, of course, that modern business-cycle theory has been to any significant extent influenced by Marx.

X

REALIZATION CRISES

If the decline in profitability which is immediately responsible for the outbreak of a crisis results from capitalists' inability to realize the full value of the commodities which they produce, we shall speak of a 'realization crisis.' In Marxist literature discussion has centered upon two types of crises which may be classified under this general heading: (1) crises arising from 'disproportionality' among the various lines of production; and (2) crises arising from the 'underconsumption' of the masses. Let us examine each of these in turn.

1. Crises Arising from Disproportionality

Marx regarded it as elementary, and none of his followers has ever denied, that a general crisis and overproduction can result from partial disturbances in the process of production and circulation. If all commodities sold at their values, this would mean that the relative proportions in which the various articles were produced would be 'correct.' But the correct proportions are not known to capitalists *a priori*, nor are they prescribed in a master plan. Each capitalist produces for a market the size of which he can only estimate on the basis of very incomplete knowledge, with the result that now 'too little,' now 'too much' is produced. This manifests itself in selling prices which are either above or below values. A compensating tendency now goes into operation; production of commodities which have been sold below their values is contracted, while production of commodities which have been sold above their values is expanded. If conditions (methods of production, wants of consumers, productivity of labor, et cetera) never changed, eventually the correct proportions would be discovered by trial and error, and thenceforth all selling prices would correspond to values. In practice, however, conditions continually change, so that conformity of selling prices to values is at best but approximate and temporary.

This is common knowledge and generally accepted by all schools of economic theory. But the classics implied, if they did not always openly state, that the processes of adjustment would be smooth and continuous so that no general disturbances could arise from these situations of partial over- and underproduction. There is no guarantee that this condition will in general be fulfilled. If, for example, the capitalists in the steel industry overestimate the demand for steel and produce more than the market can absorb at remunerative prices, they will contract their production and in so doing reduce the demand for labor power, iron, coal, transportation, et cetera. There is no reason to suppose that there must take place a simultaneous expansion in the production of other commodities of such a nature as to make good the deficit in demand created by the cut in steel production. If there is not, the error of the steel-makers will give rise to an interruption in the circulation process which, as we know from the discussion in Chapter VIII, will tend to spread from its point of origin. Moreover, if steel production is sufficiently important so that the initial disturbance is a large one, it may engulf the whole economy in a general crisis. As Marx put it, 'That a crisis (and hence also overproduction) be general, it is enough that it seize hold of the leading articles of commerce.' [1]

Such a crisis is easily traceable to what we have called disproportionality between the various branches of production, and this disproportionality in turn has its roots in the planless, anarchic character of capitalist production.* Disproportionality is always a possible cause of crises, and it is almost certainly a complicating factor in all crises whatever their basic cause may be. It is partly for this reason—the behavior of the credit system is an additional reason—that the real crisis *never* conforms exactly to a fixed theoretical pattern. But disproportionalities arising

* Some writers have ascribed crises of this type to the 'anarchy of capitalist production.' This is correct, but it should be remembered that 'anarchy' in this connection is not synonymous with 'chaos.' Anarchy does not necessarily imply absence of order but only absence of conscious regulation. In the long run, capitalist production, in spite of its anarchic character, is subject to definite and objectively valid laws of motion.

from the planlessness of capitalism are by nature not amenable to explanation in terms of general laws. For this reason their treatment falls outside the scope of Marx's theoretical system. Thus, having mentioned the possibility of disproportionality, Marx in one place proceeds as follows:

> Nevertheless we do not here speak of the crisis so far as it rests upon disproportional production [*unproportionierter Produktion*], that is to say upon a faulty distribution of social labor among the individual spheres of production. This can come into consideration only so far as the discussion concerns the competition of capitals. There, as has already been said, the rise or fall of market value as a consequence of this faulty relation has as a result the withdrawal of capital from one sphere of production and its carrying over to another, the migration of capital from one branch to another. Nevertheless it is already implied in this process of equilibration that it assumes the opposite of equilibration and hence can contain within itself the seeds of the crisis, that the crisis itself can be a form of equilibration.[2]

Since the 'competition of capitals' was a subject which he did not pretend to analyse in any detail, it was only natural that disproportionality as a cause of crises should have received no more than passing attention at his hands. Moreover, early followers of Marx, as well as commentators on his economic writings, appear to have ignored this 'theory' of crises altogether. It may, therefore, seem surprising that many spokesmen of German Social Democracy in the years before and after the First World War put forward a disproportionality explanation of crises as though it were the one and only Marxist theory of the subject.* The reasons for this deserve some attention.

The man who was chiefly responsible for the popularity of the disproportionality theory among socialists was the Russian economist, Michael Tugan-Baranowsky. Tugan was perhaps the most influential and original of the economic thinkers produced

* A good example is afforded by Julian Borchardt's essay on 'The Theory of Crises' appended to the same author's abridgment of Marx's *Capital*, which was published in English under the title *The People's Marx* and is available in The Modern Library's *Capital, The Communist Manifesto and Other Writings*, edited by Max Eastman. Borchardt's abridgment had a wide currency in Germany and enjoyed the official approval of the Social Democratic party.

by the so-called 'revisionist' movement which began to make headway in all branches of European socialism after the death of Engels in 1895. The propriety of calling Tugan a revisionist might be questioned, since he never claimed to be a Marxist of any kind and in this respect differed from those who, like Eduard Bernstein, thought (or at least said they thought) they were merely 'revising' Marx in the light of up-to-date experience. For all practical purposes, however, Tugan was one with the revisionists, and it would be misleading not to classify him as such so far as the present inquiry is concerned. It should be added, however, that Tugan also exercised a considerable influence on the development of modern business-cycle research, his work on the history of commercial crises in England being one of the pioneer pieces of empirical investigation in this field.[3]

Tugan rejected what he took to be the two explanations of crises advanced by Marx, namely, (1) that crises are produced by the falling tendency of the rate of profit, and (2) that crises result from the underconsumption of the masses. The first of these he disposed of on the alleged ground that a rising organic composition of capital, far from leading to a falling rate of profit as Marx supposed, must lead to a rising rate of profit.* The second he attempted to refute by an elaborate demonstration that there could be no overproduction or shortage of demand regardless of what happens to consumption, so long as production is correctly proportioned to the various branches of industry. The disproportionality theory was, therefore, in a sense a corollary of his criticism of Marx and was not in the least intended as an exposition of Marx's theory. But in order to explain what he meant by proportional production, which was supposed to be immune from all underconsumption difficulties, he drew heavily on the reproduction schemes which Marx had expounded in Volume II. Tugan was the first to put the reproduction schemes to this use, and, in so doing, he established a fashion which spread rapidly among Marxist writers. Soon the theory of disproportionality, developed in connection with the reproduction schemes, came to be regarded as Marx's own theory instead

* Tugan's 'proof' of this proposition is based upon a purely arbitrary assumption about what happens to the rate of surplus value and must therefore be regarded as invalid.

of as Tugan's; its real origin was overlooked or forgotten. What finally fixed the seal of authenticity on this new version of the disproportionality theory was its acceptance, at least in its positive implications, by Hilferding in his well-known book on finance capital several years later.[4] Hilferding was an 'orthodox' Marxist, looked up to as perhaps the outstanding economist of the German-speaking socialist movement; his book was certainly one of the most important since *Capital* itself. When Hilferding espoused the disproportionality theory its position was secure.

Marx would never have denied the validity of the theory. Probably he would have thought the use of the reproduction schemes to illustrate it a good idea. But he would have strongly resented the overtones and implications of the theory, and, to tell the truth, it is these rather than its rather meagre content that account for the popularity which it enjoyed. For, in fact, Tugan and most of those who followed, however unwittingly, in his footsteps, meant the disproportionality theory to be the only possible explanation of crises, and if this conclusion is accepted, the implications are indeed far-reaching. Let us examine this more closely.

If the development of capitalism is inseparable from a falling tendency of the rate of profit or a consumption demand which tends to lag ever further behind the requirements of production, or both, then the ills of the system can be expected to grow with age and the time when capitalist relations become a fetter on the further development of society's productive forces must come as certainly as night follows day.* Then, indeed, must the crises which periodically interrupt the economic life of society be regarded as a *memento mori* of the existing social order. But if these dire forebodings rest on a purely imaginary foundation, and if crises are really caused by nothing more intractable than disproportionalities in the productive process, then the existing social order seems to be secure enough, at least until people become sufficiently well-educated and morally advanced to want and deserve a better one. Meanwhile, not only need there be no collapse of capitalism, but much can be done even under capitalism to iron out the disproportionalities which are the cause of

* This problem is considered in detail below. See Chapters XI and XII.

much needless suffering. More than that: much is already being done, for as industry becomes organized in trusts and as government supervision over economic affairs progresses, is it not clear that the anarchy of capitalist production is increasingly removed? If the first of these alternative views is accepted, socialists must prepare for stormy weather ahead; they must even be ready, if need be, to force through a revolutionary solution of the contradictions of the existing order. But if the second alternative is accepted, socialists can look forward to an indefinite period of quiet educational work which, they can at least hope, will eventually be crowned with success in the peaceable adoption, by common consent, of the co-operative commonwealth.

Now there can be no doubt that at the heart of revisionism lay a will to believe that the latter is the only rational view. To bolster up and justify this will to believe became the main function of revisionist theorizing. From this point of view Tugan's disproportionality theory of crises, constructed on the basis of the very arguments which purported to disprove the falling rate of profit and the underconsumption theories, was very attractive. When it is recalled that in the years before the First World War the great majority of the intellectuals associated with German Social Democracy gravitated towards the revisionist camp—though many of them, like Kautsky and Hilferding, would have resented any questioning of their orthodoxy—the popularity of the disproportionality theory is not difficult to understand.

All this is now a part of the history of socialist thought, and it may seem like an attempt to revive dead issues to devote so much attention to the disproportionality theory today. For its intrinsic interest is not great, and recent Marxist literature on the crisis problem has shown a sound disposition to relegate it once again, as Marx himself did, to a position of secondary importance.* Nevertheless, there is still a very good reason for a careful analysis of Tugan's argument because in elaborating the disproportionality theory, Tugan was at the same time attempting to undermine all versions of the underconsumption explanation of crises. And in so doing he unknowingly provided the best key to an interpretation of Marx's own fragmentary and

* For a good recent criticism of disproportionality theories, see Natalie Moszkowska, *Zur Kritik Moderner Krisentheorien* (1935), Chapter v.

somewhat enigmatic statements on the relation between consumption and crises. We shall therefore find it useful to examine Tugan's reasoning as an introduction to the underconsumption theory of crises.

2. Crises Arising from Underconsumption

We have already had occasion to make use of reproduction schemes. In Chapter v a two-department scheme (Department i producing means of production, or constant capital, and Department ii producing consumption goods) was constructed on the assumption of simple reproduction (absence of capital accumulation). In Chapter vii three-department schemes (the consumption goods department being broken into two, producing respectively wage goods and capitalists' consumption goods) were utilized in analysing the relation between values and prices of production. In these the assumption of simple reproduction was retained. Tugan-Baranowsky always worked with three-department schemes, but the gist of his argument can be presented somewhat more simply with only two departments. We must now drop the assumption of simple reproduction, and examine the nature of the equilibrium conditions for expanded reproduction (capital accumulation). First, however, let us recall the equilibrium condition for simple reproduction.

$$\text{I} \qquad c_1 + v_1 + s_1 = w_1$$

$$\text{II} \qquad c_2 + v_2 + s_2 = w_2$$

If the supply of constant capital is to equal the demand arising from the need to replace worn-out constant capital, we must have

$$c_1 + v_1 + s_1 = c_1 + c_2$$

and if the supply of consumers goods is to absorb the entire income of both capitalists and workers, we must have

$$c_2 + v_2 + s_2 = v_1 + s_1 + v_2 + s_2$$

Each of these equations reduces to the simpler form

$$c_2 = v_1 + s_1$$

and if this condition is satisfied, equilibrium exists between the two departments. An amount of constant capital equal to c_1

must always be returned to the production process in Department I and hence never enters into the exchange with Department II; and similarly an amount of consumption goods equal to $v_2 + s_2$ is always consumed by the workers and capitalists of Department II and hence likewise does not enter into the exchange between the two departments.

In passing to expanded reproduction we shall assume, as Marx always does,* that workers continue to consume their entire incomes but that capitalists invest a part of theirs in enlarging the process of production. This means that capitalists lay out a part of their surplus value in purchasing additional means of production and additional labor power. If this is to be accomplished without difficulties, means of production over and above what is necessary to replace constant capital used up in the current production period must be produced, and consumption goods for additional workers must also be produced. We also assume that, with expanding incomes, capitalists raise their own consumption from year to year, though by less than the full amount of the increase in surplus value.

Surplus value can now conveniently be divided into four parts: first, an amount spent on consumption which is just sufficient to maintain capitalists' consumption at the level of the preceding period—call this s_c; second an increment of consumption—call this $s_{\Delta c}$; third, accumulation which serves to augment variable capital—call this s_{av}; and, fourth, accumulation which goes to purchase additional constant capital—call this s_{ac}. If we add the numerical subscripts to differentiate the items belonging to Department I from those belonging to Department II, the total reproduction scheme looks as follows:

$$c_1 + v_1 + \overbrace{s_{c1} + s_{\Delta c1} + s_{av1} + s_{ac1}}^{s_1} = w_1$$

$$c_2 + v_2 + \underbrace{s_{c2} + s_{\Delta c2} + s_{av2} + s_{ac2}}_{s_2} = w_2$$

* See above, p. 140 n.

The six terms included in the box correspond exactly to the scheme constructed on the assumption of simple reproduction; the remainder are added by passing to expanded reproduction.*

In order to discover the equilibrium condition for expanded reproduction we must proceed as before, that is to say, by equating all the items which represent a demand for constant capital to the total output of constant capital, and all the items which represent a demand for consumption goods to the total output of consumption goods. This gives us the following two equations:

$$c_1 + s_{ac1} + c_2 + s_{ac2} = c_1 + v_1 + s_{c1} + s_{\Delta c1} + s_{av1} + s_{ac1}$$

$$v_1 + s_{c1} + s_{\Delta c1} + s_{av1} + v_2 + s_{c2} + s_{\Delta c2} + s_{av2}$$
$$= c_2 + v_2 + s_{c2} + s_{\Delta c2} + s_{av2} + s_{ac2}$$

After simplification both of these reduce to the single condition

$$\boxed{c_2} + s_{ac2} = \boxed{v_1 + s_{c1}} + s_{\Delta c1} + s_{av1}$$

This is considerably more complicated than the simple reproduction case, but the two equilibrium conditions display, as might be expected, a definite structural similarity. The items enclosed in boxes on each side of the equation, in fact, constitute *ex definitione* the equilibrium condition for simple reproduction and must be equal independently of the rest of the items. Moreover, as before, a considerable number of items do not enter into the exchange between the two departments. An ever increasing amount of constant capital, produced in Department I, remains in Department I; while, of course, the expanding consumption of workers and capitalists in Department II is entirely supplied by the output of Department II.

Now, according to Tugan, the expanded reproduction

* Bukharin, in his formal presentation of the expanded reproduction scheme, makes the error of assuming that capitalists' consumption remains always the same. Hence he omits the item $s_{\Delta c}$. The same mistake crops up in his reasoning where he seems incapable of imagining an increase in capitalists' consumption. N. Bukharin, *Der Imperialismus und die Akkumulation des Kapitals*, pp. 10, 29 ff.

scheme * shows two things: first, if the part of surplus value which is annually added to capital is not divided among the various industries and departments in the correct proportions, a crisis is sure to be the result; and, second, if the increment to capital is divided in the correct proportions, no possible grounds for a crisis exist. Thus, the reproduction scheme at one and the same time demonstrates what is the cause of crises (disproportionality) and what is not (restricted consumption of the masses). Let us examine these two claims.

Tugan believed that the danger of disproportionality leading to a crisis really only arises in connection with newly accumulated capital. 'If it were not necessary to find investment for new capitals, if production were not spurred on by the capitalization of profits, the proportional division of social production would offer no great difficulties.' [5] But in the case of new investment, there can be no sound basis in experience for judging the pattern of new demand, each capitalist is making his own decisions without knowledge of what the others are doing, the correct proportions are, as the expanded reproduction scheme shows, related to one another in a complicated fashion: all in all the chance that the process will go forward smoothly and without interruptions is practically nonexistent. Since, as Tugan was careful to emphasize, accumulation is inseparable from capitalism, this is virtually the same as saying that crises are inevitable, at least until some effective form of planning can be introduced into the production process. Though it is not germane to the present inquiry, it may be added, for the sake of completeness, that Tugan builds this up into a theory of the business cycle by bringing in the workings of the credit system. Crisis and depression constitute a period during which idle loan capital piles up and interest rates are depressed. Presently new investment activity is once again embarked upon. For various reasons, among them the length of time necessary to complete many of the new projects, the latent disproportionality in the division of

* Tugan's reproduction schemes are presented in numerical terms, and the equilibrium conditions are in effect described rather than stated in equational form. Our purpose is to give the essence of his argument in briefer, more easily comprehensible, and at the same time more general form. For Tugan's exposition, see *Handelskrisen*, esp. Chapter I, and *Theoretische Grundlagen des Marxismus* (1905), Chapter IX.

the newly invested capital does not come to the surface until a considerable period of prosperity has been enjoyed. But eventually, when the new projects are in running order, the disproportionality becomes evident and soon precipitates the inevitable crisis. From this point the process merely repeats itself.

This theory is chiefly vulnerable on the grounds of its superficiality. But since it is not our intention to criticize Tugan's positive contribution to business-cycle theory, let us turn to his second contention, namely, that the expanded reproduction scheme also serves to demonstrate the impossibility of underconsumption. 'If social production were organized in accordance with a plan,' Tugan claimed, 'if the directors of production had complete knowledge of demand and the power to direct labor and capital from one branch of production to another, then, *however low social consumption might be*, the supply of commodities could never outstrip the demand.' [6]

It must be said at once that Tugan's 'proof' of this statement is purely formal and rests on manipulation of the reproduction schemes. Boiled down to its simplest terms it comes to this, that if the proportional division of output is precisely that which is prescribed by the equilibrium condition for expanded reproduction, then supply and demand must be in exact balance. When it is recalled that the equilibrium condition was derived by *assuming* a balance of supply and demand, this is hardly surprising.

At first sight, however, it might appear that even such tautological reasoning fails to support the conclusion that expanded reproduction can proceed indefinitely 'however low social consumption might be.' For if the capitalists of both departments accumulate at approximately the same rate—and there is no reason to make any other assumption—the reproduction scheme itself seems to show that equilibrium can be maintained only if both departments expand in a co-ordinated fashion, and of course the expansion of Department II necessarily implies an expansion of consumption. Let us try to construct a case of accumulation in both departments with social consumption remaining constant. All accumulation must take the form of purchase of additional constant capital, and capitalists must not increase their own consumption; otherwise social consumption would rise. This means that the $s_{\Delta c}$ and s_{av} items in the reproduction scheme are all zero. The scheme then looks as follows:

$$\text{I} \quad c_1 + v_1 + s_{c1} + s_{ac1}$$

$$\text{II} \quad c_2 + v_2 + s_{c2} + s_{ac2}$$

And the equilibrium condition reduces to the following form:

$$v_1 + s_{c1} = c_2 + s_{ac2}.$$

But we already know that v_1, s_{c1}, and c_2 are by definition the elements in expanded reproduction which correspond to simple reproduction, and hence that

$$v_1 + s_{c1} = c_2$$

must in any case be true. From this it follows that s_{ac2} must be zero; in other words, no accumulation takes place in Department II. Since this contradicts our original assumption, it seems that we must conclude that the case is an impossible one.

In reality, however, this conclusion arises from a certain inflexibility in the set-up of the reproduction scheme, for we have implicitly assumed that none of the capital and labor already employed in the previous period can migrate from one department to the other. If this assumption is dropped, some of the newly accumulated constant capital can go into each department while some variable capital (along with the laborers which it supports) can be shifted from Department II to Department I. If the proper proportions are maintained, the upshot will be that the output of Department I expands because more labor and means of production are employed there, while the output of Department II remains constant, the loss of labor being exactly offset by an increased utilization of constant capital. The organic composition of the total social capital rises, and production of means of production expands relative to production of consumption goods.

Essentially the same reasoning can be employed to construct a case of expanded reproduction, showing an increase in production of means of production coincident with an absolute but smaller decline in production of consumption goods, and this is what Tugan does.[7] Such a case, it should be noted, implies an absolute decline in the number of workers employed, hence contracting consumption by the working class as a whole, and no change in the consumption of the capitalists. Total output, however, steadily expands, and the proportion made up by means of production grows always larger. From the point of view of the workers, matters get worse and worse; but Tugan insists that capitalism is run by and for capitalists, and from their point of view there is never any shortage of demand for what they produce and hence no danger of a crisis. The only requisite is that the proper proportions must always be maintained among the various branches of production. Tugan pushes his reasoning to its logical conclusion:

If all workers except one disappear and are replaced by machines, then this one single worker will place the whole enormous mass of machinery in motion and with its assistance produce new machines—and the consumption goods of the capitalists. The working class will disappear, which will not in the least disturb the self-expansion process [*Verwertungsprozess*] of capital. The capitalists will receive no smaller mass of consumption goods, the entire product of one year will be realized and utilized by the production and consumption of the capitalists in the following year. Even if the capitalists desire to limit their own consumption, no difficulty is presented; in this case the production of capitalists' consumption goods partially ceases, and an even larger part of the social product consists of means of production, which serve the purpose of further expanding production. For example, iron and coal are produced which serve always to expand the production of iron and coal. The expanded production of iron and coal of each succeeding year uses up the increased mass of products turned out in the preceding year, until the supply of necessary minerals is exhausted.[8]

Few economists have gone to such extremes in denying the interdependence of production and consumption.* But at any

* It would be wrong, however, to suppose that in holding this opinion Tugan presents an isolated case among reputable economists. In a passage to which Dobb calls attention, J. B. Clark once wrote: 'If capitalists were . . . resolved to save all of their incomes, present and future, beyond a fixed amount, they would capitalize, first, a part of their present means, and then all later income from the capital so created. They would build

rate it is impossible to charge Tugan with inconsistency. He began playing with reproduction schemes, established certain rules of the game, and discovered that by persistence in writing one row of figures after another he could produce the most surprising results. It was not easy, even for Tugan, to take the final step of attributing the characteristics of his schemes to the real world, but, after a moment's hesitation, he took the plunge:

> This may all sound very strange, yes perhaps like the greatest nonsense. Perhaps—truth is certainly not always an easy thing to understand; nevertheless it remains truth. As truth naturally I do not mean the wholly arbitrary and unreal assumption that the replacement of manual labor by machinery leads to an absolute diminution in the number of workers (this hypothesis has only served to show that my theory, even if driven to the limit of unreality, does not break down), but rather the thesis that, given a proportional distribution of social production, no decline in social consumption is capable of producing a superfluous product.[9]

The reception which Tugan's theory was accorded by Marxist writers was unanimously and emphatically unfavorable. Not all of them by any means regarded a shortage of consumption as an inevitable or even a very important cause of crises, but none could stomach the idea that production could expand indefinitely without any regard to the level or trend of consumption. It may not be unprofitable to run over very briefly some of the reactions which Tugan's theory called forth.

One of the earliest to review Tugan's first book was Conrad Schmidt, one of the ablest of the revisionists. Writing in the

more mills that should make more mills for ever. This case presents no glut; but it is an unreal case.' Introduction to Karl Rodbertus, *Overproduction and Crisis* (English trans. 1898), p. 15. More recently, Knight has stated: 'Given accurate planning . . . the speed at which the market will absorb funds in the process of real investment can never be less than the rate at which funds are forthcoming . . . It is a purely technological matter, and there is no reason why the entire productive capacity of society should not be used to construct new capital goods, if the population should decide to save all its income!' F. H. Knight, 'The Quantity of Capital and the Rate of Interest,' *Journal of Political Economy*, October 1936, p. 639. These statements reflect a view very similar to that of Tugan, but neither of the two writers went much beyond the bare statement of principle.

theoretical organ of the revisionists, Schmidt, while agreeing fully with Tugan that the breakdown of capitalism was a most unlikely eventuality, nevertheless took issue sharply with the latter's view on the connection between production and consumption. 'The "purposes of production," for which production takes place,' Schmidt wrote, 'are purposes which in the final analysis and in one way or another proceed from the demand for consumption goods, purposes which are comprehensible only when taken in connection with and continuously referred back to consumption demand. Definitive or consumption demand is the enlivening force which, throughout the entire economy, keeps the huge appartus of production in motion.' [10]

A little later Kautsky, at the time universally regarded as the authoritative spokesman of Marxism, published a review of the same book in the official theoretical organ of the Social Democratic party. Kautsky was no less severe than Schmidt:

> The capitalist may equate men and machines as much as he likes, society remains a society of men and never one of machines; social relations remain always relations of man to man, never the relations of men to machines. It is for this reason that in the final analysis human labor remains the value-creating factor, and it is for this reason also in the final analysis that the extension of *human* consumption exercises the decisive influence over the expansion of production . . . Production is and remains production for human consumption.[11]

Louis B. Boudin, the outstanding American Marxist theorist in the years before the First World War, a member of the orthodox school, joined in the attack on Tugan. Calling the latter's theory 'an utter absurdity' and 'the veriest rot,' Boudin claimed that 'means of production . . . are nothing more than MEANS to the *production of consumable goods*. Where, therefore, there is no demand for the consumable goods ultimately to be produced by their means, their production is overproduction, and is so found to be when the ultimate test is applied.' [12]

Even Hilferding, though his own crisis theory owed much to Tugan, was in sharp disagreement on this important point:

> [Tugan] sees only the specific economic forms of capitalist production and therefore overlooks the natural conditions which

are common to all production whatever its historical form; in this way he arrives at the strange notion of production which has nothing but production in view while consumption appears only as a troublesome accident. If this is 'madness' it still has 'method' and even Marxist method, since the analysis of the historical form of capitalist production is specifically Marxian. It is Marxism gone crazy, but still Marxism, that makes Tugan's theory so peculiar and so stimulating. Tugan feels this himself, though he does not realize it. Hence his sharp polemic against the 'common sense' of his opponents.[13]

That Rosa Luxemburg, the queen of underconsumptionists, should have scornfully rejected Tugan's reasoning was, of course, to be expected. 'The view that production of means of production is independent of consumption,' she wrote, 'is naturally a vulgar economic fantasy of Tugan-Baranowsky.' *

Finally, we may bring this review of opinion to a close with the measured statement of Bukharin, frequently the spokesman in matters of political economy for the Bolsheviks. Maintaining that the essence of 'Tugan-Baranowskyism' consists 'in cutting production off from consumption and completely isolating it,' Bukharin had the following to say:

> If we had to do with a market which is emancipated from consumption, thus with a closed circle of production of means of production in which the branches of production mutually serve each other, in other words, if we had a strange production system such as that pictured by the lively imagination of Tugan, then to be sure a general overproduction would be impossible . . . We reach entirely different results if, instead of the theory of Tugan-Baranowsky, we hold to the correct theory, the theory of Marx. We have then a chain of related industries providing each other with markets which follow a certain definite order determined by the technical-economic continuity of the whole process of production. This chain ends, however, with the production of consumption goods which can . . . only go *directly* into personal consumption . . .[14]

* *Die Akkumulation des Kapitals. Ein Beitrag zur ökonomischen Erklärung des Imperialismus* (1922), p. 291. This work was first published in 1912 and was followed during the war with an answer to its critics entitled *Die Akkumulation des Kapitals oder was die Epigonen aus der Marxschen Theorie gemacht haben. Eine Antikritik.* The similarity in the titles may easily lead to confusion.

Behind all these criticisms of Tugan's theory lies one single idea, namely, that the process of production is and must remain, regardless of its historical form, a process of producing goods for human consumption. Any attempt to get away from this fundamental fact represents a flight from reality which must end in theoretical bankruptcy. Tugan's ability to construct reproduction schemes which apparently demonstrate the opposite does not change matters one whit: production is production for consumption, Tugan and his reproduction schemes to the contrary notwithstanding. On this issue all shades of Marxist opinion were in absolute agreement. But the question naturally arises: does this not stand in crass contradiction to the view so frequently reiterated by Marx himself that the end and aim of capitalist production is *not* consumption but rather the expansion of values? Is it not a glaring form of the error which Marx warned against when he said: 'It is never to be forgotten that in the case of capitalist production it is not directly a question of use value, but of exchange value, and more particularly of the expansion of surplus value'? [15]

The answer is to be found in the recognition that a contradiction between the ends of production regarded as a natural-technical process of creating use values, and the ends of capitalism regarded as a historical system of expanding exchange value does exist. Not only does it exist; it constitutes the fundamental contradiction of capitalist society from which all other contradictions are ultimately derived.

Traditional political economy tries to slur over or deny this contradiction by the device of assuming that the subjective aim of capitalist production is identical with the objective aim of production in general, namely, the augmentation of utility. Tugan, on the other hand, adopted the opposite method of assuming that the indefinite expansion of exchange value is compatible with the ends of production in general. Marxian political economy, in contrast to both, not only recognizes the contradiction but proclaims it to the skies and rests on this foundation its proof that capitalism is no more permanent than the various social systems which have preceded it.

We must now attempt to trace this line of thought, in so far as it is related to the problem of crises, in the writings of Marx himself, and then, having accomplished this, to present a logically watertight formulation of the much misunderstood 'underconsumption' theory of capitalist crises.

No more than his followers did Marx share Tugan's idea that production, regarded as a natural process common to all historical epochs, could in some fashion provide its own directives. In the unfinished 'Introduction to the Critique of Political Economy,' he was explicit on this point:

> Consumption produces production by creating the necessity for new production, i.e. by providing the ideal, inward, impelling cause which constitutes the prerequisite of production. Consumption furnishes the impulse for production as well as its object, which plays in production the part of its guiding aim. It is clear that while production furnishes the material object of consumption, consumption provides the ideal object of production, as its image, its want, its impulse, and its purpose. It furnishes the object of production in its subjective form. No wants, no production. But consumption reproduces the want.[16]

Even under capitalism, where the various branches of production acquire a considerable degree of apparent independence of one another, means of production are never produced except with a view to their ultimate utilization, direct or indirect, in turning out consumption goods.

> . . . a continuous circulation takes place between constant capital and constant capital (even without considering any accelerated accumulation), which is in so far independent of individual consumption as it never enters into such consumption, but which is nevertheless definitely limited by it, because the production of constant capital never takes place for its own sake, but solely because more of this capital is needed in those spheres of production whose products pass into individual consumption.[17]

Nevertheless, the social relations of capitalist production enforce a restriction of consumption and at the same time spur the capitalists on to attempt an unlimited expansion of production. In a powerful passage, which deserves to be widely known, Marx describes this most fundamental characteristic of capitalism:

The consumption of the worker is on the average equal to his costs of production not to what he produces. The entire surplus he produces for others . . . Moreover the industrial capitalist, who drives the worker to this overproduction (i.e. production over and above his own needs) and employs every means to increase as much as possible this relative overproduction as contrasted to the necessary production, appropriates the surplus product directly. But as personified capital, he produces for the sake of production, wants enrichment for the sake of enrichment. In so far as he is a mere functionary of capital, hence a bearer of capitalist production, he concerns himself with exchange value and its enlargement, not with use value and the increase of its size. It is a question of the expansion of abstract wealth, of the increasing appropriation of the labor of others. He is driven by exactly the same urge to get rich as the miser, only he satisfies it not in the illusory form of building a hoard of gold and silver, but in capital formation which is actual production. If the overproduction of the laborer is *production for others*, then the production of the normal capitalist, as he should be, the industrial capitalist, is *production for the sake of production*. The more his wealth grows, the more he falls behind this ideal and becomes wasteful himself for the sake of displaying his wealth. But he always enjoys his wealth with a bad conscience, with the check of economy and enrichment. He remains, in spite of all spending, like the miser, essentially greedy. When Sismondi says that the development of the productive power of labor makes it possible for the worker to enjoy ever more consumption which, however, if he actually were to receive it, would render him unfit for work (as a wage laborer), it is no less true that the industrial capitalist becomes more or less unsuited for his function as soon as he thinks of enjoying his wealth, as soon as he wants accumulation for the sake of enjoyment instead of the enjoyment of accumulation. He is thus also a producer of *overproduction*, production for others.*

Here, then, we can see the elements of what Marx in one place calls 'the fundamental contradiction' of capitalism: production

* *Theorien über den Mehrwert* I, pp. 377-9. Marx goes on to note that over against the producers, whose consumption is limited to a minimum, stand pure consumers in the form of landlords, the state, the church, et cetera. The treatment of these and other 'third parties' who consume without producing is reserved until Chapter XII below. That they are, in practice, of great importance goes without saying.

entirely lacks an objective unless it is directed towards a definite goal in consumption, but capitalism attempts to expand production without any reference to the consumption which alone can give it meaning. 'He [Sismondi] feels the fundamental contradiction: on the one hand unfettered productive power and increase of wealth which at the same time consists of commodities and must be turned into money; on the other hand as a foundation the limitation [of the consumption] of the mass of producers to the necessary means of subsistence.'[18]

Against this background, the more familiar passages in which Marx relates crises and stagnant production to the magnitude of consumption acquire a meaning and significance which they might otherwise lack. The most substantial, and in some ways the most explicit of these passages is the following:

> The creation of . . . surplus value is the object of the direct process of production. As soon as the available quantity of surplus value has been materialized in commodities, surplus value has been produced . . . Now comes the second act of the process. The entire mass of commodities . . . must be sold. If this is not done, or only partly accomplished, or only at prices which are below the prices of production, the laborer has been none the less exploited, but his exploitation does not realize as much for the capitalist. It may yield no surplus value at all for him, or only realize a portion of the produced surplus value, or it may even mean a partial or complete loss of his capital. The conditions of direct exploitation and those of the realization of surplus value are not identical. They are separated logically as well as by time and space. The first are only limited by the productive power of society, the last by the proportional relations of the various lines of production and by the consuming power of society. This last-named power is not determined either by the absolute productive power or by the absolute consuming power, but by the consuming power based on antagonistic conditions of distribution, which reduces the consumption of the great mass of the population to a variable minimum within more or less narrow limits. The consuming power is further restricted by the tendency to accumulate, the greed for an expansion of capital and a production of surplus value on an enlarged scale. This is a law of capitalist production imposed by incessant revolutions in the methods of production . . . , the resulting

> depreciation of existing capital, the general competitive struggle and the necessity of improving the product and expanding the scale of production for the sake of self-preservation and on penalty of failure. The market must, therefore, be continually extended, so that its interrelations and the conditions regulating them assume more and more the form of a natural law independent of the producers and become ever more uncontrollable. This internal contradiction seeks to balance itself by an expansion of the outlying fields of production. But to the extent that the productive power develops, it finds itself at variance with the narrow basis on which the condition of consumption rests. On this self-contradictory basis it is no contradiction at all that there should be an excess of capital simultaneously with an excess of population. For while a combination of these two would indeed increase the mass of the produced surplus value, it would at the same time intensify the contradiction between the conditions under which this surplus value is produced and those under which it is realized.[19]

Here Marx indicates a belief that an interruption of production may result from capitalists' inability to sell commodities at their values. The trouble is traced to a restricted volume of consumption demand—restricted by low wages plus capitalists' 'tendency to accumulate.' This does not necessarily mean, however, that a decline in output must occur first in the consumption-goods department. Whether it will or not depends upon the form of the relation existing between production of means of production and production of consumption goods. Marx's silence on this issue merely shows that he had never worked the 'underconsumption' theory out in any detail.

In the preceding quotation depression is pictured as a period in which expansion of production is held up by an insufficient demand for the final fruit of production, namely, consumption goods. The corresponding view of prosperity envisages a period in which more means of production are produced than can ultimately be utilized. Thus,

> the epochs in which capitalist production exerts all its forces are always periods of overproduction, because the forces of production can never be utilized beyond the point at which surplus value can be not only produced but also realized; but the sale

of commodities, the realization of the commodity capital and hence also of the surplus value, is limited not only by the consumption requirements of society in general, but by the consumption requirements of a society in which the great majority are poor and must always remain poor.*

The last two statements quoted from Marx contain the implication that stagnation of production, in the sense of less-than-capacity utilization of productive resources, is to be regarded as the normal state of affairs under capitalist conditions, for it is only from this standpoint that periods of full utilization can be rationally designated as 'periods of overproduction.' If this view is adopted, the whole crisis problem appears in a new light. Emphasis shifts from the question: 'What brings on crisis and depression?' to its opposite: 'What brings on expansion?' While the two questions are in no way mutually exclusive, business-cycle literature has always in the past tended to emphasize the former; in the course of our further inquiry we shall find that the latter leads to results of at least equal importance. Here again, however, it cannot be maintained that Marx developed the implications of his own suggestion.

Finally, we may quote what appears to be Marx's most clear-cut statement in favor of an underconsumption theory of crises:

> The last cause of all real crises always remains the poverty and restricted consumption of the masses as compared to the tendency of capitalist production to develop the productive forces in such a way that only the absolute power of consumption of the entire society would be their limit.[20]

In its context this statement has the character of a parenthetical remark; and the interpretation which ought to be placed

* *Capital* II, p. 363 n. The clause 'because the forces of production can never be utilized beyond the point at which surplus value can be not only produced but also realized' reads in the original, 'weil die Produktionspotenzen nie soweit angewandt werden können, dass dadurch mehr Wert nicht nur produziert, sondern realiziert werden kann.' Taken either literally or in accordance with the translation of the Kerr edition, this passage says the opposite of what Marx clearly intended to say. For it appears to mean that production can never be carried *as far as* the point at which the additional value can be realized, whereas the sense of the whole passage obviously requires that it should mean that production can never be carried *beyond* this point. I have therefore made this correction in the version presented in the text.

upon the expression 'the last cause of all real crises' remains unclarified. The principle involved, however, is obviously identical with that enunciated in the two preceding quotations.

Other passages stressing the contradiction between capitalism's urge to expand production and its correlative concern to limit consumption could be presented,[21] but they would add little to what has already been brought out. How far can we go, then, in saying that we have here a developed underconsumption theory of crises? No clear-cut answer to this question seems possible. Certainly the passages quoted have been taken from widely scattered parts of Marx's economic writings, and at no point is the problem subjected to the kind of prolonged and painstaking analysis which one frequently meets in his work. On this ground it could be maintained that Marx regarded underconsumption as one aspect, but on the whole not a very important aspect, of the crisis problem. This appears to be the opinion of Dobb,[22] and there is no doubt much to back it up. Another view is possible, however, namely, that in these scattered passages Marx was giving advance notice of a line of reasoning which, if he had lived to complete his theoretical work, would have been of primary importance in the overall picture of the capitalist economy. Many of his followers have evidently been of this opinion, and, on the whole, it seems to me the more reasonable of the two alternatives.

If this is so, however, it ought to be possible to construct, with the aid of Marx's analytical concepts, a logical and detailed theory where Marx himself left only very general directives. Yet it cannot be said that any Marxist writer has been very successful along this line. Rosa Luxemburg's attempt, certainly the most elaborate and probably the one to attract more adherents than any other, was a clear failure from a logical standpoint.* Kautsky did little more than repeat the statements of Marx concerning the general dependence of production on the market for consumption goods. Writing in 1902, Kautsky described 'the crisis theory which "orthodox" Marxists generally attribute to Marx' in the following terms:

* For further consideration of Rosa Luxemburg's theory, see pp. 202 ff.

> The capitalists and the laborers whom they exploit provide, with the growth of the wealth of the former and of the number of the latter, what is, to be sure, a steadily growing market for the means of consumption produced by capitalist industry; the market grows, however, less rapidly than the accumulation of capital and the rise in the productivity of labor. Capitalist industry must, therefore, seek an additional market outside of its domain in non-capitalist nations and strata of the population. Such a market it finds and expands more and more, but not fast enough . . . In this way every period of prosperity, which follows a significant widening of the market, is foredoomed to short life, and the crisis becomes its necessary end.[23]

Beyond bringing in the 'non-capitalist nations and strata of the population'—incidentally an interesting foreshadowing of Rosa Luxemburg's theory—Kautsky has here nothing to add to the statements already quoted from Marx. It is even true that Kautsky's formulation of the relation between consumption and production is less specific, and hence less satisfactory than Marx's own.

Failure to make any significant progress with the underconsumption theory, to which should perhaps be added the repeated attacks of hostile critics, tended more and more to divert the attention of Marxist writers from this approach to the problem of crises. One of the weightiest treatises written in Germany during the '20s, that of Henryk Grossmann,* flatly denied the possibility of insufficient consumption; and, as we have already noted, the outstanding present-day English Marxist economist, Maurice Dobb, assigns a role to underconsumption which is distinctly secondary to that of the falling tendency of the rate of profit.

If the underconsumption theory is to regain prestige and take a place among the important and accepted principles of Marxian economics, it seems clear that a careful formulation, free of the objections which have been levelled at earlier versions, is needed. In the remainder of this chapter an attempt will be made to provide such a formulation. The logical argument is based upon the algebraic appendix at the end of the chapter. In general, no con-

* *Das Akkumulations- und Zusammenbruchsgesetz des kapitalistischen Systems* (1929). Grossmann's own theory is considered below, pp. 209 ff.

cepts or assumptions are involved which are not implicitly or explicitly present in the main body of Marx's theory. Thus the intention is neither to construct an 'original' theory, nor to revise Marx's theory, but rather to supplement his work at a point where it is incomplete.

The real task of an underconsumption theory is to demonstrate that capitalism has an inherent *tendency* to expand the capacity to produce consumption goods more rapidly than the demand for consumption goods. To put the point in another way, it must be shown that there is a tendency to utilize resources in such a way as to distort the relation between potential supply of and potential demand for consumption goods. This tendency may manifest itself in one of two ways. Either (1) capacity is actually expanded and the difficulty becomes apparent only when an increasing volume of consumption goods begins to come on the market. There will then be a point beyond which supply exceeds demand at normally profitable prices, and as this point is passed production of consumption goods, or production of additional capacity, or more likely both, will be curtailed. In this case, then, the tendency in question manifests itself in a crisis. Or (2) there are idle productive resources which are not utilized to produce additional capacity, because it is realized that the additional capacity would be redundant relative to the demand for the commodities it could produce. In this case, the tendency does not manifest itself in a crisis, but rather in stagnation of production. It follows that if the tendency to underconsumption can be established, it can serve to explain both crises and periods of stagnation. At the same time, however, it must be expected that there are many forces which counteract the tendency to underconsumption, so that for long periods the latter may remain latent and inoperative. For the present we shall attempt only to establish the tendency to underconsumption, leaving the counteracting forces and their mutual interaction for consideration in Chapter XII.

The procedure is the following: to assume that all productive resources are continuously fully utilized and then to demonstrate that, in the absence of counteracting forces, this leads to a contradiction. The conclusion is then indicated that the contradiction can be 'solved' only by a violation of the original assumption, which, in turn, must mean in practice, by crises and stagnations.

We assume, as before, that workers consume all of their wages and that the surplus value accruing to capitalists, which steadily grows larger, can be divided into four parts: a first which maintains their consumption at its previous level; a second which increases their consumption; a third which is accumulated and serves to employ additional workers; and a fourth which is accumulated and adds to the stock of constant capital. The third and fourth parts constitute *accumulation* in Marx's sense of the term; the fourth alone is *investment* in the usage of modern business-cycle literature. It will be convenient to follow this terminology here; the reader should, therefore, be careful to keep in mind that accumulation by capitalists is in part consumed by workers, and in part invested in additional means of production. The classical economists very often made the mistake of assuming that all accumulation is consumed; modern theorists not infrequently go to the opposite extreme by assuming that all accumulation is invested.*

Now the basic fact of capitalism, on which the behavior of the system ultimately depends, is the drive of capitalists to get rich. Satisfying this desire requires two steps: (1) making as much profit as possible, and (2) accumulating as large a part of it as possible. The first involves steadily improving the methods of production, chiefly by using more and more machines and materials per worker; the second involves accumulating larger and larger proportions of a growing profit total. Translating this into the terminology of the previous paragraph we get the following: that accumulation rises as a proportion of surplus value and that investment rises as a proportion of accumulation. All the while consumption is rising because capitalists increase their own consumption and lay out a part of their accumulation in increased wages. But, and this is the significant point, since the increment of capitalists' consumption is a diminishing proportion of total surplus value, and since the increment of wages is a diminishing proportion of total accumulation, it follows that the rate of growth of consumption (i.e. the ratio of increment of

* For a fuller discussion of this problem, see Appendix A below.

consumption to total consumption) declines relative to the rate of growth of means of production (i.e. the ratio of investment to total means of production). In other words, *the ratio of the rate of growth of consumption to the rate of growth of means of production declines.* This is a result which flows logically from the characteristic pattern of capitalists' behavior.

If we now change our angle of vision and look upon production as a natural technical process of creating use values, we see that a definite relation must exist between the mass of means of production (assuming, it will be remembered, that they are fully utilized) and the output of consumption goods. Moreover, a definite relation must similarly exist between changes in the stock of means of production (investment) and changes in the output of consumption goods. These relations are ultimately determined by the technical characteristics of production and accordingly can vary with the progressive development of methods of production. Such evidence as we have, however, strongly suggests a remarkably high degree of stability for a reasonably well-developed capitalist economy. In other words, it appears that over long periods a given percentage increase in the stock of means of production will generally be accompanied by approximately the same percentage increase in output.* On this basis we are justified in making the assumption that the technically determined relation between stock of means of production and output of consumption goods remains constant. If we start from a position of equilibrium, it then follows that a given rate of increase of means of production will be accompanied by an equal rate of increase in the output of consumption goods. In other words, *the ratio of the rate of growth in the output of consumption goods to the rate of growth of means of production remains constant.* This conclusion follows from a consideration of production as an organized and synchronized process of making useful articles for human consumption.

The essence of the underconsumption theory can now be very briefly stated. Since capitalists, who control the direction of re-

* See the statistical study of Carl Snyder, 'Capital Supply and National Well-Being,' *American Economic Review,* June 1936. The fact that Snyder's conclusions are for the most part both illogical and irrelevant unfortunately mars what is otherwise a very valuable piece of work.

sources and funds, act in such a way as to produce a steady decline in the ratio

$$\frac{\text{rate of growth of consumption}}{\text{rate of growth of means of production}}$$

and since the nature of the production process enforces at least approximate stability in the ratio

$$\frac{\text{rate of growth in the output of consumption goods}}{\text{rate of growth of means of production}}$$

it follows that there is an inherent tendency for the growth in consumption to fall behind the growth in the output of consumption goods. As has already been pointed out, this tendency may express itself either in crises or in stagnation, or in both.

We have spoken of a tendency for consumption to lag behind the output of consumption goods. Since, however, the numerator and denominator, in both of the foregoing ratios, are functionally related in such a way that it would be impossible to subtract from one without adding to the other, it is equally logical to speak of a tendency for the provision of means of production to exceed the requirements for means of production. Properly understood, therefore, 'underconsumption' and 'overproduction' are opposite sides of the same coin. If this is kept in mind, it should not be a cause of surprise that an 'underconsumption' crisis may first break out in the sphere of production of means of production, while an 'overproduction' crisis may first break out in the sphere of production of consumption goods. The label used is a matter of taste, the point of origin a relatively unimportant detail dependent upon a multitude of particular circumstances.

It must be emphasized again that we have here to do with a *tendency* to underconsumption, which is always present but which may be fully or partially offset by counteracting forces of which as yet no account has been taken. The nature of these counteracting forces and their relative strength at various stages of capitalist development will be treated in Chapter XII.

A significant point emerges from this discussion, namely that it is incorrect to oppose 'disproportionality' to 'underconsumption' as a cause of crises; and that, in so doing, Tugan-Baranowsky succeeded only in confusing the real issues. For it now appears that underconsumption is precisely a special case of disproportionality—disproportionality between the growth of demand for consumption goods and the growth of capacity to produce consumption goods. This disproportionality, however, in contrast to the kind envisaged by Tugan, arises not from the uncoordinated and planless character of capitalism, but from the inner nature of capitalism, namely 'that capital and its self-expansion appear as the starting and closing point, as the motive and aim of production; that production is merely production for *capital*, and not vice versa, the means of production mere means for an ever expanding system of the life process for the benefit of the *society* of producers.' [24]

The only Marxist writers, aside from Marx himself, who correctly understood the general relation between disproportionality, underconsumption, and crises were Lenin and his followers, particularly Bukharin. Lenin's own writings * on the subject were not extensive and were almost wholly embodied in a series of polemics against the populist authors (*Narodniki*) who exercised a considerable influence in Russian intellectual circles during the 1890s. The *Narodniki* were extreme and dogmatic underconsumptionists who maintained that capitalism could never expand on the basis of the internal market and therefore must rely for its continued growth on capturing an ever-larger foreign market. Russia, they argued, had appeared on the stage too late to compete successfully for the foreign market with the older industrial nations of Western Europe and America. Hence Russian capitalism was doomed to degeneration and decay from its very birth and could under no circumstances be considered a progressive force. From this they deduced that Russian socialism could not rely on the growth of a revolutionary working class but must rather draw its support from the countryside—from the peasantry with its age-old institutions of common property and its bitter hatred for a land-owning aristocracy which lived from the most brutal kind of exploitation.

This whole conception of the role of capitalism in Russia was

* The most important passages relating to crises are collected in an appendix to Volume II of the Marx-Engels-Lenin edition of *Capital* (in German).

energetically opposed by Lenin. To him, capitalism was, under the specific conditions existing in Russia at the time, a progressive force which was calling into being the bearers of the socialist future, the industrial working class. In order to support this position he attacked the populist theory at its roots, namely, in the doctrine of the inexpansibility of the internal market. But in doing so he refused to go to the opposite extreme, represented by Tugan-Baranowsky and Bulgakov,* which maintained the indefinite expansibility of the internal market so long as the correct proportions between the individual branches of production were observed. Lenin held that a contradiction between production and consumption, in other words a tendency to underconsumption, certainly does exist in capitalism. 'Between the limitless striving for expansion of production, which is the very essence of capitalism, and the restricted consumption of the masses . . . there is undoubtedly a contradiction.'[25] This was a denial of the Tugan position. But it did not lead to the populist conclusion:

> . . . there is nothing more stupid than to deduce from the contradictions of capitalism its impossibility, its unprogressive character, etc.—that is flight from an unpleasant but undoubted reality into the cloud world of romantic fantasies. The contradiction between the limitless striving for expansion of production and the limited capacity for consumption is not the only contradiction of capitalism, which in general can neither exist nor develop without contradictions. The contradictions of capitalism testify to its historical-transitional character, explain the conditions and causes of its downfall and its transformation into a higher form—but they exclude neither the possibility of capitalism nor its progressiveness in comparison with earlier systems of social economy.[26]

In crisis theory Lenin took a closely related position, though he seems not to have worked it out in any detail. He avowed himself an adherent of the theory of disproportionality arising from the anarchy of capitalist production, but emphatically de-

* I have not had access to any of the works of Bulgakov, though it appears that some, at any rate, were translated into German. Judging from the quotations and comments of Lenin and Rosa Luxemburg, Bulgakov was a very able theorist, possibly superior to Tugan-Baranowsky.

clared that this did not deny the importance and relevance of the tendency to underconsumption, stating clearly that underconsumption, so far from contradicting the disproportionality explanation, is merely one aspect of it: 'The "consuming power of society," and "the proportionality of the various branches of production"—these are absolutely not individual, independent, unconnected conditions. On the contrary, a certain state of consumption is one of the elements of proportionality.' [27]

Bukharin followed closely in the footsteps of Lenin. He distinguished two types of crisis theory. The first, which he rejected, holds that 'crises arise from disproportionality between the individual branches of production. The factor of consumption plays no part.' The second, that of 'Marx, Lenin and the orthodox Marxists,' which Bukharin accepted, holds that 'crises arise from disproportionality in social production. The factor of consumption, however, forms a part of this disproportionality.' [28]

In principle, the position of Lenin and Bukharin, like that of Marx himself, is unobjectionable. But, again like Marx, their demonstration of the tendency to underconsumption is fragmentary and incomplete. It is to be hoped that the exposition of this chapter will serve to remove the doubts and hesitations which have hitherto prevented many Marxist economists from accepting the theory of underconsumption as one aspect—and a very important aspect—of the whole crisis problem.

Appendix to Chapter X

The following treatment of underconsumption is based upon the last book published by Otto Bauer before his death.[1] Bauer's highly interesting suggestions are essentially correct though they are not presented quite accurately and they do not bring out with sufficient clarity the connection between underconsumption and the basic characteristics of capitalist production.*

If I is the net national income in value terms, w the total wage bill (= workers' consumption), l the part of surplus value consumed by capitalists, and k the part of surplus value added to

* It is interesting to note that in none of his earlier writings did Bauer show any inclination to accept an underconsumption theory.

constant capital ($=$ investment), then we have the following equation:

$$I = w + l + k \qquad (1)$$

All of these concepts, of course, represent rates of flow per unit of time. In the case of investment, this means that k is essentially the rate of growth of the total stock of means of production. In other words, if K is the total stock of means of production, then $k = dK/dt$.

We assume that the national income steadily rises and that each of its three component parts also rises. Thus if we regard w and l as functions of k, it will always be true that as k increases w and l will also increase. But since it is a fundamental feature of capitalism that an increasing proportion of surplus value tends to be accumulated and an increasing proportion of accumulation tends to be invested, both w and l must grow less rapidly than k. Hence we have:

$$w = f(k) \text{ such that } 0 < f'(k) < 1 \text{ and } f''(k) < 0 \qquad (2)$$

and similarly:

$$l = \phi(k) \text{ such that } 0 < \phi'(k) < 1 \text{ and } \phi''(k) < 0 \qquad (3)$$

Let us now assume, in accordance with the argument put forward in Chapter x, that the output of consumption goods must be proportional to the stock of means of production. This implies that the rate of growth of means of production ($=$ investment) is proportional to the increase in consumption goods output. Hence if the increase in consumption in the time dt is $dw + dl$, there will be required an addition to means of production, say c, such that

$$c = \lambda(dw + dl) \qquad (4)$$

where λ is the factor of proportionality.* (Note that c, like k above, is essentially a derivative with respect to time.)

If a smooth and uninterrupted development is to take place, it is clear that c, the rate of investment required by the growth of consumption, must behave in the same way as k, the rate of

* λ is essentially the relation described in modern business cycle literature as 'the acceleration principle' or simply as 'the relation.'

investment dictated by the typical capitalist behavior pattern. Hence if $dc/dt \neq dk/dt$ we shall have a contradiction.

From (1) we have:

$$\frac{d^2I}{dt^2} = \frac{d^2w}{dt^2} + \frac{d^2l}{dt^2} + \frac{d^2k}{dt^2} \tag{5}$$

And since from (4):

$$\frac{dc}{dt} = \lambda\left(\frac{d^2w}{dt^2} + \frac{d^2l}{dt^2}\right) \tag{6}$$

We can write:

$$\frac{dc}{dt} = \lambda\left(\frac{d^2I}{dt^2} - \frac{d^2k}{dt^2}\right) \tag{7}$$

Now, taking account of (2) and (3):

$$\frac{d^2I}{dt^2} = [f'(k) + \phi'(k) + 1]\frac{d^2k}{dt^2} + [f''(k) + \phi''(k)]\left(\frac{dk}{dt}\right)^2 \tag{8}$$

If the national income is increasing at a constant or declining rate, i.e. if $d^2I/dt^2 \lesseqgtr 0$, then it follows from (8) and the conditions imposed in (2) and (3) that

$$\frac{d^2I}{dt^2} - \frac{d^2k}{dt^2} < 0 \tag{9}$$

From (7) and (9) then:

$$\frac{dc}{dt} < 0 \tag{10}$$

But since

$$\frac{dk}{dt} = \frac{\frac{dI}{dt}}{f'(k) + \phi'(k) + 1} \tag{11}$$

it is evident that

$$\frac{dk}{dt} > 0$$

Taken together (10) and (12) indicate a contradiction. Capitalists tend to increase the rate of investment ($dk/dt > 0$), but the way they allow consumption to grow warrants only a declining rate of investment ($dc/dt < 0$). Hence if the rate of investment actually does increase, the output of consumption goods will display a continuous tendency to outrun the demand.

It will be noticed that this conclusion is reached on the assumption that national income in value terms is growing at a constant or declining rate. If the national income grows at an increasing rate, dc/dt may be positive and it may be equal to dk/dt, though neither of these things is necessarily true. It is quite possible that national income should grow at an increasing rate in a 'young' capitalist country where manpower is abundant or rapidly increasing. Our analysis therefore suggests that such a country is unlikely to be beset with serious underconsumption difficulties. But in an 'old' capitalist country—and all the advanced capitalist countries with the possible exception of Japan certainly deserve this designation today—national income is almost certain to be growing at a declining rate. So far as capitalism is concerned we are undoubtedly justified in calling underconsumption a disease of old age. For further arguments supporting this conclusion the reader is referred to Chapter XII below.

XI

THE BREAKDOWN CONTROVERSY

1. Introduction

We are now in a position to pose a question which could be no more than suggested at an earlier stage. Are crises capitalism's *memento mori?* Do they tend to become more and more severe and eventually to result in a breakdown of the system itself? Ever since the late 1890s, this has been one of the most widely and earnestly discussed topics in the whole realm of Marxist thought. But before attempting to assess the significance for this problem of the foregoing analysis of crises, it will be useful to sketch some of the chief issues and theories in what may properly be called the breakdown controversy.

The general framework of the controversy was established by Marx's scattered statements concerning the end of capitalism and the coming of socialism. In broad outline, his position was unambiguous and consistently maintained. At a certain stage, capitalist relations of production will cease to foster the development of the forces of production and will instead turn into so many fetters on the further expansion of the forces of production. This will mark the beginning of a revolutionary period during which the working class, at once oppressed and disciplined by its special position in society, will overturn the existing relations of production and establish in their stead higher, socialist, relations of production. Moreover, according to Marx, this is not a process which *may* happen; it *must* happen with all the inevitable force of a natural law.

Marx, however, did not trace out in detail the course of events which would mark the transformation of capitalism into a fetter on the further development of productive forces. Crises would become more and more severe 'putting the existence of the entire bourgeois society on trial, each time more threateningly'; the means adopted to overcome them ('on the one hand by enforced destruction of a mass of productive forces; on the other, by the conquest of new markets, and by the more thorough exploitation of the old ones') achieve results only at the cost of 'paving the way for more extensive and more destructive crises, and . . . diminishing the means whereby crises are prevented.' This was the view put forward in the *Communist Manifesto*. A similar conviction that crises must continue to grow worse, though less explicitly expressed, can be detected in the discussion of the falling rate of profit in Volume III.* These are all, however, statements of a very general character; they leave open the question of capitalist 'breakdown' in any usual meaning of the term.

Another and distinct line of thought, which will be examined more closely in Part IV, points also to increasing obstacles in the path of capitalist expansion. There is, according to Marx, a strong tendency for capital to become centralized in fewer and fewer hands. Eventually,

> The monopoly of capital becomes a fetter upon the mode of production, which has sprung up and flourished along with, and under it. Centralization of the means of production and socialization of labor at last reach a point where they become incompatible with their capitalist integument. This integument is burst asunder. The knell of private property sounds. The expropriators are expropriated.[1]

This is, however, not so much a prediction as a vivid description of a tendency. For, in another place, speaking of the 'centralization of already existing capitals in a few hands and a decapitalization of many,' Marx issues an implied warning against too rigid deductions. 'This process,' he says, 'would soon bring about the collapse † of capitalist production, if it were not for counteracting tendencies which continually have a decentralizing effect by the side of the centripetal ones.' [2]

In a real sense it can be said that Marx's entire theoretical system constitutes a denial of the possibility of indefinite capitalist expansion and an affirmation of the inevitability of the socialist

* See the passage quoted above, p. 97.

† The German word here is *Zusammenbruch*. Throughout the present work this is translated by the more literal 'breakdown.'

revolution. But nowhere in his work is there to be found a doctrine of the specifically economic breakdown of capitalist production. Whether this is to be accounted a weakness or not, we shall consider in due course. At any rate, it is clear that his treatment of the problem, both in its positive and in its negative aspects, prepared the ground for a long-drawn-out controversy which cannot be regarded as fully settled to this day.

In the years prior to Engels' death (1895) the problem of capitalist breakdown was not often discussed as such. Occasional remarks which appeared to rest upon a definite breakdown theory were actually little more than an attempt to give emphatic expression to the general conception of an inevitable transition from capitalism to socialism. For example, in 1891 Kautsky wrote: 'Irresistible economic forces lead with the certainty of doom to the shipwreck of capitalist production. The substitution of a new social order for the existing one is no longer simply desirable; it has become inevitable.' [3] Yet a few years later, in his polemic against Bernstein,[4] Kautsky vigorously denied that there were any traces of a breakdown theory in his earlier work. He even maintained, and there seems to be no good reason to doubt his accuracy, that the very conception of a breakdown theory as well as the term itself (*Zusammenbruchstheorie*) were inventions of Bernstein. This requires some explanation.

2. Eduard Bernstein

Eduard Bernstein was for many years a close friend and collaborator of Engels, generally regarded as an orthodox Marxist and an outstanding representative of German Social Democracy. Soon after Engels' death, however, Bernstein launched the so-called revisionist movement, which will always be associated with his name. Articles published in *Die Neue Zeit* in 1896 and 1897 were elaborated in book form in 1899 under the title *The Presuppositions of Socialism and the Tasks of Social Democracy*.[5] This was, as Kautsky correctly remarked, the first sensational writing in the literature of social democracy. For the first time a big-name Marxist saw the 'wisdom' of revising Marx; naturally the press was delighted, and the book attained a large circulation and much weighty approval.

Bernstein, motivated by a deep-seated dread of violence, a contempt for theory, and an absorption in the practical details of every-day living, was in almost every sense the antithesis of Marx. 'Revisionism,' applied to the works of Bernstein, is an extreme euphemism. His real aim, though he may not have been fully conscious of it, was to eradicate Marxism, root and branch, from the socialist movement. In place of Marx's basic conception of socialism as the necessary outcome of an objective historical process, Bernstein wished to substitute the idea of socialism as the goal of civilized mankind, free to choose its future to conform to higher ethical and moral standards. Where Marx would have held that men learn to deserve what they get, Bernstein held the reverse, that they get what they deserve. Hence for struggle and revolutionary training, Bernstein would substitute persuasion and education as the means to socialism.

In order to be effective in his environment, Bernstein realized that he could not simply throw Marxism overboard; its appeal was too great and its influence too profound. It was necessary to proceed more cautiously, by way of modernizing and revising Marxism. In pursuing his goal thus deviously, Bernstein found the 'breakdown theory' one of his most convenient points of attack. His argument runs somewhat as follows. One of Marx's doctrines was the inevitable and catastrophic breakdown of capitalism—it goes without saying that Bernstein was unable to adduce proof of this. In the light of economic developments since Marx's death (growth of the world market, rise of cartels, perfection of the credit system, et cetera) the theory of catastrophic breakdown is no longer tenable and must be abandoned. In its place we must recognize a meliorative trend in capitalist development; the severity of crises diminishes, class struggles grow less sharp, et cetera—characteristically, Bernstein 'establishes' the meliorative trend in a purely descriptive fashion. And now comes the real point of the argument. Revolutionary tactics are justified only on the assumption that capitalism will break down and that the continued existence of society will absolutely demand a new economic order—in this case, of course, whatever is necessary at the time will also be justified. But if, as Bernstein believed, capitalist breakdown is the outcome not of real capitalist development but of an outworn theory, it follows that all excuse for revolution has vanished. In reality, peaceful and gradual elimination of the evils of capitalism is possible; it is therefore also politically expedient and morally right. In this way Bernstein comes to the same positive conclusion as his Fabian contemporaries in England who, because of a different intellectual heritage, were able to take the wisdom of gradualism for granted without going through the laborious preliminary of revising Marx.

3. The Orthodox Counter-Attack

The reaction of the orthodox Marxists to Bernstein's attack was by no means uniform. The first full-dress counterblast to his economic arguments was delivered by Heinrich Cunow in the official theoretical organ of the Social Democratic party. This effort is interesting chiefly for its title: 'On the Breakdown Theory.' [6] That Marx and Engels believed in the breakdown of capitalism was taken for granted by Cunow; he makes no effort, however, to give specific content to the concept. Indeed, as the term is most frequently used, it appears merely to stand for the opposite of Bernstein's cheerful predictions about the future of economic conditions under capitalism. As for Cunow's own ideas on the progressive deterioration of economic conditions, there is nothing but a crude 'shortage-of-markets' theory, which might find support in certain of Engels' popular writings but which has no foundation in Marx.

Kautsky's reaction to Bernstein was quite different from that of Cunow. Instead of debating the issue of capitalist breakdown on its merits, Kautsky attempted to pooh-pooh it out of existence. Marx and Engels had no breakdown theory in Bernstein's sense—i.e. of 'the great, all-embracing economic crisis' as 'the unavoidable way to socialist society.' [7] On the contrary, though they believed that economic conditions must get worse under capitalism, the essential and original element in their theory was that the decisive factor bringing about the transition to socialism would be the 'growing power and maturity of the proletariat.' [8] As to the tactics of the Social Democratic movement, Kautsky rejected Bernstein's gradualism in favor of maximum flexibility. It is necessary to be 'armed for every eventuality': 'Social

Democracy reckons with crisis as with prosperity, with reaction as with revolution, with catastrophes and with slow, peaceful development.' [9]

4. Tugan-Baranowsky

Bernstein had sought to wield the breakdown theory as a club over the heads of the orthodox Marxists. Kautsky's attempt to rob the weapon of its potency was singularly unsuccessful. Increasingly, the revisionist offensive took the form of disproving the inevitability of capitalist breakdown; the other side of the coin was always the endless expansibility of capitalism and hence the wickedness and destructiveness of revolution. We have already had occasion to examine at some length Tugan-Baranowsky's contribution to the revisionist case—from the economist's standpoint it is certainly the most interesting. According to Tugan, Marx had not one but two breakdown theories, one resting on the falling tendency of the rate of profit and the other on underconsumption. Tugan thought that he had succeeded in disproving both of these theories. His final conclusion, therefore, was that the breakdown of capitalism was in no sense an economic necessity. 'Mankind will never achieve socialism as a gift of blind, elementary economic forces but must, conscious of its goal, work for the new order—and struggle for it.' [10] The problem was thus relegated to a far-off time when 'mankind' should at last be ready to adopt socialism.

Tugan never attempted to distinguish between breakdown theory and crisis theory. A chapter entitled 'Marx's Theory of Crises' in his earlier work on the theory and history of crises corresponds closely in content to a chapter entitled 'The Breakdown of the Capitalist Economic Order' in the later book on the principles of Marxism. Apparently Tugan believed that Marx's theory envisaged a steady increase in the severity of crises so that eventually one of breakdown intensity would be sure to occur. In essentials this view is probably not far removed from that of Bernstein; needless to say it does not provide a very specific or readily usable concept of breakdown.

5. Conrad Schmidt

In criticizing Tugan's views Conrad Schmidt (revisionist) made a valuable contribution to the breakdown controversy. Taking it for granted that 'Marx and the Marxists' had a breakdown theory, Schmidt attempted to show that its essential core was underconsumption: 'It is from this point of view that the theory that capitalism is hastening toward a general economic catastrophe may be developed most simply and clearly.' General economic catastrophe apparently meant to Schmidt what breakdown did to Bernstein: a very severe all-embracing economic crisis. The argument, which is developed with admirable clarity, is worth quoting at some length:

> . . . do not the capitalists, by their opposition to all wage increases, conduct a struggle which has the tendency to keep the income—hence also the purchasing power—of the masses as low as possible, while they, the capitalists, on the other hand, raise their own income—and therewith the mass of accumulated capital seeking productive investment—in rapidly increasing progression? Will, under such circumstances, the increase in consuming power . . . be able to keep step with the tempo of capital accumulation? And if not, must not then the sale of commodities become always more difficult the more consumption demand, the basis of production, lags behind the rapidly increasing accumulation of capital and expansion of production—with only export, unproductive state expenditures, etc., to slow down the process? In this way, then, capitalism would tend to create in and of itself a steadily growing state of overproduction. Intensified competition on the market as a result of the growing difficulty of sales would have a tendency to manifest itself in a growing pressure on prices and therewith in a *fall of the rates of return* or of the *average rate of profit*, a fall in consequence of which the capitalist mode of production becomes even for the majority of private entrepreneurs ever more unprofitable and risky, while at the same time the labor market gets progessively worse for the workers, and the ranks of the *industrial reserve army* swell ever more terribly. The path of development of capitalist society would thus be likewise the path to its own bankruptcy, the transition to a new socialist order would be prescribed by a forced situation [*Zwangslage*] of society itself.[11]

As a description of the tendency to underconsumption, this is excellent. The weakness of Schmidt's analysis is nevertheless obvious. He treats the falling rate of profit and the growing industrial reserve army as *derivative* from underconsumption instead of as *parallel* tendencies of capitalist development. On this basis he is able to reject the whole breakdown theory along with its revolutionary implications. For, if all the difficulties of capitalism spring from underconsumption, then they can all be eliminated by sufficiently raising the purchasing power of the masses. Thus, asks Schmidt,

How . . . can one determine in advance the degree to which the laboring masses may be able, through trade union and political struggles against the capitalists, to raise their income (and hence definitive consumption demand)? How, thus, can one predict that the increase in workers' income must always necessarily lag behind the income increase and the accumulation of the capitalist class, which indeed was the basis of this entire prophecy of catastrophe? [12]

According to this view, the program of the reformist socialists was calculated to keep capitalism going indefinitely. Eventually, Schmidt believed in common with his fellow-revisionists, the working class would be strong enough and educated enough to achieve socialism without the spur of intolerable economic conditions. Unfortunately, the entire argument overlooks the direct relation which exists between wages and the rate of profit. Schmidt proposes to overcome the tendency to underconsumption by speeding up the falling tendency of the rate of profit. We already know that either is capable of causing crises; so far as capitalist breakdown is concerned—if indeed we really have to reckon with such an eventuality—there seems little reason to suppose that the one is ultimately less dangerous than the other.

6. Kautsky's Position in 1902

In 1902 Kautsky published his longest and most important contribution to crisis theory in the form of a review article [13] criticizing Tugan's book, *Theory and History of Commercial Crises in England.* This time the issues involved in the breakdown theory—though not the term itself—receive substantial treatment at Kautsky's hands, nearly a third of the whole article being devoted to investigating the question 'whether and to what extent the character of crises is changing, whether they display a tendency to disappear or to become milder, as several revisionists, in agreement with liberal optimists, still insisted two or three years ago.'[14] Drawing on Tugan's own descriptive and statistical material, Kautsky comes to a clear-cut answer: 'One can say in general that crises are becoming ever more severe and extensive in scope.'[15] Moreover, theoretical considerations lead him to believe that capitalism is headed for a 'period of chronic depression':

> According to our theory this development is a necessity, and it is proved by this alone that the capitalist method of production has limits beyond which it cannot go. There must come a time, and it may be very soon, when it will be impossible for the world market even temporarily to expand more rapidly than society's productive forces, a time when overproduction is chronic for *all* industrial nations. Even then up- and downswings of economic life are possible and probable; a series of technical revolutions, which devalue a mass of existing means of production and call forth large-scale creation of new means of production, the discovery of rich new gold fields, etc., can even then for a while speed up the pace of business. But capitalist production requires uninterrupted, rapid expansion if unemployment and poverty for the workers and insecurity for the small capitalists are not to attain an extremely high pitch. The continued existence of capitalist production remains possible, of course, even in such a state of chronic depression, but it becomes completely intolerable for the masses of the population; the latter are forced to seek a way out of the general misery, and they can find it only in socialism.
>
> . . . I regard this forced situation [*Zwangslage*] as unavoidable *if economic development proceeds as heretofore*, but I expect that the victory of the proletariat will intervene in time to turn the development in another direction before the forced situation in question arrives, so that it will be possible to avoid the latter.[16]

The analysis on which this conclusion rests leaves much to be desired; the conclusion itself, however, is very much superior in saying just what it means to earlier versions of the breakdown theory. In place of a cataclysmic but very loose and indefinite conception of capitalist breakdown, we have here for the first time a definite and clear-cut picture of 'chronic depression.' Temporary upswings are still possible, and anything like the automatic disappearance of capitalism is out of the question, but growing economic hardships drive the people on to seek a way out and, so far as the great majority is concerned, the only hope of salvation lies in a socialist direction. To be sure, Kautsky expresses the belief that what, in his polemic against Bernstein, he had called the 'power and maturity of the proletariat' will be strong enough to bring on socialism before capitalism has degenerated to such a sorry state of affairs. But whether this should prove true or not is now seen, as it was not in the earlier work, to be irrelevant to the fundamental economic tendencies of capitalist production, for Kautsky was far from sharing Schmidt's complacent view that the struggle of the proletariat against the capitalists would operate to remove the barriers to capitalist expansion.

Whether or not Kautsky's theory of 'chronic depression' should be classified as a version of the 'breakdown theory' is a debatable question. At any rate, from the point of view of bearing on practical questions of strategy and tactics, there is a close similarity. Kautsky closes his article with an admirably clear discussion of the relation between his theory and the tactics of the socialist movement. The revisionists, he says, would change Social Democracy from a party of proletarian class struggle into a democratic party of socialist reforms. 'Such a revival of the old petty-bourgeois democracy can be regarded as possible only by those who believe that the class antagonism between the proletariat and the possessing classes is growing steadily weaker.'[17] Kautsky points out, however, that

> the conception of a melioration of class antagonisms is incompatible with our theory of crises. If the latter is correct the capitalist mode of production is headed for a period of continuous depression, and if the proletariat does not conquer political power sooner, economic development must intensify class antagonisms right up to the time when this state of continuous depression is reached.[18]

Moreover, not only domestic class struggles but also international conflicts become ever more severe, since, as the state of chronic depression approaches, each nation strives to expand its share of world trade at the expense of others, 'to which end the chief means are colonial conquest, protective tariffs and cartels, and the result is a steady sharpening of the antagonisms among the great industrial states.' [19] The only path for the proletariat to pursue, therefore, is the path of class struggle, making use of the knowledge which sound theory can provide and resolutely turning away from the illusions of revisionist gradualism.

> Crises, conflicts, catastrophes [*Krisen, Kriege, Katastrophen*] of all kinds, it is this lovely alliteration that the course of development places in prospect for the next decades. Just as so many dreams have gone up in smoke in the last few years—the dream of the elimination of crises through cartels, the dream of an unnoticed, peaceful, step-by-step conquest of political power through experiments *à la* Millerand, and finally the dream of the saturation of the English ruling class with a socialist spirit . . . —so the events of the coming years will lead to the disappearance of that dream that now floats before our eyes, that wars and catastrophes are a thing of the past while before us stretches ahead the level road of peaceful, quiet progress.[20]

7. Louis B. Boudin

For a full decade after the appearance of Tugan's book and the important review articles of Schmidt and Kautsky, no strikingly new points of view were introduced into the breakdown controversy. Writing his *Theoretical Principles of Marxism* in 1905, Tugan noted, with evident disapproval, that nearly all socialists, whatever their differences might be, were in general agreement that 'there must come a time when overproduction will become chronic, and the capitalist economic order will break down because of the impossibility of finding outlets for its newly accumulated capital.' [21] Tugan was certainly exaggerating the extent of agreement among socialists; his attempt to portray Schmidt as a breakdown theorist, and in this way to give the impression that the view in question enjoyed support even among the revisionists, was little more than a debating trick.

Among the orthodox Marxists, however, there undoubtedly was little serious difference of opinion at this time. Out of the ferment of the Bernstein debates had come a relatively stabilized version of orthodox Marxist theory; as regards crises and capitalist breakdown it followed closely the views which Kautsky had put forward in 1902.

Louis B. Boudin was an adequate spokesman of this period of theoretical stabilization. His book, *The Theoretical System of Karl Marx* (1907), while containing little new or original, is none the less a substantial work which summarizes better than any other the theoretical views held by the accredited representatives of international socialism in the first decade of the century. In crisis theory, Boudin accepted a crude underconsumption explanation; he was confident that crises must grow more severe and that there were definite objective limits to the expansibility of capitalism; he even speaks of the 'purely economico-mechanical breakdown of the capitalist system.'[22] He was not inclined, however, to emphasize the breakdown problem; his general position is more adequately expressed in the following passage:

> According to the Marxian philosophy a system of production can only last as long as it helps, or at least does not hinder, the unfolding and full exploitation of the productive forces of society, and must give way to another system when it becomes a hindrance, a *fetter*, to production. That a system has become a hindrance, and a fetter to production when it can only exist by preventing production, and by *wasting* what it has already produced, goes without saying. Such a system can not therefore last very long, quite irrespective of the purely mechanical possibility or impossibility of its continuance. Such a system has become *historically impossible*, even though mechanically it may still be possible.[23]

The similarity between this view and that expressed by Kautsky in his criticism of Tugan is apparent. In general, it can be said that Boudin's analysis is distinguishable from that of Kautsky only by the more markedly primitive character of its underconsumptionism.

After Boudin the breakdown issue tended to fade into the background of theoretical controversy. Hilferding, who was much influenced by Tugan, declared that 'economic breakdown is in no sense a rational conception,' [24] but he did not elaborate on the theme. Nor did Kautsky, in writing a long review of Hilferding, feel called upon to raise the issue. Kautsky, indeed, was in no mood for sterile controversy. 'Theoretical–though not practical–revisionism has been defeated, and we Marxists can devote all our energy and time . . . to the great task of building up and adapting to recent times the structure which our masters left behind in incompleted form.' [25] All was quiet on the theoretical front–but it was not long to remain so. Hardly more than a year after Kautsky had written these lines, Rosa Luxemburg set off a bomb in the midst of the complacent theorists of Social Democracy. The reaction was one of shocked surprise–and ill-concealed rage.

8. Rosa Luxemburg

Rosa Luxemburg attempted to prove that capital accumulation is impossible in a closed capitalist system. Marx's failure to understand this was due to the unfinished state of his work. She would now supply the missing proof, close the most important remaining gap in the Marxian system, and in this way explain the hitherto inexplicable phenomena of modern imperialism.

At the heart of the problem of capital accumulation, according to Rosa Luxemburg, lies the realization of surplus value. In simple reproduction the realization of surplus value presents no difficulties: it is all sold to capitalists for their own consumption. But in expanded reproduction, matters are different. The value of all commodities, and hence of the total social output, consists of constant capital plus variable capital plus surplus value. The constant capital is realized through the replacement purchases of capitalists themselves; the variable capital is realized through the expenditure by workers of their wages; so much is clear. But how is it with surplus value? A part is purchased by the capitalists for their own consumption; another part they wish to accumulate, and here is the difficulty: 'where is the demand for the accumulated surplus value?' [26] The capitalists certainly cannot realize the surplus value which they wish to accumulate by selling it to workers, for the latter exhaust their wages in realizing the variable capital. They cannot sell it to themselves for consumption, for then we should be back in simple reproduction. 'Who, then, can be the taker or consumer for the social portion of commodities the sale of which is a necessary prerequisite of capital accumulation?'[27] It might be thought that the part of surplus value in question exists in the form of additional means of production which the capitalists buy from each other and in this way make accumulation possible. But, then, who would buy the still larger quantity of goods produced in the following period? If it is answered that this just keeps up for ever, then

we have before us a merry-go-round which revolves around itself in empty air. That is not capitalist accumulation, i.e. heaping up of money capital, but the opposite: production for the sake of production, thus, from the standpoint of capital, utter nonsense.[28]

By this reasoning Rosa Luxemburg concludes that the problem which she has posed is insoluble and that the only way out is to drop the assumption with which she started, namely, the assumption of a closed system made up exclusively of capitalists and workers. Having done this, she proceeds to argue that the part of surplus value which is to be accumulated can be realized only by sale to non-capitalist consumers, that is to say, to consumers who are altogether outside the capitalist system either because the country in which they live is still untouched by capitalism or because the section of the population to which they belong (e.g. peasants) still lives on the level of simple commodity production. The very process of expansion, however, draws these backward nations and strata of the population into the orbit of capitalism. Eventually they will all be absorbed, and when this occurs the theoretical impossibility of a closed capitalism will manifest itself in practice; the system will break down of its own accord.

On the basis of this theory, imperialism emerges as a striving on the part of all capitalist nations to get control over as much as possible of the still-remaining non-capitalist world; and high protective tariffs appear as the means by which each seeks to bar the others from access to its own internal non-capitalist market. Thus the most striking phenomena of the latest stage of capitalist development are explained as arising from the approaching exhaustion of the non-capitalist market; by the same token, they are shown to be harbingers of the impending breakdown of capitalism which no power in the world can stave off.

Rosa Luxemburg's theory is open to criticism from several different angles; one error in particular, however, overshadows the rest *: in discussing expanded reproduction she implicitly retains the assumptions of simple reproduction. The dogma, which she never questions for a moment, that the consumption of workers can realize no surplus value implies that the total amount of variable capital, and hence also the consumption of workers, must always remain fixed and constant as in simple reproduction. Actually accumulation typically involves adding to variable capital, and when this additional variable capital is spent by workers it realizes a part of the surplus value which has the physical form of consumption goods. † Since Rosa Luxemburg did not understand this, it seemed to her that consumption could not increase within the framework of capitalism. From this it was a short step to the conclusion that additions to the stock of means of production could have no function whatever. Given her premise about the constancy of consumption, this would undoubtedly be correct—it could be denied only by one who believed in the complete independence of production and consumption *à la* Tugan-Baranowsky: continued additions to means of production would then indeed be 'a merry-go-round which revolves around itself in mid-air.' Since, however, the constancy of consumption rests on nothing more substantial than Rosa Luxemburg's own logical inflexibility, the whole theory collapses like a house of cards. Bukharin's witty remark is still the most telling criticism of her theoretical structure: 'If one excludes expanded reproduction at the *beginning* of a logical

* We leave out of account altogether purely monetary problems of capital accumulation though she devotes a great deal of attention to them, frequently even confusing the question, where does the *demand* come from? with the question, where does the *money* come from? It is in discussing the latter question that she shows to least advantage; but it is, after all, a minor problem which is essentially irrelevant to her main thesis.

† In terms of the reproduction schemes used in Chapter x, the additional variable capital which realizes surplus value is designated as S_{av} (see p. 163).

proof,' he wrote, 'it is naturally easy to make it disappear at the end; it is simply a question of the simple reproduction of a simple logical error.'[29]

Beside the fundamental error involved in misunderstanding and misusing reproduction schemes, other weaknesses and confusions in Rosa Luxemburg's thinking are of subsidiary importance. For present purposes it is only necessary to point out that if the analysis were correct in denying the possibility of accumulation in a closed system, her non-capitalist consumers could in no way change the situation. It is not possible to sell to non-capitalist consumers without also buying from them. So far as the capitalist circulation process is concerned, the surplus value cannot be disposed of in this way; it can at best change its form. Who is to buy the commodities 'imported' from the non-capitalist environment? If there could have been, as a matter of principle, no demand for the 'exported' commodities there can be just as little a demand for the 'imported' commodities. The whole distinction between 'capitalist' and 'non-capitalist' consumers is, in this context, quite irrelevant. If the dilemma were a real one it would prove more than she bargained for: it would demonstrate, not the approaching breakdown of capitalism, but the impossibility of capitalism. Rosa Luxemburg, unlike the *Narodniki* in Russia a decade and a half earlier, had much too keen a sense of economic and political realities to follow her logic to such an absurd conclusion. She was never in danger, in Lenin's phrase, of fleeing 'from an unpleasant but undoubted reality into the cloud world of romantic fantasies.' She saved herself, however, only by the doubtful expedient of inventing a false solution to a specious problem.

On the whole *The Accumulation of Capital* is devoted to theoretical analysis, and only incidentally to the drawing of political inferences. Nevertheless, Rosa Luxemburg expressed the hope in a Foreword that, outside of its purely theoretical interest, the work might have 'some significance for our practical struggle against imperialism,' and she left no doubt about what she regarded as the general character of its political implications.

The more violently capital, through military methods in the outer world, and also at home, cleans out non-capitalist elements and depresses the living conditions of all working people, the more does the day-by-day history of capital accumulation on the world stage become transformed into a continuous chain of political and social catastrophes and convulsions which, together with periodic economic catastrophes in the form of crises, will make impossible the continuation of accumulation and will make necessary the rebellion of the international working class against the domination of capital even before the latter smashes itself against its own self-created economic barriers.[30]

The reception accorded to *The Accumulation of Capital* in the Social Democratic press was a genuine surprise to its author. She expected all Marxists to be convinced by her arguments, to say that hers was 'the only possible and thinkable solution to the problem.'[31] Instead most of the reviewers were sharply critical; more than that they were openly hostile. The review in the *Vorwärts,* official party newspaper, 'presents a strange appearance even to the reader unfamiliar with the material, but it is even stranger when account is taken of the fact that the criticized book is of a purely theoretical character, polemicizes against no living Marxist, and sticks strictly to its job.'[32] Unfavorable reviews were not the end of the matter. Any one who praised the book felt the displeasure of the party higher-ups; only those who criticized it could be considered 'experts'—'an unprecedented and in itself somewhat comic performance,' she thought.

The reaction of the official spokesmen of Social Democracy to Rosa Luxemburg's book did not include any significant theoretical contributions and is interesting chiefly for the state of mind which it revealed. In the German movement, fear of revolution had by now become quite as characteristic of the 'orthodox' as of the revisionist. It was still fashionable to talk revolution—to take place some time in the indefinite future. For this purpose, paradoxically enough, one needed a theory which could guarantee capitalism's lasting power. Hence all breakdown theories had to be combatted and the indefinite expansibility of capitalism, regarded simply as an economic system, had to be affirmed. Revolution could then be treated as a deliberate act of the proletariat for which, however, the proletariat would be a very long time preparing. In practice this position is indistinguishable from that of the revisionists and diametrically opposed to that of Rosa Luxemburg. Small wonder that she was regarded as a dangerous and irresponsible woman.

In spite of serious analytical errors and notwithstanding the hostility of official Marxism, Rosa Luxemburg was a more genuine Marxist than any other member of the German movement. As a historical materialist, if not as an economic theorist in the narrower sense, she stood head and shoulders above her critics. She wrote:

If we assume, along with the 'experts,' the limitlessness of capital accumulation then the solid soil of objective historical necessity is cut from under the feet of socialism. We take refuge in the fog of pre-Marxian systems and schools which pretend to derive socialism out of the mere injustice and wickedness of the present world and out of the mere revolutionary will of the working class.[33]

Unlike Marx, Rosa Luxemburg, in rejecting 'the limitlessness of capital accumulation,' set up a concept of mechanical breakdown. But this is, after all, a relatively minor difference of opinion when set alongside of their fundamental agreement on the nature of the historical process itself.

9. Post-war Attitudes

The war and its aftermath interrupted the breakdown debate; not until world capitalism had reached the relative stabilization of the middle 1920s did the question of the theoretical limits of capitalist expansion once again occupy the attention of Marxist economists. There now appeared roughly three main points of view.

First there was the position of the Social Democratic party, nearly all of whose spokesmen had come around, more or less frankly, to a reformist point of view. Here we find arguments similar to those put forth by the revisionists around the turn of the century, only now the erstwhile leading orthodox theorists, Kautsky and Hilferding, openly joined forces with the revisionists to form a united front against the breakdown theory. Kautsky, writing in 1927, repudiated his own earlier theory of chronic depression from which capitalism would be unable to find an escape: 'The expectation that crises would someday become so extensive and long-drawn-out as to render the continuation of capitalist production impossible and its replacement by a socialist order unavoidable finds no more support today.' [34] And Hilferding, speaking before the annual Social Democratic Party Conference in 1927, put the case even more explicitly:

I have always rejected every economic breakdown theory. . . . After the war such a theory was championed chiefly by the Bolshevists who believed that we were now on the very verge of the breakdown of the capitalist system. We have no reason to fear that. We have always been of the opinion that the overthrow of the capitalist system is not to be fatalistically awaited, nor will it come about through the workings of the inner laws of the system, but that it must be the conscious act of the proletariat.[35]

Second, there was the view held by the Bolsheviks. There can be little doubt that Hilferding was wrong in attributing to them a specifically economic breakdown theory. Ever since the theoretical struggle against the *Narodniki,* in which Lenin took a leading part, Bolshevik theorists had been very reluctant to give even qualified support to predictions of purely economic catastrophe. On the other hand, they clearly believed in the inevitable end of capitalism, but they expected it to result from wars which were not so much the outgrowth of a tendency to economic breakdown as of an ever more intense hunt for monopoly profits by the great trusts in rival capitalist countries. The war and the Russian revolution obviously provided a strong stimulus to this line of reasoning, which will be dealt with at greater length in Part IV. In terms of the problem posed at the outset of this chapter, the Bolsheviks cannot be classified as breakdown theorists.[36]

Third, there were those who continued to maintain the breakdown thesis. With the erstwhile leaders of orthodox Marxist thought, like Kautsky and Cunow, in open or thinly disguised alliance with the revisionists, this position was left to the followers of Rosa Luxemburg to defend. Fritz Sternberg's *Imperialism* [37] is the outstanding product, in the economic field, of this school of Marxist thought. In essentials Sternberg repeated the arguments of Luxemburg, including her errors, but succeeded in adding little of his own.

On the whole, then, the decade after the war saw little advance towards a clarification of the breakdown issue. This was the situation which existed when Henryk Grossmann published, in 1929, the most detailed and elaborate examination of the problem which had yet appeared: *The Accumulation and Breakdown Law of the Capitalist System*. A brief consideration of this work will bring us substantially up to date, for the 1930s were not a period of substantial progress in Marxist economics, a fact which may be accounted for by the well-nigh impossible conditions of work in many parts of the Continent, the preoccupation of Russian theorists with a new set of problems, and the relative backwardness of Anglo-American Marxism, particularly in questions of economic theory.*

10. Henryk Grossmann

Grossmann's own theory of capitalist breakdown—we need not take seriously his claim to be the first to exhume the true doctrine of Marx himself—has at the very least the merit of originality. For Grossmann the realization problem does not exist; just as little as Tugan-Baranowsky does he worry about the relation between production and consumption. How, then, does he bring the capitalist system to its doom? The method is nothing if not ingenious.

At the basis of Grossmann's reasoning is a reproduction scheme devised by Otto Bauer for use in his critique of Rosa Luxemburg's *Accumulation of Capital*.[38] This scheme has the following characteristics: the working population and the amount of variable capital both grow at the rate of 5 per cent per annum; the

* This does not mean that interesting and important theoretical work on the analysis of capitalist crises was altogether lacking during the 1930s. A few books may be mentioned. In Central Europe: Otto Bauer, *Zwischen Zwei Weltkriegen?* (1936), Natalie Moszkowska, *Zur Kritik Moderner Krisentheorien* (1935); in England: Maurice Dobb, *Political Economy and Capitalism* (1937); and in America: Lewis Corey, *The Decline of American Capitalism* (1934). None of these works, however, is primarily concerned with the problem of this chapter.

rate of surplus value remains always at 100 per cent, so that the total quantity of surplus value grows also at a 5 per cent rate; the organic composition of capital rises—to bring this out it is assumed that constant capital grows at a rate of 10 per cent per annum. The way in which surplus value is divided into its three basic parts—capitalists' consumption, additional variable capital, and additional constant capital—is rigidly determined by these assumptions. So much must go for additional constant capital and so much for additional variable capital as to maintain the presupposed rates of increase; the remainder is left for capitalists to consume. Now it is obvious that if this scheme is pushed far enough it will lead to strange results, for the increments to constant capital, though themselves derived from surplus value, are assumed to grow more rapidly than surplus value. Bauer developed the scheme for only four years, which was not enough to bring out its potential curiosities. But Grossmann pushes resolutely ahead until he has 35 years. In the twenty-first year, the amount of surplus value left over for capitalists to consume begins to decline, and by the thirty-fourth year it is nearly all gone! From this point on, not only do the capitalists starve, but even by such heroic sacrifices they are no longer able to maintain the preordained rate of accumulation in the preordained proportions of constant and variable capital. The scheme, in other words, breaks down from a shortage of surplus value; given its assumptions, it is literally impossible to carry it beyond the thirty-fourth year.*

Bauer's scheme breaks down from a shortage of surplus value. By a breath-taking mental leap Grossmann concludes that the capitalist system must also break down from a shortage of surplus value. Rosa Luxemburg's theory of an excess of surplus value is thus turned on its head. 'The difficulty lies rather in the expansion of capital: the surplus value does not suffice for the continuation of accumulation at the assumed rate of accumula-

* The number of years for which the scheme can run is naturally determined by the absolute size of the figures assumed for the first year as well as by the relative rates of growth of constant and variable capital. Bauer's first year is given by the formula $200{,}000c + 100{,}000v + 100{,}000s$. The 34th year shows $4{,}641{,}489c + 500{,}304v + 500{,}304s$. The quantity of s (500,304) is here less than 10% of 4,641,489 plus 5% of 500,304. Hence the scheme must come to an end with the 34th year.

tion! Therefore the catastrophe.'[39] Despite certain qualifications and refinements, this 'shortage-of-surplus value' theory, as derived from Bauer's scheme, remains throughout his work the essence of Grossmann's thinking on the breakdown problem.*

Grossmann's theory exhibits in extreme form the dangers of mechanistic thinking in social science. Reproduction schemes, including that of Bauer, are useful as a method of making comprehensible the character of a certain set of relations. But to take any particular, and necessarily arbitrary, scheme and assume that it faithfully represents the essentials of the real process of capital accumulation is to invite theoretical disaster. Lenin once remarked in criticizing Tugan-Baranowsky that 'schemes can prove nothing; they can only *illustrate* a process *when its separate elements have been theoretically clarified*.'[40] It would have been well for Grossmann to heed the warning; his failure to clarify the elements of his scheme leads to a serious distortion of the real accumulation process and to a conclusion which has no claim to acceptance. Here we can point out only a few of the more obvious shortcomings of Grossmann's theory.

In the first place, Bauer's scheme makes the rate of accumution dependent upon two factors, the rate of population growth and the assumed necessity for constant capital to increase twice as rapidly as variable capital. The rate of population growth is then set at a very high figure, namely, at a compound rate of 5 per cent per annum.† Under almost any circumstances, the assumption that constant capital grows twice as rapidly as variable capital seems highly unrealistic. But it is nothing short of fantastic when coupled with the assumption that the working force is growing at the enormous rate of 5 per cent per annum, for a rapid growth in the size of the working force is precisely the factor operating most strongly to keep down the ratio of con-

* It may be remarked, parenthetically, that the falling tendency of the rate of profit, while of course exhibited in Bauer's scheme, has nothing whatever to do with Grossmann's breakdown theory, though numerous remarks made in the course of the work might lead to an opposite impression. Moszkowska (*Zur Kritik Moderner Krisentheorien*, Ch. IV) is misled into interpreting Grossmann's theory as a falling-rate-of-profit theory.

† By way of comparison with actual historical conditions, it may be pointed out that even in the United States during the years 1839 to 1915, a period of extremely rapid population growth, the compound annual rate of increase was no higher than 2.28%.

stant to variable capital. This is so because an abundant labor supply prevents wages from rising and hence holds in check the tendency to substitute machinery for labor power. It follows that if we assume a very rapid growth in the labor supply it would be only reasonable to assume an increase in constant capital approximately equal to the increase in variable capital. On this hypothesis, the scheme can be expanded indefinitely; using Grossmann's method of reasoning we should have to conclude that capitalism can go on for ever.

Grossmann would object that an increasing organic composition of capital is an essential feature of capitalism which cannot be assumed away. Quite so, but what causes the rising tendency of the organic composition of capital? The answer is that the price of labor power tends to rise under the stimulus of accumulation—the organized efforts of workers may at certain times play quite as important a part as actual shortages in this respect—and that this induces a continuous substitution of machines for labor power. In other words, the rate of accumulation is the *independent variable;* the division of accumulation between constant and variable capital is by no means fixed but depends in good part on the relation between the rate of accumulation and the rate of growth of the labor force; in general this relation is such as to produce a relatively greater rate of increase of constant than variable capital. Of all this, which is basic to the Marxian analysis of capitalism, we find not a word in Grossmann. When it is taken into account, the idea that the increasing organic composition of capital, like a Frankenstein monster, must eventually force capitalists to throw all of their surplus value into accumulation is seen to involve a complete inversion of the causal links within the accumulation process. Bauer's scheme was satisfactory for the purpose for which it was devised, namely, to demonstrate the possibility of realizing surplus value within a closed system; as a representation of the accumulation process, however, its use is misleading and unjustified.

Numerous other criticisms can be made of Grossmann's theory. For example, assume for a moment that his use of Bauer's scheme were legitimate. Even so, why and in what sense would the thirty-fifth year be a year of breakdown from a capitalist standpoint? True, surplus value is not present in sufficient volume to employ *all* the additional workers and also add 10 per cent to constant capital. But why should this mean idle capital, as Grossmann assumes it would? Suppose surplus value were sufficient to add 4 per cent more workers and 8 per cent more constant capital. Would the capitalists hesitate out of sorrow for the 1 per cent of workers who could find no employment? Of course not. In fact, under Grossmann's assumptions, each year after the thirty-fourth would see an increase in unemployment, but there would be nothing to prevent the capitalists from continuing to invest their accumulations—and even from going back to a reasonable standard of consumption on their own account if they should want to. Mounting unemployment would have, again from a capitalist standpoint, a salutary effect in reducing wages and raising the rate of surplus value and hence the rate of profit. If the workers should insist on multiplying at so rapid a rate in spite of steadily worsening conditions, well, then, they could be left to a Malthusian fate—certainly no one ever suggested that capitalism would break down on that account.

So far as Grossmann's theory is concerned, we may regard it as sufficient to have shown, first, that the use made of Bauer's reproduction scheme is illegitimate; and second, that even if this were not so the conclusions which Grossmann draws are unwarranted. By denying the existence of a realization problem and by ignoring the real significance of the falling rate of profit, Grossmann in effect puts himself in the same school of thought with Tugan-Baranowsky. This is perhaps a harsh judgment to pass on one who spares no energy in castigating Tugan, but historical accuracy justifies no other.

With this we may bring to a close our review of the breakdown controversy. The results are inconclusive; much remains still to be clarified. To what extent can the analysis of crises presented in this Part contribute to the task of clarification?

XII

CHRONIC DEPRESSION?

1. Introduction

Neither the breakdown theorists nor their critics seem to have had a clear and unambiguous conception of the meaning of capitalist 'breakdown.' Some, like Bernstein, thought in terms of a very severe and all-embracing economic crisis from which there could be no escape. Others, like Rosa Luxemburg and Grossmann, apparently thought in terms of a sudden going to pieces of the whole social order,

> All at once, and nothing first,—
> Just as bubbles do when they burst.

But these ideas, which are obviously derived from analogies—the individual pursued by a relentless fate, or the machine which has come to the end of its useful life—lose their concreteness when applied to a social order. Any severe crisis may be, of course, and not infrequently is, described as a breakdown. But in this sense the expression loses the connotation of finality which attaches to it in the context of the breakdown controversy. The breakdown of capitalism is supposed to be the end of capitalism; it marks the point beyond which capitalism is impossible. This is the implication; yet it is just here that it becomes very difficult to be more specific. A particular form of society, that is to say a certain set of social relations, can become extremely onerous, but what does it mean to say that it is impossible?

The difficulty of answering suggests that there is something wrong with the question. Historically, the end of a social order comes about in one of two ways: either it disintegrates over a long period of time, partly as a result of internal decay, partly as a result of attacks from without; or it is more or less rapidly replaced by a new social order. Despite obvious dissimilarities, these two processes have much in common, and neither is aptly described by the term 'breakdown.' What the two cases have in common is that the old order has lost its progressive character, it saps the vitality of society, its beneficiaries are forced to resort to extreme methods in an effort to protect their position; in short, to use Marx's telling phrase, it has become a 'fetter' on the further development of society's productive forces. Which path will be followed, whether the path of decay or the path of reconstruction, depends primarily on whether the old order has, within its lifetime, produced a class which is both ready and able to cut loose from its existing ties and build a new society.

Applying these considerations to the case of capitalism, we see that the really significant questions cannot be grouped around the concept of capitalist breakdown—the term means either too little or too much. What we want to know is what, if any, are the disintegrating forces at work in capitalist society. As related to economic crises, this question can be made more specific: do the crisis-producing forces tend to become more severe in the course of capitalist development, so that eventually depression tends to be the rule rather than the exception? If so, we may account this a chief element in the transformation of capitalist relations 'from forms of development of the forces of production . . . into their fetters.' And we may feel certain that the melioration of social conflicts to which the revisionists so confidently looked forward is the forecast of wishful thinking and not of scientific analysis.

In a sense, this was always the underlying issue at stake in the breakdown controversy. Neither Rosa Luxemburg nor Grossmann, the most extreme breakdown theorists, ever believed that the development of capitalism would proceed to what they regarded as its logical conclusion. As Rosa Luxemburg expressed it, class struggles and international wars must lead to revolution 'long before the ultimate consequence of economic development is reached.' [1] Once this is granted, the conclusion can hardly be avoided that it is the direction of development and not the 'ultimate consequence' which is of primary importance; the breakdown problem appears as an essentially extraneous issue which has received an undue amount of attention. It is probably safe to assume that this is the reason why Marx did not concern himself with capitalist breakdown; he preferred to analyse the actual trends of capitalist development rather than to spin theories about a hypothetical outcome which would in any case never be reached. The incompleteness of his work is not to be found —as Rosa Luxemburg thought—in the absence of a breakdown theory, but rather in the unfinished analysis of capitalist tendencies.

Of all the attempts to revise, supplement, interpret, and correct Marx which were passed in review in the last chapter, that contained in Kautsky's 1902 article stands out as the most important. Kautsky attempted to carry one stage forward what he understood to be Marx's crisis theory by asking the question, whether in the long run crises tend to become more or less severe. His answer was that they tend to grow more severe, so much so, in fact, that a period of 'chronic depression' must sooner or later set in unless the victory of socialism should intervene. According to our own interpretation, Kautsky was certainly asking the right question. With the aid of a more adequate analysis of crises than was at Kautsky's disposal, let us test the correctness of his answer.

2. The Conditions of Capitalist Expansion

That capitalist production normally harbors a tendency to underconsumption (or overproduction) was demonstrated in Chapter x, and the reasoning will not be repeated here. In principle this tendency may manifest itself in a crisis or in stagnation of production. Both are methods, the one sudden and perhaps temporary, the other steady and continuous, whereby accumulation is prevented from outrunning the requirements of the market for consumption goods. This should not be taken to imply that depression leaves consumption unaffected and operates only to reduce accumulation. Both are affected unfavorably but the latter is to a proportionately greater extent. To take an extreme case, in a severe depression, profits may give way to losses for the system as a whole and capitalists may be obliged to live from their past accumulations instead of adding to them. In this manner accumulation can actually become negative for a time, while of course consumption must always be positive and substantial even if society is to do no more than continue to exist in a purely physical sense. The relatively greater contraction of accumulation as compared to consumption is the factor which, in a general way, establishes the lower limit to a decline in productive activity.

Since the tendency to underconsumption is inherent in capitalism and can apparently be overcome only by the partial non-utilization of productive resources, it may be said that stagnation is the norm towards which capitalist production is always tending. But we know that over the past four centuries, more or less, capitalism has expanded prodigiously with only periodic crises and occasional lapses into stagnation to mar the upward trend. What is the explanation of this apparent paradox? The answer is to be found primarily in the level of abstraction to which we have so far confined our analysis of the underconsumption problem. Up to this point we have neglected those forces which have the effect of counteracting the tendency to underconsumption, forces which evidently have been powerful enough to dominate the actual historical course of capitalist development. In order to reach an answer to the question which at present concerns us—is capitalism in fact headed for a state of chronic depression?—we must alter this procedure and focus our attention on the counteracting forces. If it appears that they are likely to operate in the future with the same strength as in the past, then we should have to conclude that the ever-present tendency to underconsumption would not in itself constitute a bar to indefinite capitalist expansion.* If, on the other hand, it can be shown that the counteracting forces are becoming relatively weaker, then we can expect the tendency to underconsumption to assert itself to an increasing extent, and Kautsky's prediction of an imminent period of chronic depression will be supplied with a solid foundation.

Generally speaking, the counteracting forces may be grouped together into two main categories: those which have the effect of raising the rate of growth of consumption relative to the

* It should be explicitly stated that we are here not concerned with difficulties which might arise from the falling tendency of the rate of profit even in the absence of insuperable underconsumption problems.

rate of growth of means of production, and those which deprive a disproportionate growth in means of production of its economically disruptive consequences. In the latter category fall (1) new industries, and (2) faulty investment; in the former, (3) population growth, (4) unproductive consumption, and (5) state expenditures. We shall attempt, in the case of each one of these items, to explain its meaning, analyse its mode of operation and weigh its probable future importance, as against its actual past importance, in counteracting the tendency to underconsumption.

3. Forces Counteracting the Tendency to Underconsumption

1. *New Industries.* During the formative period of a new industry there is no clearly defined relation between additions to means of production and additions to the output of finished products. For example, a railroad must be built before it can be used. During the construction period investment proceeds while the provision of actual transportation service is not increased; only when the railroad is finished does the relation between means of production and output of finished product assert itself. Once this point has been reached, however, it is generally the case that further additions to means of production (new rolling stock, double tracking, heavier rails, et cetera) will be closely related to changes in output (ton-miles of transportation). From this we may deduce the important principle that for the economy as a whole the relation between investment and changes in output of consumption goods will be greatly affected by the *relative* share of total investment going into the establishment of new industries.

If we start from an economy which possesses virtually no industry (aside from handicraft) it is apparent that it is capable of undergoing a transition, usually called *industrialization,* during which the greater part of its energies are devoted to building new means of production. It may even be that establishment of new industries is on such a scale *relative to total production* that for a time an actual curtailment in the output of consumption goods is required. During a process of industrialization all of what we commonly call the 'basic' industries appear as new industries, and their establishment absorbs newly accumulated capital without adding correspondingly to the output of consumption goods. It is only when the process of industrialization is completed that it becomes clear that the capacity to produce consumption goods has been greatly expanded, and the necessary connection between means of production and output of consumption goods comes to the fore again.

From this we may conclude that industrialization (establishment of new industries) counteracts the tendency to underconsumption, and does so roughly *in proportion to the relative share of total investment for which it is responsible.* That this was a factor of first importance during the eighteenth and nineteenth centuries goes without saying. From our present point of view, however, the crucial question is whether new industries have already become and whether they will continue to be relatively less important than formerly. The answer seems to be unqualifiedly in the affirmative. This does not mean that new industries no longer appear or that they are unimportant. What it does mean is that the advanced capitalist countries have undergone a process of transformation which has brought them from a predominantly agrarian-handicraft status to their present highly industrialized condition. It is difficult even to imagine a series of new industries which would today have a *relative* importance comparable to that of the textile, mining, metallurgical, and transportation industries in the eighteenth and nineteenth centuries. Still less is it possible to discern any actual or potential development of the required magnitude.

This, of course, does not apply to those parts of the world in which the process of industrialization has hardly begun or is still in full progress. There the establishment of new industries is still capable of absorbing enormous amounts of capital without adding simultaneously to the output of consumption goods. It might be supposed that this capital could be supplied from the accumulations of the already industrialized regions so that in reality the field of new industries ought to be regarded as far from exhausted. To a certain extent this is undoubtedly the case, but there are many complicating factors which have to be taken into account. One very large part of the world, European and Asiatic Russia, is rapidly industrializing itself under socialist relations of production and without benefit of outside capital. Even with respect to the remaining extensive regions of Asia, Africa, and Latin America which have so far been but lightly touched by capitalism, certain not easily surmountable barriers stand in the way of a large-scale absorption of foreign capital. The growth of monopoly within the older capitalist countries strengthens a resistance to the industrialization of new regions which has always been present to some extent; continual quarreling over the right to exploit the various areas virtually excludes the possibility that any country should enjoy the full benefits of peaceful expansion; finally, the peoples of the backward lands are becoming increasingly hostile to foreign domination and are more and more resisting incorporation into the older capitalist economies. These topics will receive fuller treatment in Part IV; merely to mention them is a sufficient warning against the easy assumption that the effects of the substantial completion of the process of industrialization at the center of capitalist production can be compensated by more rapid expansion at the periphery. That there is and will continue to be pressure in this direction is sure; whether and to what extent it will prevail and have the hoped-for effect, however, is a difficult problem which must be reserved for later and separate discussion.

So far as the older capitalist regions are concerned there is little doubt that the relative importance of new industries is on the decline. This is exactly what one would expect, and if one forgets the special characteristics of capitalism, one would be inclined to argue that it is an altogether welcome development. Having built our basic industries we are now in a position to enjoy their fruits in the form of increased mass consumption. It must not be overlooked, however, that the basic accumulation-consumption pattern of capitalism has no relation to the possibility of producing use values. Hence the substantial completion of the process of industrialization leads under capitalist conditions not to a great increase in social consumption but rather to the removal of one of the most powerful forces counteracting the ever-present tendency to underconsumption. This is what Lenin meant when he said that 'the historical mission of capitalism . . . consists in the development of society's productive forces; its structure prevents the useful application of these technical achievements for the benefit of the masses of the people.' [2] Here is one reason, perhaps the most important reason, in favor of the view that capitalism is headed for a period of chronic depression.

2. *Faulty Investment.* Under capitalist conditions investment is always undertaken with a view to supplying an uncertain demand. Inevitably there is a certain amount of investment which turns out to have been based on miscalculation and which has to be wholly or partly abandoned, to the loss and sometimes even the ruin of the capitalist undertaking it. This we can call 'faulty investment.' It absorbs a part of capitalists' accumulation without adding to the output of consumption goods and in this way counteracts the tendency to underconsumption. It is likely to be more important the less well-informed and the more sanguine are the individual capitalists. These qualities, in turn, will be most in evidence in a period which for other reasons is one of rapid expansion. Hence, in general, faulty investment is a force which counteracts the tendency to underconsumption most strongly when it is least needed and hardly at all in a period of stagnation when it would be most helpful. There is another reason why faulty investment becomes less important as a counteracting force, namely, the growth of monopolistic combines which are in a position to estimate and even perhaps influence the demand for their products where the older individualistic promoter or entrepreneur was operating largely in the dark. The greater reluctance of capital to take risks today, which is often commented upon, is probably due in no small part to a more realistic appraisal of what the risks really are. It is one of the many contradictions of capitalism that better knowledge may impair its functioning.

One should not, of course, overestimate the quantitative importance of faulty investment at any stage of capitalist development. Yet, for the reasons suggested, it may at one time have exercised a not inappreciable effect in counteracting the tendency to underconsumption, although there is little to indicate that it is of much importance today.

We now pass on to a consideration of those counteracting forces which operate by raising the rate of growth of consumption relative to the rate of growth of means of production.

3. *Population Growth.* The fully-developed Marxian underconsumption theory enables us to understand a problem which has so far eluded economists, namely, the relation of population growth to the expansion of capitalist production. In this context population growth should not be thought of in a narrow demographic sense; what is significant is rather growth in the size of the labor force at the disposal of capitalist industry, whether this results from a natural increase in numbers or from bringing within the orbit of capitalist production workers who were previously outside it. As a first approximation, however, we may consider a closed and completely capitalist system in which expansion of the labor force takes place concurrently with growth in the population at large.

If, in such a system, population growth is rapid, an equally rapid growth of variable capital is possible without any upward pressure on the wage level and hence without an adverse effect on the rate of profit. Constant capital must increase too, and for technological reasons it seems unlikely that its rate of growth should lag behind the growth of variable capital. But under the supposed circumstances there is little if any pressure continually to economize labor power by substituting constant for variable capital. Earlier theorists have generally overlooked the relevance of this set of relations to the underconsumption problem. The point especially to be noted is that the growth of variable capital constitutes an outlet for accumulation and *at the same time* signifies a growth in consumption.* Thus in the case under consideration a high rate of accumulation is compatible with a rapid growth in consumption on the one hand and no decline in the rate of profit on the other. Moreover, the danger of underconsumption is removed since there is no tendency for the rate of growth of constant capital (means of production) to outstrip the rate of growth of consumption. We already know that it is this tendency which lies at the root of underconsumption difficulties.

Let us now consider a system in which the growth of population is slow. If accumulation were still to take the form of proportional increments to constant and variable capital, this

* Cf. the exposition in Appendix A below.

could continue only if part of the additional variable capital went into increasing the wages of workers already employed. Since this would depress the rate of profit, capitalists would attempt to economize labor power by directing an ever larger proportion of their accumulation into expanding constant capital at the expense of variable. In this way unemployment would be created and the rate of profit might be maintained, but the growth of means of production would be accelerated and the growth of consumption retarded: the dilemma of underconsumption would be thus presented in full force.

This line of reasoning was indicated by Marx himself in an incisive comment on the classics' advice to workers to limit their numbers relative to the accumulation of capital. 'Such a limitation of the increase in the working population,' he wrote, 'through diminishing the supply of labor and hence through raising its price, would only accelerate the use of machinery and the transformation of circulating into fixed capital and in this fashion would create an artificial surplus population, a surplus which as a rule is not called forth by a lack of means of subsistence, but by a lack of . . . demand for labor.' * From this it is but a short step to the conclusion that any slowing down in the rate of population growth not only has the paradoxical effect of creating unemployment but also strengthens the tendency to underconsumption.

From the foregoing the following general principle may be deduced: the share of accumulation which can go into variable capital without depressing the rate of profit depends in large part on the rate of population growth; the more rapid the growth of population, the larger the share going to variable capital; hence the more rapid the increase in consumption; hence also the smaller the danger of underconsumption. This means that the strength of the tendency to underconsumption stands in inverse relation to the rapidity of population growth, being weak in periods of rapid growth and becoming stronger as the rate of growth declines. We may, therefore, for the sake of con-

* *Theorien über den Mehrwert* II/2, p. 373. This passage occurs in the course of an analysis of the views of Barton and Ricardo as the terminology indicates ('labor' instead of 'labor power,' 'circulating' and 'fixed' capital instead of 'variable' and 'constant' capital).

venience, speak of the law of inverse relation between population growth and the tendency to underconsumption.

If we drop the assumption of a closed and completely capitalist system, the scope of this law is extended. From the standpoint of capitalist production, new population includes not only natural increase in numbers but also the absorption of groups which for the first time become available for employment as wage workers. Particularly in its earlier phases, capitalism expands largely on the basis of a labor force recruited through more or less violent destruction of more primitive economic relations. In this stage of development, the 'population problem' is primarily a question of the obstacles which have to be overcome in making wage workers out of peasants and independent handicraftsmen. Later on, this same process persists in the form of an extension of capitalism to embrace so-called backward peoples in all parts of the world.

Looking back over the last four centuries, we must recognize that the population factor has been extremely favorable to rapid and uninhibited expansion of capitalism. Large reserves of manpower for impressment into the service of capital have never been lacking, while since roughly the middle of the eighteenth century the natural growth of numbers within the major capitalist nations has gone forward at an unprecedented rate. The conclusion is clearly indicated that population growth, taken in its broader sense, has been a most important factor in counteracting the tendency to underconsumption which is always striving to retard and arrest the expansion of capitalist production.

If population has been important in the past, it will be no less so in the future. It is in this connection that the well-known downward trend in the rate of population growth, which is characteristic of all highly developed capitalist countries, acquires special significance. This trend, stemming immediately from a declining birth rate, is in no sense accidental. The important contributing factors, such as urbanization, a rising standard of living,* insecurity of livelihood, and diffusion of knowledge

* In the earlier stages of development, rising living standards and increased knowledge operated chiefly to depress the death rate and hence to accelerate the growth of population. This was easily the most important factor in the great increase of the late eighteenth and nineteenth centuries.

among the masses, to mention only the most obvious, appear to be unavoidable products of capitalist development. Furthermore, attempts on the part of various countries to reverse the trend of the birth rate have not, at least as yet, met with striking success. A full discussion of this problem would carry us too far afield, but even without detailed analysis it seems safe to assume that no drastic reversal of present population trends is probable in the visible future. It follows that, from the standpoint of capitalist expansion, the situation appears to be growing increasingly unfavorable.* So far as natural growth in numbers is concerned, therefore, resistance to underconsumption is steadily diminishing; and on this count the drift of capitalism towards a state of chronic depression seems difficult to controvert.

With respect to the other aspect of the population problem, namely, the incorporation of new groups into the capitalist system, the outlook is less clear. Internally, the major countries have pretty well exhausted their reserves of non-capitalist labor power, but there are still very large aggregates of population, particularly in Asia, Africa, and Latin America, which have so far remained outside the orbit of capitalist relations. Here we meet exactly the same problem as we met before in the discussion of new industries. Once again the solution for capitalism would seem to lie in an expansion into the non-capitalist, industrially backward regions of the world. Here we can only note

Later on, however, rising living standards, in conjunction with other factors, some of which are mentioned in the text, became an equally important factor in depressing the birth rate. The apparent paradox that rising living standards could at one time accelerate and at another time retard the growth of population is thus easily explained.

In order to avoid confusion, it should be pointed out that a rise in the standard of living does not necessarily imply an increase in consumption as consumption is defined for purposes of theoretical analysis. Consumption, like accumulation and its component parts, has to be measured in value terms. Given an increase in labor productivity, it is clear that the *quantity* of goods consumed can rise while consumption in *value* terms remains constant or even declines.

* From other standpoints, e.g. the optimum population in a planned socialist society, the decline in the rate of population growth might well be a good thing; and, indeed, it is obvious that an indefinite continuation of the rate of growth exhibited by western countries in the nineteenth century must from any standpoint sooner or later be attended with disastrous consequences. These considerations, however, do not affect the conclusion reached in the text.

that the same obstacles stand in the way.* To what extent they may be overcome, and with what consequences, we shall consider in Part IV.

Let us now summarize what has been said about the role of the population factor in capitalist expansion. The Marxian analysis of the accumulation process leads—particularly because of its emphasis on the distinction between variable and constant capital, which is so often ignored or slurred over by non-Marxian theory—to the law of inverse relation between population growth and the tendency to underconsumption. On the basis of this law, we can see that both from the point of view of the availability of new strata and new regions on the one hand and from the point of view of natural increase in numbers on the other, the conditions for capitalist expansion have been extremely favorable in the past. For the same reason the decline in the rate of population growth which commenced relatively recently in the more advanced countries is certain to have serious consequences in the future, and, these serious consequences will not easily be offset by more rapid absorption of still undeveloped countries. So far as the population factor is concerned, the outlook for capitalist expansion is definitely unfavorable.

Three forces which counteract the tendency to underconsumption have now been discussed, namely, new industries, faulty investment, and population growth. The first and third have obviously been of enormous importance in determining the actual course of capitalist development; all three still operate but with diminishing strength. This is strong support for the Kautskyan thesis that capitalist expansion inevitably leads to a strengthening of the tendency to underconsumption until it finally bogs down in a state of chronic depression. But before we commit ourselves to this view we must examine the two remaining counteracting forces, for in both cases it will be shown that they have become more, and not less, powerful in recent times.

4. *Unproductive Consumption.* The basic structure of capitalist society presupposes only two classes: capitalists and workers. Since all others are in principle dispensable, we have so far

* See above, pp. 219 f.

abstracted from them in our analysis of value and accumulation. In considering the magnitude and direction of total consumption this procedure is no longer justified. As consumers, there are many 'third classes of persons' alongside the capitalists and workers who 'must either receive money for their services from these two classes, or, to the extent that they receive it without any equivalent services, they are joint owners of the surplus value in the form of rent, interest, etc.'[3] Marx here mentions two kinds of so-called 'third persons' which have traditionally been typified, on the one hand by menial servants, and on the other hand by the landed aristocracy and the church. Each receives and consumes part of the surplus value which we have hitherto assumed to be exhausted by the consumption and the accumulation of the capitalists themselves. Since these third persons do not play a direct role in the process of producing surplus value, they may be called unproductive consumers and their consumption unproductive consumption. This is the original, though generally misunderstood, sense in which Adam Smith applied the term 'unproductive' to that class of laborers which, though its services are highly useful and perhaps even indispensable, yet yields no profit to capitalist employers.* The category of unproductive consumers is broader than that of unproductive laborers in that it includes those who, like landlords, consume without performing labor of any sort. Moreover, it seems wise to extend the category still further to take in the consumption of those engaged in unproductive commercial activity,† even

* The fact that productive laborers (in the sense of those who are employed by capitalists with a view to selling their products at a profit) usually produce a material commodity led Adam Smith to identify 'productivity' with the production of material commodities. Modern writers have certainly been correct in criticizing Smith for this definition of productivity, but they have generally overlooked that their criticisms do not touch his real position. Under capitalism, productivity is a matter of producing surplus value. This Adam Smith, in spite of his logical error, knew very well, while modern economists, with their usual neglect of the specific characteristics of capitalism, have actually gone backwards from Smith by substituting a definition in terms of use value. This definition serves to obscure rather than illuminate the functioning of capitalism.

† As will be explained in greater detail below (pp. 278-80), commercial activity is unproductive because it does not create surplus value but rather absorbs it from the other sectors of the economy.

though formally they may be indistinguishable from the productive consumers (i.e. capitalists and workers) in industry, agriculture, and transport. The commercial group, while naturally never altogether absent in a capitalist system, acquires peculiar importance when the growth of monopoly obliges capitalists to place ever more emphasis on selling at the expense of production. For this reason, analysis of the so-called 'new middle class,' which includes many salesmen and others engaged in distribution as well as third persons of the more familiar type (e.g. professionals), is best undertaken only after we have considered the monopoly problem in Part IV.

The problem of unproductive consumption has long been recognized as important by those economists who have regarded the magnitude of total consumption as one of the factors determining the behavior of the capitalist system. Malthus, among the classical economists, was particularly conscious of the dangers of underconsumption, and he built upon this basis a defense of the economic role of the aristocracy and the clergy who, by their consumption, aid in preventing the general glut which, according to Malthus, would otherwise be inevitable. To Marx also it appeared that unproductive consumption helps to furnish the final objective without which continued expansion of production would be impossible. After pointing out that workers and capitalists are both 'producers for others,' the former because of their proletarian status, the latter because of their passion for accumulation, Marx proceeds as follows:

> Over against this overproduction on the one side must stand overconsumption on the other, consumption for the sake of consumption contrasted to production for the sake of production. What the individual capitalist must hand over to the landlord, the state, the creditors of the state, the church, etc., all of whom merely consume revenue, reduces his wealth absolutely but maintains his desire to get rich in a healthy state and thus supports his capitalist soul. If the landlords, money capitalists, etc., were to consume their revenue in productive instead of unproductive labor [i.e. if they were to accumulate instead of consume their incomes], the purpose would be entirely lacking. They would become themselves industrial capitalists, instead of representing the function of consumption as such . . .[4]

Marx did not elaborate this theme any more than he elaborated the theory of crises based on underconsumption, and doubtless for the same reasons. Nevertheless, it can hardly be doubted that in taking account of unproductive consumption as one of the factors conditioning the expansibility of capitalism, we are doing no more than carrying on a line of reasoning the importance and relevance of which were perfectly clear to him.

Not all unproductive consumption constitutes a net addition to the consumption of workers and capitalists. Both classes regularly elect to spend a part of their incomes for the services of doctors, teachers, servants, et cetera, instead of for consumable commodities. For most purposes it is convenient to regard the consumption of third persons of this type as an integral part of the consumption of capitalists and workers themselves. The number of people sharing in the social output of consumable goods, or in other words the total volume of employment, is certain to be influenced by the volume of unproductive consumption of this kind, but the effect on the total demand for consumable goods is not likely to be large, nor is it probable that the rate of accumulation will be materially affected.* The total volume of employment naturally exercises an indirect influence on the reproduction process, but it is not our present purpose to investigate such indirect effects. By and large our conclusion must be that the unproductive consumption of those who provide personal services can have little significance for the problem of underconsumption.

Such is not the case with other categories of unproductive consumption, however. In the England of the classical economists, for example, vast quantities of surplus value in the form of rent flowed into the pockets of a landed aristocracy which formed a separate and distinct social class. Because of their still strong feudal traditions and habits, the landed nobility and gentry did not share the capitalists' passion for accumulation; rather they poured out their incomes, and not infrequently more

* It was clearly this case which Ricardo had in mind when he expressed the much misunderstood opinion that, 'As the laborers . . . are interested in the demand for labor, they must naturally desire that as much of the revenue as possible should be diverted from expenditure on luxuries, to be expended in the support of menial servants,' *Principles*, pp. 384-5.

than their incomes, in supporting a scale of living which the industrial capitalist regarded as improvident and wasteful. Here was a form of unproductive consumption which evidently constituted a drain on the quantity of surplus value available for accumulation. Under these conditions, any change in the proportionate division of surplus value between profits and rent (e.g. as a result of the repeal of the Corn Laws) should have a decided effect upon both the total volume of consumption and the rate of accumulation. It must be said, however, that conditions in this connection have changed greatly in the last hundred years, so that today in the advanced capitalist nations it is hardly justifiable to speak any longer of a separate class of landlords whose consumption and accumulation habits differ markedly from those of the capitalists. Ownership of land and capital is now often vested in the same persons or groups of persons, perhaps through the agency of a business corporation; so far as the division of surplus value between consumption and accumulation is concerned, the distinction between rent and profit seems no longer to be an important factor. The aristocracy has become thoroughly capitalist; at the same time, however, the capitalists, thanks to their greater wealth and more important social position, have become more aristocratic and are obliged to display their wealth somewhat more lavishly than was necessary for the 'middle class' of the nineteenth century. Thus, while today the abstraction which assigns all surplus value to one homogeneous class of capitalists is more justified by real conditions than ever before, it may still be true that the historical development leading to this result has contained opposing tendencies which have largely neutralized one another with respect to the general pattern of consumption and accumulation.

While in principle the case of the earlier landed aristocracy shows most clearly the way in which unproductive consumption can affect the general level of consumption and hence operate to counteract the tendency to underconsumption, in our own time the consumption of those engaged in unproductive commercial pursuits is of far greater practical significance. This problem, as has already been suggested, is closely connected with the growth of monopoly and the rise of a so-called 'new middle class,' and for this reason analysis of its more complex aspects must be postponed until we reach these subjects in Part IV.* For the present, we shall be content to state, without proof, (1) that a considerable fraction of unproductive consumption of this kind constitutes, like that of the landed aristocracy, an addition to total consumption and a deduction from surplus value otherwise available for accumulation; (2) that unproductive consumption of this kind has been steadily growing in importance for at least the last half-century and gives every indication of continuing to grow in the future; and (3) that, from the point of view of offsetting the tendency to underconsumption, this seems to be easily the most significant trend in the field of unproductive consumption.

Our conclusion with respect to unproductive consumption is that its growth, particularly due to expansion of the distributive system, operates as a check on the tendency to underconsumption. Here, then, we have a factor which, from an economic standpoint, weakens the presumption in favor of Kautsky's theory of an approaching period of chronic depression.

5. *State Expenditures.* The classical economists, followed by Marx, treated state expenditures as a category of unproductive consumption. This was predicated upon two unspoken assumptions, namely that the state does not engage in productive activity, that is to say, lay out money in the expectation of getting it back from the sale of commodities; and that transfer expenditures (chiefly interest on the public debt) go into the hands of unproductive consumers. Given these assumptions, there is no question that state expenditures directly, and indirectly through the consumption of state employees and bondholders, operate to withdraw values from the reproduction process definitively, and this is the function of consumption which gives it a special and vital importance in the operation of the economy. Even in the nineteenth century these assumptions were no more than rough approximations to the real situation,† but they cannot have been so wide of the mark as to make the direct identification of state expenditures with unproductive consumption seriously misleading. The enormous expansion in the volume and

* See below, Chapter XV, Section 4.

† In particular it is probable that a not inconsiderable part of the interest on the public debt was regularly accumulated by its recipients.

variety of state expenditures which has been such a marked characteristic of the twentieth century, however, makes it desirable to separate state expenditures from unproductive consumption and to analyse them somewhat more carefully than formerly seemed necessary.

From the standpoint of the reproduction process, there are three fundamental categories of state expenditures: State Capital Outlays, State Transfers, and State Consumption. Let us consider each in turn.

State Capital Outlays include all outlays on labor and materials which are undertaken with a view to the production of goods or services for sale. Here the criterion of consumption, namely the withdrawal of values from the reproduction process, is not satisfied, and since state enterprises of this nature usually aim to make enough surplus value to cover the going rate of interest on government obligations, it seems proper to classify these outlays as capital and the state to this extent as a capitalist.* Expenditures for public works evidently fall within the category of state capital outlays only in so far as they are of the so-called self-liquidating type. Partially self-liquidating public works should be divided between state capital outlays and state consumption. An increase in state capital outlays, which may be called state accumulation, is, from the standpoint of the reproduction process, similar to any other form of accumulation. If state accumulation merely takes the place of private accumulation, the effect on the tendency to underconsumption is nonexistent or at most negligible; while if state accumulation proceeds at the expense of private or state consumption, the tendency to underconsumption is aggravated. Since the former case seems the more likely, it is probably safe to assume that state accumulation is not a very important influence on the tendency to underconsumption.

'State Transfers' is a convenient term to apply to that large group of payments from the public treasury which have no connection with the sale of commodities or the rendering of services

* There are, of course, differences between the state as capitalist and the private capitalist, chief of which is probably a weaker psychological and social incentive to maximum profit making and accumulation on the part of the state.

to the state: interest on the public debt, social-security and relief payments, subsidies, et cetera. Whether these transfers involve a net shift from accumulation to consumption is a question which can never be answered accurately since there is no method of isolating the sources of state revenue which are to be associated with the transfer payments. Nevertheless certain qualitative judgments are possible. Throughout the nineteenth century, the tax structure in all capitalist countries was highly regressive in its incidence, while transfer payments largely found their way into the hands of the wealthier sections of the population. Under these circumstances, there is little doubt that the state, through the mechanism of transfer payments, was acting as an engine of accumulation, siphoning purchasing power out of the pockets of consumers into the pockets of accumulators. In recent decades, however, the increasing use of corporation, income, and estate taxes and the growing volume of social-security payments have combined to shift the balance. That the transfer mechanism as a whole produces a net balance in favor of consumption is unlikely, but at any rate it is clear that it constitutes less of a drag on consumption than was formerly the case. We are therefore justified in saying that transfer payments have been evolving in a direction to offset the tendency to underconsumption.

Finally, the most important category of expenditures covers what we have called State Consumption, namely, the ordinary legislative, judicial, and executive activities of the state; public works of a non-self-liquidating character; and military establishments. Since expenditures undertaken for these purposes involve a definitive withdrawal of values from the reproduction process, they perform the same function as the individual consumption outlays of capitalists and workers. Let us assume that it is possible in a rough way to identify the revenues which are associated with expenditures for state consumption. If these revenues mean merely that the incomes of productive or unproductive consumers are diminished by an equal amount, then obviously no net increase in consumption is produced. To the extent, however, that revenues come out of surplus value which would otherwise have been accumulated, there is a clear gain for consumption. (It should be remembered that, unlike state transfers, state consumption cannot result in a decrease in total consumption.) The growing absolute and relative importance of state consumption, and the greater reliance placed by capitalist states on taxes which fall at least in part on surplus value both point to the conclusion that state consumption has been to an increasing degree responsible for a growth in total consumption. Since the same conclusion emerged from our discussion of transfer payments, we may classify state expenditures as an increasingly significant counteracting force to the tendency to underconsumption.

4. Must Underconsumption Triumph?

It appears that of the five counteracting forces which have been discussed, three (new industries, faulty investment, and population growth) have been weakening, and two (unproductive consumption and state expenditures) have been growing stronger. The balance, however, is less even than the three-to-two ratio might suggest. New industries and population growth have pretty clearly dominated the expansion of capitalism throughout the greater part of its history. Their decline in relative importance certainly tends to overshadow all the other factors singly or in combination. On the whole, there seems to be little doubt that the resistance to underconsumption is on the decline in the chief centers of world capitalism. This is no accident which happens to be true today, but which may be reversed tomorrow; the transitional character of industrialization and population growth on the nineteenth-century scale is indeed obvious to everyone. Kautsky's theory of the inevitable drift of capitalism into a period of chronic depression due to underconsumption would seem to be vindicated. But there is still another factor which has to be taken into account.

So far we have assumed that state expenditures are financed entirely by taxation. Borrowing from individuals introduces no new question of principle. But there is another possibility, namely, that the state spends money which is not taken from anyone's income but which is created either directly or by borrowing from banks. If all productive resources are fully utilized this method of financing state expenditures leads, via the mechanism of price inflation, to a subtraction from individual incomes. In this case the effect on total consumption is unlikely to be great, the increase in state consumption being as a rule largely offset by a reduction in individual consumption. But if the economy is depressed and resources are not fully utilized the additional state consumption financed by creation of purchasing power will have favorable secondary effects on private accumulation and consumption. Hence by instituting and continuing a sufficient rate of state consumption out of newly created purchasing power, it would seem that the state is in a position to bring the economy to a level of full employment and hold it there. Moreover it follows from the earlier discussion that once a condition of full employment has been attained the state can, through altering the pattern and volume of taxation and expenditure, influence total consumption and total accumulation in any desired direction.

These possibilities pose a new question. Previously, we had the problem of discovering the effects on the economy of certain state policies which were presumably adopted for reasons other than that they might have the effects in question. For example, more extensive social services and more progressive taxation were not instituted to counteract the tendency to underconsumption, though they have that effect. Now, however, we have to consider the possibility and implications of state policies which may be specifically designed to produce a certain effect on the functioning of the economy, namely, to offset the tendency to underconsumption. Modern economists quite generally advocate this course of action, and it is even common to interpret much of what capitalist governments have done in the last ten years in this light. But if it is possible for capitalist governments deliberately to counteract the tendency to underconsumption when the other counteracting forces grow too weak to prevent a state of chronic depression, then we may ask what is left of Kautsky's theory. The tendency to underconsumption, instead of translating itself into chronic depression at a certain stage of development, becomes merely a tendency to chronic depression which may be counteracted by a new force, the deliberate action of the state. Perhaps it can be said that this is more an extension than a repudiation of Kautsky. However that may be, it is clear that if the extension is accepted Kautsky's own deductions from his theory must be discarded, or at any rate regarded as unproved. If the drift to economic stagnation can be successfully countered, then why must we assume that unemployment, insecurity, sharper class and international conflicts are in prospect for capitalism? Why not, on the contrary, a 'managed' capitalist society, maintaining economic prosperity through government action and perhaps even gradually evolving into a full-fledged socialist order? When Kautsky himself, in later life, rejected the theory of chronic depression,* it was to just such a revisionist perspective that he turned. Was he, perhaps, justified?

It would be futile to attempt to answer these questions on the level of abstraction to which our analysis has so far been confined. The state cannot simply be dragged in as a *deus ex machina* to solve the demonstrated contradictions of the accumulation process. Its position and function in capitalist society must be examined to see what can and what cannot be expected of it. Moreover, the model capitalism of the foregoing analysis lacks many features which are of the greatest importance in the modern world. The assumption of a closed competitive system is a useful, even a necessary, theoretical device, but it must not be confused with the real world. To do so is to commit, in a particularly egregious form, the 'fallacy of misplaced concreteness.' The diagnosis and prognosis of the case of capitalism requires, in addition to a dissection of the accumulation process, a careful study of the state, monopoly, and world economy.

It goes without saying that such a careful study is impossible within the confines of one relatively brief volume. But we may be able to direct attention to some of the most important factors at work, and in this way to lay the basis for a better understanding both of what has been happening in recent years and of what the future holds in store.

* See above, pp. 207 f.

PART FOUR

IMPERIALISM

XIII

THE STATE

1. The State in Economic Theory

PROBABLY few would deny that the state plays a vital role in the economic process. There are still many, however, who would argue that the state can and should be kept out of economic theorizing.

From one point of view, this is not difficult to understand. So long as economics is regarded as a science of the relations between man and nature in the manner of the modern school, the state requires consideration only at the level of application and not as a part of the subject matter of the science. There is no state on Robinson Crusoe's island, yet economics is as relevant to Robinson as it is to twentieth-century America. From this standpoint the state cannot logically be a concern of theoretical economics; it must be regarded as one of the factors which shape and limit the application of economic principles to any given set of actual conditions.*

All this is changed when we take the position that economics is the science of the social relationships of production under historically determined conditions. Failure to include the state in the subject matter of economics then becomes an arbitrary and unjustifiable omission. In view of this, and after what has been said about Marx's fundamental approach to economics in earlier chapters, no further explanation seems required to justify the inclusion of a chapter on the state in our examination of Marxian economics. A word of caution is, however, necessary before we proceed.

As in the case of crises, Marx never worked out a systematic and formally complete theory of the state. That he originally

* See the Introduction above, pp. 3-8.

intended to do so is clear. For example, he opens the Preface to the *Critique of Political Economy* with the following words:

> I consider the system of bourgeois economy in the following order: Capital, landed property, wage labor; state, foreign trade, world market . . . The first part of the first book, treating of capital, consists of the following chapters: 1. Commodity; 2. Money, or simple Circulation; 3. Capital in general. The first two chapters form the contents of the present work . . . Systematic elaboration on the plan outlined above will depend upon circumstances.[1]

The plan underwent substantial alterations in the course of time, as an examination of the three volumes of *Capital* makes clear, but the state always remained in the background and never received the 'systematic elaboration' which Marx evidently had hoped to accord it. It follows that a neat summary of his views is out of the question. Instead we shall try to present a summary theoretical treatment of the state which is consistent with Marx's numerous and scattered remarks on the subject and which at the same time provides the necessary supplement to the main body of theoretical principles dealing with the development of the capitalist system.*

2. The Primary Function of the State

There is a tendency on the part of modern liberal theorists to interpret the state as an institution established in the interests of society as a whole for the purpose of mediating and reconciling the antagonisms to which social existence inevitably gives rise. This is a theory which avoids the pitfalls of political metaphysics and which serves to integrate in a tolerably satisfactory fashion a considerable body of observed fact. It contains, how-

* Among the most important Marxist writings on the state the following may be mentioned: Engels, *The Origin of the Family, Private Property and the State*, particularly Ch. IX; Lenin, *The State and Revolution;* Rosa Luxemburg, 'Sozialreform oder Revolution?' *Gesammelte Werke*, Vol. III. An English translation of the latter work is available (*Reform or Revolution?*, Three Arrows Press, N. Y., 1937), but it is unfortunately not a very satisfactory one. A reasonably adequate survey of a large body of Marxist literature on the state is contained in S. H. M. Chang, *The Marxian Theory of the State* (1931).

ever, one basic shortcoming, the recognition of which leads to a theory essentially Marxian in its orientation. A critique of what may be called the class-mediation conception of the state is, therefore, perhaps the best way of introducing the Marxian theory.

The class-mediation theory assumes, usually implicitly, that the underlying class structure, or what comes to the same thing, the system of property relations is an immutable datum, in this respect like the order of nature itself. It then proceeds to ask what arrangements the various classes will make to get along with each other, and finds that an institution for mediating their conflicting interests is the logical and necessary answer. To this institution powers for maintaining order and settling quarrels are granted. In the real world what is called the state is identified as the counterpart of this theoretical construction.

The weakness of this theory is not difficult to discover. It lies in the assumption of an immutable and, so to speak, self-maintaining class structure of society. The superficiality of this assumption is indicated by the most cursory study of history.* The fact is that many forms of property relations with their concomitant class structures have come and gone in the past, and there is no reason to assume that they will not continue to do so in the future. The class structure of society is no part of the natural order of things; it is the product of past social development, and it will change in the course of future social development.

Once this is recognized it becomes clear that the liberal theory goes wrong in the manner in which it initially poses the problem. We cannot ask: Given a certain class structure, how will the various classes, with their divergent and often conflicting interests, manage to get along together? We must ask: How did a particular class structure come into being and by what means is its continued existence guaranteed? As soon as an attempt is made to answer this question, it appears that the state has a function in society which is prior to and more fundamental than

* Many theorists recognize this up to a point, but they believe that what was true of past societies is not true of modern society. In other words, capitalism is regarded as the final end-product of social evolution. See the discussion of this point in Chapter 1 above.

any which present-day liberals attribute to it. Let us examine this more closely.

A given set of property relations serves to define and demarcate the class structure of society. From any set of property relations one class or classes (the owners) reap material advantages; other classes (the owned and the non-owners) suffer material disadvantages. A special institution capable and willing to use force to whatever degree is required is an essential to the maintenance of such a set of property relations. Investigation shows that the state possesses this characteristic to the fullest degree, and that no other institution is or can be allowed to compete with it in this respect. This is usually expressed by saying that the state, and the state alone, exercises sovereignty over all those subject to its jurisdiction. It is, therefore, not difficulty to identify the state as the guarantor of a given set of property relations.

If now we ask, where the state comes from, the answer is that it is the product of a long and arduous struggle in which the class which occupies what is for the time the key positions in the process of production gets the upper hand over its rivals and fashions a state which will enforce that set of property relations which is in its own interest. In other words any particular state is the child of the class or classes in society which benefit from the particular set of property relations which it is the state's obligation to enforce. A moment's reflection will carry the conviction that it could hardly be otherwise. As soon as we have dropped the historically untenable assumption that the class structure of society is in some way natural or self-enforcing, it is clear that any other outcome would lack the prerequisites of stability. If the disadvantaged classes were in possession of state power, they would attempt to use it to establish a social order more favorable to their own interests, while a sharing of state power among the various classes would merely shift the locale of conflict to the state itself.

That such conflicts within the state, corresponding to fundamental class struggles outside, have taken place in certain transitional historical periods is not denied.* During those long pe-

* For an example, see the discussion of 'The Conditions of Fascism,' pp. 329-32, below.

riods, however, when a certain social order enjoys a relatively continuous and stable existence, the state power must be monopolized by the class or classes which are the chief beneficiaries.

As against the class-mediation theory of the state, we have here the underlying idea of what has been called the class-domination theory. The former takes the existence of a certain class structure for granted and sees in the state an institution for reconciling the conflicting interests of the various classes; the latter, on the other hand, recognizes that classes are the product of historical development and sees in the state an instrument in the hands of the ruling classes for enforcing and guaranteeing the stability of the class structure itself.

It is important to realize that, so far as capitalist society is concerned, 'class domination' and 'the protection of private property' are virtually synonymous expressions. Hence when we say with Engels that the highest purpose of the state is the protection of private property,[2] we are also saying that the state is an instrument of class domination. This is doubtless insufficiently realized by critics of the Marxian theory who tend to see in the notion of class domination something darker and more sinister than 'mere' protection of private property. In other words they tend to look upon class domination as something reprehensible and the protection of private property as something meritorious. Consequently, it does not occur to them to identify the two ideas. Frequently, no doubt, this is because they have in mind not capitalist property, but rather private property as it would be in a simple commodity-producing society where each producers owns and works with his own means of production. Under such conditions there are no classes at all and hence no class domination. Under capitalist relations, however, property has an altogether different significance, and its protection is easily shown to be identical with the preservation of class dominance. Capitalist private property does not consist in things —things exist independently of their ownership—but in a social relation between people. Property confers upon its owners freedom from labor and the disposal over the labor of others, and this is the essence of all social domination whatever form it may assume. It follows that the protection of property is fundamentally the assurance of social domination to owners over non-owners. And this, in turn, is precisely what is meant by class domination, which it is the primary function of the state to uphold.

The recognition that the defense of private property is the first duty of the state is the decisive factor in determining the attitude of genuine Marxist socialism towards the state. 'The theory of the Communists,' Marx and Engels wrote in the *Communist Manifesto*, 'can be summed up in the single sentence: Abolition of private property.' Since the state is first and foremost the protector of private property, it follows that the realization of this end cannot be achieved without a head-on collision between the forces of socialism and the state power.*

3. The State as an Economic Instrument

The fact that the first concern of the state is to protect the continued existence and stability of a given form of society does not mean that it performs no other functions of economic importance. On the contrary, the state has always been a very significant factor in the functioning of the economy within the framework of the system of property relations which it guarantees. This principle is generally implicitly recognized by Marxist writers whenever they analyse the operation of an actual eco-

* The treatment of the relation between the state and property has of necessity been extremely sketchy. In order to avoid misunderstanding, the following note should be added. The idea that the state is an organization for the maintenance of private property was by no means an invention of Marx and Engels. On the contrary, it constituted the cornerstone of the whole previous development of political thought from the breakdown of feudalism and the origins of the modern state. Bodin, Hobbes, Locke, Rousseau, Adam Smith, Kant, and Hegel—to mention but a few outstanding thinkers of the period before Marx—clearly recognized this central function of the state. They believed private property to be the necessary condition for the full development of human potentialities, the *sine qua non* of genuine freedom. Marx and Engels added that freedom based on private property is freedom for an exploiting class, and that freedom for *all* presupposes the abolition of private property, that is to say the achievement of a classless society. Nevertheless, Marx and Engels did not forget that the realization of a classless society (abolition of private property) is possible only on the basis of certain definite historical conditions; without the enormous increase in the productivity of labor which capitalism had brought about, a classless society would be no more than an empty Utopia.

nomic system, but it has received little attention in discussions of the theory of the state. The reason for this is not difficult to discover. The theory of the state has usually been investigated with the problem of transition from one form of society to another in the foreground; in other words, what we have called the primary function of the state has been the subject of analysis. Lenin's *State and Revolution*—the title clearly indicates the center of interest—set a precedent which has been widely followed.* Consequently, the theory of the state as an economic instrument has been neglected, though evidently for our purposes it is necessary to have some idea of the essentials of Marx's thinking on the subject.

Fortunately Marx, in his chapter on the length of the working day,[3] provides a compact and lucid analysis of the role of the state in relation to one very important problem of capitalist economy. By examining this chapter in some detail we can deduce the guiding principles of Marxist teaching on the role of the state within the framework of capitalist property relations.

The rate of surplus value, one of the key variables in Marx's system of theoretical economics, depends on three factors: the productivity of labor, the length of the working day and prevailing subsistence standards. It is therefore a matter of importance to discover the determinants of the length of the working day. This is clearly not a question of economic law in any narrow sense. As Marx put it,

> apart from extremely elastic bounds, the nature of exchange of commodities itself imposes no limits to the working day, no limit to surplus labor. The capitalist maintains his rights as a purchaser when he tries to make the working day as long as possible . . . On the other hand . . . the laborer maintains his right as a seller when he wishes to reduce the working day to one of definite normal duration. There is here, therefore, an antimony, right against right, both equally bearing the seal of the law of exchanges. Between equal rights force decides. Hence it is that in the history of capitalist production, the determination of what is a working day presents itself as the result of a struggle, a

* For example, Chang's book, cited above, follows Lenin's outline very closely.

struggle between collective capital, i.e. the class of capitalists, and collective labor, i.e. the working class.[4]

After describing certain forms, both pre-capitalist and capitalist, of exploitation involving the duration of the working day, Marx examines 'The Struggle for a Normal Working Day' in the historical development of English capitalism. The first phase of this struggle resulted in 'Compulsory Laws for the Extension of the Working Day from the Middle of the 14th to the End of the 17th Century.'[5] Employers, straining to create a trained and disciplined proletariat out of the available pre-capitalist material, were frequently obliged to resort to the state for assistance. Laws extending the length of the working day were the result. For a long time, however, the extension of the working day was a very slow and gradual process. It was not until the rapid growth of the factory system in the second half of the eighteenth century that there began that process of prolonging hours of work which culminated in the notorious conditions of the early nineteenth century:

After capital had taken centuries in extending the working day to its normal maximum length, and then beyond this to the limit of the natural day of 12 hours, there followed on the birth of machinism and modern industry in the last third of the 18th century a violent encroachment like that of an avalanche in its intensity and extent . . . As soon as the working class, stunned at first by the noise and turmoil of the new system of production, recovered in some measure its senses its resistance began.[6]

The beginnings of working-class resistance ushered in the second phase of the development: 'Compulsory Limitation by Law of the Working Time, The English Factory Acts, 1833 to 1864.'[7] In a series of sharp political struggles, the workers were able to wring one concession after another from their opponents. These concessions took the form of laws limiting hours of work for ever wider categories of labor, until by 1860 the principle of limitation of the working day was so firmly established that it could no longer be challenged. Thereafter progress pursued a smoother course.

The limitation of the working day was not simply a question of concessions by the ruling class in the face of a revolutionary threat, though this was undoubtedly the main factor. At least two other considerations of importance have to be taken into account. Marx noted that,

> Apart from the working class movement that daily grew more threatening, the limiting of factory labor was dictated by the same necessity which spread guano over the English fields. The same blind eagerness for plunder that in the one case exhausted the soil had, in the other, torn up by the roots the living forces of the nation.[8]

Moreover, the question of factory legislation entered into the final phase of the struggle for political mastery between the landed aristocracy and the industrial capitalists:

> However much the individual manufacturer might give the rein to his old lust for gain, the spokesmen and political leaders of the manufacturing class ordered a change in front and of speech toward the workpeople. They had entered upon the contest for the repeal of the Corn Laws and needed the workers to help them to victory. They promised, therefore, not only a double-sized loaf of bread, but the enactment of the Ten Hours Bill in the Free Trade millennium . . .[9]

And after repeal of the Corn Laws had gone through, the workers 'found allies in the Tories panting for revenge.'[10] Thus factory legislation derived a certain amount of support from both sides to the great struggle over free trade.

Finally Marx concluded his treatment of the working day with the following statement:

> For 'protection' against 'the serpent of their agonies' the laborers must put their heads together and, as a class, compel the passing of a law, an all-powerful social barrier that shall prevent the very workers from selling, by voluntary contract with capital, themselves and their families into slavery and death. In place of the pompous catalogue of the 'inalienable rights of man' comes the modest Magna Charta of a legally limited working day, which shall make clear 'when the time which the worker sells is ended, and when his own begins.' *Quantum mutatus ab illo!*[11]

What general conclusions can be deduced from Marx's discussion of the working day? The principle of most general bearing was stated by Engels. Answering the charge that historical materialism neglects the political element in historical change, Engels cited the chapter on the working day 'where legislation, which is surely a political act, has such a trenchant effect' and concluded that 'force (that is, state power) is also an economic power' and hence is by no means excluded from the causal factors in historical change.[12] Once this has been established, it is necessary to ask under what circumstances and in whose interest the economic power of the state will be brought into action. On both points the analysis of the working day is instructive.

First, the state power is invoked to solve problems which are posed by the economic development of the particular form of society under consideration, in this case capitalism. In the earlier period a shortage of labor power, in the later period over-exploitation of the laboring population were the subjects of state action. In each case the solution of the problem required state intervention. Many familiar examples of a similar character readily come to mind.

Second, we should naturally expect that the state power under capitalism would be used first and foremost in the interests of the capitalist class since the state is dedicated to the preservation of the structure of capitalism and must therefore be staffed by those who fully accept the postulates and objectives of this form of society. This is unquestionably true, but it is not inconsistent to say that state action may run counter to the immediate economic interests of some or even all of the capitalists provided only that the overriding aim of preserving the system intact is promoted. The legal limitation of the working day is a classic example of state action of this sort. The intensity of class antagonism engendered by over-exploitation of the labor force was such that it became imperative for the capitalist class to make concessions even at the cost of immediate economic advantages.*

* This example makes clear the concession character of state action favoring the working class, since it could not possibly be maintained that the workers had a share in state power in England at the time the main factory acts were passed. In this connection it is sufficient to recall that the Reform Act of 1832 contained high property qualifications for voting and it was not until 1867 that the franchise was next extended. By this time the most important victories in the struggle for factory legislation had already been won.

For the sake of preserving domestic peace and tranquility, blunting the edge of class antagonisms, and ultimately avoiding the dangers of violent revolution, the capitalist class is always prepared to make concessions through the medium of state action. It may, of course, happen that the occasion for the concessions is an actual materialization of the threat of revolution.* In this case their purpose is to restore peace and order so that production and accumulation can once again go forward uninterruptedly.

Let us summarize the principles underlying the use of the state as an economic instrument within the framework of capitalism. In the first place, the state comes into action in the economic sphere in order to solve problems which are posed by the development of capitalism. In the second place, where the interests of the capitalist class are concerned, there is a strong predisposition to use the state power freely. And, finally, the state may be used to make concessions to the working class provided that the consequences of not doing so are sufficiently dangerous to the stability and functioning of the system as a whole.

It should be noted that none of these conclusions lends support to the revisionist view that socialism can be achieved through a series of piecemeal reforms. On the contrary, they grow out of and supplement the basic principle that the state exists in the first instance for the protection of capitalist property relations. Reforms may modify the functioning of capitalism but never threaten its foundation. Rosa Luxemburg stated the true Marxian position succinctly in the following words:

> 'Social control' . . . is concerned not with the limitation of capitalist property, but on the contrary with its protection. Or, speaking in economic terms, it does not constitute an attack on capitalist exploitation but rather a normalization and regularization of this exploitation.[18]

Marx never said anything to contradict this, and to cite his chapter on the working day, as revisionists frequently do, in

* For example, Marx remarked that in France, 'the February [1848] revolution was necessary to bring into the world the 12 hours' law.' *Capital* I, p. 328.

support of the gradualist standpoint is simply to betray a misunderstanding of his entire theoretical system.

4. The Question of the Form of Government

Up to this point nothing has been said about the form of government in capitalist society. Is it possible that the principles of state action which have been examined do not hold in a fully democratic capitalist society? (By 'fully democratic' we mean no more than what exists today in most of the English-speaking world: parliamentarism combined with universal suffrage and organizational freedom in the political sphere.)

If Marxist theory answers this question in the negative, this must not be interpreted to mean that the question of democracy is regarded as of no importance, but only that democracy does not alter the basic significance of the state in relation to the economy. The existence of democracy is, of course, a matter of prime importance particularly to the working class. Only under a democratic form of government can the working class organize freely and effectively for the achievement of its ends, whether they happen to be socialist or merely reformist in character. It is for this reason that one of the first demands of the labor movement in all non-democratic countries has always been the establishment of democratic forms of government. Moreover, for the ruling class democracy has always constituted a potential threat to the stability of its position and has consequently been granted grudgingly, with limitations, and usually only under severe pressure. Marx stated the main issues very forcibly in discussing the democratic French constitution of 1848:

> The most comprehensive contradiction of this constitution consisted in the following: the classes whose social slavery the constitution is to perpetuate, proletariat, peasants, petty bourgeois, it puts in possession of political power through universal suffrage. And from the class whose old social power it sanctions, the bourgeoisie, it withdraws the political guarantees of this power. It forces its rule into democratic conditions, which at every moment help the hostile classes to victory and jeopardize the very foundations of bourgeois society.[14]

Democracy brings the conflicts of capitalist society into the open in the political sphere; it restricts the freedom of the capitalists to use the state in their own interests; it reinforces the working class in demanding concessions; finally, it even increases the possibility that the working class will present demands which threaten the system itself and so must be rejected by the capitalists and their state functionaries regardless of the consequences. As we shall see later on, these are all matters of the greatest importance in determining the actual course of capitalist evolution; but they do not contradict the principles set forth in the preceding section. There is, in other words, nothing in the nature of democracy to make us change our view of the fundamental functions and limits of state action in capitalist society. Again, we must insist that the revisionists, in holding the opposed view, that socialism can be gradually substituted for capitalism by the methods of capitalist democracy, were in reality abandoning Marx altogether.

The fallacy of the revisionist position was never more clearly pointed out than by Rosa Luxemburg in her polemic against Bernstein and Schmidt in 1899:

> According to Conrad Schmidt, the achievement of a social democratic majority in parliament should be the direct way to the gradual socialization of society . . . Formally, to be sure, parliamentarism does express the interests of the entire society in the state organization. On the other hand, however, it is still capitalist society, that is to say, a society in which capitalist interests are controlling . . . The institutions which are democratic in form are in substance instruments of the dominant class interests. This is most obvious in the fact that so soon as democracy shows a disposition to deny its class character and to become an instrument of the real interests of the people, the democratic forms themselves are sacrificed by the bourgeoisie and their representatives in the state. The idea of a social democratic majority appears therefore as a calculation which, entirely in the spirit of bourgeois liberalism, concerns itself with only one side—the formal side—of democracy but which leaves out of account the other side, its real content.[15]

The spread of fascism in the last two decades, particularly in those countries where working-class organization had reached its greatest development, has done much to weaken the belief in the possibility of a gradual transition to socialism through the methods provided by capitalist democracy. Otto Bauer, one of the outstanding representatives of the Second International and long leader of the Austrian socialists, expressed a widespread view when he wrote, in 1936, that the experience of fascism 'destroys the illusion of reformist socialism that the working class can fill the forms of democracy with socialist content and develop the capitalist into a socialist order without a revolutionary jump.'[16] Rosa Luxemburg's warning that in an extremity 'the democratic forms themselves are sacrificed by the bourgeoisie and their representatives in the state' has turned out to be well-founded. We shall return to this question in greater detail in Chapters XVIII and XIX below.

5. Evaluating the Role of the State

It might seem that we are now ready to consider the problem of the state in relation to chronic depression, which was raised at the end of the last Part. But this would be an error. Chronic depression is only one of the problems of capitalism requiring state action, and to treat it in isolation would be certain to lead to false conclusions.

It must be recalled once again that the analysis of the preceding chapters has been carried through on a relatively high level of abstraction in several important respects. In particular we have assumed, except in occasional *excursi*, a closed and freely competitive capitalist system. In reality present-day capitalism is neither closed nor freely competitive. What we see around us is an interrelated world economy consisting of numerous capitalist, semi-capitalist, and non-capitalist nations in which varying degrees of monopoly are a common phenomenon. As we shall see, these facts are not accidental; they belong to the very nature of capitalism as a phase of world history. To abstract from them was a necessary, but at the same time, provisional stage in our analysis. The time has now come to go beyond this position, to take account of a variety of aspects of capitalist development which have so far been omitted from consideration. In so doing we shall find that new problems and conditions are introduced which profoundly affect our view of the future of capitalism and the role of the state therein.

Our next tasks must, therefore, be to analyse the structural and institutional tendencies of capitalism which modify its competitive character; and to analyse the developing characteristics of world economy. We shall find the two tasks interrelated in the closest way. Only when these tasks have been completed will we be in a position to apply the principles brought out in the present chapter and to evaluate concretely the role of state activity in deciding the fate of the capitalist order.

XIV

THE DEVELOPMENT OF MONOPOLY CAPITAL

THE tendencies in capitalism which lead away from free competition among producers and towards the formation of monopolies are closely connected with the rising organic composition of capital which has been discussed in earlier chapters. Two aspects have to be taken into consideration: first, the growth in constant relative to variable capital; and second, the growth in the fixed portion of constant capital, i.e. in buildings and machines relative to raw, processed, and auxiliary materials. The result of both of these trends is a rise in the average size of the productive unit. Marx noted that this could come about in two ways, which we must now examine.

1. Concentration of Capital

If individual capitalists accumulate, so that the quantity of capital under each one's control increases, this makes possible an enlarged scale of production. Marx called this process 'concentration of capital.' Concentration in this sense is a normal accompaniment of accumulation and obviously cannot take place without accumulation. The converse, however, is not necessarily true, since it is possible to imagine accumulation at the same time that individual capitals are declining in magnitude, perhaps through repeated subdivisions among heirs at death. Despite counteracting tendencies of this sort, concentration by itself would undoubtedly be sufficient to account for a steady rise in the scale of production and for a tendency, at least in some lines, towards the limitation of competition. Alongside of concentration there is a second and even more important process which Marx called 'centralization of capital.'

2. Centralization of Capital

Centralization, which is not to be confused with concentration, means the combining of capitals which are already in existence:

> This process differs from the former in this, that it only presupposes a change in the distribution of capital already to hand and functioning; its field of action is therefore not limited by the absolute growth of social wealth, by the absolute limits of accumulation. Capital grows in one place to a huge mass in a single hand because it has in another place been lost by many. This is centralization proper, as distinct from accumulation and concentration.[1]

Marx did not attempt to expound 'the laws of this centralization of capitals' but rather contented himself with 'a brief hint at a few facts.' This was due to the plan of his work and not to any belief that the phenomenon was unimportant. Even so, his brief hint is instructive and will bear examination.

The primary and underlying factor in centralization is found in the economies of large-scale production. 'The battle of competition is fought by cheapening of commodities. The cheapness of commodities depends, *ceteris paribus*, on the productiveness of labor, and this again on the scale of production. Therefore the larger capitals beat the smaller.'[2] Some of the smaller capitals disappear, others pass into the hands of the more efficient concerns which in this way grow in size. Thus the competitive struggle itself is an agent of centralization.

There is another force making for centralization which operates in a different manner, and this is the 'credit system.' As Marx uses the term, the credit system is to be understood in a broad sense to include not only banks but the entire financial machinery of investment houses, security markets, and so on.

> In its beginnings the credit system sneaks in as a modest helper of accumulation and draws by invisible threads the money resources scattered all over the surface of society into the hands of individual or associated capitalists. But soon it becomes a new and formidable weapon in the competitive struggle, and finally

it transforms itself into an immense social mechanism for the centralization of capitals.[3]

Centralization via the credit system, in its developed form, does not imply the expropriation of smaller capitalists by larger, but 'the amalgamation of a number of capitals which already exist or are in the process of formation . . . by the smoother road of forming stock companies.'[4] This is by far the most rapid method of extending the scale of production. 'The world would still be without railroads if it had been obliged to wait until accumulation should have enabled a few individual capitals to undertake the construction of a railroad. Centralization, on the other hand, accomplished this by a turn of the hand through stock companies.'[5]

The end of centralization in any line of industry is reached when there is only one firm left,* but for society as a whole the utmost limit would not be reached 'until the entire social capital would be united either in the hands of one single capitalist, or in those of one single corporation.'[6] It is clear from this remark, and indeed from Marx's whole discussion of centralization, that he did not regard the process from the point of view of legal ownership—which might be distributed among a large number of shareholders—but rather from the point of view of the magnitude of capital under unified direction.

The main effects of centralization, and to a lesser degree of concentration proper, are three in number. In the first place, it leads to a socialization and rationalization of the labor process within the confines of capitalism; in this connection Marx speaks of 'the progressive transformation of isolated processes of production carried on in accustomed ways into socially combined and scientifically managed processes of production.'[7] Secondly, centralization, itself the consequence of technical change and the rising organic composition of capital, acts to hasten technical change forward. 'Centralization, by thus accelerating and intensifying the effects of accumulation, extends at the same time the

* To the 4th German edition, Engels added the following footnote: 'The latest English and American "trusts" are aiming to accomplish this by trying to unite at least all the large establishments of a certain line of industry into one great stock company with a practical monopoly.' *Capital* I, p. 688.

revolutions in the technical composition of capital which increase its constant part at the expense of its variable part and thereby reduce the relative demand for labor.' * The third effect, which did not concern Marx at the particular stage of his inquiry where he treated centralization, is an obvious corollary, namely, the progressive replacement of competition among a large number of producers by monopolistic or semi-monopolistic control over markets by a small number.

3. Corporations

We have seen that Marx recognized the corporation as an essential instrument of centralization. He was also aware that corporations had certain further, and far-reaching, implications for the character and functioning of capitalist production. These are pointed out in one of the draft manuscripts which Engels put together to form Volume III of *Capital;*[8] sketchy as the analysis is, it nevertheless shows Marx to have been far ahead of his time in recognizing the significance of this problem.

Marx makes three main points in connection with stock companies:

> 1. An enormous expansion of the scale of production and enterprises, which were impossible for individual capitals . . .
> 2. Capital . . . is here directly endowed with the form of social capital . . . as distinguished from private capital, and its enterprises assume the form of social enterprises as distinguished from individual enterprises. It is the abolition of capital as private property within the boundaries of capitalist production itself.
> 3. Transformation of the actually functioning capitalist into a mere manager, an administrator of other people's capital, and of the owners of capital into mere owners, mere money capitalists.[9]

The first of these points has already been dealt with. The second and third summarize tersely the gist of a large body of literature on corporations of the last two or three decades.

* *Capital* I, p. 689. This is not the only effect of centralization on technological change. See below, p. 276.

Private production, already weakened with the coming of the factory system, disappears almost entirely in the large corporation, and the actual owner of capital withdraws more or less completely from the productive process. Marx, however, does not make the mistake, which many modern writers on the subject have made, of regarding the corporation as a direct step towards social control over production. On the contrary, the consequence of this new development is 'a new aristocracy of finance, a new sort of parasites in the shape of promoters, speculators, and merely nominal directors; a whole system of swindling and cheating by means of corporation juggling, stock jobbing, and stock speculation. It is private production without the control of private property.'[10]

The Marxian theory of corporations was elaborated and extended by Rudolf Hilferding in his important work *Finance Capital*, published in 1910. Economically the most important aspect of the corporate form of organization is the dissolution of the unifying bond between ownership of capital and actual direction of production, 'the freeing of the industrial capitalist from the function of industrial entrepreneur,' as Hilferding expressed it.[11] It was in developing the implications of this phenomenon that Hilferding made his most important contribution to the theory of corporations.

It is not the corporate form as such which transforms the industrial capitalist into a money capitalist; a private firm can go through the legal procedure of incorporation without changing anything essential from an economic standpoint. What is decisive is the growth of a reliable market for corporate securities, itself a long historical process which cannot be analysed here. The reason for this is clear: only through the securities market does the capitalist attain independence of the fate of the particular enterprise in which he has invested his money. To the extent that the securities market is perfected the shareholder resembles less and less the old-fashioned capitalist-operator and more and more a lender of money who can regain possession of his money on demand. One difference always remains, namely, that the shareholder runs a greater risk of loss than the pure lender and hence the yield on shares can be expected to exceed interest on money by a variable risk premium. With this qualification, the transformation of the shareholder from an industrial capitalist receiving profit into a money capitalist receiving interest is in principle complete.

The first consequence of this transformation is the appearance of 'promoter's profit' (*Gründergewinn*), which Hilferding correctly designates as 'an economic category *sui generis*.'[12] If an enterprise (already in existence or projected) will yield, say, 20 per cent on the capital invested in it, and if the yield on shares in enterprises of comparable risk is ten per cent, then by incorporating the enterprise and 'floating' it on the market promoters will be able to sell shares to double the amount of actually invested capital. The difference goes directly or indirectly into the pockets of the promoters who are thereby enriched and strengthened for further operations. Promoter's profit is both an incentive to the formation of corporations and a source of great fortunes; in both ways it fosters the growth in the scale of production and the centralization of capital.

The act of promotion is consummated in the issuance and sale of new securities to those who dispose over free money capital. It is for this reason that the specialist in selling new securities comes to occupy a key position in the formation of corporations, frequently performing directly the functions of promotion and reaping the lion's share of promoter's profit. In Germany the large commercial banks, with their extensive resources and financial contacts, early went into the business of selling new securities and established for themselves the primary place in the field of promotion. In the United States, on the other hand, it was the private bankers, dealers in domestic and foreign exchange, who first entered the field of new securities and in this way gradually evolved the institution of investment banking as distinct from commercial banking, though at a later stage of development the commercial banks entered the investment banking business through the medium of so-called securities affiliates. In spite of the somewhat divergent paths of development, which were probably due as much as anything to differing legal limitations on the freedom of commercial banks, the result in both Germany and the United States, the two countries which Hilferding took as the basis for his generalizations, was substantially the same. Financiers played the dominant role in promotion and in this way achieved a highly significant, and even for a time dominant, position in the corporate structure. It was on the basis of this phenomenon that Hilferding entitled his book *Finance Capital*. We shall see below, however, that Hilferding erred in the direction of overestimating the importance of financial dominance in the latest stage of capitalist development.

Besides laying the foundation for promoter's profit, the separation of the individual capitalist from his role in the productive process leads to a further centralization of control over capital. Nominally control in the corporation rests in the hands of the body of shareholders. But even legally the owners of a majority of the shares have virtually complete control over the capital contributed by all the shareholders, and in practice the proportion required is ordinarily much less than a majority, 'no more than a third to a fourth of the capital and even less.' [13] Because of this fact the big capitalist who can command a large block of shares in one or more corporations is able to bring under his control an amount of capital several times what he owns. This brings out clearly an attribute of the corporate form of organization which Hilferding did not make explicit enough, namely, that while ownership of shares as such is divorced from the control and direction of production, nevertheless ownership of a sufficiently large quantity of shares carries with it control over production on a multiplied scale.*

Even this, however, understates the possibility of centralization of control through use of the corporate form, for it must be remembered that one corporation can own the shares of one or more other corporations. Thus a capitalist may control corporation A by owning, say, one-third of its shares. Part of the capital of A may be used to gain control over corporations B, C and D, and the capital of these in turn to bring into the fold still further corporations. 'With the development of the corporate form there comes into existence a special financing technique which has the purpose of assuring to the smallest amount

* We have here an apt illustration of the dialectical principle that under certain circumstances a change in quantity beyond a definite point leads to a change in quality.

of one's own capital dominance over the greatest possible amount of other people's capital.' *

We have now to notice the final step in the centralization process made possible by the corporate form. On the one hand, promoter's profit puts vast wealth in the possession of a relatively few capitalists and banking institutions; on the other hand this wealth can be invested in such a way as to secure control over a far larger aggregate of capital. In this fashion, as Hilferding expressed it,

> there is formed a circle of persons who, thanks to their own possession of capital or as representatives of concentrated power over other people's capital (bank directors), sit upon the governing boards of a large number of corporations. There thus arises a kind of personal union [*Personalunion*], on the one hand between the different corporations themselves, on the other between the latter and the banks, a circumstance which must be of the greatest importance for the policy of these institutions since among them there has arisen a community of interests [*gemeinsame Besitzinteresse*].[14]

In many cases this personal union among 'insiders' is the parent, or at least forerunner, of still closer organizational unification, in the form of cartels, trusts, or mergers, aimed directly at monopolistic control over the market. These organizational forms will be considered separately in the next section.

The general consequences of the spread of the corporate form can be summarized as follows: intensification of the centralization process along with an acceleration of accumulation in general, on the one hand; on the other, formation of a relatively small upper layer of big capitalists whose control extends far beyond the limits of their ownership. The latter point has been so generally misunderstood by modern writers that it is perhaps worth a further word.

In recent years we have read much about separation of ownership from control in the large corporation. This is a correct description of actual trends if it is taken to mean that concen-

* *Das Finanzkapital*, pp. 130-31. Hilferding noted that 'this technique has reached its perfection in the financing of the American railroad systems' (p. 131). We should have to say today that even this level, high as it was, was surpassed in the public-utility field during the 1920s.

tration of control over capital is not limited by the concentration of ownership. If, however, it is interpreted as implying that control passes out of the hands of owners altogether and becomes the prerogative of some other group in society, it is completely erroneous. What actually happens is that the great majority of owners is stripped of control in favor of a small minority of owners. The large corporation means, thus, neither the democratization nor the abrogation of the control functions of property, but rather their concentration in a small group of large property owners. What many property owners lose, a few gain. Hilferding was perfectly correct when he said that 'capitalists form a society in the direction of which most of them have nothing to say. The actual disposal over productive capital belongs to those who have contributed only a part of it.' *

4. Cartels, Trusts, and Mergers

The final stage in the development of monopoly capital comes with the formation of combinations which have the conscious goal of controlling competition. This stage is reached only on the basis of a relatively high degree of centralization which, by reducing the number of enterprises in a given line of production, makes competition increasingly severe and perilous for the survivors. Competition tends to turn into cutthroat competition which is beneficial to no one. When this happens the ground is ready for the combination movement.

Marx completed his economic writings before the combination movement got under way and consequently there is no analysis of it from his pen in the three volumes of *Capital*. By the time Engels undertook the editing of Volume III in the middle '80s, however, the direction of events was already clear. In a long note inserted into Marx's discussion of corporations, Engels spoke of 'the second and third degree of stock companies' in the form

* *Das Finanzkapital*, p. 145. Factual proof of this thesis, so far as the United States is concerned, is now abundantly available in two carefully documented reports issued by the Temporary National Economic Committee, namely, Monograph No. 29, *The Distribution of Ownership in the 200 Largest Nonfinancial Corporations;* and Monograph No. 30, *Survey of Shareholdings in 1,710 Corporations with Securities Listed on a National Securities Exchange.*

of cartels and 'in some lines . . . the concentration of the entire production of this line in one great stock company under one joint management.' 'The long cherished freedom of competition,' Engels remarked, 'has reached the end of its tether and is compelled to announce its own palpable bankruptcy.'[15]

Hilferding, with the rich experience of Germany and America in the years from 1890 to 1910 before him, was able to build this insight into the body of Marxian economics. Our analysis follows that of Hilferding in general outline though with appropriate modifications for readers more familiar with American than with German conditions.

The specific characteristic of the organization forms which are now under examination, which distinguishes them from corporations as such, is that they are deliberately designed to increase profits by means of market controls of a monopolistic character. The achievement of this aim involves the limitation or abrogation of the independence of action of the enterprises concerned and their co-ordination under a definite unified policy. Since there is a wide range of degrees of limitation it follows that many different forms of monopolistic combination are possible. We shall mention some of the most important, beginning with the loosest form of association and proceeding to the complete merger of the competing firms. It must be kept in mind throughout that a community of interest between competitors, based on interlocking directorates or common banking connections, if it exists, smooths the way for and greatly strengthens the tendency towards combination. Indeed, it might even be said that a community of interest is in a sense a type of combination which easily leads to more binding forms.

Perhaps the weakest form of combination is the so-called 'gentlemen's agreement' which is essentially the articulation of a common policy agreed upon by competitors but without binding force for any of them. The incentive for each individual firm to break the agreement, however, is strong, and arrangements of this nature rarely last beyond a short period.

A further stage is reached with the formation of a 'pool' in which business is allocated according to a formula agreed upon among the participants. The pool agreement is generally reduced to writing, but its enforcement depends primarily on the voluntary co-operation of its members. Hence like the gentlemen's agreement, the pool is unstable and generally no more than a transitional phenomenon.

Certain types of cartel closely resemble the pool and share its weaknesses. The latter are overcome by extending the control of the cartel over its members and introducing sanctions against those who refuse to abide by its terms. A typical cartel has a central committee with the duty of fixing prices and production quotas and the power to punish violators by fines or otherwise. The independence of the members may be further restricted by centralizing purchases and sales in a single agency, thus breaking the direct relation between the individual firms and their customers, and even by giving to the central committee power to close down inefficient plants and to allocate aggregate profits according to some established formula. When this last step has been taken, the cartel approaches closely in many respects to the outright merger.

A tighter form of organization than the cartel is the 'trust' in the strict sense of the word, which enjoyed great favor in the United States for a time until it was outlawed. Under the trust form the owners of a majority of the stock of a number of independent corporations turn their holdings over to a group of trustees in exchange for trust certificates. The trustees vote the stock and the holders of the certificates receive the dividends. In this way a complete unification of the policies of the companies is achieved while the legal and business identity of the constituents is left undisturbed as in the cartel. The trust in this sense must not be confused with the common meaning assigned to the term according to which it is a generic designation covering pretty much the entire range of monopolistic combinations.

Finally we come to the complete merger in which the independence of the participating firms is abolished. The merger may take place in various ways, chief of which are the swallowing up of all the firms by one large one, and the disappearance of all the old firms in favor of a new business entity. In any case the result is the same: complete organic unity under a single direction. This is obviously the most effective form of combination from the standpoint of carrying out a monopolistic policy.

The factors determining which forms of combination will be adopted under varying circumstances of time and place constitute a special branch of applied economics. In general it can be said that they relate to the particular conditions prevailing in the different lines of industry, the weaknesses of the looser forms of association, and the legal provisions in force in the different countries. Thus, for example, in the United States laws prohibiting combinations of the cartel and trust types operated to increase greatly the use of the outright merger as a method of achieving monopolistic ends; while in Germany, where the cartel was accorded a recognized legal status, the latter form flourished.

From our standpoint, these differences are of secondary importance. The decisive fact is that the combination movement swept over all the advanced capitalist countries during the two decades, more or less, surrounding the turn of the century, and brought with it a qualitative change in the character of capitalist production. Free competition, which had been the dominant (though, of course, not exclusive) pattern of capitalist market behavior, was definitely superseded by varying degrees of monopoly, again as the dominant pattern. The consequences of this transition for the general laws of motion of capitalist society will have to be carefully examined in the next two chapters.

5. The Role of the Banks

We have already noted that banks, because of their strategic position in the issuance and sale of new securities, play a peculiarly important role in the formation of corporations, and the same applies to the merger of corporations already formed. Banks appropriate to themselves a major share of promoter's profit, appoint their own representatives to sit on the directorates of corporations, and come to exercise a great influence in the policies adopted.

In what direction will this influence be exercised? Always towards the abolition of competition. An individual company may, if it feels strong enough, welcome a knock-down-and-drag-out fight with its competitors, expecting to undergo a temporary period of reduced earnings in the hope of more than making up its losses later on. But for a bank which has relations with many companies such a course must inevitably seem futile and self-defeating. The gains of one company are offset by the losses of others. As Hilferding pointed out,

> Therefore the striving of banks to eliminate competition among the firms in which they are interested is absolute. Every bank also has an interest in the highest possible profit. Other things being equal this aim is achieved in a particular branch of industry when competition has been completely excluded. Hence the striving of banks for monopoly.[16]

The more extensive the connections of a bank and the more powerful its voice, the more effectively is it able to pursue its aim of eliminating competition and erecting monopolies. Hence the centralization of capital in the industrial sphere finds a counterpart in the growth of larger and larger banking units. On this basis there arises that inner personal union of interlocking directorates and communities of interest which binds together the most important banking and industrial magnates in all the advanced capitalist countries.

Up to this point it is possible to accept Hilferding's analysis with few reservations. But he goes considerably further, sometimes openly stating and always implying that in the partnership between industrial and banking capital it is the latter which occupies the dominant position. 'Finance capital' is defined at one point as 'capital controlled by the banks and utilized by the industrialists,'[17] and the trend of capitalism is pictured as involving the increasing subjection of all aspects of economic life to an ever narrower circle of huge banks. This comes out clearly in the following passage:

> With the development of banking, with the ever closer relation between banks and industry, the tendency grows, on the one hand for competition among the banks to be excluded, on the other hand for all capital to be concentrated in the form of money capital and to reach productive outlets only through the instrumentality of the banks. In the final analysis this tendency would lead to a situation in which the entire money capital would be at the disposal of one bank or group of banks. Such a 'central bank' would then exercise control over the whole of social production.[18]

There can be little doubt that this view is fundamentally misleading. Hilferding mistakes a transitional phase of capitalist development for a lasting trend. It is true that during the period of the combination movement itself, when corporations and mergers are in the process of formation, the banks are in a strategic position which enables them to extend their sway over the key areas of the productive system. The process of combination, however, cannot continue indefinitely. The ultimate limit would be reached in any given industry when only one firm is left, but as a rule the process comes to a halt considerably before this ultimate limit is actually reached. Competition of a dangerous kind is generally effectively abolished when something of the order of three-fourths to four-fifths of a given industry is in the hands of a few large companies. Beyond this point the tendency to further combination is greatly weakened and may even be altogether offset by counteracting forces. Rival groupings of large capitalists continue to exist and each always hopes to be able to improve its position at the expense of the others; each needs bases in the most important industrial sectors as a source of strength and as possible counters in a game of bargaining with the others. Once the spectre of cutthroat competition has been banished and a *modus vivendi* for the most general and necessary monopolistic ends has been discovered, further combinations occur less frequently and may soon cease altogether.

When this stage has been reached the position of the banks undergoes a sharp change. The function of issuing new securities, on which their power was originally founded, becomes much less important. The large monopolistic corporations find themselves, in direct proportion to their success (i.e. profitability), in possession of internal sources of funds, not only in the form of profits which can be accumulated instead of being distributed as dividends to shareholders, but also in the form of depreciation, depletion, obsolescence, and other so-called 'reserve' accounts which are to an ever increasing extent turned to the purposes of accumulation. With these internal sources of additional capital at their disposal, corporate managements are to a greater or less degree freed from dependence on the market for new securities as a source of capital, and by the same token they are freed from their dependence on bankers. To be sure, where the influence of banks is firmly entrenched this does not mean an immediate decline in their power. But in the long run, economic power which is related to no economic function is bound to weaken and eventually disappear. This is exactly what happens to the power of the banks in so far as it is based on control over the issuance of new securities. The function itself atrophies and the power to which it gave rise declines, leaving the banks in a secondary position. Bank capital, having had its day of glory, falls back again to a position subsidiary to industrial capital, thus re-establishing the relation which existed prior to the combination movement. This does not mean that capitalism in general returns to its earlier state; on the contrary, monopoly and the dominance of a small upper layer of big capitalists become solidified and gradually extended to take in ever larger sectors of the productive and distributive system. Only their base is industrial capital and not, as Hilferding thought it would be, bank capital. The dominance of bank capital is a passing phase of capitalist development which roughly coincides with the transition from competitive to monopoly capitalism.*

Hilferding's error is a serious one in at least two respects. For one thing the preconception of financial dominance precludes an understanding of the most important recent changes in the character of the accumulation process, particularly the growth of internal corporate financing. † And for another thing, it leads to profound illusions about the nature and difficulty of the task involved in achieving a socialist society. Already in 1910 Hilferding expressed the view that 'the seizure of six big Berlin banks would mean the seizure of the most important spheres of big industry.' [19] Even at the time this was far from the truth, though unquestionably the seizure of the big banks could have

* The clearest recognition, by a Marxist writer, of the transitional character of financial dominance is in Grossmann, *Das Akkumulations- und Zusammenbruchsgesetz des kapitalistischen Systems*, pp. 572 ff. For a brief outline of the weakening of financial power in the United States, see the present writer's article, 'The Decline of the Investment Banker,' *Antioch Review*, Spring, 1941.

† It is interesting to note that in spite of all changes in the years between 1910 and 1930, nevertheless in the latter year Hilferding was repeating, almost word for word, the arguments of *Das Finanzkapital*. See his article 'Die Eigengesetzlichkeit der kapitalistischen Entwicklung,' in Bernhard Harms ed., *Kapital und Kapitalismus* (1931), Vol. I.

seriously disrupted the industries dependent upon them. But today the entire banking system could be 'seized' in the United States, for example, without causing more than a temporary ripple in the ranks of big capital. It is clear that if the theory of finance capitalism is interpreted to imply the dominance of banks, it is a poor foundation on which to build a socialist policy.

In concluding this discussion, however, we should note that the expression 'finance capital' does not necessarily have the implications which Hilferding attached to it. Lenin, in particular, criticized Hilferding's definition of finance capital on the ground that it 'is silent on one of the most important points, namely, the growth of concentration of production and of capital to such a great extent that the concentration leads and has led to monopoly.' For Hilferding's 'capital controlled by the banks and utilized by the industrialists,' Lenin substituted the following:

> The concentration of production, the monopolies arising therefrom, the merging or concrescence of banks with industry: this is the history of the rise of finance capital and the content of this concept.[20]

Lenin's theory is thus certainly not open to the criticisms which have been directed at Hilferding's. Nevertheless it is doubtful whether the term 'finance capital' can be divested of the connotation of banker dominance which Hilferding gave it. This being the case, it seems preferable to drop it altogether and substitute the term 'monopoly capital,' which clearly indicates what is essential to Lenin's concept of 'finance capital' and yet is not so likely as the latter to mislead the unwary reader.

XV

MONOPOLY AND THE LAWS OF MOTION OF CAPITALISM

In the last chapter we investigated how and why competitive capitalism at a certain stage in its development turns into monopoly capitalism. This metamorphosis, in its turn, reacts on the functioning of the system, altering some of its laws and modifying others. To analyse the alterations and modifications in the laws of capitalist motion must, therefore, be our next task. In this chapter we shall confine ourselves to those effects which emerge under the assumption of a closed system; in the following chapter the problems of world economy will be subjected to inquiry.

1. Monopoly and Price

'When we speak of a monopoly price,' Marx wrote, 'we mean in a general way a price which is determined only by the eagerness of the purchasers to buy and by their solvency, independently of the price which is determined by the general price of production and by the value of the products.'[1] This being the case it appears to be obvious, as Hilferding said, that 'the realization of Marx's theory of concentration, of monopolistic merger, seems to result in the invalidation of Marx's value theory.'[2]

This observation is certainly not without a certain justification. Under conditions of monopoly, exchange ratios do not conform to labor-time ratios, nor do they stand in a theoretically demonstrable relation to labor-time ratios as is the case with prices of production. When the power of limiting supply is in the hands of producers so also is the power of setting prices, and to determine theoretically, and with a useful degree of generality, at what point prices will be set is impossible; too many diverse factors enter into the determination of a given price to permit the construction of a precise theory with any but the most limited applicability. This is fully proved by the attempts of orthodox economic theory in recent years to establish objective laws of price under conditions of total or partial monopoly. Aside from a few empty propositions, such as that price will be set where profit is maximized, monopolistic price theory rapidly turns into a catalogue of special cases, each with its own particular solution. This is not the fault of the economists, nor is it, as some maintain, merely a sign of the backwardness of the science; the difficulty is inherent in the subject matter. No reasonably general laws of monopoly price have been discovered because none exist.

The fact that it is useless to search for a theory of monopoly price which can stand on an equal footing with the theories of value and production price should not, however, be a cause for despair. For it is possible to say with a great deal of generality and assurance that, as compared to the situation which would exist under competition, equilibrium output is smaller and equilibrium price is higher when elements of monopoly are introduced. Since this is so, we can start from the theory of value (or production price) as a base and analyse the kind, if not the extent, of modifications which monopoly brings with it. This is extremely important since it allows us to develop the theory of monopoly along genuinely useful lines, something which would not be possible if the deviations of monopoly price from competitive price were purely arbitrary in regard both to direction and to extent.

Even in relation to the extent of the deviation of monopoly price from competitive price, certain judgments of the 'more-or-less' type are often possible. Thus it is usually safe to assume that the price will be higher the less responsive, relatively, the quantity purchased to changes in price (i.e. the less elastic the demand), and the more complete the monopoly. These are factors about which it is frequently possible to make a rough but serviceable judgment, particularly when it is a question of estimating the effects of technical and organizational changes on prices. We must not, however, expect to be able to reduce the theory of monopoly price to quantitative precision; any one attempting to do so will only succeed in getting lost in a maze of special cases.

It goes almost without saying that the validity of measuring commodities in value terms, that is to say by the yardstick of socially necessary labor time, is independent of the particular exchange ratios which happen to be established on the market, whether under competitive or monopolistic conditions. As we shall see presently, this fact is of first importance in developing the theory of monopoly beyond the sphere of mere prices.

2. Monopoly and the Rate of Profit

So far as the individual enterprise is concerned the transition from competition to monopoly brings with it an increase in profit; this is, indeed, the whole aim and end of monopoly. But the total value produced by the social labor force is in no way increased by the formation of monopolies, and hence the extra profit of the monopolist is in the nature of a transfer of values from the incomes of other members of society. Out of whose pockets does the extra profit of monopoly come? Marx stated the two most general possibilities in the following terms:

> The monopoly price of certain commodities would merely transfer a portion of the profit of the other producers of commodities to the commodities with a monopoly price. A local disturbance in the distribution of the surplus value among the various spheres of production would take place . . . but they would leave the boundaries of the surplus value itself unaltered. If a commodity with a monopoly price should enter into the necessary consumption of the laborer, it would increase the wages and thereby reduce the surplus value if the laborer would receive the value of his labor power the same as before. But such a commodity might also depress wages below the value of labor power, of course only to the extent that wages would be higher than the physical minimum of subsistence. In this case the monopoly price would be paid by a deduction from the real wages . . . and from the profits of the other capitalists.[3]

In short, either the extra profit is a deduction from the surplus value of other capitalists or it is a deduction from the wages of the working class. Generally speaking, however, at any given time and place wages gravitate around a level which is socially recognized as a minimum standard of subsistence. Trade unions are one of the most powerful agents in the achievement of this result; * and since unions are already well developed by the time of the combination movement it seems reasonable to suppose that deductions from wages caused by monopoly extra profit will be rapidly restored. If this reasoning is valid, it follows that the extra profit of the monopolist comes primarily from the pockets of his fellow capitalists. In what follows we shall work with this assumption except where a qualification is specifically introduced.

The tendency to an equality of profit rates which is a characteristic feature of competitive capitalism is thus doubly disrupted by monopoly: the profits of some are raised, while the profits of others are reduced. Naturally there is still a tendency for capital to try to move out of the disadvantaged and into the favored fields, but the very essence of monopoly is the existence of effective barriers to such free movement of capital. A new form of the tendency to equal profit rates now comes into play therefore, a form which is much stressed by Hilferding in his discussion of monopoly.[4] This is the *spreading* of monopoly from every point where it makes an appearance. To the extent that monopoly becomes general, the gains of the individuals are to a certain degree offset by their losses and the profit rates are brought more nearly to equality—though an exact equality could never be achieved by this path. The principle of spreading may be clarified as follows. A certain industry, say iron ore production, is monopolized and the price raised. Part of the resulting loss is borne by the pig-iron producers, who now have an increased incentive to combine both to raise their prices to the steel industry and to bargain for lower prices from the ore industry. In this way combination will spread in concentric circles from any given point of origin, seizing upon those industries where circumstances are favorable to the establishment and maintenance of monopoly conditions.

The spreading process, however, works very unevenly, for

* This should not lead us to overlook the fact that in the long run unionism is one of the significant determinants of the conventional subsistence level itself.

there are always industries in which it is difficult or even impossible to effect a stable combination. These are the industries in which only a small capital investment is required; numerous firms are necessary to fill the demand and entry into the field is easy for any one with the required minimum of capital. Here competitive conditions persist despite the advantages to be had from combination. It follows that we can expect a general equalization of profit rates neither from the mobility of capital nor from the spreading of monopoly. We get instead a hierarchy of profit rates ranging from highest in the industries of large-scale production where close well-protected combinations are relatively easy to establish, to lowest in the industries of very small-scale production where numerous firms co-exist and the ease of entry precludes stable combinations.

3. Monopoly and Accumulation

Monopoly profoundly affects the accumulation process, first in its effect on the rate of accumulation out of a given amount of surplus value, and second in its effect on the outlets for accumulated capital. Let us consider these problems in turn.

The total surplus value of society is divided into numerous segments each corresponding in size to the portion of the total social capital from which it springs. It is a general rule that the proportion accumulated increases with the size of the segment of surplus value. From this it follows that centralization by itself, since it decreases the number and increases the size of the segments, will have the effect of raising the rate of accumulation from a given total of surplus value.* Monopoly intensifies this

* The question might be raised whether the segments of surplus value should be measured in accordance with the size of the productive units to which they first accrue or in accordance with the size of the ultimate and much more numerous ownership units to which they finally flow. If the latter is the proper method, centralization of production, since it can proceed by way of the corporate form without centralization of ownership, might be largely without effect on the relative size of the segments and hence on the rate of accumulation. With the growth of internal corporate financing, however, the units of production (corporations) acquire enormous significance as units for purposes of accumulation. Therefore while the absence, or at least slower rate, of centralization of ownership as compared with centralization of production must be taken into account,

effect by transferring surplus value from the smaller capitals to the larger. The increment of accumulation arising from the addition to the larger segments must be larger than the decrement attributable to the subtraction from the smaller segments. We see, therefore, that on two counts the rate of accumulation under monopoly capitalism tends to be higher than the rate under competitive capitalism.

Let us now turn to the effects of monopoly on the requirements for newly accumulated capital. Here the decisive factor is that the very maintenance of monopoly necessitates the blocking off of investment from the monopolized, and hence most profitable, fields of industry. We observe the following apparent paradox, namely, that a monopolist making large profits will nevertheless refuse to invest more capital in his own industry and will search for outside opportunities for investment even though the rate of profit obtainable be much lower. The paradox disappears as soon as we realize that the monopolist's investment policy cannot be dominated by his overall profit rate or by the rate obtainable on the additional investment taken by itself. He must rather be guided by what we may call the marginal profit rate, that is to say the rate on the additional investment after allowance has been made for the fact that the additional investment, since it will increase output and reduce price, will entail a reduction in profit on the old investment.* The overall

it nevertheless does not by any means signify that centralization of production has no power to raise the rate of accumulation.

* The following illustration will help to clarify the concept. A monopolist with a capital of $1,000 produces 100 units annually at a cost of $5 per unit and sells at a price of $10 per unit. His profit is $500 or 50 per cent on his capital. The addition of $100 to his capital will allow him to produce 10 more units, still at a cost of $5 per unit. In order to sell 110 units, however, the price will have to be reduced from $10 to $9. The profit on the additional investment would be $90 – $50 = $40, or 40 per cent on the additional capital involved. However the monopolist has to take account of the fact that the price of $9 applies to all the units and not only to the additional units. Since he has been selling 100 units at $10 he will lose $100 when the price goes down to $9. This loss is to be set alongside of the gain of $40 from the additional units to be sold. Obviously the loss more than outweighs the gain; the marginal profit rate is actually negative. The monopolist will do better to invest his $100 outside his own industry so long as he can get any profit at all, and if that is impossible it will be better for him to hold the $100 in cash rather than put it into his own business.

rate of profit may be high while the marginal rate is low or even negative. The monopolist will therefore search for outside outlets so long as the rate to be earned anywhere is greater than the marginal rate in his own field. It is, of course, true that the outsider will not be governed in his actions by the marginal rate of profit to the monopolist; but the existence of the monopoly means that the outsider is not free to enter the field no matter how much he might like to do so.

The principle that the monopolist is guided in his investment decisions by the marginal rate of profit is of fundamental importance. In addition to explaining the cessation of investment in monopolized fields while the rate of profit still appears to be high, it helps us to understand how and why the attitude of monopoly capital towards technological change differs from that of competitive capital. Just as in the case of an expansion of output the monopolist must take account of the effect on his old business, so in the case of a technological innovation he cannot neglect the depreciation in value which his already invested capital may suffer through being outmoded. Under competition, on the other hand, the gain is enjoyed by the innovator while the loss, if any, is borne at least in large part by his competitors. This does not mean that technological change will cease under monopoly; the elaborate research facilities which the great monopolistic combines maintain are something new and make it certain that in range and comprehensiveness technological advance receives a powerful stimulus from the centralization of capital. What it does mean is that labor saving becomes more than ever the goal of capitalist technology and that the rate of introduction of new methods will be so arranged as to minimize the disturbance to existing capital values. In other words, new methods will have an even stronger labor-saving bias, and for the most part new equipment will be put in the place of old only when the latter wears out and needs to be replaced anyway.* Consequently monopoly steps up the rate of flow of

* In certain cases this may result in the complete suppression of an invention, for by the time it would be profitable to introduce it even more highly developed techniques may be at hand. In other words, certain inventions may be by-passed because of the absence of competitive pressures to introduce them as they became available. I am indebted to Dr. Robert K. Merton for pointing this out to me.

workers into the industrial reserve army and reduces the outlet for newly accumulated capital provided by technological progress.

We have seen that monopoly stops up the demand for new capital in the monopolized industries in two ways: because output is restricted in the interest of maintaining the maximum possible overall profit rate; and because the rate of introduction of technological innovations is consciously regulated in such a way as to minimize the need for new capital.* The counterpart of this stoppage of investment in the monopolized industries is a crowding of capital into industries where entry is free, or at least less restricted, with a consequent depression of profit rates in these areas. Thus the immediate effect of accumulation is simply to intensify the distortions in the pattern of profit rates which monopoly originally brings with it.

What is the significance of monopoly for the problems of crisis and depression? In so far as the rate of accumulation is increased, the effect obviously is to hasten the falling tendency of the average rate of profit and to strengthen the tendency to underconsumption. But this is not all. Since the monopolist is guided by the marginal profit rate in his own industry, and since the rate in the remaining competitive spheres is depressed, the net result is a depression of the rate of profit which is controlling for investment decisions. This is a factor contributing to crises and depressions independent of and additional to the falling tendency of the average rate of profit and the tendency to underconsumption. Thus, besides intensifying the old contradictions of the accumulation process, monopoly introduces new ones.

One further point in this connection is to be noted. If any part of monopoly extra profit constitutes a deduction from labor income the effect is to raise the total of surplus value at the expense of the share of the social output going to the working class. This, in turn, raises the rate of accumulation and lowers the rate of consumption and in this fashion strengthens the tendency to underconsumption.

* The last point may be clarified for some readers if it is put as follows: the monopolist tends to finance his technological progress from depreciation accruals instead of from net saving.

4. Monopoly and the Rising Costs of Distribution

In order to analyse the relation between monopoly and the costs of distribution it is first necessary to indicate the main outlines of Marx's theory of commercial capital and commercial profit.[5]

Commerce is to be understood in a narrow sense to include only buying and selling activities and to exclude transportation, storage, and delivery. The latter, in Marx's theory, are aspects of production proper and consequently do not require separate theoretical treatment. In practice the merchant performs a part of these productive functions so that the isolation of his commercial functions is never easy, Nevertheless in principle the distinction is clear and must be made for theoretical purposes.

From the point of view of society as a whole commerce is unproductive; it adds nothing to the total of values produced but rather is concerned with the transformation of already existing values from the money form to the commodity form or *vice versa*. This principle is perfectly plain to the individual industrial capitalist who knows very well that an increase in the costs of buying and selling, other things remaining equal, does not raise the value of his products but instead reduces his profit. But when the commercial function is separated from the industrial function and is carried on by an independent group of merchants, it appears that the value of the products is enhanced by the amount of the merchants' profits plus any expenses incidental to carrying out the commercial operations. This, however, is an illusion which disappears upon analysis. The mere separation of commerce from production is powerless to change the character of either.

Assume for a moment that the merchant has no expenses. Nevertheless for the purpose of buying commodities and selling them again he requires a certain amount of capital, and this capital, since he is free at any time to transfer it to other lines of activity, must draw the going rate of profit. How is this possible if no surplus value originates in the sphere of commercial operations? Marx solved the problem by showing that commercial capital appropriates a part of the surplus value produced in the industrial sphere. The merchant buys commodities from the industrialist at less than their value by the amount of his profit margin and sells them at their value. He is enabled to do this because under capitalism commerce cannot be dispensed with; in an unplanned economy the bringing together of buyers and sellers is an absolutely necessary function. Consequently capital must be invested in this field. But capital will not be invested in commerce unless it earns the average rate of profit. Competition ('supply and demand') consequently forces down the industrialist's price to the point where commercial capital can come into the field at the ruling rate of profit. The net result is that an unchanged quantity of surplus value is spread over a larger amount of capital; the average rate of profit is reduced. As Marx expressed it, 'The larger the merchant's capital in proportion to the industrial capital, the smaller is the rate of industrial profit and *vice versa*.' [6]

In practice, the merchant does have expenses to meet both for labor power (clerks, typists, bookkeepers, et cetera) and for office space, fixtures, and auxiliary materials. Marx's treatment of these expenses is not altogether unambiguous; the relevant passages have the earmarks of a rough first draft in which he was working his way through the problem without a clear picture at the outset of the conclusions which would emerge. Nevertheless we can attempt to indicate the solution which seems most in keeping with the general logic of his theory.

From the point of view of the merchant, expenses have the character of capital quite as much as do his outlays on commodities for resale. Hence the margin between the purchase and sale prices of the commodities in which he deals must be sufficiently large not only to provide for commercial profit in the sense already explained, but also to reimburse him for the outlays involved in meeting his expenses plus a normal profit on these outlays. No part of the margin between purchase price and sale price is value produced in the commercial sphere; this principle is in no way altered by the introduction of the merchant's expenses. Consequently it must be in its entirety a deduction from the surplus value which would otherwise accrue to the industrial capitalists.

Since the employees in the commercial sphere are paid out of surplus value and do not themselves create any value, it follows that they must be classified as unproductive laborers and their consumption as unproductive consumption. This analysis thus provides the justification for the procedure adopted in Chapter XII, of including commercial workers along with servants, landlords, and the like in the category of unproductive consumers.*

Commerce has a threefold effect on accumulation. (1) Since the expenses of commerce constitute a deduction from surplus value there is less surplus value available for accumulation. Part of the expenses are wages which are spent by their recipients on consumption goods; to this extent social consumption is increased. Part of the expenses are outlays on buildings, equipment, and materials which do not raise social consumption either directly or indirectly. Nevertheless the effect on the reproduction process is the same as though consumption were increased; values are used up and disappear from the reproduction scheme. The first effect of commerce is therefore to reduce surplus value and hence accumulation and to increase correspondingly the rate of consumption. (2) Since the commercial capitalists share in the remaining surplus value along with the industrial capitalists, it follows that the number of segments into which the total is divided is larger and the average size smaller. It has already been noted that this reduces the rate of accumulation. (3) The expansion of the reproduction process requires a growth in commercial capital which therefore offers an investment outlet. In summary: commerce increases consumption, reduces accumulation, and provides an investment outlet. It therefore counteracts the tendency to underconsumption.†

We are now ready to analyse the effect of monopoly on the commercial sphere of the capitalist economy.

The most evident consequence of centralization and the growth of monopoly is a decline in the relative importance of the independent merchant. This arises from two causes: on the

* See above, p. 231.

† In an earlier stage of capitalist development, when the counteracting force of population growth and new industries was very strong and there often seemed to be a shortage rather than a plethora of capital seeking investment, commerce would be thought of as a drag on the expansion of capitalist production. Conditions have so changed, however, that this attitude is no longer justified.

one hand vertical combinations eliminate transactions between independent capitals which otherwise would have been unavoidable; on the other hand, the large firms do more and more of their own buying and selling since their business is extensive enough to permit them to maintain specialized departments for the purpose which are at least as efficient as the independent merchant. Hilferding stressed this aspect of monopoly: 'Monopolistic combination . . . effects an elimination of independent trade. It makes a part of the trading operations entirely superfluous and reduces the expense of the rest.' [7] Unfortunately, since he stopped here he concluded that the costs of buying and selling were on the decline and hence gave a completely incorrect impression of the true state of affairs. Actually there is another and much more important connection between monopoly and the costs of circulating commodities.

Under competition high profits lead to an expansion of production. The extra profits of monopoly, however, do not have this consequence; in fact they are conditioned on the restriction of output. Nevertheless they are not without their effect on the behavior of the monopolists, each one of whom now concentrates his attention on trying to increase his share of the available business and hence of the extra profit. It is very important that this be done without resort to the method of price cutting which nearly always leads to retaliation, expansion of total output and reduction or even abolition of extra profit. The alternative to price cutting is to attract buyers away from rival sources of supply by more effective selling methods. Two cases have to be distinguished, though they present closely interconnected aspects of the same general phenomenon. First, there are the efforts of firms in the same industry to take business away from each other. In this connection it must be remembered that centralization rarely proceeds to the point of bringing an entire industry under the control of a single firm. And second, there are the efforts of all the producers in one industry to persuade consumers to spend more money on their products at the expense of the products of other industries. As between these two cases selling techniques vary somewhat, but basically they follow a similar pattern and do not require separate analysis.

In the efforts of monopolists to enlarge their sales without jeopardizing the existence of extra profits we find the fundamental explanation of the enormous development of the arts of salesmanship and advertising which is such a striking characteristic of monopoly capitalism. This development takes on many forms including the attempt to attract customers through alluring packaging and labeling, the maintenance of staffs of salesmen and publicists, and perhaps most important of all the continuous emission of enormous quantities of advertising through newspapers, magazines, and radio. But direct methods of salesmanship and advertising are only a part of the picture. Indirectly the effect is a multiplication of the channels of distribution and a vast amount of duplication in the fields of transporting, storing, and delivering commodities. These activities are, as we know, a part of the process of production proper. But now they become expanded far beyond the limits of what would be socially necessary under competitive conditions.* Under monopoly only a part of distributive activities can be considered as productive of value; the rest are essentially similar to selling in the strict sense and share with the latter the attribute of using up value without producing any.

Recent studies of distribution costs give some indication of the extent to which monopoly has resulted in an expansion of the machinery of selling and distribution. For example, on the basis of its report *Does Distribution Cost Too Much?* (1939), the Twentieth Century Fund makes the following statements:

> Distribution—not production—is now the great frontier of the American business system. Distribution takes 59 cents of the consumer's dollar as compared with only 41 cents for production processes. Workers in distribution increased nine times between 1870 and 1930, while the population increased only three times.[8]

Too much significance should not be attached to the precise figures quoted. Quite apart from criticisms which have been directed at the statistical methods employed, they do not provide a measure of the growth of *unproductive* activities in selling and distribution. Some increase in the relative importance of trans-

* A good example is provided by the effects of the widespread practice of resale price maintenance, which allows large margins to distributors and hence encourages the entrance of a greater number than would otherwise be necessary.

port, storage, and delivery is certainly to be expected as production becomes more diversified and geographically specialized. How much of the increase is thus socially necessary could be established only after a long investigation and even then only within fairly wide limits. In spite of all qualifications, however, both the direction and importance of the general trend is clear.

The theoretical principles which emerge from the Marxian analysis of commercial capital and commercial profit are fully applicable to the growth of selling and unproductive distribution costs under the influence of monopoly. Surplus value which would otherwise be available for accumulation is instead diverted into supporting a swollen selling and distributing mechanism. The extra profits of monopoly are reduced in this fashion, often to the point where they appear to be no greater than average competitive profits so that the very existence of monopoly is obscured from view. Many new segments of surplus value are created, for example in the form of profits of advertising firms or of duplicate and socially unnecessary retail stores. Consumption is raised by the amount paid as wages to additional unproductive workers, and the same effect, so far as the reproduction process is concerned, is brought about by the outlays on materials and equipment necessary for carrying on selling and much of distribution activities. The net effect of all this is a slowing down in the rate of expansion of capital and the emergence of a powerful counteracting force to the tendency to underconsumption.

There is another aspect of the growth of the distributive system in the period of monopoly capitalism which deserves brief consideration. The entire trend is predicated upon a substantial and continuing rise in the productiveness of labor. Only if this condition is satisfied is it possible for the proportion of the labor force engaged in unproductive pursuits to increase without serious adverse consequences for the general standard of living. Conversely, given a steady increase in the productiveness of labor the stage is set for an expansion of surplus value and the social classes which are maintained out of surplus value. In his discussion of the views of Barton and Ricardo on machinery, Marx was at great pains to bring out this aspect of rising labor productivity.

> The mass of articles entering into gross income * can increase without a concomitant increase in the part of this mass going to variable capital. The latter can even become smaller. In this case more is consumed as revenue by the capitalists, landlords, their hangers-on, the unproductive classes, the state, the intermediate classes (employees in trade) etc.[9]

To this we need only add that the expansion of the sphere of distribution under the influence of monopoly constitutes a specific form of a development which Marx treats here only in the most general terms.

The rise in labor productivity and the disproportionate growth in the distributive sphere to which it leads under monopoly capitalism constitute a development with far-reaching social and political implications. The so-called 'new middle class' of industrial bureaucrats, professionals, teachers, state employees, and the like, which inevitably grows up in the wake of centralization and rising living standards, is augmented by the army of salesmen, advertising agents, publicists, and salaried employees who form such a large proportion of those engaged in distributive activities. These elements of the population are relatively well paid and hence enjoy a standard of living which, from a subjective standpoint, ties them more or less closely to the ruling class of capitalists and landlords. Moreover since under capitalism a large proportion of them derive their incomes directly or indirectly from surplus value, so that a diminution of surplus value would necessarily react upon them unfavorably, there also exists an objective bond linking their fortunes with those of the ruling class. For both of these reasons the new middle class tends to provide social and political support for the capitalists rather than for the workers; its members constitute, so to speak, a mass army which readily accepts the leadership of capitalist generals. Contrary to widespread opinion, Marx was fully aware of this role of the new middle class. In his critique of Ricardo's theory of machinery Marx put the matter as follows:

* 'Gross income' is here used in its Ricardian meaning, not in the sense assigned to it by modern theorists. Translated into Marxian concepts, Ricardian gross income equals the sum of variable capital plus surplus value.

What he [Ricardo] forgets to bring out is the steady growth of the middle classes standing between the laborers on the one side and the capitalists and landlords on the other, for the most part supported directly from revenue, which weigh as a burden on the laboring base and enhance the security and power of the upper ten thousand.[10]

If this was a highly important trend already in Marx's time, how much more so has it become in the period of monopoly capitalism! Subsequently we shall see how it constitutes one of the component forces which decide the actual course of capitalist development.

5. Conclusion

Let us now attempt a brief schematic summary of the most important general effects of monopoly on the functioning of the capitalist system.

1. Prices of monopolized commodities are raised.

2. The equal profit rates of competitive capitalism are turned into a hierarchy of profit rates, highest in the most completely monopolized industries, lowest in the most competitive.

3. Small segments of surplus value are reduced, large segments increased. This raises the rate of accumulation and hence accentuates both the falling tendency of the average rate of profit and the tendency to underconsumption.

4. Investment in monopolized industries is choked off; capital crowds into the more competitive areas. The rate of profit which is relevant to investment decisions is therefore lowered. This is a factor in causing depressions independent of both the general falling tendency of the rate of profit and the tendency to underconsumption.

5. The labor-saving bias of capitalist technology is enhanced, and the introduction of new techniques is so arranged as to minimize the need for new capital.

6. The costs of selling are raised and the distributive system is expanded beyond what is socially necessary. This in turn has the following consequences:

   a. Monopoly extra profits are reduced, in many cases to no more than the competitive level.

b. New segments of surplus value are created, and a large number of unproductive consumers are brought into existence. Therefore the rate of accumulation is reduced and the rate of consumption increased. This acts as an offsetting force to the tendency to underconsumption.
c. The new middle class which provides social and political support for the capitalist class is enlarged.

It will be noted that the effects listed under (6) in a measure counteract numbers (3), (4), and (5). This, however, is not a case of simple cancellation of opposed forces. The contradictions of the accumulation process, which are accentuated by (3), (4), and (5), are basically symptomatic of the difficulty of containing rapidly expanding productive forces within the framework of capitalist property relations. The growth of the distributive system under monopoly eases the difficulty and softens the contradictions, but it does so not by making it possible for capitalism to harness the expanding productive forces, but rather by diverting their use into socially unnecessary and hence wasteful channels. There is an important difference here which should not be overlooked. When it is appreciated, the 'favorable' effects of monopoly appear in anything but a favorable light.

XVI

WORLD ECONOMY

1. General Considerations

There never has been and never will be a closed capitalist system such as we have been assuming in the greater part of the foregoing analysis. This does not mean that we are not justified in making the assumption of a closed system, nor does it mean that the laws and tendencies of capitalism which have been discovered on the basis of this assumption are non-existent. What it does mean is that we have been abstracting from certain aspects of reality in order the more clearly to identify and analyse others. In dropping the assumption of a closed system we do not give up what we have already learned; rather we make it possible to extend and deepen our knowledge along paths which we have so far deliberately refrained from following.

The real world is one in which a number of nations co-exist and have relations with one another. Some of these nations are well-developed capitalist societies; some are rapidly becoming capitalist; some have hardly as yet been touched by capitalism; one is a socialist society. Their mutual relations are not arbitrary or accidental; no nation could continue to exist in anything like its present form and for an extended period of time in isolation from the others. Just as the individuals in society are economically necessary to each other and hence form an integrated economy, so the nations of the world are economically necessary to each other and hence form an integrated world economy. Let us examine the character of these international economic relations.

The basic economic relations of world economy are the exchange relations of commodity production. Historically, commodities originated in the sphere of inter-communal trade,* and the relations among the members of a community have never been so completely dominated by exchange as have the relations among the communities themselves. In a single country, even one in which commodity production is highly developed, there is always a wide range of non-exchange economic relationships; this is the case, for example, with the relations existing among managers and workers within a factory or corporation. In the international sphere, however, non-exchange relations, generally speaking, play a less prominent role. This fact determines our approach to the problems of world economy.

Exchange in general arises from a particular form of the social division of labor. In the same way international exchange corresponds to a particular form of the international division of labor. The bases of international division of labor at any given time are in part naturally, in part historically, conditioned. For example, one country exports commodities for the production of which it possesses advantages of climate and natural resources; another, industrially more advanced, exports commodities which require a high level of technique and a skilled labor force, and so on. There are certain near-constants in the pattern of international division of labor, but there are also highly important elements which are continually changing because of the different stages and rates of development of the countries involved. This must never be lost from mind. World economy, being a commodity-producing economy, is not regulated according to a plan which calls for the synchronized growth of its various component parts; rather the parts develop by fits and starts and at uneven rates. Any balance which may result is an accidental resultant of their mutual interaction which possesses a purely temporary character.

To the extent that capitalism develops in various parts of the world economy, international economic relations are no longer confined to simple commodity exchanges; these are supplemented by capital movements, i.e. the export by some countries and the import by others of commodities which have the specific

* As Marx expressed it, 'the development of products into commodities arises through the exchange between different communities, not through that between members of the same commune.' *Capital* III, p. 209.

characteristics and functions of capital. For example, capitalists in country A send means of production to capitalists in country B with which the latter can employ labor power for the purpose of producing surplus value. The surplus value, however, does not belong to the capitalists of B, or at least not all of it does; it must be regularly sent back to the capitalists in A.* Through transactions of this sort the spread of capitalism is greatly accelerated and the economic relations between countries are complicated. No longer need the exports of a country balance its imports; movements of capital in one direction and of surplus value in the other must also be taken into account.

To what extent do the laws governing value, the rate of surplus value, and the rate of profit apply to world economy? Let us first consider the case of trade alone, leaving capital export for subsequent treatment. Given competition and mobility of resources within the individual countries, commodities will sell domestically at their values or prices of production—in what follows this qualification will not be repeated—and both rates of surplus value and rates of profit will be equalized as between different lines of industry. As between different countries, however, no such equilibration can be effected by the processes of trade alone. The commodities exchanged between two countries on equal terms need not contain equal quantities of labor; indeed it would be purely accidental if they did. Exactly the same would be true of the products of two industries within a country if transfer of labor from one to the other were impossible. In other words, the law of value holds only among commodities which are the products of one and the same homogeneous and mobile labor force; in the case of commodities produced in different countries this condition is generally not satisfied. Similarly, when we speak of the tendency of rates of surplus value to an equality under capitalist production, we imply free mobility of labor † which, again, is lacking in international economic relations. Hence the rate of surplus value (or, alterna-

* Capital export is correctly defined by Hilferding as 'export of value which is destined to breed surplus value abroad. It is essential that the surplus value remain at the disposal of the domestic capital.' *Das Finanzkapital*, p. 395.

† See above, p. 65.

tively, the rate of exploitation) need not be the same in different countries. Finally, equalization of profit rates presupposes mobility of capital and this we have provisionally ruled out by assumption. It does not follow, because the laws in question are valid inside each of the trading countries and not between the countries, that no effect is produced by international trade. Trade must in any case increase the mass of use values at the disposal of all the countries concerned, and it may influence the height of both the rate of surplus value and the rate of profit in one or more of them. For example, if country A can get wage goods more cheaply (in terms of its own labor time) by exchange with other countries than it could by producing them at home, then the same real wage will be manifested in a higher rate of surplus value, and hence also a higher rate of profit, with trade than without trade. This was the main burden of Ricardo's defense of free trade and explains in good part why the English capitalists, in the particular circumstances of the mid-nineteenth century, were so strongly opposed to the Corn Laws. Further, if trade results in a 'cheapening of the elements of constant capital,' to use Marx's phrase, the rate of profit is raised.*

It should be particularly noted that trade between two countries can affect the distribution of the value produced within either one or both of them—for example by altering the rate of surplus value in the manner already explained—but that it cannot transfer value from one to the other. A more advanced country, for example, cannot extract value from a less advanced country by trade alone; it can do so only through the ownership of capital in the latter. Several Marxian writers have argued to the contrary, that trade does constitute a method whereby value is transferred from backward lands to more highly industrialized countries. Thus Otto Bauer, in discussing a trade relation of this sort, has the following to say:

> The capital of the more highly developed country has the higher organic composition of capital . . . Now Marx has made it possible for us to understand that—thanks to the tendency to an equalization of profit rates—the workers of each country do

* It will be recalled that this is one of the 'counteracting causes' to the falling tendency of the rate of profit discussed by Marx.

> not produce value only for *their own* capitalists; rather the surplus value produced by the workers of *both* countries is divided between the capitalists of both countries, not according to the quantity of labor performed in each of the two but according to the quantity of capital active in each of the two countries. Since, however, in the more highly developed country *more* capital goes with the same quantity of labor, therefore the more highly developed country attracts to itself a larger share of surplus value than corresponds to the quantity of labor performed in it. It is as though the surplus value produced in both countries were first heaped up in a single pile and then divided among the capitalists according to the size of their capitals. *The capitalists of the more developed country* thus exploit not only their own workers, but *continually appropriate also a portion of the surplus value produced in the less developed country.**

The trouble with Bauer's argument is that it assumes what it is intended to prove. It takes for granted that the equalization of profit rates as between countries can be brought about through trade alone, and then deduces that this must imply a transfer of surplus value from the country with relatively less capital to the country with relatively more capital. The conclusion indeed follows from the premise, but the premise is incorrect. It is no more true that trade equalizes profit rates between two countries than it is that trade equalizes profit rates between two monopolized industries within a single country. Bauer applies Marx's theory of the equalization of profit rates, which is based on competition and mobility of capital, to trade between countries without noticing that the conditions necessary for its validity are absent.

The situation changes, of course, as soon as we drop the assumption excluding capital exports. Clearly the capitalists in low-profit countries—generally speaking the countries in which accumulation has already gone farthest—will export capital to the

* *Die Nationalitätenfrage und die Sozialdemokratie*, pp. 246-7. The same position is taken by Grossmann, *Das Akkumulations- und Zusammenbruchsgesetz des kapitalistischen Systems*, pp. 431 ff. Grossmann's attempt to show that this was also Marx's view is unconvincing. For a discussion of Marx's stand, relative to the conflicting arguments put forward by Smith and Ricardo on this question, see Dobb, *Political Economy and Capitalism*, pp. 229-30. Dobb himself reaches conclusions substantially similar to those set forth in the text above.

higher-profit countries. The rates of profit will now tend towards a single level, allowing as always for necessary risk premiums. Moreover the capitalists in the low-profit countries will benefit doubly. As Dobb explains the matter in reference to investment in colonial areas:

> Not only does it [investment in colonial areas] mean that the capital exported . . . is invested at a higher rate of profit than if it had been invested, instead, at home; but it also creates a tendency for the rate of profit at home . . . to be greater than it otherwise would have been. The latter occurs because the plethora of capital seeking investment in the metropolis is reduced by reason of the profitable colonial outlet, the pressure on the labor market is relieved and the capitalist is able to purchase labor-power at home at a lower price . . . Capital thereby gains doubly: by the higher rate of profit it reaps abroad and by the higher 'rate of surplus value' it can maintain at home . . .[1]

It should be noted that international equality of profit rates does not imply international equality of rates of surplus value. So long as free mobility of labor across national borders is restricted, for whatever reason, the workers of some countries will continue to be more exploited than others even if the rate of profit obtainable by capital should be everywhere the same.

The general effect of capital export is to retard the ripening of the contradictions of the accumulation process in the capital-exporting countries and to hasten their appearance in the capital-importing countries. In short there is a tendency for the rate of development of capitalism in the various parts of world economy to be evened out by capital movements.

The foregoing analysis pictures a world economy in which freedom of trade and freedom of capital movements are the rule. If this were a realistic assumption we should be justified in concluding that the results of our closed-system analysis require but slight modification to take account of the fact that the world is divided into politically separated regions. Actually, the assumption is far from realistic. The relations between countries have, since the beginning of the capitalist epoch, constituted to a peculiar degree the domain of economic policy, that is to say of state action directed to the achievement of definite economic goals. Since, for historical reasons which cannot be examined here, there have always been not one but numerous capitalist states operating in the international sphere, we have to take account not so much of the effects of a particular, even if changing, economic policy as of a clash of divergent and often conflicting economic policies. This circumstance has a profound influence on the course of international economic relations; even more important, perhaps, it reacts upon and modifies the internal structure of the countries concerned. When we speak of world economy, therefore, we do not mean merely the extension of the relations of commodity production (increasingly capitalist) to the widest conceivable area; we imply also qualitative changes in the component parts of world economy.

Before proceeding to an examination of the nature and consequences of international economic policies it is desirable to note some of the basic determinants of state action in this field. It has already been pointed out in Chapter XIII that the state is brought into action to solve economic problems as they arise in the course of capitalist development and that, since the capitalist class controls the state apparatus, the pressure to this end is increased in proportion to the importance of the capitalist interests involved. In the international sphere new problems are continually emerging, partly, because it is the nature of capitalism to change, but even more because the different parts of world economy change at varying tempos so that their positions relative to one another are all the more unstable. Moreover, each country has to adapt itself to the changing policies adopted by the others. Those whose interests are involved in international trade and capital movements comprise as a rule large and influential sections of the capitalist class often with the addition of other important groups, like large landed-proprietors and independent peasants or farmers who rely on the sale of commodities without being themselves capitalists. The latter groups commonly have some share in state power. The working class has little direct interest in international matters, since the commodity which it has to sell, namely labor power, by its nature must be sold locally and cannot be dealt in across national boundaries. Consequently the working class exerts little pressure on the formation of international economic policy, which is left in the hands of those immediately concerned who are members of the ruling class and have access to the state power. Under the circumstances opposition to the use of state power is at a minimum, and the actual content of economic policy depends upon the outcome of a conflict of interests among different sections of the ruling class. Finally, it is very important to note that in international relations any policy which is adopted is at least in part directed against outsiders and that on this ground it may easily be possible, by appeal to sentiments of nationalism, patriotism, and hostility to the foreigner, to secure the acquiescence and even support of substantially the whole community. It is much more difficult to portray state intervention in the internal life of a nation in this light, and this is unquestionably one of the decisive reasons why the state has always tended to be much more active in the international sphere.

2. Economic Policy in the Period of Competition

In the period of competitive capitalism—roughly the first seven decades of the nineteenth century—the economic policy of capitalist countries with respect to foreign trade conformed more or less closely to one of two basic patterns. The first, which was practiced only in England, was the policy of free trade; the second, which held sway throughout the rest of the capitalist world, was the policy of limited protection for industrial production. For our purposes the policy of limited protection may be illustrated by the case of the United States. Let us examine the two in turn.

England emerged from the eighteenth century with her industry far in advance of that of any other country. The textile, mining, and metallurgical industries, which were the spearheads of the industrial revolution, were almost from the outset dependent for their prosperity upon the export market and had nothing to fear from foreign competition. On the other hand the still politically dominant landed interests were well protected by a system of tariffs and export bounties: tariffs to check the import of foreign grain when the English harvest was poor and prices high, bounties to reduce the domestic supply and keep the price up when the harvest was good. With the growth of population and its concentration in industrial centers, it became necessary regularly to import agricultural products, and it soon became clear that the whole system of agricultural protection stood in sharp contradiction to the interests of industrial capital. There began the famous struggle for the repeal of the Corn Laws which ended in 1846 with the victory of free trade and the stripping of much of its remaining political power from the landlord class. Hilferding described the underlying issues in this struggle with admirable clarity:

> The manufacturers had nothing to fear from the import of foreign industrial products since their establishments were technically and economically far superior. On the other hand, however, the price of grain constituted the most important element in the 'price of labor,' and this factor was all the more important in determining industrial costs because the organic composition of capital was still low and the share of living labor in the value of the total product correspondingly high. The openly avowed motive of the English tariff campaign was the cheapening on the one side of raw materials, on the other side of the price of labor power.[2]

Ricardo, with his usual frankness, justified free trade largely in these terms, though for the most part its adherents rested their case on the advantages, in terms of multiplied use values, which would allegedly accrue to the great majority of the peoples in all the trading countries. It is noteworthy that the working class took little direct part in the struggle, though it utilized the split between industrialists and landlords to further its own campaign for factory legislation.

While the victory of free trade was being won in England a similar struggle, though with the roles reversed, was going on in the United States. Here industry was in its infancy and unable to compete successfully, except on a very restricted basis, with English products. On the other hand agriculture, and particularly cotton, the mainstay of the southern slave economy, was to an increasing degree dependent upon the export market. Moreover the agricultural classes were interested in buying industrial products as cheaply as possible. As a result incipient American industrialism, particularly in the northeastern states, clamored for protective tariffs, while agriculture, led by the old south, upheld the system of free trade. For a considerable period the issue was partially resolved through a series of compromises. Tariffs were imposed, but they were notably more effective in filling the public treasury than in fostering the growth of industry; on the whole the system remained more one of free trade than of protection, but it was genuinely satisfactory to no one. Under the circumstances the tariff question became one of the central points of conflict between the north and the south leading to the Civil War. With the victory of the north the backbone of the free-trade interest was broken, and the United States entered upon a course of greatly increased protection for its rapidly expanding industries.

We see that the achievement of political dominance by industrial capital led in England to a policy of free trade and in the United States to a policy of protection at a time when the industrial structure of both countries was largely competitive. It is therefore incorrect to speak of 'the' economic policy of competitive capitalism in the international sphere. There are two basic policies (of course with minor variants), and which one is adopted depends upon the stage of development in which a country finds itself and its position *vis-à-vis* the other countries with which it maintains relations. There is one further point which needs to be stressed in this connection. The underlying theories advanced by the spokesmen of industrial capital in the two countries were fundamentally identical. Such adherents of protection in this country as Henry Carey did not disagree with the English free traders as to the ultimate superiority of free trade. They held, however, that an industrially backward country like the United States ought to use protection as a transitional device to catch up with England (the so-called infant-industries argument). When capital equipment and skills had been built up to equality with the more advanced country, the tariffs should be abandoned in favor of free trade and each country should be allowed to enjoy the full benefits of the international division of labor. Hence we may say that free trade is the ideology of competitive capitalism even though it is actually put into practice only under special conditions.

A second aspect of economic policy in the period of competition concerns the relations between the economically advanced countries and the backward areas of the world with economic systems still very largely pre-capitalist. In this connection the main characteristics of the Mercantilist period, from the sixteenth century well into the eighteenth century, must be recalled. The major trading nations (Spain, Holland, France, and England) had built up colonial empires of world-wide scope, a process involving frequent armed conflict between two or more of the participants. The underlying purposes of the colonial system were three in number: to secure the safety and property of the merchants engaged in the colonial trade (primarily monopolistic trading companies), to exclude the competition of foreign merchants, and to regulate the terms of trade between mother country and colony in such a way as to ensure that the lion's share of the benefit would accrue to the former. Mercantilism was thus characterized by the pursuit of an active and aggressive colonial policy.

The nineteenth century witnessed a sharp change. Spain and Holland had already been reduced to the rank of second-rate powers no longer able to exercise a decisive influence on the development of world economy. France, after her defeat in the Napoleonic wars, turned to the intensive development of her internal economy on an industrial basis. England, alone among the great colonial powers, was apparently in a position to extend the scope of her imperial interests and intensify the exploitation of the backward areas of the world almost at will. But nothing of the sort happened; on the contrary, the rise to dominance of competitive industrial capital altered the tenor of colonial policy. The elaborate restrictions and regulations of the Mercantile system were felt to be so many fetters on the freedom of capital to expand and enter whatever line of activity it chose; the products of English factories needed no exclusive privileges to conquer the world; the maintenance of the empire was costly and seemed to many to be unnecessary. Almost every aspect of Mercantilism, including its colonial policy, came in for severe attack, along with the Corn Laws, at the hands of the free trade party. To be sure the actual setting free of the colonies remained no more than a demand of the radical free traders. The requirements of security of life and property made hasty action undesirable, and the vested interests in jobs and pensions of important elements of the governing class could hardly be ignored. It is even true that important new areas were brought under British rule in the middle years of the century. Nevertheless relations with the colonies were significantly liberalized, and people everywhere looked forward confidently to the day when the backward areas, better educated to the rights and obligations of civil society, could take their place as self-governing units in a world commonwealth of nations.

As to export of capital in the period of competition, it seems reasonable to say that this had not yet achieved the status of a major problem influencing the pattern of economic policy. The rapid growth of population and the advance of industrialization which characterized the period created vast opportunities for the accumulation of capital in most of the countries where stable capitalist relations had been established. Under the circumstances, and considering the inevitable risks involved, capitalists generally were not disposed to search for profitable opportunities for investment outside the boundaries of their own countries. England again was an exception—Holland and certain financial centers in a still disunited Germany should be added for the sake of completeness—but English capital had little trouble in finding lodgment abroad under satisfactory conditions which required a minimum of attention from the English government. A very large part of English capital export during this period, it should be remembered, went to the Americas and particularly the United States where it mingled with the rising tide of American accumulation. The problem of creating favorable conditions for capital investment, by destroying pre-capitalist forms of economy or warding off the dangers of awakened nationalism in backward areas, was still largely for the future.

Let us now summarize the main characteristics of economic policy in the period of competitive capitalism. Clearly the decisive factor overshadowing all others on a world scale was the pre-eminence of English industrialism. This produced a policy of free trade in England and a policy of limited protection (over the opposition of agricultural producers) in the less developed industrial states. In the colonial sphere, England, even though she had far outstripped or vanquished her chief rivals, turned away from the aggressive and expansionist path of the previous period. Along with the Corn Laws and the monopolistic privileges and restrictions of Mercantilism, the colonial system itself fell into disrepute with the spokesmen of industrial capital, though, for a variety of reasons, its actual abandonment remained no more than a hope for the future. Finally, capital export had not yet become a major problem influencing economic policy.

3. The Transformation of Economic Policy

During the final quarter of the nineteenth century there occurred a sea change in the methods and objectives of economic policy throughout the capitalist world. Three basic factors were responsible: (1) the rise of other nations, notably Germany and the United States, to a position from which they could challenge England's industrial supremacy; (2) the emergence of monopoly capitalism; and (3) the maturing of the contradictions of the accumulation process in the most advanced capitalist states. For theoretical purposes it is necessary to analyse these three factors separately, though in practice they are inextricably interrelated. Let us begin with the effects of monopoly on economic policy in the international sphere.

The objective of monopoly is the reaping of extra profits through raising price and limiting supply. If foreign producers have access to the monopolist's market, however, it may be impossible to achieve this objective. Consequently monopoly capital demands tariffs. Moreover it demands tariffs not only high enough to equalize advantages enjoyed by foreigners—such advantages indeed may already belong to the monopolist rather than to his rivals—but rather tariffs high enough to exclude the foreigner from the market under all conditions. For the monopolist, 'the striving for higher tariffs is just as unlimited as the striving for profits.'[8] This fact alone signifies a fundamental change in the character of protectionism, which is well described by Hilferding:

> The old tariff policy had the task . . . of accelerating the growth of an industry within the protected borders . . .
>
> It is otherwise in the period of capitalist monopolies. Now the mightiest, most-able-to-export industries, about whose capacity to compete on the world market there can be no doubt and for

which according to the old theory tariffs should have no interest, demand high protective duties.[4]

This is not the end of the story. The restriction of supply which the monopolist is forced to practice has serious disadvantages. It inhibits the optimum utilization of plant capacity and prevents the full enjoyment of the benefits of large-scale production; moreover it forces the accumulated capital of the monopolist to seek outside investment outlets instead of serving the purpose of expanding his own production facilities. Consequently he seeks to overcome these disadvantages by entering the export trade, and in order to assure to himself as large a share as possible of the world market he is ready to undersell his foreign competitors. This he can afford to do because he is fortified by the extra-profits of the protected domestic market; but it must not be assumed that he loses as a result. The lower costs of larger-scale production may raise the profit on domestic business and make it possible for him to show more profit on the foreign sales than he would be able to earn had he invested his capital in some non-monopolized home industry. This system of 'subsidizing' foreign sales from the profits of domestically protected monopoly is known as 'dumping.' Hilferding described its implications as follows:

> With the development of the subsidy system, protective tariffs completely change their function, even turn it into its opposite. From being a means of defense against foreign conquest of domestic markets they become a means of conquering foreign markets, from a weapon of protection for the weak they become a weapon of aggression for the strong.[5]

When several national monopolies in the same industry are simultaneously engaged in strenuous rivalry on the world market, perhaps each of them resorting to the practice of dumping in an effort to enlarge its share, the kind of cutthroat competition which was eliminated by the formation of a monopoly at home is reproduced on an international scale. The result frequently is the same, namely, the reaching of an agreement, perhaps in the form of an international cartel, to partition the available business among the contending parties. Some writers have seen in these international cartels a sign of a growing harmony of interests among the capitalist countries. This is an error. Such an agreement is more in the nature of a peace treaty which is observed only until one signatory feels strong enough to break it with advantage. Since the different countries develop at uneven rates such a time is sure to come. The international cartel is merely the means of temporarily stabilizing an existing situation so that all the members may avoid useless losses; it is never a means of wiping out the underlying conflict of interests between national monopolies.*

Two other effects of monopoly must be mentioned. We have noted that monopoly restricts the field for capital accumulation and that this heightens the interest of the monopolist in expanding his export market. It also stimulates the search for profitable foreign fields for the investment of capital; in other words it gives an impetus to capital export. In so far as the capital seeking foreign lodgment is that of the monopolist himself, capital export often takes the special form of 'direct investment,' that is to say, the establishment of branch factories in foreign countries. This is particularly likely to be the case when the monopolist is prevented, by tariffs or otherwise, from expanding his exports into the areas in question. Finally, the highest desiderata of monopoly capital must always remain the extension of the range of monopolized products on the one hand and the expansion of the protected market on the other. Both of these objectives call for expansion of the territory under the political domination of the monopolist's own country. The desire of monopolists to have exclusive access to scarce raw materials which can be used to exact tribute from the whole world is particularly strong, and this can be accomplished much more expeditiously when concessions and protection from the state are readily forthcoming, that is to say, if the raw material producing region is under the control of the monopolist's state. Colonies producing valuable raw materials are not only or even primarily sought after to ensure a *source of supply* to the mother country, as is often argued; the purpose is more often to ensure a *source of extra profit* to the monopolists of the mother country. The expansion of the monopolist's protected market likewise requires terri-

* The point is ably argued by Hilferding, *Das Finanzkapital*, pp. 392-3 and was stressed by Lenin, *Imperialism*, Chapter v.

torial annexations since only in this way can new customers be brought within the confines of the national tariff system. In this connection, it makes no difference in principle whether the additional territory is industrially backward or advanced so long as the monopolist believes he will be able to take over the market for his own products. Near-by industrial states and far-away colonies are equally grist to the monopolist's mill. Consequently in the matter of colonial and territorial policy monopoly capital is expansionist and annexationist.

The significance of the appearance in the world arena of nations competent to challenge England's industrial supremacy requires but little emphasis. If one were to search for turning points in this development one would unquestionably select the Civil War in the United States and the Franco-Prussian War (as the culmination of the German wars of unification) on the continent of Europe. These events marked the emergence of the United States and Germany, and to a lesser extent of France in spite of her military defeat, as powerful industrial nations. Under the new circumstances, English capital, though it still had little to fear so far as its domestic market was concerned, had to look forward to increasingly severe competition on the international market. It could no longer safely regard the world as its preserve; not only did it have to face the possibility of competition in new areas, there was even the danger, not immediate perhaps, of being dislodged from positions in which it had long been entrenched.

The immediate outcome was a tightening of the bonds of empire and a revival on all sides of an aggressive colonial policy. Africa, which had been less than 10 per cent under outside domination in 1875, was almost completely partitioned by the European nations during the next twenty-five years. Even the United States, still deeply engaged in settling the open spaces of the North American continent, entered the colonial lists before the close of the century as a result of the Spanish-American War.

Much of this renewed activity in empire building was of a protective or anticipatory character. When one country lays claim to an area, it follows as a matter of course that the nationals of other countries will at the very least be at a serious disadvantage in doing business there. Consequently, though English capitalists may have little to gain through annexation by their own country, they may have much to lose through annexation by France or Germany. As soon as rivals appear on the scene, each country must make every effort to protect its position against the incursions of the others. The result may appear to be a net loss, but this is only because the measurement is made from an irrelevant base. What is important is not the loss or gain compared to the pre-existent situation, but rather the loss or gain compared to the situation which would have prevailed had a rival succeeded in stepping in ahead. This is a principle of wide application in the economics of monopoly; when applied to the building of colonial empires it may appropriately be referred to as the principle of protective annexation.* Closely related in some ways is the urge to annex territories which, though of little or no present value, nevertheless may become valuable in the future. This may be called the principle of anticipatory annexation. Protective and anticipatory annexations played a very important part in the late-nineteenth-century scramble for still unclaimed parts of the earth's surface. Finally, we must not forget considerations of a strategic nature. An empire must be defensible from a military standpoint, and this obviously implies the need for well-placed land and sea bases, lines of communication, and so forth.

The change in attitude towards colonies which we have been discussing originated with the appearance of serious rivals to England's world industrial supremacy. Our previous analysis of the effect of monopoly on economic policy should make it clear that the new colonial policy received a mighty impetus from the development of monopoly capitalism in the closing decades of the nineteenth century.

The third fundamental factor contributing to the transformation of economic policy is the maturing of the contradictions of the accumulation process in the advanced capitalist countries. The underlying theory has been presented in detail in Part III

* Marxian writers on imperialism have not as a rule sufficiently stressed this factor in the extension of colonial empires. A notable exception is Grossmann, *Das Akkumulations- und Zusammenbruchsgesetz des kapitalistischen Systems*, pp. 450 ff.

and will not be repeated here. We need only recall that both the falling tendency of the rate of profit and the tendency to underconsumption put ever-growing obstacles in the path of accumulation. To an increasing extent accumulation in the advanced countries takes the form of capital export * to backward regions where wages are low and profits high, where the potential abundance of labor supply and the low level of industrialization obviate, at least for the time, the dangers of underconsumption. But it must not be supposed that capital finds everything in readiness to receive it in the backward regions. The native populations have their own accustomed ways of making a living and are far from eager to enlist in the service of foreign capital at meager wages. Consequently the areas must be brought under the jurisdiction of the capitalist state and conditions favorable to the growth of capitalist relations of production must be forcibly created. Hilferding wrote:

> As always, when capital finds itself for the first time face to face with relations which stand in the way of its need for self-expansion and which would be overcome by economic processes only gradually and much too slowly, it appeals to the state power and puts the latter into the service of forcible expropriation which creates the necessary free wage proletariat, whether it is a case, as in the early days, of European peasants or the Indians of Mexico and Peru, or whether it is a case, as today, of the negroes of Africa.[6]

This is the first, but not the only, reason why capital export to backward countries makes for an active colonial policy. A second reason is that, as more and more advanced countries reach the stage of capital export, rivalry for the most profitable fields of investment becomes intense, and the capitalists of each nation appeal to their own governments for assistance. This is most easily given by turning the backward regions into colonies from which the nationals of other countries can be wholly or partially excluded. Here again protective and anticipatory motives play a role. Finally, a third motive for a colonial policy emerges. To quote again from Hilferding:

* As Lenin expressed it, 'The necessity for exporting capital arises from the fact that in a few countries capitalism has become "over-ripe" . . .'. *Imperialism*, p. 58.

In the newly opened lands themselves the imported capitalism . . . arouses the ever-growing opposition of the people, awakened to national consciousness, against the intruders . . . The old social relations are completely revolutionized, the agrarian, thousand-year-old unity of the 'nations without a history' is rent asunder . . . Capitalism itself gradually gives to the oppressed peoples the means and the method of achieving their own liberation. The goal, which once was the loftiest of the European nations, the creation of a national state as a means to economic and cultural freedom, now becomes theirs. These independence movements threaten European capital precisely in its most valuable . . . fields of exploitation, and to an ever increasing degree the latter finds that it can maintain its mastery only through the continual increase of its instruments of force.

Consequently the cry of all capitalists interested in foreign countries for a strong state power, the authority of which can protect their interests in the farthest corners of the globe . . . But export capital feels best satisfied with the complete domination of the new regions by the state power of its own country. For then the capital from other countries is excluded, it enjoys a privileged position, and its profits are guaranteed by the state. Thus capital export too makes for an imperialist policy.[7]

It must not be supposed from anything that has been said about capital export that it directly contributes to a rapid *industrialization* of backward areas. The fields into which capital tends to flow are rather government-guaranteed loans for various kinds of public works, railroads, public utilities, exploitation of natural resources, and trade: in short, activities which do not compete with commodity exports from the industrially advanced countries. Capital export therefore leads to a very one-sided development of the economies of the backward areas. A native bourgeoisie emerges and attempts to foster the growth of native industries, but the obstacles are formidable and progress is at best slow. Meanwhile the destruction of handicraft industry by cheap manufactured imports drives a larger proportion of the native population onto the land. In this way we see the genesis of the fundamental economic contradiction of backward regions, the ever-mounting agrarian crisis. The interests of both native bourgeoisie and native masses are sacrificed to the needs of capital in the advanced countries. Both classes consequently unite in a genuinely national movement for freedom from foreign domination. It is this movement, as Hilferding points out in the quotation above, which forces the imperialist powers to a continual strengthening of their grip on the backward areas.*

It should be obvious that in so far as monopoly stimulates capital export—and we have seen that there is every reason to believe that it does—it contributes to the new colonial policy through this channel as well as through those which have already been discussed.

We have now seen how monopoly, the challenge to England's world economic supremacy, and the maturing of the contradictions of the accumulation process in the advanced countries combined to effect a complete transformation in the character of economic policy in the closing decades of the nineteenth century. For free trade or limited protection there was gradually substituted unlimited protection; for free competition on the world market there was substituted the cutthroat competition of national monopolies now and again mitigated by international combines of a more or less stable character; for indifference and even hostility to the colonial empires inherited from the days of Mercantilism there was substituted a renewed and doubly aggressive colonial policy designed to corner valuable sources of raw materials, extend the scope of protected markets, and guarantee profitable investment outlets for exported capital. We have, in short, surveyed the emergence of those features of the latest stage of capitalist development which led Lenin to give to it the name of 'Imperialism.' But it goes almost without saying that such a fundamental overturn in the relations of world economy could not but have profound effects upon every other aspect of capitalist economics and capitalist politics. Therefore in the next chapter we shall devote further attention to the nature and consequences of imperialism.

* This whole problem is discussed at greater length in the next chapter.

XVII

IMPERIALISM

1. Introduction

Imperialism may be defined as a stage in the development of world economy in which (a) several advanced capitalist countries stand on a competitive footing with respect to the world market for industrial products; (b) monopoly capital is the dominant form of capital; and (c) the contradictions of the accumulation process have reached such maturity that capital export is an outstanding feature of world economic relations. As a consequence of these basic economic conditions, we have two further characteristics: (d) severe rivalry in the world market leading alternately to cutthroat competition and international monopoly combines; and (e) the territorial division of 'unoccupied' parts of the world among the major capitalist powers (and their satellites). With minor qualifications, this is the definition of imperialism proposed by Lenin.* Lenin's book on imperialism,

* A correct definition of imperialism, according to Lenin, 'will include the following five essential features:

'1. The concentration of production and capital, developed to such a high stage that it has created monopolies which play a decisive role in economic life.

'2. The merging of bank capital with industrial capital and the creation, on the basis of this "finance capital," of a financial oligarchy.

'3. The export of capital, as distinguished from the export of commodities, becomes of particularly great importance.

'4. International monopoly combines of capitalists are formed which divide up the world.

'5. The territorial division of the world by the greatest capitalist powers is completed.' *Imperialism*, p. 81.

Lenin evidently presupposes our point (a), and we have omitted his item (2). It has already been explained (above, p. 269) that what is sound in the concept of 'finance capital,' including the dominance of a small oligarchy of big capitalists, is comprehended in our concept of 'monopoly capital.' Consequently, to retain Lenin's second feature would be either redundant or misleading.

it should be remembered, was brief and much of it was devoted to summarizing supporting facts and figures. The more detailed theoretical analysis of the preceding chapters may help to demonstrate the consistency and appropriateness of Lenin's conception of imperialism.

The international antagonisms of imperialism are fundamentally the antagonisms of rival national capitalist classes. Since in the international sphere the interests of capital are directly and quickly translated into terms of state policy, it follows that these antagonisms assume the form of conflicts between states and thus, indirectly, between whole nations. The resultant profound effects upon the internal economic and social structure of the capitalist countries must now be examined.

2. Nationalism, Militarism, and Racism

In the formative period of capitalist society, nationalism and militarism together played an indispensable role. Nationalism was the expression of the aspiration of the rising middle class for economic unity and cultural freedom as against the separatism and obscurantism of feudal society; militarism was the inevitable means to the end. There are those who do not like to admit that militarism ever played a constructive historical role, but, as Rosa Luxemburg put it, 'if we consider history as it was—not as it could have been or should have been—we must agree that war has been an indispensable feature of capitalist development.' [1]

In the period of imperialism, nationalism and militarism, still bound together like Siamese twins, undergo a change in their character in the advanced countries, though retaining their earlier function and significance in the case of oppressed nationalities and acquiring these characteristics for the first time in the backward and colonial areas of the world. In the advanced countries, nationalism and militarism cease to serve the purpose of realizing internal unification and freedom on a capitalist foundation and instead become weapons in the world struggle among rival groups of capitalists. Militarism, the use of organized force, is a necessary aspect of such a struggle, though as long as unclaimed territory still remains to be occupied it may not lead to open conflict between the powers. Nationalism is no less vital, for without the goals of national honor and greatness, the masses would lack the enthusiasm and willingness to sacrifice, so necessary to success in the imperialist struggle. This is not to argue, though the contrary is often implied, that nationalism is an artificial sentiment deliberately stirred up by capitalists for their own ends; on the contrary, it is precisely the deep roots which nationalism struck in wide strata of the people in the formative period of modern society that makes it such an important factor in the period of imperialism. In this connection Hilferding correctly speaks of the 'remarkable twisting of the national idea' away from a recognition of the right of self-determination and independence and towards the glorification of one's own nation as against others.* In spite of this, it is significant that nationalism continues to bear the marks of its origin. Even when it is most obvious that it is being invoked in the interests of domination, the vocabulary of 'freedom,' 'liberation,' 'self-determination,' and so on, is faithfully retained.

The rise of militarism to a position of permanent and steadily growing importance in all the imperialist nations has far-reaching economic consequences. In the first place, it fosters the development of a group of specially favored monopolists in those industries, like steel and shipbuilding, which are most important to the production of armaments. The munitions magnates have a direct interest in the maximum expansion of military production; not only do they benefit in the form of state orders but also they are afforded safe and lucrative outlets for their accumulated profits. Hence it is these elements of the captalist class which take the lead in calling for an aggressive foreign policy. In the second place, since military expenditures perform the same economic function as consumption expenditures,† the expansion of armies and navies constitutes an increasingly important offsetting force to the tendency to underconsumption. From the point of view of the functioning of the economy as a whole, therefore, it becomes ever more dangerous to restrict the magnitude of

* *Das Finanzkapital,* p. 427. Several pages by Hilferding on the ideology of imperialism, including the passage cited here, have been translated and are presented as Appendix B below.

† See above, p. 233.

military outlays. Finally, to the extent that production of armaments utilizes labor power and means of production for which there would otherwise be no demand, militarism actually provides the capitalist class as a whole with increased opportunities for profitable investment of capital. For all these reasons, and quite apart from the necessities engendered by imperialist rivalries, militarism tends to develop its own expansionist dynamic in capitalist society. As Rosa Luxemburg, writing in 1899, very truly said:

What demonstrates best the specific character of present-day militarism is the fact that it develops generally in all countries as a consequence, so to speak, of its own internal mechanical motive power, a phenomenon which was completely unknown several decades ago. We recognize this in the fatal character of the impending explosion which is inevitable in spite of the complete inconclusiveness of the objectives and motives of the conflict. From a motor of capitalist development militarism has turned into a capitalist disease.[2]

Along with the transformation in the character of nationalism and militarism there emerges a new, pseudo-scientific justification for the policy of imperialist expansion, namely the theory of racial superiority. The relation of racial ideology to imperialism was clearly explained by Hilferding:

Since the subordination of foreign nations proceeds by force, that is to say in a very natural way, it appears to the dominant nation that it owes its mastery to its special natural qualities, in other words to its racial characteristics. Thus in racial ideology there emerges a scientifically-cloaked foundation for the power lust of finance capital, which in this way demonstrates the cause and necessity of its operations. In place of the democratic ideal of equality there steps the oligarchical ideal of mastery.[3]

It is true that the doctrine of racial superiority as such was not novel. The Frenchman Gobineau, writing in the 1850s, was one of the earliest and most influential exponents of the modern pseudo-science of race. Gobineau's purpose, as he frankly admitted, was to combat the rising tide of democratic opinion on the European continent and to establish the natural right of the aristocracy to rule over France. The French aristocracy, Gobineau argued, was originally of Germanic extraction while the mass of the French people were Gallic or Celtic. Since the Germanic race is 'superior' it followed that the aristocracy ruled by virtue of its inherent characteristics. This theory was not calculated to arouse much support in France, but several decades later it was enthusiastically taken up by the exponents of German expansion and in this way became the starting point of modern German racial ideology. At about the same time in England, and to a lesser extent in America, the 'white man's burden' was being somewhat belatedly discovered and turned into a 'humanitarian' justification of Anglo-Saxon world domination.

The usefulness of the theory of racial superiority, it was soon discovered, is not limited to the justification of foreign conquest. The intensification of social conflict within the advanced capitalist countries, which will be more fully analysed presently, has to be directed as far as possible into innocuous channels—innocuous, that is to say, from the standpoint of capitalist class rule. The stirring up of antagonisms along racial lines is a convenient method of directing attention away from class struggle, which, as Hilferding points out in another connection, 'for the possessing class is both fruitless and dangerous.'[4] Consequently anti-Semitism, which during the nineteenth century was generally believed to be disappearing from the more advanced capitalist countries, is revived and takes its place among the 'scientific' discoveries of the new racism. Discrimination against real or imaginary racial minorities, moreover, has the full sanction of monopolistic economics, for in this way jobs and investment opportunities can be denied to the disadvantaged groups, their wages and profits can be depressed below prevailing levels, and the favored sections of the population can reap substantial material rewards.

3. Imperialism and the Classes

In order to analyse the impact of imperialism on the internal social conflicts of capitalist society, it is necessary to digress briefly to call attention to certain characteristics of advanced capitalism which have so far remained largely unremarked.

In the first place, there is a marked tendency for the interests of large property-owners to merge under the leadership of monopoly capital. Under a regime of corporations, the ancient conflict between industrialists and big landowners tends to disappear; all sorts of physical assets are merged in the corporate balance sheet, and corporate securities are a common medium for the investment of surplus value whether its source be one type oi property or another. Moreover with the development of monopoly in industry on the one hand, and the opening up of new agricultural countries on the other, the old dispute over tariff policy loses its meaning; all sections of the propertied class unite in demanding protective duties. This is not to say that conflicts of interest among large property owners can ever be eliminated; their severity, however, is reduced and has a diminishing significance for the formation of ruling-class policy. Hilferding gives an acute analysis of this trend for the case of Germany;[5] in spite of differences in national conditions, which may assume great importance in times of crisis, the trend goes forward *pari passu* with the accumulation process all over the capitalist world.

Secondly, along with the unification of propertied interests goes the unification of the interests of the workers. In their struggle for higher wages, shorter hours, and better working conditions the workers in one industry after another discover that their strength lies in organization and co-operation. Consequently trade unionism grows up and spreads to ever wider sections of the working class. On the basis of experience in cooperation for the attainment of common ends the workers form their own political parties to win concessions which lie outside the reach of the economic struggle alone. On these foundations there arises a class consciousness and solidarity among the workers which fosters common action and common policies in all fields and makes possible the achievement of economic gains and political concessions which would otherwise be unattainable.*

* It is beyond the scope of the present work to investigate in detail the consequences for the functioning of capitalism of trade unions and legislation favoring the working class. It may be noted in passing, however, that the specific introduction of these factors does not suspend any of the fundamental laws of the accumulation process which have already been discussed. The primary effect is to raise wages. Since a slowing down in the rate of population growth also has the tendency to raise wages, the analysis of the two phenomena is essentially similar. The rate

This process was already well under way in England by the middle of the nineteenth century, but in the capitalist world at large it develops fully only during the imperialist epoch. Thus so far as capitalists and workers are concerned, imperialism is characterized by a tightening of class lines and an intensification of class struggle. This occurs independently of the special international characteristics of imperialism.

Thirdly, between capitalists and workers there stands an array of middle groups belonging to neither of the basic classes of capitalist society. Some of these are declining in importance, for example the independent farmers who are gradually succumbing to the spread of capitalist agriculture and hence tend to become (in a very few cases) capitalists or (in the vast majority of cases) wage workers or propertyless tenants; handicraftsmen and genuinely independent tradesmen also decline in numbers and importance: these are, in short, the groups which Marx and Engels had in mind when they spoke in the *Communist Manifesto* of the disappearance of 'the lower strata of the middle class—the small tradespeople, shopkeepers, and retired tradesmen generally, the handicraftsmen and peasants.' Alongside these declining sections of the middle class, however, there are the 'new middle classes' which are brought into being by rising living standards, centralization of capital, and the growth of monopoly. The new middle classes include such diverse groups as industrial and governmental bureaucrats, salesmen, publicists, dealers who are in

of surplus value and hence also the rate of profit is reduced. Capitalists react to this by stepping up the rate of introduction of new machinery; the reserve army is swelled. But since trade unions, unemployment insurance, et cetera, prevent the reserve army from exercising its full depressing effect on wages, the process now becomes more or less continuous. Mechanization leads to a rapid growth of the means of production, but consumption is not appreciably stimulated since the higher wage rates are offset by the greater volume of unemployment. Hence, paradoxically, trade-union action tends to intensify the tendency to underconsumption. (For a fuller exposition of the effects of a declining rate of population growth, see above, pp. 222 f.)

The fact that trade-union action does not greatly improve the position of the working class as a whole is one of the most important forces driving it on to political action. When it is discovered that here too capitalism puts definite limits to the gains which can be realized, the working class is at length forced by experience to change its goals from reform within the framework of capitalism to the overthrow of capitalism and the establishment of a socialist economy.

fact if not in form employees of big capital, professionals, teachers, and so forth. In the period of imperialism, particularly because of the expansionary effect of monopoly on the distributive machinery, these groups grow not only absolutely but also as a proportion of the total population. The numerical importance of the middle classes, old and new, should not, however, lead us to evaluate their role as we do that of the capitalists and workers. Instead of a growing solidarity of interests expressed in closer organizational unity and more conscious and effective political action, we find among the middle classes the utmost confusion and diversity of interests and aims. An objective basis for organizational unity and consciously oriented policy is lacking except in the case of relatively small groups which are too weak to be effective and often work at gross purposes into the bargain. Hence it is the fate of the middle classes in the period of ripening capitalist contradictions to be squeezed between the extortions of monopoly capital on the one hand and the demands of the working class for better conditions and greater security on the other hand; this much, at any rate, they all have in common, and it is this which determines the basic attitude characteristic of nearly all sectors of the middle classes. The attitude in question is hostility to both organized capital and organized labor which can manifest itself in seemingly contradictory ways. On the one hand the middle classes are the source of various degrees of non-proletarian anti-capitalism; on the other hand of Utopias in which all organized class power is dissolved and the individual (i.e. the unattached member of a middle-class group) becomes the basic social unit as in the lost days of simple commodity production. We shall see in the next chapter how under certain circumstances the former of these ideologies is harnessed to the needs of monopoly capital in the form of fascism.

Let us now attempt to assess the impact of the special features of imperialism on the various social classes.

As far as the propertied class, under the leadership of monopoly capital, is concerned, little needs to be added to what has already been said in this and earlier chapters. Monopoly capital needs to expand abroad, and for this purpose it requires the assistance and protection of the state. It is, therefore, here that we find the roots of imperialist policy with all its manifold implications.

The interests of the working class in an aggressive and expansionist foreign policy are more complex. In so far as foreign trade and capital export make possible the importation of cheap wage goods and enlarge the profits of the capitalist class, it is clear that opportunities are opened up for the workers to improve their standard of living without necessarily arousing the bitter hostility of their employers. In this sense the workers gain. Moreover if, in the absence of capital export and the military expenditures incident to an imperialist policy, an advanced capitalist country would suffer from the effects of a low rate of profit and underconsumption, then it may be said that the working class benefits from a higher level of employment than would otherwise obtain. Against this, however, is to be set the loss in real wages which the workers bear if military expenditures go beyond a certain point and especially if inter-imperialist rivalries lead to actual armed conflict. It appears from these considerations that the working class of any country can gain most from an extension of foreign trade and capital export if the profits of the capitalists are enhanced, cheap imports of wage goods are fostered, and there is little danger of a collision with rival countries. This was precisely the peculiar situation in which the English working class found itself throughout the greater part of the nineteenth century, a fact which amply accounts for the complacent and even favorable attitude which the British working-class movement adopted towards the extension of British interests abroad in the years before the First World War.

Even in England conditions gradually changed in this respect. As Kautsky pointed out as early as 1902:

> So long as English industry ruled the world market the English workers could agree with their capitalists that live and let live is the best policy. That came to an end as soon as equal, frequently even superior, competitors appeared on the world market in the shape of Germany and America. Now begins again in England too the struggle against the trade unions which becomes the more intensive in proportion to the sharpness of the competition among these great industrial powers.[6]

As soon, in other words, as international rivalry becomes acute, each capitalist class attempts to hold its position without sacrificing its profits by depressing wages and lengthening hours in its own country. Moreover, it must not be forgotten, as Dobb has stressed, that capital export keeps wages from rising at home as they would if the capital were invested domestically: Dobb even regards this as 'the reason why, fundamentally, the interest of capital and of labor in this matter are opposed.'[7] And finally, with the intensification of imperialist rivalries it becomes increasingly clear to the working class that the end of the process can only be war, from which it stands to lose much and gain little. While, therefore, there may be times when the economic interests of the working class are benefited by an imperialist policy, this cannot last long and ultimately the more fundamental and lasting opposition of the workers must come to the surface. On this, as on other issues, the interests and policies of capital and labor are fundamentally antagonistic.

Few worthwhile generalizations about the economic interests of the middle classes can be made, and this holds true of their relations to imperialism. Some groups no doubt stand to gain, others to lose; in still other cases the balance depends upon particular circumstances or is altogether indeterminate. Lacking common interests and a common organizational base, the middle classes are peculiarly unstable and become easily attached to vague ideals of national greatness or racial superiority, a propensity which is magnified by the difficult position which they occupy between organized capital and organized labor in advanced capitalist society. The nation or the race becomes the substitute for the solidarity of class interests which their isolated position in society denies to the middle classes, and at the same time it offers to them a kind of psychological escape from the frustrations of their everyday life. Objectively, therefore, wide sectors of the middle classes are ripe for enlistment in the cause of foreign expansion. Monopoly capital appreciates these susceptibilities of the middle classes and, moreover, knows how to take advantage of them for its own ends. In this connection it is a fact of great importance that the vast sums which monopoly causes to be spent on advertising and publicity bring all the channels of public opinion under the direct influence of the top oligarchy of the ruling class. By playing on the susceptibilities of the middle classes, and to a less extent of the unorganized sections of the working class, it is possible to build up formidable mass support for an aggressive imperialist policy. It is in this connection that the nationalist and racist ideologies, which were analyzed in the preceding section, acquire their greatest importance. The advantages to the propertied interests are even greater than this would indicate. Since, as we have seen, the working class tends to be hostile to imperialist expansion, its organizations and policies can be made to appear 'unpatriotic' and 'selfish.' In this fashion the hostility of the middle classes to the working class, which is present in any case, can be intensified. Thus the net result of imperialism is to bind the middle classes closer to big capital and to widen the gulf between the middle classes and the working class.

4. Imperialism and the State

It goes without saying that the renewed rise of empires and the growth of militarism imply an augmentation in the power of the state and an extension of the scope of its functions. The maturing contradictions of the accumulation process in the epoch of imperialism provide additional grounds for increased state activity, particularly in the economic sphere.

From the standpoint of the capitalist class there are two basic methods of countering the growing power and unity of the working class: repression and concession. Though these two methods may appear to be contradictory they are in fact complementary, being mixed together in varying proportions at different times. Both necessitate an expansion in the power and functions of the state. Thus we observe simultaneously the growth of the instruments of force designed to guarantee internal 'law and order' and the extension of social legislation in the form of workmen's compensation, unemployment insurance, old-age benefit payments, and so forth.

An additional factor impelling the state to interference in the economic process is the centralization of capital and the growth of monopoly. The revisionists believed that monopoly would have the effect of regulating the anarchy of capitalist production, an opinion which, like so much of revisionist theorizing, has the remarkable quality of being the precise opposite of the truth. Actually monopoly intensifies the anarchy of capitalist production: * the various monopolized industries attempt to go their own way in defiance of the requirements of the system as a whole. In this way disproportionalities are multiplied and the equilibrating force of the market is prevented from exercising its influence. The state is obliged to step in and attempt to substitute its own action for the 'law of supply and demand.' Moreover the strategic position of the so-called natural monopolies (railroads and public utilities) is so strong that the state finds it necessary to curb their exercise of monopoly power. This is frequently interpreted as state action in the interests of consumers, and to a degree of course it is; but a more important consideration is the protection of the vast majority of capitalist enterprises, which are absolutely dependent on electric power and transportation, from the exactions of a small number of very powerful monopolists. The history of railroad regulation in the United States, for example, would be quite unintelligible in any other terms. It is interesting to note that Marx recognized the connection between monopoly and state intervention; the growth of joint-stock companies, he remarked, 'establishes a monopoly in certain spheres and thereby challenges the interference of the state.'[8]

Finally, we may note in this connection that the contradictions of the accumulation process and the uneven development as between branches of industry bring it about that now one line of production, now another, ceases to expand and becomes actually unprofitable. In the days of competitive capitalism the result was a disappearance of numerous firms, the bankruptcy and ruin of many capitalists. When a declining industry, however, is the home of great monopolistic combines with ramifications throughout the economic system, failures and bankruptcies are a much more serious matter; it becomes necessary for the state to take a hand by way of loans of public funds, subsidies, and even in some cases government ownership of the no-longer

* As Lenin expressed it, 'when monopoly appears in some branches of industry, it increases and intensifies the state of chaos inherent in capitalist production as a whole.' *Imperialism,* p. 27.

profitable enterprises. In this fashion capitalist states are forced to go in for an ever greater degree of 'socialism.' What is socialized is almost invariably the losses of the capitalists involved. 'A state monopoly in capitalist society,' Lenin drily remarked, 'is nothing more than a means of increasing and guaranteeing the income of millionaires in one branch of industry or another who are on the verge of bankruptcy.' [9]

Along with the expansion of the power of the state and the scope of its economic functions goes a decline in the effectiveness of parliamentary institutions. In the words of Otto Bauer, 'Imperialism reduces the power of the legislature [*Gesetzgebung*] as against the executive [*Verwaltung*].' [10] The reasons for this are not far to seek. Parliament grew out of the struggle of the capitalist class against the arbitrary exercise of power by the centralized monarchies which characterized the early modern period; its function has always been to check and control the exercise of governmental power. Consequently parliamentary institutions flourished and reached the peak of their prestige in the period of competitive capitalism when the functions of the state, particularly in the economic sphere, were reduced to a minimum. At that time it was possible to look forward to a day when all the nations of the world would be under parliamentary governments on the English or American model. In the period of imperialism, however, a sharp change occurs. With the tightening of class lines and the increasing severity of social conflict, parliament becomes more and more a battle ground for contending parties representing divergent class and group interests. While on the one hand parliament's capacity for positive action declines, on the other hand there emerges an increasing need for a strong centralized state ready and able to rule over distant territories, to direct the activities of fleets and armies, and to solve difficult and complex economic problems. Under the circumstances, parliament is forced to give up one after another of its cherished prerogatives and to see built up under its very eyes the kind of centralized and uncontrolled authority against which, in its youth, it had fought so hard and so well.

So far as the effect of imperialism on the capitalist state is concerned, we observe on the one hand a vast expansion in the power and functions of the state, on the other hand the decline of parliamentarism. These are not two separate movements but rather two aspects of one and the same development which is connected in the closest way with the economic and social characteristics of imperialism in general.

5. Wars of Redivision

Writing of the last quarter of the nineteenth century, Lenin pointed out that

> the characteristic feature of this period is the final partition of the earth, final not in the sense that a *re-partition* would be impossible—on the contrary, re-partitions are possible and inevitable—but in the sense that the colonial policy of the capitalist countries *has completed* the seizure of unoccupied land on our planet. For the first time the world is now divided up, so that in the future *only re-divisions* are possible; i.e. a transfer from one 'owner' to another, and not of unowned territory to an 'owner.'[11]

The underlying reasons for this have already been sufficiently elucidated in these pages; but we may well ask why 're-partitions' should be 'inevitable.' Why should not the various capitalist powers, once the great scramble is over, settle down to a peaceful exploitation of what they have? The answer is that capitalism, by its very nature, cannot settle down but must keep expanding, and since the various sectors of the world capitalist economy expand at very different rates, it follows that the balance of forces is bound to be upset in such a way that one or more countries will find it both possible and advantageous to challenge the *status quo* with respect to territorial boundaries. The rival national capitalist classes show by their concern over armies, navies, strategic bases, allies, and so forth, how well they understand this basic fact of the imperialist period, for it is self-evident that a redivision of the world can be effected only by armed force.

It should be clear from the analysis of the preceding chapter that the annexationist urge of imperialist nations is by no means confined to backward, non-industrialized regions. To include new markets and new sources of raw materials within the protective tariff walls of one's own nation is a desideratum of imperialist policy whether the areas concerned are pre-capitalist or capitalist, backward or highly industrialized. This is important to keep in mind in examining the course of events of the last three decades, for any theory which denies it is clearly inadequate to account for what has actually taken place. It may be remarked in passing that we here touch upon one of the glaring weaknesses of the theory of imperialism put forward by Rosa Luxemburg and her followers. It must also be emphasized that a picture of world economy which displays only a handful of advanced imperialist nations surrounded by backward colonial areas is an oversimplification. In reality there are other elements to be taken into account: on the one hand small and relatively advanced industrial nations, some with and some without empires of their own; on the other hand formally independent backward countries which in fact occupy a semi-colonial position relative to the great powers. In both cases such independence as these areas enjoy is essentially the outcome of rivalry among the major imperialist nations.* In peace time these countries constitute, so to speak, the focal points of imperialist conflict; when the balance of forces shifts and the weapons of diplomacy give way to the weapons of force, they form the major battle grounds of wars of redivision.

Let us now attempt a very brief summary of the international conflicts of the twentieth century on the basis of our theory of imperialism. Such a summary should enable us to get a clearer view of the limits of imperialism than would otherwise be possible.

The first war for redivision of the world began in 1914 and came to an end with the peace treaties of 1918 and 1919. On both sides it was a war of coalition in which the major contestants were respectively England and Germany, the two most powerful and advanced capitalist nations of Western Europe.

* China, which since the middle of the nineteenth century has been one of the main areas of imperialist conflict, is a case in point. One of the most discerning students of Chinese history has very truly noted that 'all that prevented foreign imperialism from mastering China outright was rivalry among the imperial powers.' Owen Lattimore, *Inner Asian Frontiers of China* (1940), p. 144.

It is impossible to localize the underlying issues, though it is clear that the area of most immediately severe rivalry was Southeastern Europe and the Near East, including the Eastern Mediterranean. The decay and dissolution of the pre-capitalist Turkish Empire, which had been in process for some time, created a welter of international problems and ambitions which involved all the European imperialist powers. The actual occasion for the outbreak of the struggle was connected with the aspirations of the oppressed nationalities of the Balkan region for national independence and statehood. As the war spread, however, the issues likewise broadened to include the entire question of redivision of the world. The peace treaties show more clearly what the war was about than the particular and relatively minor disputes which set off the conflagration.

From the outset all the European imperialist nations except Italy were involved, and Italy joined as soon as her statesmen believed they could tell which side would emerge victorious. The two major non-European imperialist powers, the United States and Japan, were also drawn in. In 1917 the breakdown of the Tsarist regime in Russia was followed by the Bolshevik revolution, the establishment of the world's first socialist society, and Russia's withdrawal from the imperialist arena. The following year the war came to an end with the collapse of German and Austro-Hungarian resistance. The Treaty of Versailles, the major imperialist peace treaty, was dominated by England and France which took for themselves the lion's share of Germany's colonial empire. Important raw-material-producing areas on the east and west of Germany were awarded to a reconstructed Poland and to France and Belgium respectively; Germany was stripped of her navy and merchant marine, and her army was reduced to a size which it was thought would be sufficient to maintain the system of capitalist property relations within her new frontiers. Austria-Hungary broke up into pieces, and a ring of new states was established in Southeastern and Eastern Europe to isolate the Soviet Union and to act as a counterweight against a possible German risorgimento. The United States, while not profiting from the war in a territorial sense, emerged as economically the most powerful nation in the world, a creditor on a vast scale where a few years before she had still been a heavy debtor to the European capital-exporting nations. It was already clear that the United States would play a key role in future imperialist conflicts. Italy was too weak at the end of the war to collect what had been promised her for her entrance on the Allied side. Finally Japan, which was involved in the hostilities only peripherally, took advantage of the preoccupation of the Western powers to extend her territory and sphere of influence in the Far East; she was, however, as yet too weak to hold all of her gains and was forced to disgorge by the United States and England after peace was re-established in Europe.

From the point of view of the structure of world imperialism, the results of the first major war of redivision may be summed up as follows: (1) German power was temporarily smashed, and her colonial empire was taken over by the victorious nations (chiefly England and France); (2) Austria-Hungary was eliminated from the imperialist scene; (3) the United States emerged as the economically strongest nation in the world; (4) Italy and Japan, though on the winning side, were frustrated in their imperial ambitions; and, finally, (5) Russia withdrew entirely from the arena of imperialist rivalry and commenced the task of building the world's first socialist society. The basic pattern of the second war of redivision was already discernible in the results of the first.

Some of the most important developments of the period between wars of redivision will be analysed in detail in the next chapter. From our present point of view the course of events was straightforward. Those nations which were left out in the first partition of the world, and lost or failed to benefit from the first war of redivision, the nations in which capital had the least opportunity for internal expansion, soon set about preparing for a second redivision. The actual campaign began with the Japanese invasion of Manchuria in 1931 and continued through the Italian absorption of Ethiopia (1935), the Spanish Civil War (1936),* the renewed push of Japan into China (1937), and

* The inclusion of the Spanish Civil War perhaps requires a word of explanation. The Franco rebellion was in reality an instrument of German and Italian policy; without the support of the fascist nations it would have been quickly suppressed. Germany and Italy were interested in establishing control over Spanish resources and in strengthening their strategic position *vis-à-vis* Britain and France.

finally the series of direct German aggressions on the European continent, beginning with the occupation of Austria in 1938 and continuing in an unbroken succession to the present time. The Second World War as a whole, however, is not, like the first, a simple inter-imperialist struggle for redivision of the world. It is in reality three distinct wars which are merged together only in a military sense and even in this respect incompletely. The first of these three wars is a war of redivision on the 1914-18 pattern with Germany, Italy, and Japan on one side and Great Britain and the United States on the other side; the second is a war between capitalism and socialism with Germany on one side and the Soviet Union on the other; the third is an anti-imperialist war of national independence waged by China against Japan.*

The special characteristics of the present war, of which there are many, can be comprehended only when the fact is grasped that it is not one war which is being fought but three. It is not, however, our purpose to pursue this question further here but only to point out that the three-in-one character of the war brings into sharpest possible relief the limits to the expansion and even to the continued existence of imperialism as a system of world economy. Whereas the first period of world-wide hostilities was a period of exclusively *inter*-imperialist rivalry, at the present time *anti*-imperialist struggle is at least as important a component of the total pattern of conflict. The causes and implications of this will be examined in the next section.

6. The Limits of Imperialism

If we consider the system of imperialism as a whole, rather than single imperialist nations, it is apparent that it raises up against itself two types of opponent and that its expansion enhances their potential power of opposition. It is here that we must seek for the factors which will ultimately set the limits of imperialism and prepare the way for its downfall as a system of world economy.

The first opposition force arises, as we have already seen, from

* From the Japanese standpoint it is, of course, an imperialist war to subjugate a semi-independent backward area.

the internal development of the imperialist countries. Class lines are drawn ever more tightly and class conflict grows in intensity. Eventually the working class is forced to adopt an anti-capitalist position and to set as its goal the attainment of socialism. But in the era of imperialism, anti-capitalism necessarily means also anti-imperialism. The special features of imperialist policy, which make for increased internal exploitation and international war, serve to enhance the opposition of workers, though the roots of this working-class attitude are to be found in the structure of capitalist society in general. We may speak in this connection of socialist opposition to imperialism. Such opposition is in itself not capable of preventing the expansion of imperialism. Its real significance emerges only in the closing stages of a war of redivision when the economic and social structure of the imperialist powers is seriously weakened and revolutionary situations mature in the most severely affected areas. Successful socialist revolutions then become possible; the chain of world imperialism tends to break in its weakest links.* This is what took place in Russia in 1917. The Bolshevik revolution established new socialist relations of production in Russia with the result that a large part of the earth's surface was withdrawn at one stroke from the world system of imperialism and formed the nucleus for a future world economy on a socialist basis. It seems safe to predict that this process will be repeated, perhaps on an even larger scale, before the present international conflict has exhausted itself. Thus we see that the first limit to imperialism is the result of the interaction of its national and international aspects. The crucial opposition force originates within the imperialist nations but the conditions for its triumph are established by the wars of redivision which are a recurring feature of imperialism considered as an international system. This is the dialectic, so to speak, of the birth and growth of socialism. Moreover the limit to imperialism implicit in the rise of socialism is in the long run a contracting limit. Some of the implications of this fact for the

* The theory that imperialism breaks first not necessarily in the countries which are most advanced but rather in the 'weakest link,' which is quite likely to be a relatively backward capitalist nation, was apparently first put forward by Lenin. See Joseph Stalin, *Leninism* (1928), pp. 101 ff.

future of world economy will be considered in the final chapter of the present work.

The second fundamental limit to imperialism arises from the relations between metropolis and colony.* The introduction of cheap manufactured commodities and the import of capital into the colonial economy revolutionize the pre-existing mode of production. Handicraft industries are dealt a crippling blow; modern means of transport and communication break down the local separatism inherent in pre-capitalist production; old social relations are dissolved; a native bourgeoisie arises and takes the lead in promoting a spirit of nationalism such as that which characterized the early development of capitalism in the now advanced industrial nations. At the same time, however, the development of colonial economy is not well balanced. Under the domination of imperialism, industrialization advances very slowly, too slowly to absorb the steady flow of handicraft producers who are ruined by the competition of machine-made products from the factories of the advanced regions. The consequence is a swelling of the ranks of the peasantry, increased pressure on the land, and a deterioration of the productivity and living standards of the agricultural masses who constitute by far the largest section of the colonial populations. Imperialism thus creates economic problems in the colonies which it is unable to solve. The essential conditions for improvement are fundamental changes in the land system, reduction of the numbers dependent upon agriculture, and increase in the productivity of agriculture, all objectives which can be attained only in conjunction with a relatively high rate of industrialization. Imperialism is unwilling to reform the land system because its rule typically depends upon the support of the colonial landlord class, both native and foreign; the interests of producers, and especially monopolistically organized producers, in the metropolis prevent the erection of colonial protective-tariff barriers and in other ways inhibit the growth of industrialism in the backward areas. The inevitable consequence is that colonial economy stagnates, and living

* The term 'colony' as used here is not to be interpreted in a legalistic sense; it applies equally to the backward areas which are the object of imperialist economic exploitation even though they may be formally independent nations.

conditions for the great majority of the people tend to become worse rather than better. All classes of the colonial populations, with the exception of the landlords and a few relatively small groups which are in effect agents of imperialist rule, are therefore thrown into the struggle for national independence. Alongside the socialist opposition to imperialism within the advanced countries we have here the nationalist opposition in the backward countries.

The relation between the two major forces opposing imperialism is a complex one which cannot be fully analysed here. We must be content with a few brief suggestions. There obviously exists a firm foundation for an alliance between the socialist opposition to imperialism in the advanced countries and the nationalist opposition in the colonial countries. The rise and spread of an independent socialist section of the world, however, introduces certain complications. It was pointed out above that the colonial bourgeoisie takes the lead in organizing and promoting movements of national independence, but the ultimate objective of the colonial bourgeoisie is the establishment of independent capitalist nations. Consequently it sees enemies in both imperialism and socialism. The colonial working class, on the other hand, though numerically small, adopts a socialist goal almost from the outset; while the oppressed agricultural masses are not unreceptive to socialist ideas and tend to follow the leadership of those who demonstrate most clearly by their actions that they mean to win a genuine improvement in conditions. The position of the colonial bourgeoisie tends more and more to unfit it for the role of leadership which it assumes in the early stages of the national movement. It wavers between accepting the support of the forces of socialism, both external and internal, against imperialism, and temporizing with imperialism in order to keep in check the socialist menace. The result is a policy which always stops short of decisive action, reverses itself and backtracks, then once again moves hesitantly forward. Since this is not the kind of policy which can make a strong appeal to the mass of the peasantry, and since without such support the national independence movement is impotent, it follows that leadership gradually tends to slip out of the hands of bourgeois elements and into the hands of the working class in alliance with the more advanced sections of the peasantry, which, though not necessarily socialist in their convictions, nevertheless have no stake in the maintenance of capitalist relations of production after independence is achieved. Eventually, therefore, it falls to the lot of the working class to lead the nationalist opposition to imperialism in the colonial countries just as it stands at the head of the socialist opposition to imperialism in the advanced countries. When this stage has been reached the two great opposition forces are united not only in their immediate objectives but also in their ultimate resolve to work for a socialist world economy as a way out of the growing contradictions of imperialist world economy. In the long run the colonial bourgeoisie is unable to play an independent historical role and must split up into two opposing factions, one of which attempts to save its own precarious privileges by means of an open alliance with imperialism, while the other remains true to the cause of national independence even though the price is the acceptance of socialism.

Hence we see, finally, that what started as two independent forces opposed to imperialism tend to merge into one great movement. Just as in the advanced capitalist countries themselves, so also on a world scale the issue becomes ever more clearly defined as Imperialism versus Socialism, with the mounting contradictions of imperialism ensuring its own decline and the concomitant spread of socialism.

XVIII

FASCISM

SPEAKING in general terms, fascism, as it exists in Germany and Italy, is one form which imperialism assumes in the age of wars of redivision. The present chapter will be devoted to the elaboration of this theme on the foundation of the theory of imperialism set forth in the preceding pages.

1. THE CONDITIONS OF FASCISM

Fascism arises under certain specific historical conditions which are in turn the product of the impact of imperialist wars of redivision on the economic and social structure of advanced capitalist nations. According to military and diplomatic usage, at the end of a war belligerent nations are put into two categories, those on the winning side and those on the losing side. The extent of the damage to the internal social structure of the various countries, however, provides a more significant basis for classification. According to the extent and severity of the damage suffered it is possible to arrange the countries in a series, ranging from those which emerge virtually unscathed or even actually strengthened to those in which the pre-existing structure of economic, political, and social relations is completely shattered. Usually the nations on the winning side stand nearer the top and those on the losing side nearer the bottom of the scale, but the correlation is far from perfect.

It is not easy to establish criteria by which to judge the extent and severity of the damage suffered by a country as a result of war, but certain related symptoms would no doubt be widely recognized as indicative: extreme scarcity of food and other necessaries of life; partial breakdown of 'law and order'; disorganization, poor discipline, and unreliability in the armed forces; loss of confidence on the part of the ruling class; and lack of regard for established habits of thought and behavior among wide sections of the population. Conditions of this sort are almost certain to give rise to revolutionary struggles which may eventuate in a decisive victory for the counter-revolution; in an overthrow of the existing structure of property relations and the establishment of socialism—as happened in Russia in 1917; or in a temporary stalemate in which neither of the major contending forces, the working class or the capitalist class, is able to gain a decisive triumph—as happened in Germany and, less unambiguously, in other parts of central and eastern Europe in 1918 and 1919. It is the last case which interests us here.

The fact that the revolution stops short of a socialist consummation is, in a very real sense, the key to subsequent developments. What emerges may best be described as a transitional condition of class equilibrium resting on a foundation of capitalist property relations. Juridically this balance of class forces tends to express itself in an ultra-democratic state form, to which the name of the 'people's republic' was applied by Otto Bauer.* The people's republic leaves the capitalists in control of the economy but at the same time affords to the working class a share in state power and freedom to organize and agitate for the achievement of its own ends. The personnel of the state apparatus is largely unchanged, but the weakness and unreliability of the armed forces at the disposal of the state obliges the capitalists to pursue a policy of temporization and compromise.

The democratic character of the people's republic gives rise to a variety of illusions. Liberals see in the sharing of state power and the compromises which necessarily result an earnest of class co-operation and the softening of social conflict; revisionists believe that the people's republic is merely a stepping stone to the gradual achievement of socialism. The reality of heightened class antagonism behind the temporary balance of forces is too often overlooked. But these optimistic diagnoses are soon discredited by events. Nothing proves so clearly the unstable and impermanent character of the people's republic as its inability to meliorate the contradictions of capitalist production. These contradic-

* *Die Osterreichische Revolution* (1923), especially Ch. 16 ('Die Volksrepublik'). Bauer was under no illusions as to the stability or permanence of the people's republic.

tions, far from being eliminated, are on the contrary intensified. The gains won by the greatly strengthened trade unions and the enactment of social legislation under working-class pressure put burdens on capitalist production which it is ill prepared and even less willing to bear. Big capital meets this situation in two ways. First, by tightening up its monopolistic organizations and squeezing the middle classes. The latter, already impoverished by the war and the subsequent derangement of economic life which, in the form of inflation, bears particularly heavily on those with small savings and no organizations to protect them, now find that their desperate position is but slightly improved by the return of 'law and order,' that they are in effect the orphan children of the people's republic. Second, the capitalists embark upon an intensive campaign of 'rationalization,' that is to say the substitution of machinery for labor power and the intensification of the labor process, which has the consequence of swelling the ranks of the reserve army. It is, of course, true that making good the economic destruction and wastage of the war period provides the basis for a considerable upswing in economic activity, an upswing which nearly everywhere in Europe during the 1920s was encouraged and supported by the importation of capital from the United States. For a time the production of means of production is severed from its dependence on the market for consumption goods, but only for a time. Once the productive mechanism has been substantially rebuilt the discovery is made that the demand for consumption goods, depressed as it is by the impoverishment of the middle classes and by technological unemployment among the workers, is inadequate to support high levels of economic activity. A crisis followed by a sharp decline of production and employment becomes unavoidable.

From the standpoint of capitalist production such a crisis could be mitigated or overcome by the normal imperialist method of expansion abroad. But it is precisely the countries which were most severely weakened by the preceding war which have the least opportunities to follow this course. Their colonies were taken from them, and their military strength is so depleted that they cannot pursue an aggressive foreign policy. Moreover the political influence of the working class under the people's republic is definitely opposed to embarking upon new imperialist adventures. Hilferding, writing in 1931 and with recent German experience in mind, was so impressed by this state of affairs that he regarded imperialist expansionism as almost a thing of the past. 'It is the stronger control over foreign policy in the democratic countries,' he wrote, 'which limits to an extraordinary degree finance capital's disposal over the state power.'[1] This was true enough at the time it was written, but unfortunately Hilferding was no longer able, as he once had been, to draw conclusions from his own analysis.

The argument of this section may be briefly summed up as follows: a nation, the economic and social structure of which is seriously disrupted as the result of an imperialist war of redivision, may, failing a successful socialist revolution, enter upon a period of class equilibrium on the basis of capitalist relations of production. Under such conditions, the intensification of the contradictions of capitalism leads to a severe internal crisis which cannot be 'solved' by resort to the normal methods of imperialist expansion. This is, so to speak, the soil in which fascism takes root and grows.

2. Fascism's Rise to Power

Both the origins and the mass base of fascism are to be found in the middle classes, which form such a large section of the population of capitalist countries in the period of monopoly capitalism. Lenin pointed out very clearly the characteristics of middle-class psychology which, under appropriate circumstances, foster and encourage the growth of a fascist movement:

> For Marxists it is well established theoretically—and the experience of all European revolutions and revolutionary movements has fully confirmed it—that the small proprietor (a social type that is very widely represented in many European countries), who, under capitalism, suffers constant oppression and very often an incredibly sharp and rapid worsening of conditions of life and even ruin, easily becomes extremely revolutionary, but is incapable of displaying perseverance, ability to organize, discipline and firmness. The petty bourgeois, 'furious' over the horrors of capitalism, is a social phenomenon which like anarchism,

is characteristic of all capitalist countries. The instability of such revolutionism, its barrenness, its ability to become swiftly transformed into submission, apathy, phantasy, and even into a 'mad' infatuation with one or another bourgeois 'fad'—all this is a matter of common knowledge.[2]

What Lenin here says of the small proprietor applies in varying degrees to wide sectors of the middle classes. It is precisely these groups which are most disastrously affected during the period of class-equilibrium capitalism which may follow an unsuccessful war of redivision. They constitute the core of fascism's popular support. Once the movement has begun to make headway, other elements of the population are attracted to it, though not always for the same reasons; these include certain groups of unorganized workers, independent farmers, part of the army of unemployed, declassed and criminal elements (the so-called *lumpenproletariat*), and youths from all classes who see ahead but meager opportunities for a normal career.

The ideology and program of fascism reflect the social position of the middle classes and in this respect are merely an intensification of attitudes which have already been shown to be characteristic of imperialism.* The chief ingredients have a negative character, namely, hostility to organized labor on the one hand and to monopoly capital on the other hand. On the positive side the middle classes compensate for their lack of common class interests and solid organizational bases by glorification of the nation and the 'race' to which they belong. Foreigners and racial minorities are blamed for misfortunes the nature of which is not understood. † So far as internal economic and social problems are concerned the program of fascism is a mass of ill-digested and often mutually contradictory proposals which are notable chiefly for their unmistakably demagogic character. Hardly any of these proposals is novel or original; almost without exception they have appeared and reappeared in earlier periods of social distress. What gives to fascism coherence and vitality is its stress on nationalism, its demand for the restoration of a strong state power, and its call for a war of revenge and

* See above, pp. 316 f.

† This is not to deny that middle-class support for discrimination against minorities also rests on grounds of immediate economic advantage.

foreign conquest. It is this which provides a firm foundation for rapprochement between fascism and the capitalist class.

The attitude of capitalists towards fascism is at first one of reserve and suspicion; they particularly distrust it for its intemperate attacks on financial capital. But as the movement spreads and gains in popular support, the attitude of capitalists undergoes a gradual transformation. Their own position is a difficult one, caught as they are between the demands of the organized working class and the 'encirclement' of rival capitalist powers. Ordinarily under such circumstances the capitalist class would make use of the state power to curb the workers and to improve its own international position, but now this course is not open to it. The state is weak and the workers share in its control. Consequently fascism, once it has proved its right to be taken seriously, comes to be looked upon as a potentially valuable ally against the capitalists' two worst enemies, the workers of their own country and the capitalists of foreign countries; for the genuineness of fascism's hatred of workers and foreigners is never open to doubt. By means of an alliance with fascism the capitalist class hopes to re-establish the strong state, subordinate the working class, and extend its vital 'living space' at the expense of rival imperialist powers. This is the reason for the financial subsidies by which capitalists support the fascist movement and, perhaps even more important, for the tolerance which the capitalist-dominated state personnel displays in dealing with the violent and illegal methods of fascism.

It must not be supposed, that the capitalists are altogether happy about the rise of fascism. Unquestionably they would prefer to solve their problems in their own way if that were possible. But their impotence forces them to strengthen fascism, and when at length conditions become generally intolerable and a new revolutionary situation looms on the horizon, the capitalists, from their positions inside the citadel of state power, throw open the gates and admit the fascist legions.

3. The Fascist 'Revolution'

Once in power, fascism sets out with ruthless energy to destroy the class equilibrium which underlies the indecision and paralysis of the people's republic. Trade unions and working-class political parties receive the first and hardest blows; their organizations are smashed and their leaders killed, imprisoned, or driven into exile. Next comes the establishment of the strong state and finally, with these necessary preliminaries attended to, the swinging into full-scale preparations for a new war of re-division. In these three steps are comprehended what is often called the fascist 'revolution.'

The building up of state power is itself a complex process which inevitably involves the sloughing off of the middle-class radical program on the basis of which fascism rose to power. Whether or not this is a deliberate choice on the part of the fascist leaders is a question which need not even be raised. The fascist program is self-contradictory and takes no account of the real character of economic laws; it would be bitterly opposed by all the powerful elements of the capitalist class. To attempt to put it into practice would be to court disaster and perhaps to make forever impossible the realization of the dreams of foreign conquest which constitute the ideological core of fascism. Not only can fascism not afford to incur the hostility of capitalists; it requires their full co-operation, since they occupy the strategic positions in the economy and possess the necessary training and experience to make it run. The capitalists, on their side, welcome the smashing of the organized power of the working class and look forward with enthusiasm to the resumption of a policy of foreign expansionism. Rebuilding the state power therefore takes place on the basis of an ever-closer alliance between fascism and capital, particularly monopoly capital in the all-important heavy industries.

Politically, the establishment of the strong state involves scrapping the paraphernalia of political parties appropriate to parliamentary democracy. But this is not all. Extremist elements within the fascist party itself are bitterly resentful at what they can only regard as a betrayal of the fascist program of social reform, and they insistently press for a 'second revolution.' The developing crisis within the ranks of fascism is met by a purge of the dissident leaders and the integration of the private fascist armies into the regular armed forces of the state. From this time on the fascist party loses its independent significance and becomes in effect a mere adjunct of the state apparatus. By these acts fascism finally and irrevocably transfers its social base from the middle classes to monopoly capital. There now takes place an *interpenetration* of the top fascist leadership and the dominant circles of monopoly capital which results in the creation of a new ruling oligarchy disposing in a co-ordinated fashion over economic and political power. The full energies of the nation are henceforth directed to rearming; all other considerations of economic and social policy are subordinated to the overriding aim of waging and winning a new imperialist war of redivision.

The accomplishments of the fascist 'revolution' are thus the smashing of the pre-existing class equilibrium, the establishment of the strong state, and the preparation of the nation for a new war of redivision. Far from overthrowing capitalist imperialism, fascism in reality lays bare its monopolistic, violent, and expansionary essence.

4. The Ruling Class under Fascism

There have been so many theories of fascism which interpret it as a novel social order, fundamentally neither capitalist nor socialist in character, that it may not be out of place to formulate somewhat more explicitly our own attitude towards this problem.* The theories in question usually concede that fascism has retained the forms of capitalism but hold that these forms merely constitute a screen under cover of which a new ruling class takes over the real controls and manipulates them for its own ends. What these ends are is commonly left somewhat vague, but it is perhaps not inaccurate to say that most writers conceive of them in terms of power. In pursuit of power the fascist ruling class, it is alleged, disregards the 'rules of the capitalist game'; consequently fascism is a new society which neither obeys the laws nor suffers from the contradictions of capitalism. A full exploration of this thesis would, of course, require an analysis of concrete fascist societies such as cannot be attempted

* Much of the following analysis is taken from the author's article, 'The Illusion of the "Managerial Revolution",' *Science and Society*, Winter 1942.

here.* But it may be a useful exercise to test the concept of the new fascist 'ruling class' in the light of the theory of capitalism set forth in this book.

Class affiliation is not a question of social origins. One who is born into the working class can become a capitalist and vice versa. Common social origins are important to the thinking and cohesiveness of a class, but they do not determine its composition. This is a matter of the position which individuals actually occupy in society, that is to say their relations to others and to society as a whole. For Marxism this means, primarily, position in the structure of economic relations which dominate the totality of social relations. It is by this path that we arrive at the definition of the ruling class as comprising those persons who individually or in combination exercise control over the means of production.

This is a general definition which is unobjectionable as far as it goes, but it is important to realize that it does not go very far and that its uncritical application can be misleading. While it is correct that the ruling class is made up of those who control the means of production, the converse is not necessarily true. Control over the means of production is by no means synonymous with exploitation of one part of society by another. If the relation of exploitation does not exist, the concept of a ruling class is inapplicable; the society is said to be classless. The most unambiguous example of a classless society is provided by what Marx called 'simple commodity production' in which each producer owns and works with his own means of production. Moreover, because of its nature as a general definition applying equally to all class societies, the definition in question furnishes no clue to the differences between them and hence no criteria for telling one ruling class from another. To put the problem crudely, suppose that a new set of individuals acquires control over the means of production. Is it a new ruling class or just a new personnel for the old ruling class? The general definition is of no assistance in answering this question.

This example should serve to warn us of the impossibility

* For an admirable study of German fascism, see Franz Neumann, *Behemoth*, 1942. Neumann's conclusions are substantially identical with those reached in the present work.

of treating the problem of the ruling class as an abstract problem of society in general. We must be historically specific if we are to make the concept a useful instrument of social analysis. This means that in the case of every particular ruling class we must carefully specify the character of the social relations in which it occupies the dominant position, and the form of control which it exercises over the means of production. It is these factors, and these factors alone, which determine the motives and objectives of the ruling class. In this way we can distinguish between ruling classes; we shall, in short, have a method of separating genuine social revolutions (shifts in class rule) from mere substitutions, more or less thorough as the case may be, of new faces for old.

Let us now apply these considerations to the case of capitalism. Here we have two basic classes, apart from intermediate groups and remnants of earlier social forms, namely, the capitalists who own the means of production and the class of free wage laborers who own nothing but their own capacity to work. The importance of the form of control exercised over the means of production cannot be overemphasized. This form is the ownership of capital, from which, of course, capitalism derives its designation; exploitation correspondingly takes the form of the production of surplus value. 'Capital' is not simply another name for means of production; it is means of production reduced to a qualitatively homogeneous and quantitatively measurable fund of value. The concern of the capitalist is not with means of production as such, but with capital, and this necessarily means capital regarded as a quantity, for capital has only one dimension, the dimension of magnitude.

We have already seen in earlier chapters that the concern of the capitalist with the quantity of capital has the consequence that the expansion of capital becomes his primary and dominant objective. His social status is decided, and can only be decided, by the quantity of capital under his control; moreover even if the capitalist as an individual were content to 'maintain his capital intact,' without increase, he could rationally pursue this end only by striving to expand. Capital 'naturally' tends to contract—the forces of competition and technological change work wholly in this direction—and this tendency can be defeated only by a continuous effort to expand. Fundamentally surplus value is an increment to capital; the fact that the capitalist consumes a part of his income is a secondary phenomenon.

The objective of expanding capital is thus not one which capitalists are free to take or leave as they choose; they must pursue it on pain of elimination from the ruling class. This holds equally for actual owners of capital and for those who, though not themselves substantial owners, come into the 'management' of capital, as not infrequently happens in the modern large corporation. Neither is in any sense a free agent. The ruling class under capitalism is made up of the functionaries of capital, those whose motives and objectives are prescribed for them by the specific historical form of their control over the means of production. It was this which caused Marx to remark, in the Preface to the first edition of *Capital:* 'My standpoint, from which the evolution of the economic formation of society is viewed as a process of natural history, can less than any other make the individual responsible for relations whose creature he socially remains, however much he may subjectively raise himself above them.'

This analysis helps us to solve the problem of the ruling class under fascism. As we have seen, the forms of capitalism are preserved: the means of production retain the form of capital; exploitation continues to take the form of production of surplus value. Consequently the ruling class is still the capitalist class. Its personnel, however, is somewhat altered. For example, Jewish capitalists may be expropriated, and many fascist leaders use their political power to acquire important positions in industry. But these new members of the ruling class do not bring with them a new set of motives and objectives which are at variance with the outlook of the incumbent capitalists. On the contrary, they soon adopt as their own the motives and objectives which inevitably flow from the position in society which they come to occupy. They are now responsible to capital; like every one else in this position they must strive to preserve and expand it. As in the case of all parvenus, however, they bring to their task greater energy and fewer scruples than those who, by training and tradition, are accustomed to fulfilling the obligations imposed upon the functionary of capital.

The infusion of new blood into the ranks of the capitalist class is thus one very significant consequence of the victory of fascism. Another, no less important, is the increasing absorption of the organs of monopoly capital into the state apparatus. Chambers of commerce, employers' associations, cartels, and other similar bodies are made compulsory and are directly clothed with the authority of the state; their activities in turn are co-ordinated through a hierarchical series of boards and committees, leading up to governmental ministries at the top. At each stage officials and experts are drawn primarily from the experienced personnel of industry and finance, with the addition, however, of many who have risen to prominence through their political activity in the fascist movement. Tendencies inherent in capitalism in its imperialist phase here reach their climax. The expanding economic functions of the state and the centralization of capital meet in what might be described as a formal marriage between the state and monopoly capital. The separate channels through which the ruling class exercises economic and political power in a parliamentary democracy are merged into one under fascism.

It is important not to misunderstand the nature and significance of this process. In particular it must be stressed that what takes place is *not* the organic unification of all capital into one gigantic trust—what Hilferding called the 'general cartel' [3]—with the government, so to speak, as the board of directors. Capital remains divided into organizationally distinct units which for the most part have the corporate form. Those who dominate the largest corporations constitute the ruling oligarchy, while those attached to smaller units of capital occupy an inferior position in the economic and social hierarchy. Moreover within the ruling oligarchy itself the position of the individual is roughly proportional to the magnitude of the capital which he represents, just as, for example, in feudal society the lords holding the greatest domains outrank their lesser rivals. For this reason the urge to self-expansion remains as strong as ever in the separate segments of capital. There are four methods of expansion open to the larger units of monopoly capital: internal accumulation, absorption of smaller capitals, expansion abroad, and expansion at the expense of each other. The last of these, if practiced to extremes, can seriously weaken monopoly capital as a whole and hence must be kept under fairly strict control by the ruling oligarchy; but no such objection applies to the first three. Consequently the great corporations and combines reinvest their profits, vie with one another in gobbling up small capitals and use the state in a variety of ways to extend their 'living space' at the expense of foreign nations. Each hopes by skilful exploitation of its opportunities to enhance its relative importance and power without, however, becoming involved in a costly and possibly even suicidal struggle with its rivals. The imperative need for a unified policy against the masses at home and against the outside world does not, therefore, prevent monopoly capitalists from carrying on a continuous, though largely unobserved, campaign for expansion and preferment within the framework of the fascist economy.

At one time I thought fascism could be aptly described as 'state capitalism,' which I defined as 'a society which is entirely capitalist in its class structure but in which there is a high degree of political centralization of economic power.'[4] The definition itself, while perhaps lacking in exactness, is not an incorrect characterization of fascism, but a consideration of the way in which other writers, and particularly Marxists, have used the term 'state capitalism' has led me to the conclusion that its application to the case of fascism is more likely to be confusing than helpful. Bukharin's description of state capitalism may be taken as more or less typical of the way in which the concept has often been understood. Starting from a society 'in which the capitalist class is unified in a single trust and we have to do with an organized but at the same time from a class standpoint antagonistic economic system,' Bukharin proceeds as follows:

Is accumulation possible here? Naturally. Constant capital grows since the consumption of capitalists grows. New branches of production corresponding to new needs are always arising. The consumption of workers grows, though definite limits are placed upon it. In spite of this 'underconsumption' of the masses no crisis arises since *the demand of the various branches of production for each other's products as well as the demand for consumption goods* . . . is laid down in advance. (Instead of 'anarchy' of production—what is from the standpoint of capital a rational plan.) If a mistake is made in production goods, the surplus is added to inventory and a corresponding correction made in the next production period. If a mistake is made in workers' consumption goods the surplus can be divided among the workers or destroyed. Also in the case of a mistake in the production of luxury goods 'the way out' is clear. Thus there can be *no kind* of crisis of general overproduction. In general, production proceeds smoothly. Capitalists' consumption provides the motive for production and for the production plan. Consequently there is in this case not a specially rapid development of production.[5]

Now whatever the merits of this model for the particular restricted theoretical purposes which Bukharin had in mind, it is clear that it does not fit the case of fascism, nor for that matter does it throw light upon any actual tendencies of capitalist production. Fascism is not a society 'in which the capitalist class is unified in a single trust,' and it is emphatically not true that 'capitalists' consumption provides the motive for production and for the production plan.' On the contrary, capital, and hence also the capitalist class, remains divided into organizationally distinct units; and accumulation remains the dominant motive of production under fascism as under all other forms of capitalist society. In the next section we shall attempt to bring out the implications of these closely related facts.

5. Can Fascism Eliminate the Contradictions of Capitalism?

The contradictions of capitalism arise, as Marx expressed it, 'from the fact that capital and its self-expansion appear as the starting and closing point, as the motive and aim of production; that production is merely production for *capital*, and not vice versa, the means of production mere means for an ever expanding system of the life process for the benefit of the *society* of producers.'[6] This characterization, as we have seen, holds good for fascism, but there is this difference, that under fascism control over the economic system is centralized, conflicts between the different branches of capital are largely suppressed in the interests of capital as a whole, and heavy risks are pooled through the instrumentality of the state. We have here what Nazi economists have appropriately called a 'steered economy' (*gesteuerte Wirtschaft*) in which the individual capitalist must subordinate himself to a unified national policy. The question naturally arises, whether complete centralization of economic control in itself provides a basis for the elimination of the contradictions of capitalism.

Those who reply to this question in the affirmative commonly argue that the correctness of their answer has already been demonstrated in practice. The chief contradiction of capitalism, according to this view, consists in economic stagnation, relatively low levels of production, and mass unemployment. It was capitalism's inability to overcome this condition which set the stage for fascism's rise to power. But once in power, fascism quickly demonstrated its ability to eliminate unemployment and step up production to maximum levels. Consequently it must be concluded that fascism has succeeded in freeing itself from the basic contradiction of capitalism. While this argument may have a certain surface plausibility, a closer examination clearly reveals its fallacious character. Actually the contradiction of capitalism consists in an inability to utilize the means of production 'for an ever expanding system of the life process for the benefit of the society or producers.' Under certain circumstances this manifests itself in stagnation and unemployment, that is to say, in the *non-utilization* of a part of the means of production. Under other circumstances, however, it manifests itself in the utilization of the means of production for the purposes of foreign expansion. Stagnation and unemployment on the one hand and militarism and war on the other are therefore alternative, and to a large extent mutually exclusive, forms of expression of the contradiction of capitalism. When this fact is understood the achievement of fascism appears in its true perspective. Fascism has given no evidence of ability to overcome stagnation and unemployment through the use of material and human resources for the expansion of use values for the mass of the people. On the contrary, it has from the beginning devoted all the resources at its disposal to the preparation and waging of an imperialist war of redivision. Under fascism enforced idleness gives way to violence and bloodshed. This is not an overcoming of the contradictions of capitalism; rather it is a revelation of how deep-seated they really are.

Let us suppose, for purposes of carrying the analysis a step further, that a fascist nation emerges from war with its social structure intact and with its territory and colonies vastly expanded. What then would be its probable subsequent development? Would it be able to create a planned and stable economic order capable alike of avoiding internal depression and of eschewing further external aggression? If it were legitimate to assume that the objective of production would, under such circumstances, be shifted from the accumulation of capital to the expansion of use values, then we should certainly have to answer this question in the affirmative, for it is impossible to question the abstract possibility of a planned economy free of the contradictions of capitalism. We are, however, not dealing with an abstract possibility but with a concrete form of society which can be understood only in terms of its own history and structure. From this standpoint there is not the slightest ground for anticipating that fascism either could or would abandon accumulation of capital as the primary objective of economic activity. On the contrary, there is every reason to assume that monopoly capital, with the full assistance and protection of the state, would set out at once to exploit for its own self-expansion any new territories or colonies which might be gained as the result of war.

Nevertheless, it is more than probable that fascism would retain a highly centralized, state-directed economy. We can therefore take it for granted that stagnation and mass unemployment would under no circumstances be allowed to appear. But this does not imply the elimination of the contradictions of capitalism any more than the suppression of a symptom implies the cure of a disease. If, and this seems a likely case, the consumption of the masses were held under strict control and accumulation were allowed to proceed at an accelerating tempo, there would intervene a period of boom conditions which might last for a considerable period of time. Eventually, however, the tendency to underconsumption would begin to make itself felt in the appearance of excess capacity not only in the consumption-goods but also in the production-goods industries. Fascism would now have to face again the very same problem which confronted it when it first achieved state power. Should means of production be diverted to raising the living standards of the masses, or should they be mobilized once more for a new war of conquest? Knowing what we do of fascism, and remembering that we have assumed that one adventure in foreign aggression turned out to be a success, it is not difficult to imagine what the decision would be.

This is not the only possible course of development. Alternatively, the fascist state might find it advisable to allow living standards to rise in the metropolis and correspondingly to check the rate of accumulation to a certain extent. Such a policy would undoubtedly be feasible for a time, but if it were persisted in, it would certainly entail a falling rate of profit. Since we have ruled out crisis and depression as a corrective of a decline in profitability, we must assume that the ruling oligarchy would find it necessary to initiate deliberate measures to reverse the trend. This could be done by reducing wages, a device which never fails to appeal to capitalists but which has the unfortunate effect of bringing to life the tendency to underconsumption. The cure is no improvement over the disease. But it is more likely that the problem would present itself in the form of a lack of national 'living space' and hence would directly result in a renewed drive for foreign conquest.

Even under the most favorable conditions, therefore, there is no reason to suppose that fascism would succeed in escaping from the economic contradictions of capitalism. But to assume these 'most favorable conditions' is really an unwarranted concession to those who believe in the stability of fascism. This explains why the foregoing analysis has been carefully couched in the conditional mode. The analysis, it will be recalled, started from the assumption that fascism emerged from a war of redivision intact and with greatly expanded territory. As it happens, the fascist nations are even now engaged in a gigantic war which was precipitated by their own drive to expansion and foreign conquest. Not only is there no assurance that they will be victorious; there is even no assurance that they will survive in their present form. In other words, fascism has already demonstrated in the clearest possible way its fundamentally self-destructive character. Under these conditions, to speculate on what will happen to fascism after the present world crisis is past can easily turn into what Lenin once described, in a similar connection, as 'a slurring-over and a blunting of the most profound contradictions of the newest stage of capitalism, instead of an exposure of their true depth.' [7]

6. Is Fascism Inevitable?

Every capitalist nation, in the period of imperialism, carries within it the seeds of fascism. The question naturally arises whether it is inevitable that these seeds should take root and grow to maturity. Marx, in writing *Capital*, drew most of his material from English experience, but he was careful to warn his native country that it could not expect to escape a similar fate—'*de te fabula narratur*.' In writing of fascism today must we issue such a warning to the peoples of the non-fascist capitalist nations?

If our analysis is correct it would seem to follow that fascism is not an inevitable stage of capitalist development. Fascism arises only out of a situation in which the structure of capitalism has been severely injured and yet not overthrown. The approximate class equilibrium which ensues at once intensifies the underlying difficulties of capitalist production and emasculates the state power. Under these conditions the fascist movement grows to formidable proportions, and when a new economic crisis breaks out, as it is bound to do, the capitalist class embraces fascism as the only way out of its otherwise insoluble problems. So far as history allows us to judge—and in questions of this sort there is no other guide—a prolonged and 'unsuccessful' war is the only social phenomenon sufficiently catastrophic in its effects to set in train this particular chain of events. It is, to be sure, not inconceivable that an economic crisis could be so profound and long-drawn-out as to have substantially the same results. But this seems unlikely unless the structure of capitalist rule has already been seriously undermined; for a capitalist state which retains relative freedom of action and disposes over strong armed forces is quite capable of initiating measures, internal or external or both, which will effectively check an economic depression before it reaches dangerous proportions.

To maintain the inevitability of fascism it would appear to be necessary to demonstrate two things: (1) that every capitalist nation must at some time have its social structure severely damaged by war, and yet (2) that capitalist relations of production must survive even though in a greatly weakened form. Clearly neither of these contentions will stand examination. We need only cite the Soviet Union and the United States to prove the point. Russia was prostrated as the result of the last war, but capitalist relations of production did not survive the debacle; a new socialist society arose on the ruins of capitalism. The United States, on the other hand, emerged from the last war stronger than ever, and so far as one can now judge, there is no necessity to suppose that the internal structure of capitalism will be irreparably damaged as a result of the present war. To be sure, if we had to anticipate an endless succession of wars in the future, matters would some day almost certainly turn out differently. But whether there will be a series of further wars in the future is a question not of a single nation but rather of the character of world economy as a whole. In this respect there are tendencies at work today which may completely change the character of international relations and therewith the course of development of each individual nation. In the final chapter we shall attempt to sketch some of the most important considerations which must be taken into account in forming an opinion about the probable future of world capitalism.

XIX

LOOKING FORWARD

In attempting to sketch the probable future course of world capitalism, we must first return to a question posed at the very end of Part III. It was there pointed out that so far as the logic of the reproduction process is concerned it should be possible for the state, by an appropriate policy of taxation and spending, so to regulate the rates of consumption and accumulation as to nullify the tendency to underconsumption. Does this fact perhaps point the way to a possible future of liberal capitalist reform?

1. The Prospects of Liberal Capitalist Reform

For our purposes it will not be necessary to consider the details of the various proposals for liberal capitalist reform which have been put forward in recent years. It is sufficient to point out that those which deserve to be taken seriously derive more or less directly from the writings of John Maynard Keynes and that their basic idea in every case is social control over consumption and investment.* Generally speaking their logical consistency cannot be challenged, either on their own ground or on the basis of the Marxian analysis of the reproduction process. The critique of Keynesian theories of liberal capitalist reform starts, therefore, not from their economic logic but rather from their faulty (usually implicit) assumptions about the relationship, or perhaps one should say lack of relationship, between

* The fundamental theoretical work is Keynes, *The General Theory of Employment, Interest and Money* (1935). The literature based on Keynes has grown to enormous proportions. A good popular presentation, which develops the implications for public policy, will be found in John Strachey, *A Program for Progress* (1940). The leading American exponent of this school of thought is Alvin H. Hansen; see his *Full Recovery or Stagnation?* (1938) and *Fiscal Policy and Business Cycles* (1941).

economics and political action. The Keynesians tear the economic system out of its social context and treat it as though it were a machine to be sent to the repair shop there to be overhauled by an engineer state. Following the analysis of this Part it should be possible to deal satisfactorily with this question in relatively brief compass.

The presupposition of liberal reform is that the state in capitalist society is, at least potentially, an organ of society as a whole which can be made to function in the interests of society as a whole. Now historically, as we know from the analysis of Chapter XIII, the state in capitalist society has always been first and foremost the guarantor of capitalist property relations. In this capacity it has been unmistakably the instrument of capitalist class rule; its personnel—bureaucratic, executive, and legislative—has been drawn from strata of the population which accept the values and objectives of capitalism unquestioningly and as a matter of course. Again speaking historically, control over capitalist accumulation has never for a moment been regarded as a concern of the state; economic legislation has rather had the aim of blunting class antagonisms so that accumulation, the normal aim of capitalist behavior, could go forward smoothly and uninterruptedly. All this, it may be said, presupposes relatively unlimited opportunities for capital to expand. When this condition no longer obtains, is it not possible that the norms of state policy should change? If we could postulate that the objectives of capital would become other than its own self-expansion, then certainly we could not deny the possibility of an alteration in state policy—even more, we should be obliged to expect such a change without any shift in the balance of political power. As a matter of fact, however, there is no reason whatever to assume any such transformation in the character of capital. Hence our problem can be reduced to the following more specific form: is it possible for the state within the framework of capitalist society to act against the interests and objectives of capital provided such action is desirable in the interests of society as a whole? Let us examine this more closely.

First it must be emphasized that we have to do here not with concessions which are designed to remove obstacles to accumulation but rather with a deliberate policy of restricting accumulation and raising consumption with a view to benefitting the society of producers. It is apparent that capitalists could not be expected to adopt such a program as their own, at least not so long as another way out exists—and another way out always does exist along the path of foreign expansion. 'Where,' as Lenin bluntly asked, 'except in the imagination of sentimental reformists, are there any trusts capable of interesting themselves in the conditions of the masses instead of in the conquest of colonies?' [1] Until this question has been satisfactorily answered, we must continue to assume that monopoly capital will, if it has the choice, decide for imperialist expansion as against internal reform. Moreover we must assume that monopoly capital and its political representatives will actively oppose any movements designed to realize a program of liberal reform.

Who, then, are to be the bearers of liberal reform and how are they to establish themselves in a position to put their proposals into practice? Clearly not the capitalists and their representatives who already hold the strategic positions; their political power must, on the contrary, be quietly reduced to negligible proportions. What is required apparently is a mass party dedicated to reform which can meet the following specifications: (a) it must keep itself strictly free of capitalist influence, not only for a time but permanently; (b) it must acquire power and eliminate capitalists and their representatives at least from all critical positions in the state appartus, and it must do so by non-revolutionary means; and (c) it must establish its position so firmly that it would be overwhelmingly plain that any resistance by capitalists in the economic sphere would be futile. In short, not only the semblance but also the reality of political power must somehow fall into the hands of the reform party and remain there; and capitalists must be put in a position of holding their position in the economy only on condition of good behavior. It can hardly be doubted that a party occupying this position could proceed without further ado to the complete elimination of capitalists and the inauguration of a system of planned production of use values. Moreover since we have assumed that its interest is the general welfare rather than the protection of capitalism as such, there seems to be no reason why it would not in fact take this final step along the path of economic reform.

The conditions outlined in the preceding paragraph will no doubt appear wildly exaggerated to the proponents of liberal reform. Judging from the historical record, however, we can say with confidence that they are in no sense overdrawn. The first two (freedom from capitalist influence and elimination of capitalists from all key positions in the state apparatus) are essential if the sharing of state power is to be avoided, and it clearly must be avoided if a long-term program of reform is to be formulated and put into practice. The third (reduction of capitalists to a position in which they hold economic power only on suffrance) is equally necessary as a means of avoiding friction and an eventual showdown between the economic power of the capitalists and the political power of the party of reform. One who has conscientiously studied the history of reform movements in capitalist countries, from English Chartism of a century ago through the Social Democratic and Labor governments, the Popular Fronts and New Deals of our own time, would find it difficult to assert that the conditions for long-term success are less stringent than these. If this be granted, a rather surprising conclusion follows, namely, that the elimination of the contradictions of capitalism via the road of liberal reform is, viewed from a political standpoint, no less a task than the gradual achievement of socialism. In fact, we are justified in saying that the two movements, liberal reformism and gradualist socialism, have virtually identical political content; by comparison the avowed difference in ultimate aims is a matter of distinctly secondary importance.

If experience shows the necessary conditions for a successful movement of reform, it also indicates no less clearly the impossibility of their fulfilment. The rise to power of a political party of the required type is conceivable only in an abstract world from which the permeating social and political power of capital has been banished. In the sober world of reality, capital holds the strategic positions. Money, social prestige, the bureaucracy, and the armed forces of the state, the channels of public communication—all these are controlled by capital, and they are being and will continue to be used to the utmost to maintain the position of capital. Movements of reform are born into and grow up in a society dominated materially and ideologically by capital. If they accept that society, even if (as they imagine) only provisionally, they must attempt to get along with it, and in so doing they are inevitably swallowed up by it. Ambitious leaders are easily corrupted (from the standpoint of their avowed aims), potential followers are frightened away by intimidation or propaganda; as a consequence we have what might easily be considered the outstanding characteristic of all movements of reform, the progressive bartering of principles for respectability and votes. The outcome is not the reform of capitalism, but the bankruptcy of reform. This is neither an accident nor a sign of the immorality of human nature; it is a law of capitalist politics.

The rule of capital would indeed be secure if it were threatened by nothing more dangerous than reform, whether of a liberal or socialist orientation. But, of course, this is not the case. The really deadly enemy of capitalism is its own self-contradictory character—'the real barrier of capitalist production is capital itself.' [2] In seeking a way out of its self-imposed difficulties, capital plunges the world into one crisis after another, finally setting loose forces which it is no longer able to control. The perspective is certainly not a pleasant one, but in our final section we shall attempt to show that it has a more hopeful side for those who care to see it.

2. The Decline of World Capitalism

If one thing should be clear from our analysis of imperialism it is that the course of capitalism in its latest phase cannot be regarded as a problem of a closed system or of a group of discrete individual countries. Each capitalist nation is a part of a world system; for each—and hence also for the system as a whole—the controlling consideration is the interaction of internal and external pressures. Expressed schematically, the basic internal contradiction of capitalist production drives to external expansion and conflict. The latter, in turn, leads to a restructurization of the internal field which now here, now there releases the forces of a new world order (socialism). So far as any single country is concerned there is, at least as yet, no ground for assuming that the birth of socialism can be either a gradual or a peaceful process; up to now socialism has come into the world as a result of a revolutionary overturn and has established its position only after a bloody civil war let loose by its enemies.

This undoubted fact may easily give rise to an over-mechanical, and hence false, picture of the probable future process of capitalist decline. Again we must insist that we are dealing with a process of world-wide scope. While the transition from capitalism to socialism in a single country may be, in its decisive phase, an abrupt one, this is by no means the case on a world scale. From a world point of view, the transition may well be long drawn-out and gradual, and it may pass through several phases differing markedly one from another. It is this problem which primarily interests us in these concluding remarks.

Before the Russian revolution of 1917, Marxists generally assumed, though without much explicit discussion of the problem, that the socialist revolution would occur more or less simultaneously in at least all of the advanced European capitalist nations. This view continued to predominate in the stormy post-war years, when it seemed likely that the revolution would succeed in central Europe, particularly in Germany, and spread from there to the rest of the continent. After the revolutionary wave had subsided, however, and the temporary stabilization of capitalism was seen to be an accomplished fact—roughly by the end of 1923—the problem in question came up for urgent reconsideration. Socialists had been able to maintain themselves in power only in Russia; the problem now was whether they could proceed to the building of a genuine socialist society in Russia alone, or whether they would have to wait until socialism triumphed in the rest of Europe, meanwhile holding the fort and devoting their best energies to strengthening and assisting their comrades abroad.

This was the setting of the famous 'socialism in one country' debate which received so much attention in the Russian Communist Party during the year 1924. There were two schools of thought; one, of which Trotsky was the outstanding spokesman, held to the traditional view that socialism could triumph only on an international scale; the other, led by Stalin, took the position that it would be possible to build up a socialist society in one country, even a country so technically backward and poor as Russia. So far as Russian policy was concerned, the debate was definitively settled in favor of Stalin's view at the Fourteenth Congress of the Communist Party of the Soviet Union, held in the middle of 1925. The policy which later developed into the five-year plans and the collectivization of agriculture was really decided upon at this time.

From our present point of view it is important to examine somewhat more closely the arguments put forward by Stalin in this debate, for they are directly related to the problem under consideration, the process of capitalist decline on a world scale. In 1926 Stalin reviewed the debate over socialism in one country. The fundamental issue, he said, must be broken down into two distinct parts:

> First of all there is the question: Can socialism *possibly* be established in one country alone by that country's unaided strength? This question must be answered in the affirmative. Then there is the question: can a country where the dictatorship of the proletariat has been established, regard itself as *fully safeguarded* against foreign intervention, and the consequent restoration of the old regime, unless the revolution has been victorious in a number of other countries? This question must be answered in the negative.*

In brief, socialism can be built up in one country, but its permanence is assured only when socialism has been victorious on an international scale. This solution of the problem, it will be seen, has the effect of setting a task for Russian socialism without diminishing its interest in the establishment of socialism elsewhere. The probable course of the world revolution remained a vital concern to the Bolsheviks. Hence it is not surprising that this question constituted, so to speak, a branch of the socialism-in-one-country problem. In a work dating from the end of 1924,[3] Stalin set forth his views concerning the path to world socialism.

* *Leninism*, p. 53. This book is a collection of writings and speeches by Stalin up to early 1926. The quotation is taken from 'Problems of Leninism,' dated 25 January 1926.

In the first place, he held, the Russian revolution has made necessary a revision of formerly received opinion on this subject.

> The roads leading to the world revolution are not so straightforward as they were wont to appear in days gone by when there had as yet been no victory of the revolution in a single land, and when a fully-fledged imperialism . . . was still in the womb of time. A new factor has come to the fore: the variations in the rate of development of capitalist countries, under the conditions that are created by a developed imperialism, conditions which lead inevitably to wars, to a general weakening of the capitalist front, and to the possibility of achieving the victory of socialism in individual countries.[4]

The old idea 'that the revolution would develop by way of the regular "maturing" of the elements of socialism, and that the more developed, "more advanced" countries would take the lead' has to be abandoned.[5] Instead the profound antagonisms among the capitalist powers, between the capitalist powers and their colonies, and finally between the imperialist world and the Soviet Union open up a new prospect:

> What is most likely to happen is that the world revolution will develop in such a way that a certain number of additional countries will cut themselves adrift from the comity of imperialist states, and that the proletariat of these countries will be supported in this revolutionary act by the proletariat of the imperialistic states . . . Further, the very development of the world revolution, the very process of separating a number of additional countries from the imperialist states, will be all the quicker and more thoroughgoing in proportion as socialism shall have struck roots in the first victorious country, in proportion as that country shall have transformed itself into the base whence the development of the world revolution can proceed, in proportion as that country shall have become the crowbar getting a solid pry and setting the whole structure of imperialism rocking.[6]

What is the probable subsequent course of this development? In Stalin's opinion,

> It is more than likely that, in the course of the development of the world revolution, there will come into existence–side by side with the foci of imperialism in the various capitalist lands and

with the system of these lands throughout the world—foci of socialism in various soviet countries, and a system of these foci throughout the world. *As the outcome of this development there will ensue a struggle between the rival systems, and its history will be the history of the world revolution.*[7]

And, finally, the Russian revolution is evaluated in the following terms:

> The worldwide significance of the October revolution lies not only in the fact that it was the first step taken by any country whatsoever to shatter imperialism, that it brought into being the first little island of socialism in the ocean of imperialism, but likewise in the fact that the October revolution is the first stage in the world revolution and has set up a powerful base whence the world revolution can continue to develop.[8]

This analysis goes considerably beyond previous Marxian thought on the larger aspects of the transition from capitalism to socialism. In place of the untenable assumption of a single international revolution, we have here the picture of a series of revolutions in separate countries building up step by step to a world-wide socialist system capable of meeting world capitalism on at least equal terms. The process culminates in a final struggle between the rival systems from which socialism at length emerges in sole possession of the field.

The question may be raised whether this theory is not somewhat overschematic. So far as the broad outlines are concerned it is not inconsistent with the conclusions reached in Chapter XVII above, namely that socialism grows up side-by-side with imperialism and gradually extends its scope at the expense of imperialism. But does this necessarily imply an eventual clear-cut and decisive conflict between the two systems? Such a possibility cannot be denied, yet there are reasons for thinking that it is far from inevitable. Let us examine a possible alternative course of development.

It is necessary to point out first of all that it would never have been possible for the Soviet Union to survive and become the nucleus of a world socialist system had it not been for the antagonisms of imperialism. These antagonisms are, as we already know, of three kinds: internal class conflicts, inter-capitalist rivalries, and antagonisms between advanced nations and backward or colonial countries. All three played an important role in permitting the Soviet Union to maintain its independence and build up its strength. Without going into the matter in detail, we may note the following well-known circumstances in support of this contention. The opposition of the European working class was perhaps of decisive importance in bringing about the failure of foreign intervention in the immediate post-war period. The resistance of China to Japanese penetration has for more than ten years been an important factor in keeping Japan from an attack on Soviet Siberia. Finally, and most important for the present situation, Anglo-German (to a lesser extent Franco-German) rivalry made it possible for the Soviet Union to avoid a united onslaught by the capitalist powers from the west. In short, by exploiting the fissures in the structure of world imperialism, the Soviet Union has managed to keep alive as a center of socialism in spite of unquestioned economic and military inferiority. Not, of course, that the Soviet Union has escaped renewed intervention, but when this intervention came it was not the joint enterprise of a united capitalist world bent upon exterminating socialism; it was rather a desperate gamble by one imperialist power which realized that to succeed at all it must eliminate the potential threat of the Soviet Union from its rear.

This means that even in a period during which socialism has been relatively weak, a mere 'island in the ocean of imperialism,' the capitalist powers have not been able to pull themselves together sufficiently to submerge it. The question now arises whether, when the socialist nucleus has grown in size and strength, the capitalist powers will then be able to compose their differences, internal and external, for a final showdown between the two world systems. This is a crucial question.

It may be said, and certainly not without justification, that hitherto the weakness of socialism has been a source of protection. So long as socialism is only an island in an ocean of imperialism, it does not exercise a decisive influence on the structure of imperialism. The antagonism between socialism and imperialism as a whole is still overshadowed by the intra-imperialist antagonisms; there thus arises the opportunity for socialism to exploit these antagonisms to its own advantage without jeopardizing its existence. So much is clear. Moreover, there seems to be little doubt that as socialism grows in extent and power it will exercise an ever stronger influence on the structure of imperialism. But here a difference of opinion becomes possible. Will the growth of socialism have on balance a consolidating or a disintegrating effect on imperialism? If the former, then Stalin's prognosis would seem to be justified. Intra-imperialist antagonisms would decline in importance, and the conflict between socialism and imperialism would come increasingly to the fore, leading eventually to a showdown for world supremacy. If, on the other hand, the growth of socialism should have a disintegrating effect on imperialism, matters would work out quite differently. In this case the obstacles to the expansion of socialism would be undermined by the very process of expansion; imperialism in retreat might here and there fight rearguard actions, but it would never be able to consolidate its dwindling forces for a final and decisive battle.

It is difficult to say which of these alternative developments is the more likely, chiefly because there are tendencies working in both directions at the same time. On the one hand, the rivalries among the imperialist powers will in all probability be mitigated by any further growth of socialism; but on the other hand internal class conflicts and the antagonisms between the advanced countries and the colonial countries will be intensified. The existence of these contradictory trends within the structure of imperialism is not a matter of conjecture; both were clearly discernible in the period preceding the outbreak of the present war. Appeasement, which was the policy of powerful elements in the ruling classes of all capitalist nations, represented fundamentally an attempt to put aside intra-imperialist conflicts, at least for the time being, in favor of a joint campaign against the Soviet Union. It can hardly be doubted that a further growth of socialism during or after the war will add to and strengthen the adherents of this policy, though naturally the form which it takes in the future will not be identical with the pre-war form. This is one side of the picture. On the other side there is strong evidence that the existence of the Soviet Union, and its consistently anti-imperialist policy, exercised a strong disintegrating effect on the cohesiveness of the total structure of imperialism, a fact which can be seen most clearly in the rapid growth of the nationalist and socialist movements in China and India, countries which it is no exaggeration to say constitute the pivot of modern colonial exploitation. Here again it can hardly be denied that this trend will also be intensified by any further growth of socialism. Particularly would this be the case if one of the advanced western European countries were to go socialist, for this would have an enormous effect on the working classes in all the other western countries.

While it is certainly impossible to speak with assurance about the outcome of a process in which so many variables are at work, nevertheless it appears not unlikely that the disintegrating effects on imperialism of a further growth of socialism will outweigh the consolidating effects. If so, the present World War may also be the last. It may turn out that imperialism has suffered a mortal wound from which it will never recover to set the world ablaze again. In order to convince ourselves that this is not an altogether fantastic perspective, it may be well to conclude by tracing out a possible—one could hardly say probable—course of development which would substantiate our theory.

We start with the assumption of a military defeat of German fascism. This happy event, it may be postulated, would be followed by the collapse of capitalist rule and the victory of socialism over substantially the entire European continent, not merely in Germany and the occupied countries, but also in France, Italy, and Spain. Anglo-American attempts at intervention are not excluded, but it seems hardly likely that they would meet with success; the opposition of the British working class would probably be the decisive factor here. Socialism would now have an impregnable base extending from the Atlantic to the Pacific and including the most advanced centers of industry outside the United States. A firm alliance with the colonial and semi-colonial countries of Asia would follow, and the expulsion of imperialist influence, both Japanese and western, from the Asiatic mainland would be only a matter of time. Japanese capitalism, which is to a peculiar degree dependent upon foreign expansion, could hardly survive such a blow. The evolution of the entire Far East, including India, China, and Japan, in a socialist direction would now be assured, though it could not be expected that the process would be free of severe internal conflicts.

Meanwhile, what about Great Britain, the non-Asiatic parts of the British Empire, and the United States? It is not impossible that Great Britain herself would go socialist along with the rest of western Europe, of which she is in a very real sense a part. If this were to happen, our subsequent analysis would hold *a fortiori*, but let us assume that capitalism succeeds in maintaining its hold in Britain. Even so, the effects of the war and the loss of a large part of the empire would so weaken Britain's position that she would no longer be capable of pursuing an independent course in world affairs; Britain, the dominions, and any remaining colonial areas would of necessity come under the protection and even domination of the United States. It seems quite clear that a victory of socialism in the United States as an immediate result of the war is out of the question; capitalism is still very firmly entrenched in the United States, and the forces of socialism are as yet of negligible importance. The United States would therefore become the center of a much shrunken imperialist system which, according to our assumptions, would include Britain, the dominions, and probably Latin American and parts of Africa.

The question now arises whether the world socialist system based on Europe and Russia and the world imperialist system based on North America would inevitably clash in a struggle for supremacy. That such a clash would be possible cannot be denied; that it would be inevitable, however, cannot be asserted. There is an alternative possibility which, by comparison, may even be said to have the character of a probability. It must be remembered that socialism is founded upon a non-antagonistic and non-exploitative economy. It follows from this that the socialist system would be able at once to turn its energies to raising living standards within its borders through the planned production of use values. Even under such conditions, and with the assistance of the most advanced techniques, however, the well-nigh bottomless pit of unsatisfied needs which will exist at the end of the war in the European and Asiatic countries would require many years to fill. During this period the socialist system would have no incentive to turn its attention outward—

whatever the case might be at a later stage of development. Consequently it may be safely assumed that the initiative in starting a new war would have to come from the imperialist side. Certainly, however, before this could occur a period of recuperation and reorganization would have to intervene, and it may even be doubted whether the imperialist sector would ever be able to recover completely from the disruption of the war, the defection of colonial areas, and the loss of foreign assets. The contradictions of capitalist production would soon make themselves felt again in a peace economy. In short, the process of stabilization would be long drawn-out and difficult at best. In the meantime what would be the effect on the social structure of imperialism of the victory of socialism in so large a part of the world and the steady rise of living standards in the areas affected? Is it not clear that the working classes in the advanced industrial areas and the masses in the backward countries still enmeshed in the imperialist system would be powerfully attracted to the new socialist system? Would not the ruling imperialist oligarchy find it increasingly difficult, and in time even impossible, to organize a crusade against the new and vastly expanded socialist system? The answer seems to be obvious.

We must conclude that, because of the differences in their underlying economies, the socialist sector of the world would quickly stabilize itself and push forward to higher standards of living while the imperialist sector would flounder in the difficulties with which we are already sufficiently familiar. Nevertheless, it must be granted that this does not finally settle the matter, for it is inconceivable that the two systems should continue to exist side by side indefinitely. It seems not unlikely that the gravitational pull, so to speak, of the fundamentally stronger and more stable socialist system would exercise a progressively disintegrating effect on the structure of the imperialist system, first paralysing its capacity for aggression and then chipping out bit by bit the cement which holds it together as a cohesive social structure. Under these circumstances, paradoxically enough, a peaceful transition to socialism would for the first time become a genuine possibility. If—and it seems by no means unthinkable—democratic forms in the Anglo-American countries were to survive even so great an upheaval as we have pictured, it would now be possible to fill them with a socialist content. Once socialism has had an opportunity to demonstrate its superiority on a large scale and under reasonably favorable conditions, the effect not only on the working class but also on the great majority of the middle classes still living under capitalist conditions can be counted upon to be unprecedently powerful. The adherents of socialism will multiply by leaps and bounds; the small oligarchy whose social existence is bound up with the old order will be weakened, deprived of its international support and eventually rendered impotent. In the later stages of the world revolution, democracy may at long last be able to fulfil the promises which have so far remained unhonored amid the frustrations of a self-contradictory economic system.

The foregoing analysis has been developed in opposition to Stalin's theory of an eventual showdown between the rival socialist and imperialist systems. This does not mean that the two views are mutually contradictory; they are merely indications of alternative possible courses of development. In this connection it is interesting to note that Stalin himself recognized the possibility of a pattern such as we have outlined. In the *Foundations of Leninism* Stalin explains why the transition to socialism cannot be expected to be peaceful, and then adds the following comment:

> No doubt in the distant future, if the proletariat has triumphed in the chief countries that are now capitalist, and if the present capitalist encirclement has given place to a socialist encirclement, it will be possible for a 'peaceful' transition to be effected in certain capitalist countries where the capitalists, in view of the 'unfavorable' international situation, will deem it advisable 'of their own accord' to make extensive concessions to the proletariat. But this is to look far ahead, and to contemplate extremely hypothetical possibilities. As concerns the near future, there is no warrant for any such expectations.[9]

Undoubtedly this skepticism was justified in 1924, and it may prove to be today as well. But if we are justified in assuming a military defeat of fascism in the present war, the relatively near future will bring a sharp change in perspectives. Yesterday's 'extremely hypothetical possibilities' may be on tomorrow's order of business.

In the meantime—and unless conditions change much more rapidly than seems likely between the time when this chapter is written and the time when it is published—the great majority of readers will no doubt feel that our analysis is far-fetched and unreal, to use no stronger terms. Underlying trends do not always show on the surface. But the issue need not be debated here; we gladly leave it to the future to decide.

Appendix A

ON REPRODUCTION SCHEMES

BY

Shigeto Tsuru

This appendix consists of a few explanatory notes on the reproduction scheme of Marx. In the first two parts, a diagrammatic presentation of the scheme is given in comparison with Quesnay's *tableau économique*. And in the last part, aggregative categories which are the elements of Marx's reproduction scheme are compared with the set of aggregates most widely used in modern economics, namely, the one associated with the economics of John M. Keynes.

1. Quesnay's Tableau

The society Quesnay visualized consists of three classes: (1) the 'productive' class of farmers whose labor alone yields a surplus, (2) the class which appropriates this surplus, including the landlords, the Church, and the state, and (3) the 'sterile' class of manufacturers. His *tableau* was intended to portray, under simplifying assumptions, how the total annual product of such a society circulates between these three classes and enables annual reproduction to take place. For this purpose it is imagined figuratively that exchanges take place in a lump sum at the end of a year, enabling the complete disposition of the goods produced during that year and at the same time placing all the factors of production in readiness where they are wanted as the new year begins. Quesnay's simple presentation of the circulation process of such a society by the use of lines has not always been readily understood. At least it led Eugen Dühring to suspect Quesnay of some mathematical fantasy. As an alternative method of presentation, we propose here a diagram for the *tableau économique*.

Diagram 1 depicts the situation before the exchange. The productive class hold five billion dollars' worth of their own gross product, three of food and two of raw materials, and in addition, two billion dollars in money which is used solely as a medium of exchange and is assumed to be held by them only for expositional reasons. The landlords hold nothing, but have a claim on the productive class for rent to the amount of two billion dollars—the amount equal to the net product arising in agriculture. The sterile class hold two billion dollars' worth of manufactured products.

To begin with, the productive class pays rent in money (two billion dollars) to the landlords—the action which is indicated in the diagram by the two arrows emanating from the solid thick line and pointing to the landlords' section. Other arrows indicate the direction in which this money flows as it effects the circulation of goods produced. The landlords buy with one billion dollars food for their consumption, thereby returning one half of the money advanced by the productive class to its point of origin. With another half of the rent revenue, the landlords purchase manufactured goods from the sterile class, who in turn use

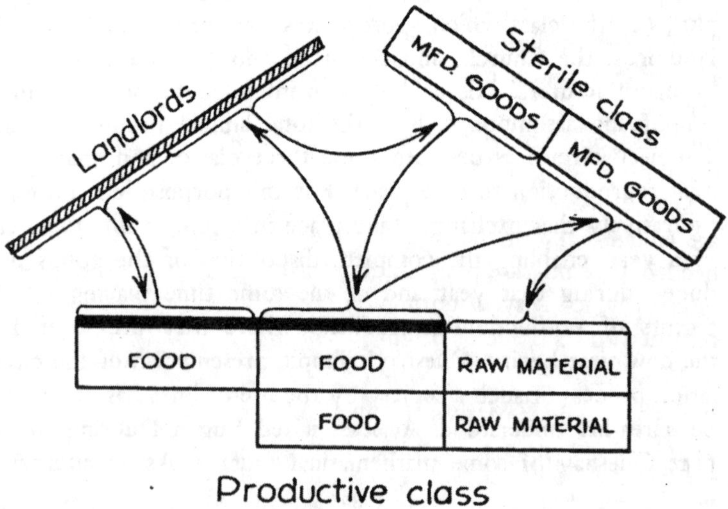

DIAGRAM 1

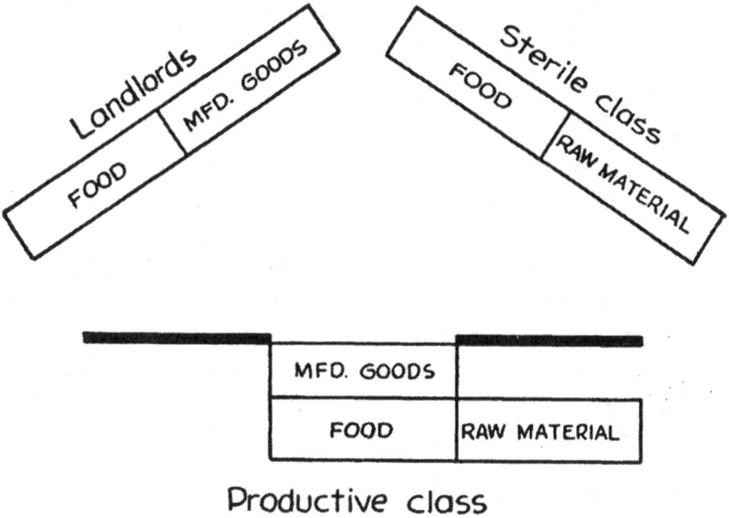

DIAGRAM 2

this money to buy food from the productive class. Thereupon the latter class purchase with that money the manufactured goods from the sterile class who in turn buy the farm product (to be used as raw materials in the next period) from the productive class, thereby returning another one billion dollars of money to its point of origin. In addition, the productive class 'buy' from themselves one billion dollars of their own product as food and another one billion dollars' worth as raw materials for the next period. These constitute internal exchange within the class, and are, therefore, placed on the second deck in the diagram.

Diagram 2 depicts the situation after all sales and purchases are ended. Each of the three classes is in possession of the goods needed to embark upon a new period of production, and the money, which served its function as a medium of exchange, has returned to its point of origin.

2. Marx's Reproduction Scheme

Marx thought highly of Quesnay's *tableau économique* and was indebted to it for developing his own reproduction scheme.

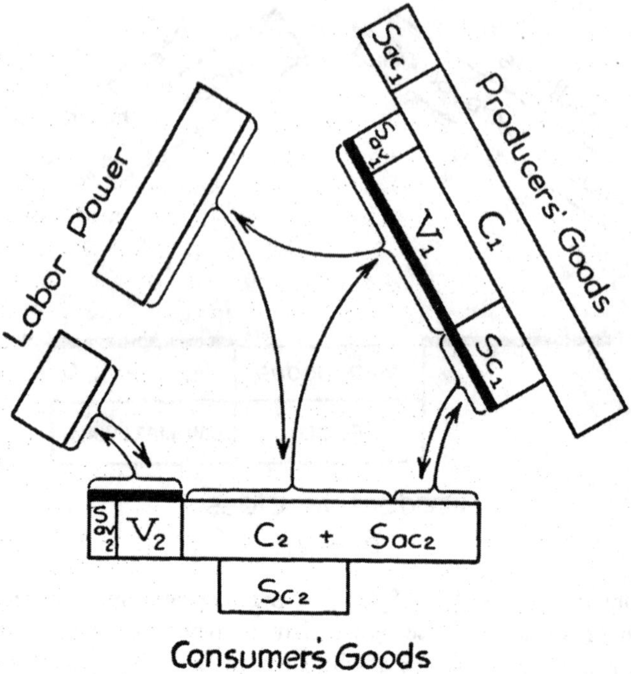

DIAGRAM 3

His first attempt along this line was also a diagram of simple reproduction making use of lines in the manner of Quesnay.* This diagram, complicated as it was with fourteen ascending and seven descending lines, was not finally used in exposition and gave way to the now familiar form of equational *tableau.* However, it may facilitate the understanding of the latter if we resort to the diagrammatic technique which we used for Quesnay's *tableau* above. Both similarities and dissimilarities between the two *tableaus* will thereby be graphically brought out.

Since the elements and principles of Marx's reproduction scheme are fully discussed in the text, it is sufficient here to state that we shall illustrate the case of extended reproduction which may be formulated equationally as follows: †

* See Marx's letter to Engels as of 6 July 1863.

† See above, p. 163. Here we have consolidated $Sc_1 + S\Delta c_1$ into Sc_1 inasmuch as we are not interested in the comparison with the case of simple reproduction.

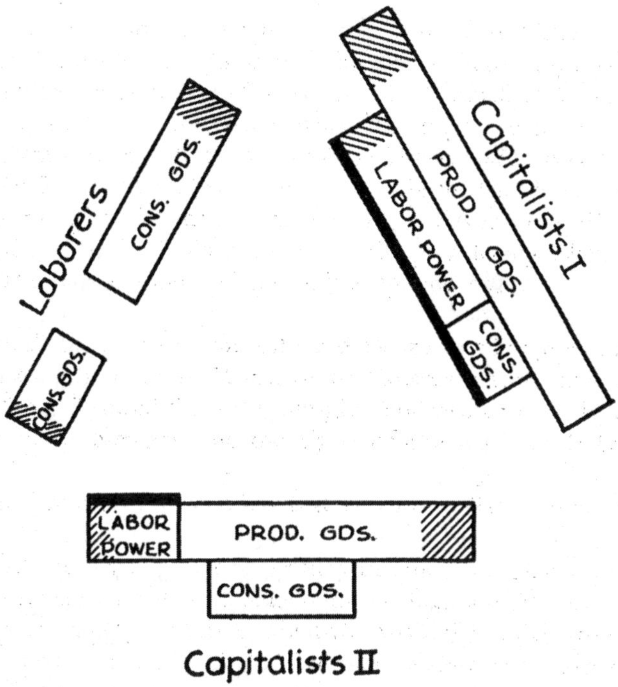

DIAGRAM 4

$$C_1 + V_1 + Sc_1 + Sac_1 + Sav_1 = W_1$$

$$C_2 + V_2 + Sc_2 + Sac_2 + Sav_2 = W_2$$

Diagrams 3 and 4 portray the circulation of commodities in this scheme. In contrast to Quesnay's *tableau*, three corners are now occupied by the holders of three basic commodities: consumers' goods, producers' goods, and labor power. Technical devices for simplification are similar to those in Quesnay's case. The solid thick line again indicates the point at which money is advanced and the arrows show the direction in which money flows. The points of origin of money, however, are somewhat arbitrary; several different patterns may be drawn with essentially the same result for our purpose. The three aggregates, C_1, Sac_1, and Sc_2, constitute demand for goods produced within their respective branches and are exchanged internally. Therefore, they are placed on the second deck. The exchange process of the other elements is clearly shown in Diagram 3. Capitalists in the first branch, or the producers' goods branch, advance money to workers who purchase with it consumers' goods from capitalists in the second branch, or the consumers' goods branch. The latter in turn purchase producers' goods in partial fulfilment of their demand for such goods, returning thereby the money originally advanced by capitalists in the first branch to its point of origin. Similarly for other exchanges. When all the transactions are completed, no commodity remains unsold, all the factors of production are again placed in readiness for the new period, and all the money is back at the point of origin. (See Diagram 4.) Reproduction on an enlarged scale is indicated by the addition of shaded areas in Diagram 4—the addition to that which was the amount for each aggregate at the end of the preceding period.

If we now revert to the equations of extended reproduction cited above, we may observe that they are a synthetic product of two logically distinct phases of social circulation. On the one hand, each equation may be interpreted as revealing the *cost* structure, or the proportion in which factor payments are made. Thus such relations as that between constant capital and variable capital and that between surplus value and variable capital may be explicitly embodied in the equation. On the other hand, the equation may be interpreted as revealing the *demand* structure, or the character and the magnitude of demand arising out of different factor payments. Thus the factor payment S_1, or the surplus value in the first branch, for example, is shown to generate three kinds of demand, Sc_1 amount of consumers' goods demanded by capitalists, Sac_1 amount of producers' goods demanded also by the same capitalists, and Sav_1 amount of consumers' goods demanded by workers.

It may further be observed that the bridge between the two phases is not characterized by a uniform number of metamorphoses for all the aggregates. C_2, e.g., exists in the first instance as an aliquot part of consumers' goods, is sold for money, and then exchanged against C_2 amount of producers' goods. V_2 too exists in the first instance as an aliquot part of consumers' goods and is then sold for money; but its next metamorphosis is against the commodity called labor power, which in turn generates demand for consumers' goods (assuming that workers do not save). Further, Sav_2 may be interpreted to involve one additional metamorphosis, if we treat the payment of surplus value as factor payment. Such difference in the number of metamorphoses needed to bridge the two phases is accounted for by the implicit manner in which the commodity labor power is treated. Diagram 3, by making the position of the commodity labor power explicit, enables us to trace clearly the process of circulation implied in the synthetic shorthand of the equations of the reproduction scheme.

3. Comparability with the Keynesian Aggregates

The foregoing analysis paves the way to a discussion of the comparability between the elements of Marx's reproduction scheme and the Keynesian aggregates. One aspect of such a problem, for example, may be phrased as follows: what corresponds in the Marxian scheme to that which is called net national income by Keynes? If some of us are tempted to reply in unguarded haste that it is variable capital plus surplus value, it only goes to show how easily we tend to forget the implicit assumptions which shroud each analytical scheme of interpretation.

Although a type of society implied in Marx's extended reproduction scheme is drastically simple, and a type of society to which the Keynesian aggregates are applied can be of any degree of complexity, the essentials may be brought out by taking as our point of departure the reproduction scheme as it is found in Marx. The latter implies, for one thing, that no fixed capital exists; and, for another, that what is not consumed is immediately invested; and thirdly, that capitalists in the first branch do not invest in the second branch and *vice versa*. Then, again, we have:

$$C_1 + V_1 + Sc_1 + Sac_1 + Sav_1 = W_1$$

$$C_2 + V_2 + Sc_2 + Sac_2 + Sav_2 = W_2$$

Adding the two equations, we obtain: ($C_1 + C_2 = C$ and so on)

$$C + V + Sc + Sac + Sav = W$$

This total, W, corresponds to what Keynes designates by A,* or

* J. M. Keynes, *The General Theory of Employment, Interest and Money*, 1936, Ch. 6.

the gross proceeds of sales both to consumers and between entrepreneurs. Transactions between entrepreneurs, or A_1 of Keynes, may be written as the sum of C and Sac. Since he defines consumption as the difference between A and A_1, we obtain:

$$\text{Consumption} = W - (C + Sac) = V + Sc + Sav$$

Now, as to investment. It may be recalled that Keynes defines investment as the difference between G', or the net value conservable from what was on hand at the beginning of the period, and G, or the value of the means of production on hand at the end of the period. In terms of the elements of the reproduction scheme, it is clear that G' consists of C amount of producers' goods and V amount of labor power,* while G consists of C and V plus Sac and Sav. Thus we obtain for investment:

$$\text{Investment} = G - G' = (C + V + Sac + Sav) - (C + V)$$
$$= Sac + Sav$$

It may strike one as peculiar that labor power is to be counted as a part of the means of production on hand. In the strict logic of capitalism, however, such treatment is perfectly consistent. Additional labor power is just as much a part of the net national product as would be, for example, a new robot-machine. True, Keynes never treats the commodity labor power as belonging to the category of investment goods. But from his standpoint, labor power may be regarded as the limiting case of goods-in-process, for the minute labor power is bought by an entrepreneur, the latter can be said to be in possession of an asset in the sense of renderable service.

Now, equivalent expressions for such other terms as user cost, saving, and national income can be derived from the above. In the definitions of Keynes, user cost, U, is equal to A_1 plus G' minus G (ignoring again B'), or:

$$U = (C + Sac) + (C + V) - (C + V + Sac + Sav)$$
$$= C - Sav$$

* We ignore Keynes' B' as insignificant in this case. B' is the sum which the entrepreneur would have spent on the maintenance and improvement of his capital equipment if he had decided not to use it to produce output.

As for saving, Keynes equates it to entrepreneurial transactions (A_1) minus user cost (U), or:

$$\text{Saving} = (C + Sac) - (C - Sav) = Sac + Sav$$

which is found to be naturally equal to investment. And finally, Keynes defines his national income as equal to the difference between the gross proceeds of sales (A) and user cost (U), or:

$$\text{National income} = W - (C - Sav)$$
$$= V + Sc + Sac + Sav + Sav$$

It is to be noted that *Sav* appears twice in the national income. In other words, it appears that *Sav* is registered twice as income and exchanged only once against goods. Such appearance is deceptive, however. Actually, *Sav* stands for three metamorphoses as follows: *

(1) C–M . . . Produced goods (C) to the amount of *Sav* are sold against money and capitalists realize their surplus value.
(2) a. M–C' . . . Capitalists buy the commodity labor power (C').
b. C'–M . . . Or, from workers' point of view, they sell their labor power against money.
(3) M–C'' . . . Workers buy consumers' goods (C'').

In this series of exchanges, the money receipt appears twice as *income*, i.e. in (1) and (2)b, and each time is subsequently exchanged against commodity, i.e. C' and C''. Since the process (2) is not made explicit in the reproduction scheme, the same symbol *Sav* is made to stand for both phases, i.e. (1) to (2) and (2) to (3). It has already been observed in the previous section that if our abstract representation of the actual circulation network is limited to a part of the realm of commodities, any exchange against a commodity which is left out will not be registered and will be indicated only *by magnitude* in the metamorphosis involving a commodity explicit in our scheme.

The foregoing discussion on the translation of the Keynesian

* Here the symbol C is used in the sense of a commodity and not in the sense of constant capital.

into the Marxian aggregates is not complete. A number of minor points are omitted entirely, such for example as the problem of inter-household transactions (or service industries), the problem of what Keynes calls the 'supplementary cost,' and so on. Such an exercise in conceptual translation, however, is in itself of little positive significance, and we need not carry through the task to the final detail.

A translation such as we have attempted should rather be looked upon as a way of enabling us to understand significant differences between the two systems of interpretation, in terms which are commensurate with both.

Appendix B

THE IDEOLOGY OF IMPERIALISM *

[The ideology of finance capital] is entirely opposed to that of liberalism; finance capital wants not freedom but dominance; it has no taste for the independence of the individual capitalist but rather demands his regimentation; it abhors the anarchy of competition and desires organization, to be sure only to be able to resume competition on a higher level. In order to achieve this and at the same time to maintain and augment its power, it needs the state to guarantee the home market through protection and thereby to facilitate the conquest of foreign markets. It requires a politically powerful state which need take no account of the opposed interests of other states in formulating its commercial policy. It needs a strong state which recognizes finance capital's interests abroad and uses political power to extort favorable treaties from smaller states, a state which can exert its influence all over the world in order to be able to turn the entire world into a sphere for investment. Finance capital, finally, needs a state which is strong enough to carry out a policy of expansion and to gather in new colonies. Where liberalism was an opponent of state power politics and wished to insure its own dominance against the older power of aristocracy and bureaucracy, to which end it confined the state's instruments of power within the smallest possible compass, there finance capital demands power politics without limit; and it would do so even if the outlays for army and navy did not directly assure to the most powerful capitalist groups an important market with enormous monopolistic profits.

The demand for a policy of expansion revolutionizes the entire *Weltanschauung* of the bourgeoisie. The bourgeoisie ceases to be peaceful and humanitarian. The old freetraders believed in

* Translated from Rudolf Hilferding, *Das Finanzkapital*, 1910, pp. 426-9. The title is added.

free trade not only as the best economic policy, but also as the beginning of an era of peace. Finance capital has long since abandoned any such notions. It does not believe in the harmony of capitalist interests, but knows that the competitive struggle approaches ever closer to a political battle for power. The ideal of peace dies out; in place of the ideal of humanity steps that of the might and power of the state. The modern state, however, had its origin in the strivings of nations toward unity. The national aspiration, which found its natural limit in the formation of the nation as the foundation of the state—because it recognized the right of every nation to its own state form and therefore saw the borders of the state in the natural borders of the nation—is now transformed into the aspiration of one nation for dominance over others. As an ideal there now appears the conquest of world mastery for one's own nation, a striving as unlimited as capital's striving for profit from which it springs. Capital becomes the conqueror of the world, and with every new land conquered sets a new border which must be overstepped. This striving becomes an economic necessity, since any holding back lowers the profit of finance capital, reduces its ability to compete and finally can make of a smaller economic region a mere tributary of a larger one. Economically grounded, it is ideologically justified by that remarkable twisting of the national idea, which no longer recognizes the right of every nation to political self-determination and independence, and which is no longer an expression of the democratic belief in the equality of all nationalities. Rather the economic advantage of monopoly is mirrored in the favored place which must be ascribed to one's own nation. The latter appears as chosen above all others. Since the subordination of foreign nations proceeds by force, that is to say in a very natural way, it appears to the dominant nation that it owes its mastery to its special natural qualities, in other words to its racial characteristics. Thus in racial ideology there emerges a scientifically-cloaked foundation for the power lust of finance capital, which in this way demonstrates the cause and necessity of its operations. In place of the democratic ideal of equality steps an oligarchical ideal of mastery.

If in the field of foreign policy this ideal seems to include the whole nation, in internal affairs it stresses the standpoint of mastery as against the working class. At the same time, the growing power of the workers increases the effort of capital to enhance the state power as security against the demands of the proletariat.

In this way the ideology of imperialism arises on the grave of the old liberal ideals. It scoffs at the naïveté of liberalism. What an illusion, in a world of capitalistic struggle where the superiority of arms alone decides, to believe in a harmony of interests! What an illusion to look forward to the reign of eternal peace and to preach international law where only force decides the fate of peoples! What idiocy to want to extend the legal relations existing within a state beyond its borders! What irresponsible business disturbances are created by this humanitarian nonsense which makes a problem out of the workers; discovers social reform at home; and, in the colonies, wants to abolish contract slavery, the only possibility of rational exploitation! Eternal justice is a lovely dream, but one never even built a railroad out of moralizing. How can we conquer the world if we want to wait for competition to get religion [*auf die Bekehrung der Konkurrenz warten wollen*]?

In place of the faded ideals of the bourgeoisie, however, imperialism injects this dissolution of all illusions only to awaken a new and greater illusion. Imperialism is sober in weighing the real conflict of capitalist interest groups which both quarrel and unite among themselves. But it becomes transported and intoxicated when it reveals its own ideal. The imperialist wants nothing for himself; he is also, however, no illusionist and dreamer who dissolves the hopeless confusion of races in all stages of civilization and with all sorts of possibilities for development into the bloodless concept of mankind. With hard, clear eyes he looks at the crowd of peoples and perceives above them all his own nation. It is real; it lives in the mighty state, always becoming greater and more powerful; and its glorification justifies all his strivings. The renunciation of individual interest in favor of the higher general interest, which constitutes the condition of every vital social ideology, is thereby achieved; the state, which is extraneous to the people, and the nation are thereby bound together; and the national idea is made the driving force of policy.

Class antagonisms are abolished in the service of the totality. Common action of the nation united for the goal of national greatness takes the place of class struggle which for the possessing class is both fruitless and dangerous.

This ideal which seems to unite shattered bourgeois society with a new bond, must receive an even more ecstatic acceptance since all the time the disintegration of bourgeois society proceeds apace.

LIST OF WORKS CITED

Bauer, Otto, 'Die Akkumulation des Kapitals,' *Die Neue Zeit*, Jhrg. xxxi, Bd. 1 (1912-13), pp. 831-8, 862-74.

—— *Die Nationalitätenfrage und die Sozialdemokratie*, Verlag der Wiener Volksbuchhandlung Ignaz Brand, Wien, 1907.

—— *Die Österreichische Revolution*, Wiener Volksbuchhandlung, Wien, 1923.

—— *Zwischen zwei Weltkriegen?*, Eugen Prager Verlag, Bratislava, 1936.

Bernstein, Eduard, *Die Voraussetzungen des Sozialismus und die Aufgaben der Sozialdemokratie*, J. H. W. Dietz, Stuttgart, 1899.

—— *Evolutionary Socialism*, Independent Labour Party, London, 1909. (A translation of the foregoing work.)

Bittelmann, Alex, and Jerome, V. J., *Leninism—the Only Marxism Today*, Workers Library Publishers, New York, 1934.

Böhm-Bawerk, Eugen von, *Karl Marx and the Close of His System*, T. F. Unwin, London, 1898.

Bortkiewicz, Ladislaus von, 'Böhm-Bawerk's Hauptwerk in seinem Verhältnis zur sozialistischen Theorie des Kapitalzinses,' *Archiv für die Geschichte des Sozialismus und der Arbeiterbewegung*, Jhrg. xi, Heft 1 u. 2 (1923), pp. 161-73.

—— 'Der Kardinalfehler der Böhm-Bawerkschen Zinstheorie,' *Jahrbuch für Gesetzgebung, Verwaltung und Volkswirtschaft im Deutschen Reich*, Jhrg. xxx, Heft 3 (1906), pp. 61-90.

—— 'Wertrechnung und Preisrechnung im Marxschen System,' *Archiv für Sozialwissenschaft und Sozialpolitik*, Bd. xxiii, Heft 1 (1906), pp. 1-50; Bd. xxv, Heft 1 (1907), pp. 10-51; Bd. xxv, Heft 2 (1907), pp. 445-88.

—— 'Zur Berichtigung der Grundlegenden theoretischen Konstruktion von Marx im dritten Band des "Kapital",' *Jahrbücher für Nationalökonomie und Statistik*, Bd. xxxiv, Heft 3 (1907), pp. 319-35.

—— 'Zur Zinstheorie,' *Jahrbuch für Gesetzgebung, Verwaltung und Volkswirtschaft im Deutschen Reich*, Jhrg. xxxi, Heft 3 (1907), pp. 370-85.

Boudin, L. B., *The Theoretical System of Karl Marx*, Charles Kerr & Company, Chicago, 1907.

Bukharin, N. I., *Der Imperialismus und die Akkumulation des Kapitals*, Verlag für Literatur und Politik, Wien-Berlin, 1926.

Chang, S. H. M., *The Marxian Theory of the State*, The University of Pennsylvania, Philadelphia, 1931.

Corey, Lewis, *The Decline of American Capitalism*, Covici Friede, New York, 1934.

Cunow, Heinrich, 'Zur Zusammenbruchstheorie,' *Die Neue Zeit*, Jhrg. XVII, Bd. 1 (1898-9), pp. 356-64, 396-403, 424-30.

Dobb, Maurice, *Political Economy and Capitalism*, International Publishers, New York, 1939.

Engels, Friedrich, *The Origin of the Family, Private Property and the State*, Charles Kerr & Company, Chicago, 1902.

— and Marx, Karl, *see* Marx, Karl and Engels, Friedrich.

Goldsmith, R. W., Parmelee, R. C. and others, *The Distribution of Ownership in the 200 Largest Non-Financial Corporations*, Temporary National Economic Committee Monograph No. 29, Government Printing Office, Washington, 1940.

Granby, Helene, *Survey of Shareholdings in 1,710 Corporations with Securities Listed on a National Securities Exchange*, Temporary National Economic Committee Monograph No. 30, Government Printing Office, Washington, 1941.

Grossmann, Henryk, 'Die Änderung des urspringlichen Aufbauplans des Marxschen "Kapital" und ihre Ursachen,' *Archiv für die Geschichte des Sozialismus und der Arbeiterbewegung*, Bd. XIV, Heft 2 (1929), pp. 305-38.

— *Das Akkumulations- und Zusammenbruchsgesetz des kapitalistischen Systems*, C. L. Hirschfeld, Leipzig, 1929.

Hansen, A. H., *Fiscal Policy and Business Cycles*, W. W. Norton & Company, Inc., New York, 1941.

— *Full Recovery or Stagnation?*, W. W. Norton & Company, Inc., New York, 1938.

Hegel, G. W. F., *The Philosophy of History*, translated by J. Sibree, Cooperative Publication Society, New York, 1900.

Hicks, J. R., *Value and Capital*, Clarendon Press, Oxford, 1939.

Hilferding, Rudolf, *Böhm-Bawerk's Marx-Kritik*, Verlag der Wiener Volksbuchhandlung Ignaz Brand, Wien, 1904.

— *Das Finanzkapital*, Wiener Volksbuchhandlung, Wien, 1923

Hilferding, Rudolf, 'Die Eigengesetzlichkeit der kapitalistischen Entwicklung,' in Vol. I of *Kapital und Kapitalismus*, 2 vols., edited by Bernhard Harms, R. Hobbing, Berlin, 1931.

Jerome, V. J., and Bittelmann, Alex, *see* Bittelmann, Alex, and Jerome, V. J.

Kautsky, Karl, *Bernstein und das Sozialdemokratische Programm*, J. H. W. Dietz, Stuttgart, 1899.

—— *Die Materialistische Geschichtsauffassung*, 2 vols., 2nd ed., J. H. W. Dietz, Berlin, 1929.

—— *The Class Struggle* (*Erfurt Program*), Charles Kerr & Company, Chicago, 1910.

—— 'Finanzkapital und Krisen,' *Die Neue Zeit*, Jhrg. XXIX, Bd. 1 (1910-11), pp. 764-72, 797-804, 838-46, 874-83.

—— 'Krisentheorien,' *Die Neue Zeit*, Jhrg. XX, Bd. 2 (1901-2), pp. 37-47, 76-81, 110-18, 133-43.

Keynes, J. M., *The General Theory of Employment, Interest and Money*, Harcourt, Brace and Company, New York, 1936.

Knight, F. H., 'The Quantity of Capital and the Rate of Interest,' *Journal of Political Economy*, Vol. XLIV, No. 4 (1936), pp. 433-63, No. 5, pp. 612-42.

Korsch, Karl, *Karl Marx*, Chapman & Hall, Ltd., London, 1938.

Lange, Oskar, 'Marxian Economics and Modern Economic Theory,' *Review of Economic Studies*, Vol. II, No. 3 (1935), pp. 189-201.

Lattimore, Owen, *Inner Asian Frontiers of China*, American Geographical Society, New York, 1940.

Lenin, V. I., *Die Entwicklung des Kapitalismus in Russland*, Sämtliche Werke Bd. III, Verlag für Literatur und Politik, Wien-Berlin, 1929.

—— *Imperialism*, International Publishers Company, Inc., New York, 1933.

—— *Left-Wing Communism: an Infantile Disorder*, International Publishers Company, Inc., New York, 1934.

—— *The State and Revolution*, International Publishers Company, Inc., New York, 1932.

Lowe, Alfred, 'Mr. Dobb and Marx's Theory of Value,' *Modern Quarterly*, London, Vol. I, No. 3 (1938), pp. 285-90.

Lukacs, Georg, *Geschichte und Klassenbewusstsein*, Der Malik-Verlag, Berlin, 1923.

Luxemburg, Rosa, *Die Akkumulation des Kapitals. Ein Beitrag zur ökonomischen Erklärung des Imperialismus*, Vereinigung Internationaler Verlags-Anstalten, Berlin, 1922.

Luxemburg, Rosa, *Die Akkumulation des Kapitals oder was die Epigonen aus der Marxschen Theorie gemacht haben*. Eine Antikritik, Frankes Verlag, Leipzig, 1921.

— *Sozialreform oder Revolution?*, Gesammelte Werke Bd. III, Vereinigung Internationaler Verlags-Anstalten, Berlin, 1925.

Marx, Karl, *A Contribution to the Critique of Political Economy*, Charles Kerr & Company, Chicago, 1911.

— *Capital*, 3 vols., Charles Kerr & Company, Chicago, 1933.

— *Capital, The Communist Manifesto and Other Writings*, edited by Max Eastman, The Modern Library, New York, 1932.

— *The Class Struggles in France*, International Publishers Company, Inc., New York, 1934.

— *The Eighteenth Brumaire of Louis Bonaparte*, International Publishers Company, Inc., New York, no date.

— *Das Kapital*, 3 vols., edited by the Marx-Engels-Lenin Institute, Ring-Verlag A. G., Zurich, 1934.

— *The Poverty of Philosophy*, International Publishers Company, Inc., New York, no date.

— *Theorien über den Mehrwert*, 3 vols., edited by Karl Kautsky, J. H. W. Dietz, Stuttgart, 1905-10.

— *Value, Price and Profit*, International Publishers Company, Inc., New York, no date.

— *Wage Labor and Capital*, International Publishers Company, Inc., New York, no date.

— and Engels, Friedrich, *Correspondence*, 1846-95, *a Selection with Commentary and Notes*, International Publishers Company, Inc., New York, 1936.

— and Engels, Friedrich, *The Communist Manifesto*, with an introduction and explanatory notes by D. Ryazanoff, M. Lawrence Ltd., London, 1930.

Mill, J. S., *Principles of Political Economy*, edited by W. J. Ashley, Longmans, Green and Co., Ltd., London, 1926.

Moszkowska, Natalie, *Das Marxsche System*, H. R. Engelmann, Berlin, 1929.

— *Zur Kritik Moderner Krisentheorien*, Michael Kacha Verlag, Prag, 1935.

Neisser, Hans, 'Das Gesetz der Fallenden Profitrate als Krisen- und Zusammenbruchsgesetz,' *Die Gesellschaft*, Jhrg. VIII, No. 1 (1931), pp. 72-85.

Neumann, Franz, *Behemoth*, Oxford University Press, New York, 1942

Parkes, H. B., *Marxism: an Autopsy*, Houghton Mifflin Company, Boston, 1939.

Parsons, Talcott, 'Wants and Activities in Marshall,' *Quarterly Journal of Economics*, Vol. XLVI, No. 1 (1931), pp. 101-40.

Petry, Franz, *Der Soziale Gehalt der Marxschen Werttheorie*, G. Fischer, Jena, 1916.

Pigou, A. C., *The Economics of Welfare*, 3rd ed., Macmillan and Company, London, 1929.

Preiser, Erich, 'Das Wesen der Marxschen Krisentheorien,' in *Wirtschaft und Gesellschaft, Festschrift für Franz Oppenheimer*, Frankfurter Societäts-Druckerei, Frankfurt a. M., 1924.

Preobrashensky, E., *Novaya Ekonomika*, Communist Academy, Economic Section, Moscow, 1926.

Ricardo, David, *Letters to Malthus*, 1810-1823, edited by James Bonar, Clarendon Press, Oxford, 1887.

—— *Principles of Political Economy and Taxation*, edited by E. C. K. Gonner, G. Bell and Sons, Ltd., London, 1929.

Robbins, Lionel, *The Nature and Significance of Economic Science*, Macmillan and Company, London, 1932.

Robinson, Joan, *The Economics of Imperfect Competition*, Macmillan and Company, London, 1933.

Rodbertus, Karl, *Overproduction and Crises*, with an introduction by J. B. Clark, S. Sonnenschein & Co., Ltd., London; C. Scribner's Sons, New York, 1898.

Schmidt, Conrad, 'Zur Theorie der Handelskrisen und der Überproduktion,' *Sozialistische Monatshefte*, Jhrg. V, Bd. 2, No. 9 (1901), pp. 669-82.

Schumpeter, J. A., *Business Cycles*, 2 vols., McGraw-Hill Book Company, Inc., New York, 1939.

—— *The Theory of Economic Development*, Harvard University Press, Cambridge, Mass., 1936.

Shibata, Kei, 'On the General Profit Rate,' *Kyoto University Economic Review*, Vol. XIV, No. 1 (1939), pp. 40-66.

—— 'On the Law of Decline in the Rate of Profit,' *Kyoto University Economic Review*, Vol. IX, No. 1 (1934), pp. 61-75.

Smith, Adam, *An Inquiry into the Nature and Causes of the Wealth of Nations*, 2 vols., edited by Edwin Cannan, Methuen & Co., Ltd., London, 1930.

Snyder, Carl, 'Capital Supply and National Well-Being,' *American Economic Review*, Vol. xxxi, No. 2 (1936), pp. 195-224.

Stalin, Joseph, *Leninism*, International Publishers, New York, 1928.

Strachey, John, *A Programme for Progress*, Random House, New York, 1940.

Sweezy, P. M., 'The Decline of the Investment Banker,' *Antioch Review*, Vol. i, No. 1 (1941), pp. 63-8.

— 'The Illusion of the "Managerial Revolution",' *Science and Society*, Vol. vi, No. 1 (1942), pp. 1-23.

Tugan-Baranowsky, Michael, *Studien zur Theorie und Geschichte der Handelskrisen in England*, G. Fischer, Jena, 1901.

— *Theoretische Grundlagen des Marxismus*, Duncker & Humboldt, Leipzig, 1905.

Twentieth Century Fund, *Does Distribution Cost Too Much?*, The Twentieth Century Fund, New York, 1939.

Veblen, Thorstein, *The Theory of the Leisure Class*, Modern Library, New York, 1934.

NOTES

INTRODUCTION

1. A. C. Pigou, *The Economics of Welfare* (3rd ed., 1929), p. 556; and Joan Robinson, *The Economics of Imperfect Competition* (1933), pp. 281 ff.

PART ONE

VALUE AND SURPLUS VALUE

I: Marx's Method

1. Georg Lukacs, *Geschichte und Klassenbewusstsein* (1923), p. 13.
2. Author's Preface to the first edition of *Capital* i, p. 14.
3. *Philosophy of History*, World's Greatest Literature ed., p. 65. Quoted by Henryk Grossmann, 'Die Änderung des ursprunglichen Aufbauplans des Marxschen "Kapital" und ihre Ursachen,' *Archiv für die Geschichte des Sozialismus und der Arbeiterbewegung*, Bd. xiv, Heft 2 (1929), p. 327.
4. *Principles of Political Economy and Taxation*, Gonner ed., p. 1.
5. *Critique of Political Economy*, p. 302. The quotation is from the unfinished 'Introduction to the Critique of Political Economy,' which was not published as a part of the *Critique* in the original edition (1859). It was written by Marx in 1857 and was first published by Kautsky in 1903. It is included as an Appendix in the English (Kerr) edition.
6. Ibid. pp. 303-4. Italics added.
7. *Capital* iii, p. 1025.
8. Ibid. i, p. 707.
9. Ibid. ii (Editor's Preface), p. 7.
10. *Geschichte und Klassenbewusstsein*, p. 7.
11. *The Eighteenth Brumaire of Louis Bonaparte*, International Publishers ed., p. 13.
12. *The Poverty of Philosophy*, p. 102.
13. *Geschichte und Klassenbewusstsein*, p. 173.

II: The Qualitative-Value Problem

1. *The Wealth of Nations*, Cannan ed., Vol. i, p. 15.
2. Ibid.
3. *Capital* i, p. 49. Italics added.
4. *Critique*, p. 19.
5. Ibid. p. 21.
6. Lionel Robbins, *The Nature and Significance of Economic Science*, p. 69. Italics added.

7. Petry, *Der Soziale Gehalt der Marxschen Werttheorie*, p. 17.
8. Marx, 'Randglossen zu Adolph Wagner's "Lehrbuch der Politischen Ökonomie,"' Appendix to *Das Kapital*, Marx-Engels-Lenin Institute ed., Vol. I, p. 853. This is Marx's last economic work, being taken from a notebook dated 1881/2. Marx died in 1883.
9. *Capital* I, p. 70.
10. Ibid. p. 55.
11. *Der Soziale Gehalt der Marxschen Werttheorie*, p. 19.
12. *Capital* I, p. 48.
13. Ibid. p. 50.
14. Ibid. p. 51.
15. Ibid. p. 54.
16. Ibid. 59 n.
17. 'Introduction to the Critique of Political Economy,' *Critique*, p. 298.
18. *Geschichte und Klassenbewusstsein*, p. 18.
19. *Capital* I, p. 51.
20. *Critique*, p. 299.
21. *Capital* I, p. 114.
22. Ibid. pp. 83-4. One serious and several minor inaccuracies in the English translation have been corrected.
23. *Critique*, p. 31. Also see *Capital* I, pp. 94-5.
24. *Capital* I, p. 93.
25. *Geschichte und Klassenbewusstsein*, p. 97.
26. J. M. Keynes, *The General Theory of Employment, Interest and Money* (1935), p. 131.

III: The Quantitative-Value Problem

1. Letter to Kugelmann, *Selected Correspondence*, p. 246.
2. *Capital* I, p. 45.
3. Ibid. p. 46.
4. Ibid. p. 51.
5. Ibid. p. 52.
6. Ibid. p. 52.
7. *Wealth of Nations* I, p. 49.
8. In his illuminating essay on 'Marxian Economics and Modern Economic Theory,' *Review of Economic Studies*, June 1935.
9. *Capital* III, p. 224.
10. International Publishers ed., p. 26.
11. *Capital* I, p. 48.
12. Ibid. III, pp. 745-6. See also pp. 209, 226.
13. Ibid. p. 214. Minor changes have been made in the translation.
14. Ibid. pp. 222-3.
15. J. A. Schumpeter, *Business Cycles* (1939), I, p. 73.
16. *Capital* III, p. 1026.
17. E. v. Böhm-Bawerk, *Karl Marx and the Close of His System* (English translation 1898, original 1896), particularly Ch. III, 'The Question of the Contradiction.'
18. *Capital* III, p. 900.

IV: Surplus Value and Capitalism

1. *Capital* I, p. 188.
2. Ibid. p. 189.
3. Ibid. III, p. 1026.
4. Ibid. I, pp. 169-70. Italics added.
5. Ibid. pp. 189-90.
6. Ibid. p. 217.
7. Ibid. p. 232.
8. Ibid. pp. 232-3.
9. Ibid. III, p. 206.
10. Ibid. p. 206.
11. Marx-Engels, *Selected Correspondence*, International Publishers ed., p. 106.
12. L. v. Bortkiewicz, 'Wertrechnung und Preisrechnung im Marxschen System,' *Archiv für Sozialwissenschaft und Sozialpolitik*, July 1906, p. 30.

PART TWO

THE ACCUMULATION PROCESS

V: Accumulation and the Reserve Army

1. *Theorien über den Mehrwert* I, p. 92.
2. *Capital* I, p. 649.
3. Ibid.
4. Ibid.
5. Ibid. I, p. 654 n.
6. Ricardo, *Letters to Malthus*, 1810-1823, Bonar ed., p. 45. Italics added.
7. *Principles*, p. 71. Italics added.
8. *Capital* I, p. 699. The whole page is important in this connection.
9. Letter to Schweitzer, *Selected Correspondence*, p. 170.
10. Letter to Kugelmann, ibid. p. 201.
11. *Capital* I, p. 675 n.
12. Ibid. p. 672.
13. Ibid. p. 701. Italics added.
14. Ibid. p. 691.
15. Ibid. p. 700.
16. Ibid. p. 693.
17. Ibid. p. 680.
18. Ricardo, *Principles*, p. 101.
19. J. S. Mill, *Principles of Political Economy*, Ashley ed., p. 746.

VI: The Falling Tendency of the Rate of Profit

1. *Capital* III, p. 304.
2. Ibid. p. 272.
3. Ibid. p. 277.
4. Ibid. p. 276.
5. Ibid. p. 278.

6. Ibid. I, p. 405.
7. Ibid. p. 662. Italics added.
8. This particular quotation is from *Capital* III, p. 255.

VII: The Transformation of Values into Prices

1. *Capital* III, pp. 181-2.
2. Ibid. p. 194.
3. *Theorien über den Mehrwert* III, pp. 200-201.
4. Ibid. p. 201.
5. 'Wertrechnung und Preisrechnung im Marxschen System,' *Archiv für Sozialwissenschaft und Sozialpolitik*, September 1907, pp. 446-7.
6. *Jahrbücher für Nationalökonomie und Statistik*, July 1907.
7. *Archiv für Sozialwissenschaft und Sozialpolitik*, July 1906, July 1907, September 1907.

PART THREE

CRISES AND DEPRESSIONS

VIII: The Nature of Capitalist Crises

1. *Capital* I, p. 26. Corrections have been made in the translation. In the English edition this Postscript is erroneously called 'Preface to the Second Edition.'
2. *Theorien über den Mehrwert* II/2, p. 286.
3. Ibid. esp. pp. 272-91.
4. *Principles*, pp. 273, 275.
5. *Theorien über den Mehrwert* II/2, p. 277.
6. Ibid. pp. 280-81.
7. *Capital* I, p. 170.
8. Ibid. p. 171 n.
9. *Theorien über den Mehrwert* II/2, p. 265. Italics added.
10. Ibid. pp. 266-7.

IX: Crises Associated with the Falling Tendency of the Rate of Profit

1. *Capital* III, Chapter XV.
2. Ibid. p. 283.
3. Ibid. p. 303.
4. *Capital* III, p. 199.
5. Ibid. I, pp. 693-4.
6. Ibid. p. 680.
7. Ibid. III, pp. 297-9.
8. Ibid. I, pp. 694-5.

X: Realization Crises

1. *Theorien über den Mehrwert* II/2, p. 293.
2. Ibid. p. 301.
3. M. Tugan-Baranowsky, *Studien zur Theorie und Geschichte der Handelskrisen in England*, 1901. The German translation is based on

the second, revised Russian edition of 1900. The first Russian edition appeared in 1894.

4. Rudolf Hilferding, *Das Finanzkapital*, 1910.
5. *Handelskrisen*, p. 33.
6. Ibid. p. 33. Italics added.
7. *Theoretische Grundlagen des Marxismus*, pp. 224 ff. See especially the footnote beginning on p. 226.
8. Ibid. p. 230.
9. Ibid. pp. 230-31.
10. *Sozialistische Monatshefte* (1901), II, p. 673.
11. *Die Neue Zeit*, Jhrg. XX, Bd. 2 (1901-2), p. 117.
12. *The Theoretical System of Karl Marx* (1907), p. 249.
13. *Das Finanzkapital*, p. 355 n.
14. *Der Imperialismus und die Akkumulation des Kapitals*, p. 76.
15. *Theorien über den Mehrwert* II/2, p. 266.
16. *Critique*, pp. 278-9.
17. *Capital* III, p. 359.
18. *Theorien über den Mehrwert* III, p. 55.
19. *Capital* III, pp. 286-7.
20. Ibid. p. 568.
21. E.g. Ibid. pp. 293, 301, 302-3.
22. *Political Economy and Capitalism*, p. 115.
23. *Die Neue Zeit*, Jhrg. XX, Bd. 2 (1901-2), p. 80.
24. *Capital* III, p. 293.
25. *Sämtliche Werke* Bd. III, p. 21.
26. Ibid. p. 22.
27. *Das Kapital*, Marx-Engels-Lenin ed., Bd. II, p. 562.
28. *Der Imperialismus und die Akkumulation des Kapitals*, pp. 79-80.

Appendix to Chapter X

1. *Zwischen zwei Weltkriegen?* (1936), especially pp. 51-66 and the appendix.

XI: The Breakdown Controversy

1. *Capital* I, p. 837.
2. Ibid. II, p. 289.
3. *The Class Struggle* (*Erfurt Program*), Kerr ed., p. 117.
4. *Bernstein und das Sozialdemokratische Programm*, 1899.
5. *Die Voraussetzungen des Sozialismus und die Aufgaben der Sozialdemokratie*. The English translation is entitled *Evolutionary Socialism*.
6. *Die Neue Zeit*, Jhrg. XVII, Bd. I (1898-9).
7. The formulation is quoted by Kautsky from Bernstein, *Bernstein und das Sozialdemokratische Programm*, p. 43.
8. Ibid. p. 45.
9. Ibid. p. 166.
10. *Theoretische Grundlagen des Marxismus*, p. 239.
11. *Sozialistische Monatshefte*, Jhrg. V, Bd. 2 (1901), pp. 675 f.
12. Ibid. p. 676.
13. 'Krisentheorien,' *Die Neue Zeit*, Jhrg. XX, Bd. 2 (1901-2).
14. Ibid. p. 133.

15. Ibid. p. 136.
16. Ibid. pp. 140-41.
17. Ibid. p. 141.
18. Ibid. p. 142.
19. Ibid. p. 142.
20. Ibid. p. 143.
21. *Theoretische Grundlagen des Marxismus*, p. 214.
22. *Theoretical System of Karl Marx*, p. 163.
23. Ibid. p. 254.
24. *Das Finanzkapital*, p. 471.
25. 'Finanzkapital und Krisen,' *Die Neue Zeit*, Jhrg. XXIX, Bd. 1 (1910-11), p. 765.
26. *Die Akkumulation des Kapitals. Ein Beitrag zur ökonomischen Erklarung des Imperialismus*, p. 114 (cited from the 1922 edition). This work will henceforth be referred to as *Akkumulation des Kapitals*. The later work, *Die Akkumulation des Kapitals oder was die Epigonen aus der Marxschen Theorie gemacht haben. Eine Antikritik*, will be cited (from the 1921 edition) as *Antikritik*.
27. *Antikritik*, p. 16.
28. Ibid. p. 17.
29. *Der Imperialismus und die Akkumulation des Kapitals*, p. 20.
30. *Akkumulation des Kapitals*, p. 445.
31. *Antikritik*, p. 5.
32. Ibid.
33. Ibid. p. 37.
34. *Die Materialistische Geschichtsauffassung* (2nd ed.), Bd. II, p. 546.
35. Quoted by Grossmann, *Das Akkumulations- und Zusammenbruchsgesetz des kapitalistischen Systems*, p. 57 n.
36. See Chapter V ('The Theory of the Breakdown of Capitalism') of Bukharin's *Der Imperialismus und die Akkumulation des Kapitals*.
37. *Der Imperialismus*, 1926.
38. Otto Bauer, 'Die Akkumulation des Kapitals,' *Die Neue Zeit*, Jhrg. XXXI, Bd. I (1912-13), pp. 831-8, 862-74.
39. Grossmann, op. cit. p. 178.
40. *Das Kapital* (Marx-Engels-Lenin ed.), Vol. II, Appendix, p. 566.

XII: Chronic Depression?

1. *Antikritik*, p. 21.
2. *Sämtliche Werke* III, pp. 20-21.
3. *Capital* II, p. 384.
4. *Theorien über den Mehrwert* I, pp. 378-9.

PART FOUR

IMPERIALISM

XIII: The State

1. *Critique*, p. 9.
2. *Origin of the Family, Private Property and the State*, Kerr ed., p. 130.
3. *Capital* I, Chapter X.

4. Ibid. p. 259.
5. Chapter x, Section 5.
6. *Capital* I, pp. 304-5.
7. Chapter x, Section 6.
8. *Capital* I, pp. 263-4.
9. Ibid. pp. 308-9.
10. Ibid. p. 311.
11. Ibid. p. 330.
12. Letter from Engels to Conrad Schmidt, 27 October 1890. *Selected Correspondence*, p. 484.
13. *Gesammelte Werke* III, p. 56.
14. *Class Struggles in France*, International Publishers ed., pp. 69-70.
15. Rosa Luxemburg, *Gesammelte Werke* III, pp. 59-60.
16. Otto Bauer, *Zwischen Zwei Weltkriegen?* p. 142.

XIV: The Development of Monopoly Capital

1. *Capital* I, p. 686.
2. Ibid. p. 686.
3. Ibid. p. 687.
4. Ibid. p. 688.
5. Ibid.
6. Ibid.
7. Ibid.
8. Ibid. III, Chapter XXVII ('The Role of Credit in Capitalist Production').
9. Ibid. p. 516.
10. Ibid. p. 521.
11. *Das Finanzkapital*, p. 112.
12. Ibid. p. 118.
13. Ibid. p. 130.
14. Ibid. p. 132.
15. *Capital* III, p. 518.
16. *Das Finanzkapital*, p. 231.
17. Ibid. p. 283.
18. Ibid. p. 218.
19. Ibid. p. 473.
20. *Imperialism*, International Publishers' Little Lenin Library ed., p. 44.

XV: Monopoly and the Laws of Motion of Capitalism

1. *Capital* III, p. 900.
2. *Das Finanzkapital*, p. 286.
3. *Capital* III, p. 1003.
4. See *Das Finanzkapital*, pp. 287 ff.
5. *Capital* III, Chapters XVI and XVII.
6. Ibid. p. 337.
7. *Das Finanzkapital*, p. 264.
8. Circular letter to economics teachers from the Twentieth Century Fund, dated 9 May 1941.
9. *Theorien über den Mehrwert* II/2, p. 353.
10. Ibid. p. 368.

XVI: World Economy

1. *Political Economy and Capitalism*, pp. 234-5.
2. *Das Finanzkapital*, pp. 377-8.
3. Ibid. p. 386.
4. Ibid. pp. 384-5.
5. Ibid. p. 389.
6. Ibid. p. 401.
7. Ibid. p. 406.

XVII: Imperialism

1. *Gesammelte Werke* III, p. 58.
2. Ibid. p. 59.
3. *Das Finanzkapital*, pp. 427-8. Also Appendix B below.
4. Ibid. p. 429.
5. Ibid. Chapter XXXIII.
6. 'Krisentheorien,' *Die Neue Zeit*, Jhrg. xx, Bd. 2 (1901-2), p. 142.
7. *Political Economy and Capitalism*, p. 235.
8. *Capital* III, p. 519.
9. *Imperialism*, p. 37.
10. *Die Nationalitätenfrage und die Sozialdemokratie*, p. 488.
11. *Imperialism*, p. 70.

XVIII: Fascism

1. 'Die Eigengesetzlichkeit der kapitalistischen Entwicklung,' in *Kapital und Kapitalismus*, Bernhard Harms, ed. (1931), Vol. I, pp. 35-6.
2. *Left-Wing Communism: an Infantile Disorder*, International Publishers ed., p. 17.
3. *Das Finanzkapital*, pp. 295 f.
4. 'The Decline of the Investment Banker,' *The Antioch Review*, Spring 1941, p. 66.
5. *Der Imperialismus und die Akkumulation des Kapitals*, pp. 80-81.
6. *Capital* III, p. 293.
7. *Imperialism*, p. 84.

XIX: Looking Forward

1. *Imperialism*, p. 76.
2. *Capital* III, p. 293.
3. 'The October Revolution and the Tactics of the Russian Communists' (preface to the work entitled *Towards October*), reprinted in *Leninism*, pp. 179-216.
4. *Leninism*, p. 213.
5. Ibid. p. 213.
6. Ibid. pp. 214-15.
7. Ibid. p. 215. Italics added.
8. Ibid. p. 216.
9. Ibid. pp. 117-18.

INDEX